INTELLIGENCE, INFORMATION PROCESSING, AND ANALOGICAL REASONING:

The Componential Analysis of Human Abilities

THE EXPERIMENTAL PSYCHOLOGY SERIES

Arthur W. Melton • Consulting Editor

MELTON AND MARTIN • *Coding Processes in Human Memory*, 1972

McGUIGAN AND LUMSDEN • *Contemporary Approaches to Conditioning and Learning*, 1973

ANDERSON AND BOWER • *Human Associative Memory*, 1974

GARNER • *The Processing of Information and Structure*, 1974

MURDOCK • *Human Memory: Theory and Data*, 1974

KINTSCH • *The Representation of Meaning in Memory*, 1974

KANTOWITZ • *Human Information Processing: Tutorials in Performance and Cognition*, 1974

LEVINE • *A Cognitive Theory of Learning; Research on Hypothesis Testing*, 1975

CROWDER • *Principles of Learning and Memory*, 1976

ANDERSON • *Language, Memory, and Thought*, 1976

STERNBERG • *Intelligence, Information Processing, and Analogical Reasoning: The Componential Analysis of Human Abilities*, 1977

INTELLIGENCE,
INFORMATION PROCESSING,
AND ANALOGICAL REASONING:

The Componential Analysis of Human Abilities

ROBERT J. STERNBERG
Yale University

LAWRENCE ERLBAUM ASSOCIATES, PUBLISHERS
1977   Hillsdale, New Jersey

DISTRIBUTED BY THE HALSTED PRESS DIVISION OF
JOHN WILEY & SONS
New York   Toronto   London   Sydney

Lawrence Erlbaum Associates, Inc., Publishers
62 Maria Drive
Hillsdale, New Jersey 07642

Distributed solely by Halsted Press Division
John Wiley & Sons, Inc., New York

Library of Congress Cataloging in Publication Data

Sternberg, Robert J
   Intelligence, information processing, and analogical reasoning.

   (The Experimental psychology series)
   Bibliography: p.
   Includes indexes.
   1. Intellect. 2. Reasoning. 3. Analogy.
I. Title. II. Series.
BF431·S738   160   77-4178
ISBN 0-470-99137-2

Printed in the United States of America

Contents

Preface   ix

PART I   PRESCRIPT   1

1 Introduction   3
   Goals of the Monograph   3
   Organization of the Monograph   3

PART II   APPROACHES TO INTELLIGENCE   9

2 The Differential Approach to Intelligence   11
   Principles of Factor Analysis   12
   Factor Theories of Intelligence   20
   Contributions of Factor Analysis   25
   The Decline of the Differential Approach   27
   Summary   34

3 The Information-Processing Approach to Intelligence   37
   The Fundamental Unit of Analysis   38
   Information-Processing Methodology   40
   Information-Processing Theories of Intelligence   44
   Advantages of the Information-Processing Approach   53
   Limitations of Information-Processing Methodology   54
   Summary   61

4 The Componential Approach to Human Intelligence   64
   Preliminaries   65
   Intensive Task Analysis   71

Extensive Task Analysis   83
Why Componential Analysis?   84
Summary   93

PART III   A COMPONENTIAL ANALYSIS OF
ANALOGICAL REASONING   97

5 Theories of Analogical Reasoning: A Literature Review   99
   Differential Theories of Analogical Reasoning   101
   Information-Processing Theories of
     Analogical Reasoning   106
   Issues Confronting Research on
     Analogical Reasoning   130
   Summary   131

6 A Componential Theory of Analogical Reasoning   134
   Nature of Analogy   134
   The Componential Theory   135
   Componential Models of Analogical Reasoning   137
   Evaluation of Componential Theory   145
   Summary   147
   Appendix: Detailed Specifications of
     Componential Models   149

7 The People Piece Analogy Experiment   173
   Method   173
   Internal Validation   181
   External Validation   206
   Integration   217
   Summary   219

8 The Verbal Analogy Experiment   222
   Method   222
   Internal Validation   226
   External Validation   240
   Integration   250
   Summary   251

9 The Geometric Analogy Experiment   255
   Method   255
   Internal Validation   260
   External Validation   277
   Integration   283
   Summary   284

10 The Animal Name Analogy Experiment 287
   Method   288
   Internal Validation   289
   External Validation   298
   Summary   301

11 Miller Analogies 303
   Method   304
   External Validation   305
   Summary   308

12 Conclusions about Analogical Reasoning 309
   Basic Unit of Information Processing   309
   Componential Theory   309
   Componential Models: Error Rate   311
   Relations Between Solution Time and
      Error Rate   312
   Relations Between Solution Time and
      Reference Abilities   312
   Relations Between Solution Time-Error
      Rate and Reference Abilities   313
   Relations Between Component Times and
      Reference Abilities   313
   Relation Between Percentage of Variance
      Accounted for and Reference Abilities   314

PART IV   POSTSCRIPT 315

13 Toward a Theory of Intelligence 317
   Preliminary Sketch of a Theory of Intelligence   317
   Current Issues in Intelligence Research   321
   Summary   325

References   326

Author Index   335

Subject Index   339

This book is dedicated
to my wife, Betty,
who first introduced me
to People Pieces.

Preface

Theories of intelligence once were defended in raging battles. Championing their competing theories, intellectual giants like Spearman and Thurstone led their armies through hard-fought campaigns. Each battle was headline news in the world of psychology.

The generals eventually passed away. The armies retreated, the soldiers deserted. The battlefield of intelligence lay quiet, strewn with the relics of a glorious but indecisive war. Some researchers disappeared into obscurity, others abandoned substantive concerns and entered the more esoteric realm of measurement theory. But the glory was not there. Younger recruits joined forces with those on livelier but altogether different psychological battlefields. They turned to areas such as memory and perception, fields in which the armaments were sophisticated and the theories hotly contested. The psychology students who once might have learned about factor analysis and the structure of intelligence learned instead about signal detection theory and the structure of memory traces.

The field of intelligence, however, did not die out altogether. Intelligence research began to focus more and more on issues such as the heritability of intelligence and racial differences in intelligence; this research quickly fell into a quagmire, partly because the research is so difficult to do properly, and partly because there seemed to be no viable theory of intelligence that might serve as a basis for the research. By 1970, Vernon was led to remark that "to the theoretical psychologist . . . intelligence seems to have outgrown its usefulness" (p. 100).

In the few years that have passed since Vernon's despairing assessment of the state of intelligence as a theoretical construct, interest in intelligence has shown a remarkable renaissance. Researchers such as Carroll, Estes, Horn, E. Hunt, and Simon, to name just a few, have again shown the viability of intelligence as an important theoretical construct. As the writing of this book neared completion, a milestone volume, *The Nature of Intelligence* (Resnick, 1976), appeared on the scene, offering a wide variety of challenging and up-to-date perspectives on intelligence as a theoretical construct. The volume shows how far the renaissance has come in just half-a-decade. The present book is intended to carry on in this new tradition of research on intelligence.

This volume has three major goals: To specify the form a theory of intelligence should take; to describe a new and general method for studying intelligence; to present the beginning of a theory of intelligence. This beginning is a theory of one important aspect of intelligence, reasoning by analogy.

With respect to the first goal, the proposed form for a theory of intelligence is called a *componential theory.* Together with a *componential model,* it specifies not only the component processes involved in performance of tasks requiring intelligence, but also the rule by which multiple component processes are combined into a single component processing strategy, the way in which multiple executions of a single component process are sequenced, and the duration and difficulty of each component process. Measures of goodness of fit are provided for both group and individual data, so that one can assess at each level the degree to which the proposed theory fits empirically derived data.

With respect to the second goal, the proposed method for studying intelligence is called *componential analysis.* Componential analysis identifies the component mental processes underlying a series of related information-processing tasks, and discovers the organization of these component processes in terms of their relationships both to each other and to higher-order constellations of mental abilities. Componential analysis builds upon both differential and information-processing methodologies, adding, at the same time, unique theory-testing operations of its own. It is believed that componential analysis capitalizes upon the strengths of the differential and information-processing approaches, while sharing the weaknesses of neither.

With respect to the third goal, the proposed *componential theory of analogical reasoning* attempts to account for both group and individual latency and error data. A single information-processing model incorporating six component processes is shown to provide an excellent fit to data from four different types of analogies, and to provide a meaningful basis for understanding individual differences in information processing. The processes identified by the theory seem to be general ones in everyday intelligent behavior.

The book is divided into four parts. The first part, Chapter 1, is an introduction to the rest of the book. The second part, Chapters 2–4, is an analysis of three perspectives on intelligence research. This section opens with a critical review of the differential approach. (Chapter 2), continues with a critical review of the information-processing approach (Chapter 3), and ends with an introduction to the proposed componential approach (Chapter 4). The third part of the book, Chapters 5–12, presents and tests a rigorously specified theory of analogical reasoning. This section includes a review of the literature on analogical reasoning (Chapter 5), a presentation of the proposed componential theory of analogical reasoning (Chapter 6), five experiments on analogical reasoning (Chapters 7–11), and a summary of major conclusions (Chapter 12). The fourth part, Chapter 13, explores the implications of the research on analogical reasoning for the understanding of intelligence and how to measure it.

Intelligence, Information Processing, and Analogical Reasoning is addressed to professionals and graduate students interested in intelligence, reasoning processes, or individual differences. Although the book was written as a monograph, I have found it useful in graduate courses as well, successfully using Parts II and IV in a course on Individual Differences in Cognition, and Parts III and IV in a course on Reasoning and Problem Solving. The volume, or parts of it, might serve equally well in courses with titles such as Human Abilities, Intelligence, Complex Processes, or Thinking.

I have acquired many intellectual debts over the years, and I can acknowledge but not repay them. I am especially grateful to Gordon Bower, my adviser through three years of graduate school, and to Roger Shepard and Lee Cronbach. As members of my dissertation committee, they plowed through the long dissertation upon which this book is based, and provided detailed feedback on it. I also owe a special debt of gratitude to my mentor from undergraduate days, Endel Tulving, whose hypnotic influence might have kept me in memory research were he not 3000 miles away from Stanford. Thanks are also due to Richard Hackman and Alexander Wearing, who advised me on research while I was an undergraduate at Yale, to David O. Herman and Jerome Doppelt, who were my supervisors during two summers at The Psychological Corporation, and to Michael Zieky, Chuck Myers, and Tom Donlon, who were my supervisors during a summer at Educational Testing Service. I also thank Sam Chauncey and John Hoskins, who allowed and encouraged me to pursue my interests in admissions research while I was an undergraduate.

Finally, I thank my wife, Betty, whose contributions to my personal and scientific development have been immeasurable, my parents, Joseph and Lillian, who encouraged me to pursue my early interest in intelligence, and the late William H. Adams, my seventh grade science teacher, who stood up for me when a school system psychologist threatened to confiscate and burn my copy of *Measuring Intelligence.*

ROBERT JEFFREY STERNBERG

INTELLIGENCE, INFORMATION PROCESSING, AND ANALOGICAL REASONING:

The Componential Analysis of Human Abilities

Part I

PRESCRIPT

1
Introduction

GOALS OF THE MONOGRAPH

This book has three major goals. The first goal is to specify the form a theory of intelligence should take. Such a specification is a metatheory of intelligence. The theory it specifies is called a componential theory. The second goal is to outline a general method for studying intelligence. The method is called componential analysis. The third goal is to present the beginning of a theory of intelligence. This beginning takes the form of a componential theory of analogical reasoning.

ORGANIZATION OF THE MONOGRAPH

Overview

This volume is divided into four parts, the first of which is this introduction. In the second part I seek to accomplish the first two goals described above, and thus this part is general and metatheoretical in intent. Here the two major approaches that have been applied to the study of intelligence – the differential and the information-processing approaches – are reviewed. A third approach, componential analysis, which is a synthesis of the other two, is also introduced.

In the third part of the volume I seek to accomplish the third goal described above, and thus this part is theoretical rather than metatheoretical in intent. It opens with a critical review of previous theories of analogical reasoning, continues with a new theory of analogical reasoning and experimental data in support of the theory, and ends with a review of the conclusions based upon the preceding discussion and experiments.

In the fourth and final part of the volume I present a preliminary sketch of a theory of intelligence and enumerate major issues facing contemporary intelligence research.

Part I: Prescript

Chapter 1   In this introduction, I describe the three goals of the book and its organization.

Part II: Approaches to Intelligence

Chapter 2   Chapter 2 is a review and critique of the differential approach to intelligence, an approach that bases theories of intelligence almost exclusively upon individual difference data. For more than half a century, the study of intelligence was inseparable from the study of individual differences (except for the research of a small number of scholars, such as Piaget). Little more than a decade ago, Quinn McNemar (1964) queried whether "two supergeniuses, being totally unaware of individual differences, [would] ever hit upon and develop a concept of intelligence" (p. 882). It seemed possible that the concept of intelligence was inseparable from the concept of individual differences.

A major contention of this volume is that the concept of intelligence can be discovered without a prior concept of individual differences. It is argued, furthermore, that the dependence of the concept of intelligence upon the study of individual differences has not been an entirely salubrious one. Although a comprehensive theory of intelligence should account for individual differences, it should not be based upon them.

The chapter concentrates on factor analysis, the primary individual-differences methodology used to study the structure of intelligence. The research of the pioneers in the factor-analytic movement – Spearman, Thomson, Thurstone, to name a few – seemed promising. It appeared to point the way toward the establishment of a solid, empirically derived foundation for the theory of intelligence. But as the first half of the twentieth century gave way to the second half, the psychometric foundation began to crumble. In this chapter I discuss why.

Chapter 3   Chapter 3 presents a review and critique of information-processing research as it pertains to the study of intelligence. Information-processing concepts promised a new foundation for many fields of theoretical psychology, but it was not immediately obvious that intelligence was among these fields. The information-processing approach was a reaction to stimulus-response psychology, not to differential psychology, and its initial applications were to problems that had baffled behaviorists, not to those that had stymied differential psychologists. The nature of intelligence was not among the behaviorists' problems, since behaviorists had never shown much interest in it, at least not in its own right. But while intelligence per se may have been neglected, intelligent behavior was not, and relevant research proceeded under labels such as reasoning and problem-solving.

Information-processing research has progressed along two somewhat different lines united by their common name and their common concern with the algorithms and heuristics people use in processing information. The first line of research has concentrated upon very complex thought processes, for example, problem solving, and has been associated with protocol analysis. On occasion, human protocols have been modeled by computer simulation. The second line of research has investigated somewhat less complex modes of thinking, for example, retrieval from semantic memory, and has been associated with response-time measurement. On occasion, human response times have been modeled by mathematical equations.

Each stream of research has made its unique contribution to the study of intelligent behavior, but neither has been shown capable of providing the kind of systematic, macrotheoretical foundation for the concept of intelligence that emerged from the early differential research. Chapter 3 considers why this is so, and why the information-processing approach by itself is inadequate for the development of a comprehensive theory of intelligence.

Chapter 4 The strengths and weaknesses of the differential and information-processing approaches to intelligence are largely complementary. The componential approach to intelligence, described in Chapter 4, attempts to draw upon the strengths of both approaches and, thereby, to avoid the weaknesses of each. In this respect, it is kindred in spirit to the approaches of Hunt, Carroll, and others. The chapter shows how componential analysis can be used to develop a theoretically and empirically adequate theory of intelligence.

Part III: A Componential Analysis of Analogical Reasoning

Chapter 5 Theories of analogical reasoning have followed lines similar to those of theories of intelligence. Consequently, Chapter 5, a literature review, is divided into two major sections. The first section reviews differential theories of analogical reasoning, and the second section reviews information-processing theories. Theories are evaluated in terms of five criteria: (1) their *completeness* in accounting for all processes involved in analogical reasoning; (2) the *specificity* with which they describe the details of each process; (3) the *generality* of the theory across different types of analogical reasoning tasks; (4) the *parsimony* of the theory's description, and (5) the *plausibility* of the theory in accounting for experimental data.

Chapter 6 In this chapter I present a componential theory of analogical reasoning—an account of the way people solve problems of the form A is to B as

C is to D. The theory also serves as the beginning of a general theory of intelligence.

The theory is general in that it specifies only: (1) the components involved in analogical reasoning; and (2) the way in which these components combine. Because of its generality, the theory does not fully account for information-processing behavior. Specific models permissible under the general theory are needed that can further specify information processing. Alternative models are presented, both for true–false and for forced-choice analogies. These models specify: (1) the order of component execution; and (2) the mode of component execution, whether the components are each executed serially or in parallel, as self-terminating or exhaustive processes, and holistically or particularistically. Flow charts are presented that describe each alternative model in detail.

Chapter 7   In Chapter 7 I present the first experimental study of the series, the People Piece Analogy Experiment. The study used People Pieces as the task material. These are simple pictures of people with well-defined binary attributes: height (tall, short); sex (male, female); color (red, blue); girth (fat, thin). The stimuli were similar to those that have been used in large numbers of concept-learning studies (e.g., Bruner, Goodnow & Austin, 1956). The advantages and disadvantages of using simple stimuli are well known. When an investigator starts out knowing almost nothing about the process under study, he wants to control as many variables as possible. Simple stimuli contribute to this goal. However, experimental control can be gained at the expense of ecological validity, and in starting simply, one runs the risk of making discoveries limited to the simple stimuli used. If the results of this experiment were limited, it should become apparent from the results of the subsequent experiments.

Chapter 8   The second experiment used fairly simple verbal analogies, such as attorney: client :: doctor : patient. These analogies, like the People Piece analogies, employed a true–false format, although they were more difficult for subjects to solve. The subjects in this experiment were the same as the subjects in the People Piece Experiment, so that it was possible to compare aspects of performance in the two experiments.

Chapter 9   The third experiment used pictorial material. The test stimuli were geometric analogies in which: (1) the number of attributes varied from one analogy to the next (and even between terms within a single analogy); and (2) the relevant attributes for analogy solution varied from one analogy to the next. The items, more difficult than those in the preceding experiments, were of the type found in many standard tests of mental ability. In fact, the items were taken, with modifications to be described, from actual college ability tests administered to high school seniors and college freshmen in past years. These items differed in another important respect from those in the first two experiments. The People Piece and verbal items were true–false: The analogy $A : B ::$

$C : D$ was presented, and the subject had to respond either "true" or "false." In the geometric analogies, responses were forced-choice: Two possible final terms were presented in an analogy of the form, $A : B :: C : D_1\ D_2$. The subject had to choose between the correct and incorrect answer.

Chapter 10 Animal name analogies, first introduced by Rumelhart and Abrahamson (1973) in their now famous study of analogical reasoning, were examined in less detail than the other three types of analogies. Indeed, the analysis was not even fully componential. However, they were investigated for two reasons.

First, the experiment permitted a limited test of the componential theory of analogical reasoning with stimuli in which the latent attributes are identifiable but not at all obvious. In the People Piece Experiment, the latent attributes are identifiable and also obvious. In the Verbal Analogy Experiment and the Geometric Analogy Experiment, the attributes are neither readily identifiable nor obvious. In the Animal Name Analogy Experiment, the latent attributes are not obvious, but they are identifiable through multidimensional scaling or other mathematical algorithms.

Second, the animal name analogies have not been shown actually to measure reasoning ability, and external validation procedures were used to determine whether they do provide a good measure of reasoning.

Chapter 11 Miller analogies of the type found on the Miller Analogies Test were studied in even less detail than the animal name analogies. The Miller Analogies Test is a difficult examination used for admission to graduate schools. Some previous research has indicated that these analogies might be more appropriate as measures of vocabulary or general information than as measures of reasoning (Meer, Stein, & Geertsma, 1955; Guilford, 1967; see also Sternberg, 1974, pp. 108–110). It was possible to investigate this hypothesis further in the present series of studies.

Chapter 12 In this chapter I present a summary and integration of the experimental findings presented in the preceding five chapters. The theoretical implications of these findings are discussed, and directions for future research are suggested.

Part IV: Postscript

Chapter 13 In the final chapter I assess the present state of the theory and metatheory of intelligence. A sketch of a componential theory of intelligence is presented. The significant unresolved questions facing contemporary intelligence research and the ways in which they might be resolved within the framework of componential analysis are then discussed.

Part II

APPROACHES TO INTELLIGENCE

2
The Differential Approach
to Intelligence

For half a century, factor analysis and related methods seemed to be the keys that would unlock the mysteries of intelligence. The methods seemed to be opening the right doors. As late as 1940, Burt was claiming that "the validity of factor analysis as such has not been seriously questioned" (Burt, 1940, p. 61). Burt conceded that there were rumblings here and there, but attributed these to the "non-statistical psychologist."

Burt's assessment of the immunity of factor analysis from criticism was probably overoptimistic to begin with, but by 1953, whatever immunity factor analysis had once possessed was a thing of the past. Eysenck (1953) remarked that "few methods of statistical analysis have encountered as much resistance among both statisticians and psychologists as has factor analysis" (p. 105). But Eysenck remained a staunch defender, arguing that "criticism of factor analysis as a whole . . . is often vitiated by (a) lack of historical perspective, (b) lack of scientific sophistication, (c) lack of understanding of the particular problem which the factor analyst is trying to solve" (p. 113). Fourteen years later, the defender had turned critic, suggesting that "the psychometric approach has become almost completely divorced from both psychological theory and experiment and that factor analysis, while an extremely useful tool, cannot by itself bear the whole burden which has been placed upon it" (Eysenck, 1967, p. 83).

The pioneers in the factor-analytic movement had not intended factor analysis to bear the heavy burdens that later were placed upon it:

The exploratory nature of factor analysis is often not understood. Factor analysis has its principal usefulness at the border line of science. It is naturally superseded by rational formulations in terms of the science involved. Factor analysis is useful, especially in those domains where basic and fruitful concepts are essentially lacking and where crucial experiments have been difficult to conceive. The new methods have a humble role. They enable us to make only the crudest first map of a new domain. But if we have scientific intuition and sufficient ingenuity, the rough factorial map of a new domain will enable us to proceed beyond the exploratory factorial stage to the more direct forms of psychological experimentation in the laboratory. (Thurstone, 1947, p. 56)

Intelligence research could not forever remain "at the border line of science," but the admonitions of Thurstone were either forgotten or ignored. At the very least, the exploratory nature of factor analysis was not understood. Scientific ingenuity and intuition went not toward proceeding "beyond the exploratory factorial stage to the more direct forms of psychological experimentation" but toward successive factorial stages.

In this chapter, I present an assessment of the differential (factorial) approach. The assessment is preceded, however, by three other sections. The first is a brief sketch of the logic and principles of factor analysis. The sketch provides only a very casual acquaintance with factor analysis. A complete statement is presented by Harman (1967). The second section provides a brief history of factor-analytic theories of intelligence. Further details can be found in Butcher (1968). The third section presents an assessment of the contributions of factor analysis. The fourth and final section is a critique focusing upon why factor analysis by itself is inadequate for ascertaining the structure of intelligence.

PRINCIPLES OF FACTOR ANALYSIS

Purpose of Factor Analysis

According to Thurstone (1947), "the factorial methods were developed primarily for the purpose of identifying the principal dimensions or categories of mentality" (p. 55). There have been two opposing schools of thought as to how this purpose should be accomplished. Both distinguish between stages of hypothesis formation and hypothesis testing. They differ in the stage at which it is believed that factor analysis is most useful.

On the one hand, there are those who have taken the position that factor analysis is a "useful tool in hypothesis formation rather than hypothesis testing" (Humphreys, 1962, p. 475). Advocates of this viewpoint regard factor analysis as a useful exploratory technique, but not as a useful technique for choosing among the theories suggested by initial exploration.

On the other hand, there are those who have taken the position that factor analysis should be regarded "not as a source of hypotheses, but merely as a method of comparing, confirming or refuting alternative hypotheses initially suggested by nonstatistical arguments or evidence" (Burt, 1970, p. 17). Advocates of this viewpoint believe that the utility of factor analysis is not in the initial exploration of hypotheses, but in the selection of a preferred hypothesis from those suggested by initial exploration.

One may also take the intermediate position that factor analysis is useful both as a means of suggesting theories and as a means of choosing among them. The intermediate position seems to be the most common one. In proposing the theories described in the next section, factor analysts generally used factor analysis both as a source of hypotheses and as a means of arguing in favor of their own theories over competing ones.

Fundamental Unit of Analysis

The fundamental unit of analysis in factor analysis is the factor. There has never been much consensus among factor analysts as to just what a factor is. Thurstone (1947) noted that "factors may be called by different names, such as 'causes,' 'faculties,' 'parameters,' 'functional unities,' 'abilities,' or 'independent measurements' " (p. 56). Royce (1963) added to this list "dimensions, determinants, . . . and taxonomic categories" (p. 522).

There have been two major opposing points of view regarding the nature of factors: the descriptive and the causal. Burt (1940) took a descriptive view, arguing that "the primary object of factorial methods is neither causal interpretation, nor statistical prediction, but exact and systematic description" (p. 63). Vernon (1971) has also taken a descriptive view, but whereas Burt likened factors to lines of longitude and latitude, Vernon regarded them as "categories for classifying mental or behavioral performances" (p. 8).

Taking a causal viewpoint, Cattell (1971) has referred to factors as "source traits," and Guilford (1967) has described a factor as "an underlying, latent variable along which individuals differ" (p. 41). "It is an intervening variable, conceived by the investigator, and has a status like that of *drive* and *habit,* which are also inferred from observed data" (p. 37).

Preliminaries to Factor Analysis

Suppose that an investigator's goal is to discover the structure of intelligence via factor analysis. How would he go about reaching this goal? He might take a series of steps.

1. *Select tests.* The investigator must select a battery of tests that taps all intellectual functions he wants to be incorporated into the model of intelligence. It is an old dictum of factor analysis that you can only get out a transformation of what you put in. One therefore wants to include a broad range of tests, so as to assure the measurement of all relevant abilities. One wants to avoid extraneous tests, however, that may blur the results.

2. *Select subjects.* The investigator must select a representative sample of subjects from the population of interest. A broad sample is particularly important, since factor analysis is based on patterns of individual differences among

subjects. Factors cannot be discovered in the absence of consistent individual differences.

3. *Administer tests to subjects.*

4. *Score tests and compute basic statistics, including intercorrelations among tests.* The intercorrelation matrix shows patterns of individual differences among subjects for the given set of tests. Advocates of the "latent trait" notion of factors will suggest that hypothetical sources of individual differences can be discovered through factor analysis.

Object of Factor Analysis

The object of factor analysis is to represent a variable z_j, usually a series of scores on a given test, in terms of underlying factors or hypothetical constructs (Harman, 1967, p. 14). In most factor models, this representation is a linear one.

Procedures of Factor Analysis

Input to factor analysis. Factor analysis begins with a matrix, usually of intercorrelations among tests. This matrix represents the interrelationships between values (usually scores) on a number of different variables (usually tests). The diagonal entries are correlations of each test with itself. The off-diagonal entries are correlations of each test with every other test. Correlations to the left of the principal diagonal are often not shown, because they form a mirror image of the correlations to the right of the diagonal.

The diagonal entries (1S) may be replaced by reliabilities or communalities (explained below). The choice of which kind of value to place in the diagonal depends upon the way in which the variance of each test (s_j^2) is to be partitioned.

Partitioning the variance within variables. The variance of each test may be partitioned in three different ways:

$$\text{Model I:} \quad \text{total variance} \qquad = \text{total variance} \qquad (2.1)$$

$$\text{Model IIA:} \quad \text{total variance} \qquad = \text{reliability} + \text{error} \qquad (2.2)$$

$$\text{Model IIB:} \quad \text{total variance} \qquad = \text{communality} + \text{uniqueness} \quad (2.3)$$

In Model I, there is only one partition. The total variance is set equal to itself and is not subdivided. For mathematical tractability, each variable is standardized to have a variance of one. This value is placed in the diagonal of the intercorrelation matrix. This standardized variance, of course, is equal to the correlation of the variable with itself.

In Models IIA and IIB, the total variance is partitioned into two parts. In Model IIA, the two parts are reliability and error. The reliability of the test (or any variable) is that part of the variance which is systematic; the error is that part of the variance which is not systematic. The reliability is placed in the diagonal of the correlation matrix.

In Model IIB, the two parts are communality and uniqueness. The communality of a variable is that part of the variance which is shared with at least one other variable; the uniqueness is that part which is not shared with any other variable. The communality is placed in the diagonal of the correlation matrix. The difference between the partitions in Models IIA and IIB, then, is that in IIA overlap with other variables is ignored, whereas in IIB it is taken into account.

Communalities are calculated by a complicated mathematical algorithm that is performed iteratively. In the initial iteration, it is necessary to estimate the communalities. A widely used initial estimate is the squared multiple correlation of the particular variable with every other variable. This squared multiple correlation represents "shared" variance between the particular variable and all the other variables.

The interrelationships among the various terms and models can be understood with reference to the following set of equations:

$$\text{Model I: total variance} = h_j^2 + b_j^2 + e_j^2 \tag{2.4}$$

$$\text{Model IIA: reliability} = h_j^2 + b_j^2 \tag{2.5}$$

$$\text{error} = e_j^2 \tag{2.6}$$

$$\text{Model IIB: communality} = h_j^2 \tag{2.7}$$

$$\text{uniqueness} = b_j^2 + e_j^2 \tag{2.8}$$

Three terms enter the equation for total variance: communality (h_j^2), specificity (b_j^2), and error (e_j^2). Communality is variance shared between a given variable and at least one other variable. Specificity is unique variance that is systematic. In other words, it is reliable variance, but it is not shared with any other variable. Error is unique variance that is not systematic.

Model I is distinguished from Models IIA and IIB by its inclusion of error in the first (and for Model I, only) partition. Model IIA, unlike Model IIB, places specificity – systematic, unshared variance – in the first partition. The models include successively less variance in their first partition (that is, the diagonal of the correlation matrix). Model I includes the total variance of the test or other variable. Model IIA includes only reliable variance of the test. Model IIB includes only reliable variance that is shared with at least one other variable.

Distributing the variance between factors.   Once variance is partitioned within each variable, factor analysis distributes it systematically between factors. There are two basic models by which this distribution can be accomplished:

1. In a full *component model,* there are n components, where n is equal to the number of tests.[1] This model distributes variance according to the following mathematical specification:

$$z_j = a_{j1}F_1 + a_{j2}F_2 + \ldots + a_{jn}F_n \qquad (j = 1, 2, \ldots, n). \qquad (2.9)$$

In this equation, z_j is a given subject's score on test (or variable) j. The subject's score can be represented as a linear combination of n factor scores, $F_1, \ldots, F_n$, where each factor score represents the level of the subject's performance on a particular component. Associated with each test and each component is a coefficient, a_{jk}, where j is the number of the test and k the number of the component. This coefficient weights each factor score in the prediction of each test score. In short, the individual's score on test j is the sum of his factor scores multiplied by their respective coefficients for test j.

2. In a full *factor model,* there are n common factors and n unique factors, where n is again equal to the number of tests. (See Footnote 1.) This model distributes variance according to the following mathematical specification:

$$z_j = a_{j1}F_1 + a_{j2}F_2 + \ldots + a_{jn}F_n + d_jU_j \qquad (j = 1, 2, \ldots, n). \qquad (2.10)$$

In this equation, z_j is again a given subject's score on test (or variable) j. The subject's score can be represented as a linear combination of n common factor scores, $F_1, \ldots, F_n$, plus a unique factor score, U_j, where each factor score represents the level of the subject's performance on a particular factor. The values of F are scores on factors common to all tests; the U is a score on a factor unique to test j. Associated with each test and each common factor is a coefficient, a_{jk}, where j is the number of the test and k the number of the common factor. Associated with each unique factor is a coefficient d_j. The coefficient weights each factor score in the prediction of the test score. In short, the individual's score on test j is the sum of his common factor scores multiplied by their respective coefficients for test j, plus his unique factor score weighted by its coefficient for the test to which the unique factor corresponds.

The two models differ in an important way. The component model does not distinguish between common and unique factors: It distributes variance in only one way — into components. The factor model does distinguish between two

[1] It is assumed that no pair of tests is perfectly correlated.

kinds of factors: It distributes variance in two ways. In fact, the component model corresponds to Model I of the previous section, and the factor model corresponds to Models IIA and IIB of the previous section. In the component model (I), 1s are placed in the diagonal of the correlation matrix, so that it is impossible to distinguish between the different types of variance. The components may include common, specific, and error variance. In the factor model (II), either reliabilities or communalities may be placed in the diagonal. If reliabilities are placed in the diagonal, then the common factors will include common variance plus specific (but not error) variance. If communalities are placed in the diagonal, then the common factors will include only common variance and neither specific nor error variance.

Output from the factor analysis.   The input to the factor analysis was a matrix of intercorrelations. The output consists of two matrices: the *factor pattern* and the *factor structure*. The factor pattern is the matrix of coefficients a_{jk} for the equations described in the preceding section. These coefficients weight the factor scores in predicting test scores. These coefficients are often called factor loadings. The factor structure is the matrix of correlation coefficients between each variable and all of the factors. The factor structure coefficients are mathematically related to the factor pattern coefficients. With uncorrelated factors, the structure coefficients equal the corresponding pattern coefficients.

Relationship between the output matrices and the input matrix.   In both the component and factor models, it is always possible to reproduce perfectly the original values of z_j (test scores in standard form). In the component model (I), the test score values will be perfectly reproduced (within rounding error) by the retention of all n components. In the factor model (II), $2n$ factors (n common factors plus n unique factors) are required to reproduce the original values (within rounding error).

If the full set of components or factors is retained, the output pattern and structure coefficient matrices are related to the input correlation matrix in a simple way:

$$R = A S',\qquad(2.14)$$

where R is the correlation matrix, A the pattern matrix, and S' the transpose of the structure matrix. If the factors are uncorrelated, the pattern and structure matrices are identical, so that we have the pattern matrix multiplied by its transpose.

Investigators rarely retain all components or factors, since the major purpose of the analysis is to obtain a *simplified* representation of the structure in the data. If the full set is not used, however, the estimated values of z_j will not equal the original values (see Footnote 1 above), and an attempt to reproduce the original correlation matrix (by intercorrelating the estimated z_j) will reproduce a correlation matrix, R^*, which is not identical to the original correlation matrix.

If only a partial set of components or factors is retained, then the input correlation matrix cannot be reproduced, but R* can be,

$$R^* = A \ S'. \tag{2.15}$$

This equation is completely general, since when all components or factors are used, R^* equals R. This equation is called the fundamental factor theorem.

Indeterminacy of output matrices. While the input correlation matrix is of course unique, the output pattern and structure matrices are not. In fact, an infinite number of pairs of pattern and structure matrices can produce R^* because, although the factor analysis uniquely determines the m-dimensional space of factors ($m \leqslant n$, the number of tests), it does not uniquely determine the frame of reference for the factor space.

Major Decisions to be Made in Factor Analysis

Method of factor analysis. There are a number of methods for performing factor analysis. The most widely used are the principal-component and principal-factor methods, which maximize the amount of variance placed into each successive component or factor of the unrotated solution. Thus, the first factor will contain the maximum possible variance, the second factor will contain as much of the residual variance as possible, and so on. Each factor will therefore account for successively less variance.

An alternative method is the centroid method, which yields a solution approximating the principal components or principal factor solution, and is much easier to perform computationally. This method is generally preferred when hand calculations must be made, but with the advent of electronic computers, it is rarely used anymore.

A number of other methods have been proposed. The choice of method will depend upon one's goals in performing the analysis and available computational facilities. The choice of method is generally less important than the choices described below.

Factor-analytic model. Two basic models were described in the preceding section: the component model and the factor model. The choice of model will depend on what types of variance one wants in factors. In the component Model I, common, specific, and error variance will enter into components. In factor Model IIA, common and specific variance will enter into the first n factors; the second n factors will contain error variance. In factor Model IIB, only common variance will enter into the first n factors. The second n factors will contain specific and error variance.

Number of factors. An investigator will usually want to retain fewer factors than there are tests, since a major purpose of factor analysis is simplification. Deciding how many factors to retain can be difficult, however. Four criteria are often used. The first is a prior theory, which may specify the number of factors to be retained. A second criterion is the proportion of variance accounted for by each factor. Factors accounting for trivial proportions of variance in the data are generally of little interest. If one plots the cumulative proportion of variance accounted for by number of factors, there may be an "elbow" in the curve, indicating that, after a certain point, subsequent factors account for much less variance than previous factors. The factor occurring at the elbow may be used as a cutoff. A third criterion is interpretability. In using this criterion, one retains only factors to which a meaningful substantive interpretation can be assigned. A fourth criterion is factorial invariance. If a certain factor reappears in study after study, it is reliable and probably of psychological interest. If a factor appears only in an isolated study, it is less likely to be of psychological interest.

Type of rotation. As stated earlier, the orientation of factorial reference axes is not unique; an infinite number of orientations are mathematically permissible. Most factor analysts agree that part of their job is to decide upon a psychologically appropriate orientation, but there has been considerable disagreement as to what rotation should be performed — or whether one should be performed at all.

The most commonly used factor-analytic methods (such as the ones described earlier) generally yield a factor structure in which the first factor is a general one, with most factor loadings having the same sign, and subsequent factors are bipolar, with approximately half of the loadings positive and half negative. Some theorists, generally British ones, have preferred to use the unrotated factor solution as the basis for psychological theorizing. Such solutions have tended to support the notion of a strong general factor pervading virtually all mental ability tasks. Other theorists, generally American ones, have preferred to use rotated factor solutions as bases for psychological theorizing. In these solutions, the general factor, or at least the appearance of one, has often been "rotated away."

Theorists preferring rotation (e.g., Guilford, 1967) have argued that the unrotated factor structure is indicative of mathematical rather than psychological regularities. According to these theorists, psychologically meaningful factors can be obtained only through rotation.

If the theorist decides to rotate, then he has two fundamental decisions to make. The first is whether to use an objective or subjective form of rotation. The second is whether to require orthogonal factor axes or to permit oblique ones.

Horn (1967) has made a useful distinction between objective and subjective rotation. An *objective rotation* is one in which all investigators who use the method on the same data will arrive at the same result, regardless of differing a priori hypotheses they may have had regarding the outcome. A *subjective rotation* is one in which investigators with different hypotheses may get different results from the same set of data. In subjective methods, investigators usually specify a target matrix that represents hypotheses about the configuration of factor loadings after rotation. The rotation is then performed so as to minimize the discrepancy of the solution from the target matrix.

Factor axes may be either *orthogonal* or *oblique.* When orthogonal axes are used, factors are uncorrelated. They may then be viewed as independent vectors. When oblique axes are used, factors may be correlated. Performance on one factor is not independent of performance on every other factor.

The most common solution to the rotational problem is rotation to what Thurstone (1947) called *simple structure.* Thurstone proposed five criteria for simple structure. The effect of these criteria is to produce a large number of trivial factor loadings and some very substantial ones, but relatively few moderate loadings. As much variance as possible from each test is confined to a single factor.

For a number of years, a precise mathematical algorithm for rotation to simple structure eluded factor analysts. Within a year of each other, Carroll (1953) and Neuhaus and Wrigley (1954) independently arrived at mathematically equivalent algorithms that provided an approximation to simple structure. Their technique, which "cleaned up" the rows (tests) of the factor structure matrix, was called the quartimax method. Kaiser (1958) developed an alternative, the varimax method, which "cleaned up" the columns (factors) of the structure matrix. Since this outcome more closely approximated simple structure and tended to yield more interpretable solutions than the quartimax method, it has become the most widely used form of rotation. It is an objective method, and results in orthogonal axes.

The question of how to rotate factor axes is of particular importance from a psychological point of view, because method of rotation is a major distinguishing element among various factor-analytic theories of intelligence. These theories will be considered in the next section.

FACTOR THEORIES OF INTELLIGENCE

Spearman's Two-Factor Theory

Charles Spearman (1904) opened the door for factor-analytic theories of intelligence with his paper "General intelligence objectively determined and measured." In the paper, Spearman proposed that "all branches of intellectual activity have in common one fundamental function (or group of functions), whereas the remaining or specific elements of the activity seem in every case to be wholly different from that in all the others" (p. 284). This statement epitomizes Spearman's two-factor theory. The theory maintains that there is a general factor that pervades all intellectual performances, and a set of specific factors, each of which is relevant to one particular task.

In *The Abilities of Man*, Spearman (1927) stated his position in detail, and contrasted the position with what then seemed to be the major competing views: the monarchic, the oligarchic, and the anarchic. According to a monarchic theory, there is just one factor of intelligence that pervades all intellectual tasks. According to an oligarchic theory, there are several distinct factors that determine intellectual performance. According to an anarchic theory, there is a set of specific abilities, each relevant to a particular task, with no general factor common to more than one task.

Thomson's Theory of Bonds

Brown and Thomson (1921) pointed out that the two-factor theory was not the only theory consistent with Spearman's factor-analytic results. They argued that the obtained general factor could be indicative of a mathematical rather than a psychological unity. Thomson (1939) proposed a theory of bonds, in which the mind is conceived of as possessing an enormous number of "bonds," including reflexes, habits, learned associations, and the like. Performance on any one task would activate a large number of these bonds. Related tasks, such as those used in mental tests, would sample overlapping subsets of bonds. A factor analysis of a set of tests might therefore give the appearance of a general factor, when in fact what is common to the tests is a multitude of bonds.

As the years passed, it became apparent that neither Spearman's two-factor theory nor Thomson's theory of bonds could withstand the test of time. There appeared to be a third kind of factor that was neither general to all intellectual tasks, nor specific to just one task. Subsequent theorizing attempted to account for this phenomenon in different ways.

Holzinger's Bi-Factor Theory

Holzinger (1938) proposed a bi-factor theory, which retained the general and specific factors of Spearman, but also permitted group factors common to some tests but not others. The theory thus expanded upon the foundation of Spearman's theory, and Holzinger and Spearman actually collaborated in developing the bi-factor theory. The theory never gained widespread support, in part because it was developed at about the same time Thurstone proposed a theory that kindled more enthusiasm.

Thurstone's Multiple-Factor Theory

L. L. Thurstone (1938) proposed a theory with seven "multiple" factors: verbal comprehension, number, memory, perceptual speed, space, verbal fluency, and inductive reasoning. Thurstone called these "primary mental abilities." They were the factors that appeared when Thurstone rotated his solutions to simple structure.

The primary mental abilities were used as the basis for the later Primary Mental Abilities tests. The composition of the tests varies somewhat at different grade levels. In the 1962 revision (Thurstone & Thurstone, 1962), the two levels of tests for secondary school students include synonyms to measure verbal comprehension, simple arithmetic problems to measure number, letter series, word classification (which word doesn't belong with the others?) and number series to measure inductive reasoning, and symbol rotation to measure space.

The most salient problem confronting the multiple-factor theory was that a general factor would not quite go away. Thus it happened that, just as Spearman was eventually obliged to concede the existence of group factors, Thurstone was obliged to concede the existence of some kind of general factor. The concessions were grudging, however. Spearman maintained until the end that group factors were relatively unimportant, while Thurstone labeled the general factor a "second-order factor," one that need appear only when factors are themselves factored.

Guilford's Structure-of-Intellect (SI) Model

Guilford (1967) proposed an extension of Thurstone's theory that incorporates Thurstone's factors. However, it splits the primary mental abilities and adds new abilities so that the number of factors is increased from 7 to 120. Whereas Thurstone permitted factors to be correlated, Guilford hypothesized that his factors are independent.

According to Guilford (1967), every mental task includes three ingredients: an operation, a content, and a product. There are five kinds of operation: cognition, memory, divergent production, convergent production, and evaluation. There are six kinds of product: units, classes, relations, systems, transformations, and implications. And there are four kinds of content: figural, symbolic, semantic, and behavioral. Since the subcategories are independently defined, they are multiplicative, so that there are 5 X 6 X 4 = 120 different mental abilities. Guilford has represented the structure of intellect as a large cube composed of 120 smaller cubes. Each dimension of the cube corresponds to one of the three categories (operation, content, product), and each of the 120 possible combinations of the three categories forms one of the smaller cubes.

Guilford and his associates have devised tests that measure many of the 120 factors required by the model. (Guilford and Hoepfner, 1971, report that the number of demonstrated SI abilities is 98.) We can consider only a few of many examples, since there are 120 abilities and usually at least two tests to measure each ability. Cognition of figural relations (abbreviated CFR), for example, is measured by tests such as figure analogies or matrices. Memory for semantic relations (MMR) is measured by presenting to examinees a series of relationships, such as, "Gold is more valuable than iron," and then testing retention in a multiple-choice format. Evaluation of symbolic units (ESU) is measured by same—different tests, in which subjects are presented with pairs of numbers or letters that are either identical or different in minor details. Subjects then have to mark each pair as either "same" or "different."

Burt's and Vernon's Hierarchical Models

Burt (1940) distinguished four kinds of factors likely to be found in the measurement of a given set of traits: general, group, specific, and error. General factors are common to all traits. Group factors are common to some of the traits. Specific factors are limited to each trait whenever it is measured. Error factors are limited to each trait on each particular occasion it is measured.

Burt (1949) proposed a five-level hierarchical model. At the top of the hierarchy is "the human mind." At the second level, the "relations level," are g (the general factor) and a practical factor. At the third level are associations, at the fourth level is perception, and at the fifth level is sensation.

Probably more sophisticated is the hierarchical model proposed by Vernon (1971). At the top of the hierarchy is g. At the second level are two major group factors, v:ed and k:m. The former refers to verbal—educational abilities of the kind measured by conventional tests of scholastic aptitude. The latter refers to spatial—mechanical abilities, such as those measured by tests of spatial and mechanical abilities. At the third level of the hierarchy are minor group factors, and at the fourth level are specific factors.

Relations among Theories

How could factor-analytic investigations support such a wide range of theories? There are a number of ways in which differences can arise:

1. *Method of factor analysis.* As stated earlier, there are many different methods for performing factor analyses, each of which generally yields a somewhat different solution for the same set of data. Ability theorists disagree as to the preferred method. Moreover, early theorists such as Spearman and even Thurstone used cruder methods than those widely used today. However, it is unlikely that method of factor analysis was a major determinant of differences among theories, since the results obtained from the different methods, although not identical, are usually comparable.

2. *Factor-analytic model.* Two basic models were described earlier, the component model and the factor model. These models yield different results. The components of the former model contain both specific and error variance, so that it is not possible to separate specific and error factors from common factors. The factors of the latter model do permit separation of common from unique (either specific or error) factors, but some theorists choose to ignore the unique factors while others do not, as was seen in the previous section. However, the model used in the analysis cannot account for the most salient differences among the theories, such as the decision about whether to include a general factor.

3. *Criteria for stopping factor extraction.* The investigator must decide how many factors to retain, and investigators use widely differing criteria for retaining factors. Guilford's criteria are obviously among the most lenient. However, the large discrepancy in the number of factors posited by Guilford as compared to other theorists is not due solely to differing criteria for stopping factor extraction. Selection of tests is also important.

4. *Selection of tests.* Spearman used a relatively restricted range of related mental tests, so that a strong general factor would be more likely to appear in his analyses. Thurstone, whose theory involves seven factors, used a wider variety of tests. Guilford, whose theory demands one hundred twenty factors, used by far the largest number of tests — several hundred. Guilford also used the most diverse sampling of tests. With larger numbers of tests and more diverse tests, finer discriminations in patterns of individual differences can be made, and hence the number of reliable factors can be increased.

5. *Subject population.* Subject populations differed across studies, both in size and diversity. Vernon (1971) has pointed out that Spearman and his followers "were seldom able to test large populations. Hence any residual overlap that did appear was usually not statistically significant; it might have arisen from chance errors in the correlations" (p. 14). Differences in range of ability in the population can also affect outcomes, as can age of the population. It is commonly believed that abilities become more differentiated with age (cf. Garrett, 1946; Vernon, 1971, pp. 29–31).

6. *Alternate interpretations of identical solutions.* Identical mathematical solutions are open to alternative psychological interpretations. Spearman's and Thomson's theories, for example, assign widely differing psychological meanings to identical factorial solutions. Both theories are consistent with a general factor and a set of specific factors. Holzinger's bi-factor theory is related in a similar way to Burt's hierarchical theory. Their general and group factors are formally equivalent, and the specific factors of Holzinger include Burt's specific factors and possibly his error factors.

7. *Method of and criteria for rotation.* Differences in rotational preferences are probably the major source of differences among theories. Spearman and Burt did not rotate factors. As a result, they usually found a general factor followed

by a succession of bipolar factors. Thurstone found such a pattern of factors lacking in psychological meaningfulness, and so he rotated factors to what he believed was a psychologically more meaningful configuration – simple structure. By definition, simple structure does not permit a general factor. The only way to show the existence of a general factor is to factor the factors, which may yield a second-order general factor. Guilford found simple structure rotations lacking in psychological meaning, and so he rotated his factors according to a subjective procedure in which the criterion was minimization of the discrepancy between the observed and the predicted pattern of factors. That rotation was used which best supported Guilford's theory. (This procedure is discussed further later in the chapter.)

Clearly, the method of rotation can have a major impact upon the theory that the factor analysis is viewed as supporting. The identical factor space can be interpreted as supporting any of an infinite number of theories, each corresponding to a different rotation. While only a limited number of these will be of psychological interest, the number is large enough to generate a diversity of theories.

While a factor analysis can support many theories, it cannot support any theory. Indeed, many investigators have had to modify their notions at least to some extent as a result of factor-analytic results that were not entirely consistent with their preconceptions. Two examples of such accommodation were cited earlier: Spearman's eventual acceptance of group factors and Thurstone's eventual acceptance of a general (second-order) factor. Many theories have not been considered seriously since Spearman's time, simply because they are inconsistent with the collective results of factor-analytic investigations. For example, no major factor-analytic investigation has supported the monarchical theory to which Spearman contrasted his two-factor theory. Furthermore, the identities of the group factors are at least somewhat constrained by factor analysis: Certain types of tests tend to cluster together consistently. Factor analysis has thus limited the number of theories that can be accepted as meeting any reasonable criterion of psychological plausibility.

CONTRIBUTIONS OF FACTOR ANALYSIS

Zeitgeist for Two Generations of Researchers

The historical sketch above should make clear that factor analysis has been much more to ability theorists than a method of data analysis. Factor analysis provided the Zeitgeist for two generations of ability theorists and other differential psychologists. While there was little agreement among theorists as to the way in which abilities are organized, there was general agreement that factor analysis was the way in which this organization could be discovered and elucidated. While it might not provide final answers, it provided enough tentative answers to support lifetime programs of research. Until recently, no alternative approach to the study of abilities could seriously compete with factor analysis for the allegiance of ability theorists.

Applicability to Complex Processes

Factor analysis not only provided a way of looking at things, it provided a way of looking at the elusive entities that intelligence researchers wanted to study — complex mental abilities. Through factor analysis, researchers were able to study the hypothetical sources of complex human behavior at a time when the two major alternative approaches, behaviorism and Gestalt psychology, were unpromising. The methods of the behaviorists were better suited to the study of animal behavior and simple human behavior, and many of these accounts deliberately ignored the mediating mental constructs that were of interest to ability researchers. Some of the accounts denied that such constructs were even objects worthy of serious study. Gestalt psychologists attempted to apply their experimental methods to the study of complex behavior, for example, Köhler's (1925) experiments on insight learning. The Gestalt approach, however, never permitted its users the level of theoretical detail and quantitative precision that was enjoyed by ability researchers. Gestalt theories were barely specified at all. The hope was for later physiological specification, but this hope has yet to be realized.

Macrotheoretical Capability

The theories of intelligence generated by factor-analytic investigations were not only specified quantitatively and in some detail; they were also specified at a macrotheoretical level. Generality was a major concern of the differential psychologists. Factorial invariance — identification of the same factors across different populations and different groups of tests — was a widely sought goal. As would be expected, it proved difficult to achieve.

Systematic Study of Individual Differences

Factor-analytic theories are built upon a foundation of individual differences: They are derived from data quantifying information about individual differences (correlations across subjects), and factors cannot be derived in the absence of individual differences among subjects. It is therefore not surprising that, whereas experimental psychologists have traditionally shied away from individual differences, ability theorists have thrived upon them. Ability theorists were not forced by the assumptions of their methods to ignore the exploration of meaningful individual differences, nor to explain them away in a few sentences reserved for inconspicuous parts of their articles and books. There has been no other approach to psychological research that has been able to handle individual differences so easily and systematically.

Concurrent Development of Theories of Measurement and Intelligence

The development of the theory of psychological measurement went hand in hand with the development of the theory of intelligence. Many theorists who made significant contributions to one also made significant contributions to the other (most notably Spearman and Thurstone). Measurement theory developed in a substantive vacuum can quickly become dry and abstruse, but in the early 1900s measurement theory developed rapidly because it was needed for substantive theory. The result was an extraordinarily productive symbiotic relationship.

Relevance to Applied Settings

Much psychological research is of little import outside the psychological laboratory. Even years of research on learning, for example, have had a surprisingly meager impact upon educational practice. Psychometric work on abilities, however, has had a tremendous impact upon educational and industrial practice, largely through mental tests. As is well known, the tests were all too often misused. Nevertheless, they have in countless instances provided valuable supplemental information to other available sources of information; when used correctly, the tests have been able to enhance significantly the quality of educational and industrial decision making.

Overview

The differential approach to intelligence, using factor analysis as its main tool for investigation, was for many years a most productive one. Many important contributions to both theory and practice have been made by users of the differential approach. Because of these contributions, and because there was for many years no viable alternative to the differential approach, it is not surprising that it thrived for as long as it did.

THE DECLINE OF THE DIFFERENTIAL APPROACH

In spite of its earlier successes, the differential approach to intelligence has not fared well in recent years. Interest in the approach has declined considerably. Why the decline? A major reason is that its principal tool, factor analysis, can no longer meet the multifarious demands placed upon it. When the demands became too great, they strained the entire differential research enterprise to a point of near collapse. The sources of strain were of two kinds: misuses of factor-analytic methods and limitations of these methods.

Misuses of Factor Analysis

Factor analysis has always been easy to misuse, and with the advent of electronic computers, it has become progressively easier to misuse. Humphreys (1962) noted that "except for the decision as to the number of factors to rotate, which is a very important subjective component in the procedure, factor analyses can now be ground out without having the basic data seen by human eye or touched by human hand" (p. 475). Today, Humphreys' remarks are outdated: The computer can decide even how many factors to rotate.

Many misuses of factor analysis stem not from failing to inspect the data, but from using poor judgment in inspecting them. McNemar (1951) has described ten of the most common problems:

1. use of samples too small to permit stability;
2. overinterpretation of small factor loadings and disregard for sample size in deciding upon the minimum loading to interpret;
3. irrational decisions regarding rotation of factors;
4. use of unreliable tests;
5. lack of experimental independence among variables that are factor analyzed;
6. selection of tests so as practically to guarantee a predetermined factor structure;
7. use of tests from domains that are too limited to demonstrate anything and use of tests from separate domains known to be uncorrelated;
8. scanning of tests in a biased fashion when interpreting and naming factors;
9. struggling to make sense out of results;
10. "varying all over the map in the use of hypotheses" — from those who "started with no hypotheses, used none in the process, and ended up with none," to those who "start with hypotheses, use them enroute, and end with hypotheses" (McNemar, 1951, p. 358).

Guilford (1952) has also described "some common faults in factor analysis." He too noted ten problems, which are listed below verbatim:

1. "Too many factors are often extracted for the number of experimental variables" (p. 27).
2. "Too many experimental variables are factorially complex" (p. 27).
3. "Sometimes a common factor fails to come out because it is substantially represented in only one experimental variable" (p. 28).
4. "Not enough factors are extracted" (p. 28).

5. "Correlation coefficients used in analysis are often spurious" (p. 29).
6. "Correlations of ipsative scores are sometimes used in an analysis"[2] (p. 30).
7. "A pair of factors is very much confined to the same experimental variables" (p. 31).
8. "The population on which the analysis is based is heterogeneous" (p. 32).
9. "Not enough attention is given to requirements for correlation coefficients" (p. 32).
10. "Difficulty levels of tests often vary substantially" (p. 33).

The only striking similarity in the lists of McNemar and Guilford is the number of items. The actual items are virtually nonoverlapping. With twenty common faults, it is no surprise that factor analysis ran into trouble. But the most serious trouble resulted not from misuses of the method, but from limitations of factor analysis.

Limitations of Factor Analysis

The limitations of factor analysis have been the major source of strain upon the differential approach to intelligence. The limitations to be described pose serious problems only when factor analysis is used for purposes for which it is not suited. Unfortunately, these are the purposes for which most ability theorists have wanted to use factor analysis. *Factor analysis is not an appropriate method for discovering the components underlying intelligence.* Four reasons are proposed for its lack of suitability, each corresponding to an intrinsic limitation of factor analysis. The first two limitations are statistical in nature; the second two are psychological. Because of the statistical limitations, factor analysis lacks inferential power for distinguishing among theories. Because of the psychological limitations, factors could not be components of intelligence.

At least the first two of the limitations to be described, the statistical ones, are not insurmountable. The relatively recent advent of confirmatory maximum likelihood methods of factor analysis makes it possible to use factor analysis for sophisticated testing of prior hypotheses, and also makes possible the attainment of a unique solution (not subject to rotation). It is possible, even likely, that the second two substantive limitations can be surmounted as well. It remains to be shown, though, that factor analysis can be performed so as to dispense with all four limitations simultaneously.

Lack of control over mathematical realization of psychological theory. A distinction must be drawn between two types of theory, the psychological theory and the mathematical one. The psychological theory states how the mind

---

[2] An ipsative score for each individual is distributed about the mean for the individual, rather than about the population mean (cf. Guilford, 1954, p. 528).

functions. The mathematical theory states the way a set of empirical data should look.

In order to clarify the discussion that follows, let us also distinguish between psychological theory-testing operations in factor analysis and in mathematical modeling of the type done in many experimental investigations. In each case, theory-testing occurs in two steps. However, the two steps occur in opposite orders.

In mathematical modeling: (1) the investigator formulates a mathematical theory on the basis of a psychological theory; and (2) mathematical procedures fit the mathematical theory to a set of empirical data. The first step is qualitative, the second step quantitative. The investigator must start with a psychological theory in order to formulate the mathematical theory, but he may or may not have experimental data when he formulates the mathematical theory.

In factor-analytic modeling: (1) mathematical procedures formulate a mathematical (factor-analytic) theory on the basis of experimental data; and (2) the investigator fits the mathematical theory to a psychological theory. The first step is quantitative, the second step qualitative. Experimental data are needed for the factor-analytic machinery to formulate the mathematical model, but the investigator may or may not have a psychological theory when this is done.

From the present point of view, the crucial difference between modeling procedures is in the locus of control over the mathematical theory. Using mathematical modeling, the investigator defines, and hence has control over, both the psychological and the mathematical theories. Using factor-analytic modeling, the investigator defines, and hence has control over, only the psychological theory. The mathematical theory is defined by the machinery of factor analysis. Control over the mathematical theory enables the mathematical modeler to perform two important theory-testing operations that the factor-analytic modeler cannot perform:

1. The investigator can compare directly two (or more) mathematical theories on the same set of data. In comparing two mathematical theories, X and Y, for example, on the same set of data, the investigator might find that Theory X accounts for 80% of the variance in the data and that Theory Y accounts for 50% of the variance in the data. The investigator would probably be justified in accepting Theory X over Theory Y.

2. The investigator can compare directly one mathematical theory on two (or more) sets of data. If Theory X accounts for 80% of the variance in Data Set A, but only 50% of the variance in Data Set B, then the investigator may conclude that the theory works quite well under certain circumstances but less well under others. The investigator must then determine what these circumstances are.

Using factor analysis, the investigator can test two mathematical theories on the same set of data if they differ in just one respect — number of factors. The comparison must be made in light of the fact that the theory with the greater number of factors will always account for the greater proportion of variance in the data. The factor analyst cannot perform the two theory-testing operations described above because the data, not the theorist, determine the mathematical theory.

Factor analysis obviously does not preclude comparisons between psychological theories. As was shown in the section summarizing factor-analytic theories of intelligence, certain psychological theories are incompatible with the results of factor-analytic research. The problem is that a rather wide variety of psychological theories may be compatible with the results of a single factor analysis, and it is not possible to distinguish among them mathematically.

Solution indeterminacy: the rotation dilemma. Guilford (1974) has called the need for rotation "the most serious weakness" (p. 498) of the factor-analytic method. The crux of the problem is that while the factor space is unique, the orientation of axes is not. The axes may be rotated in an infinite number of ways, each of which defines factors along different dimensions. The different dimensions have different psychological implications. For example, an unrotated solution will often support a theory of a general factor followed by bipolar group factors and possibly specific factors. Rotation to simple structure will often support a theory of group or multiple factors in the absence of a general factor. Subjective rotation to minimize discrepancies between predicted and observed factors can yield still different results.

Guilford has been a proponent of subjective rotational methods, the most widely used of which are a class of "Procrustean" algorithms (e.g., Cliff, 1966; Hurley & Cattell, 1962; Schönemann, 1966). (Procrustes was the Attican giant who seized travelers and either cut off their legs or stretched them until they fit an iron bed to which he had tied them.) While most American psychologists have used objective rotation to simple structure, Guilford's "experience showed that although simple structure is a useful guide, it is by no means sufficient if we want logical psychological meaning" (Guilford, 1974, p. 498). In the course of his career, Guilford "actually tried out just about every objective computerized method that existed, both orthogonal and oblique, with the same sets of data. The general results were the same: Factors were neither nicely interpretable nor were they invariant from one method to another. This is a fact of life that those who factor analyze must face" (Guilford, 1974, p. 499). Facing this fact, Guilford turned to subjective rotation. However, these methods also have a drawback, that "aiming of axes in the directions of selected tests involves forcing of data toward a better fit to theory than is justified by the data. But knowing from experience how stubborn coefficients of correlations are as data and also the principal-factor coefficients derived from them, there was not a great deal of concern on that score" (Guilford, 1974, p. 499).

Horn and Knapp (1973) have suggested that there may be cause for concern. They used Procrustean methods to test randomly generated theories. They found that

> ... the support provided for such arbitrary theories is quite comparable to that put forth as providing support for SI [Guilford's Structure-of-Intellect] theory. This pseudo-support for a theory can be obtained (a) with variables that are not random, (b) under a requirement that factors remain orthogonal, (c) when factor coefficients remain generally positive, (d) under a requirement that loadings be .30 or larger to be regarded as "significant," and (e) in samples as large as are customarily used in psychological research. (p. 42)

Horn and Knapp correctly pointed out that their results do not disconfirm SI theory. The Horn–Knapp factors will probably not replicate as well as Guilford's, and no single experiment or set of experiments is likely to undermine a supporting data base built up over a period of twenty-five years. But the Horn–Knapp results raise questions. At least where subjective rotational methods are used, heavy reliance upon factor analysis for theoretical support is a risky enterprise.

What is particularly disconcerting about the theoretical status of the psychometrically derived and tested theories of intelligence is that a major differentia among them (if not *the* major differentia) is the type of rotation used upon the initial factor matrix. Since all rotations of a given number of factors extracted from a particular set of data account for identical proportions of variance in the data, it is clear that methods other than factor analysis will have to be used to choose among alternative theories.

Failure to discover or explicate process.   Factor analysis provides no way to discover or explicate the processes that in combination constitute intelligent behavior. Thurstone (1947) realized that the goal of research into the nature of intelligence should be the understanding of process. He pointed out that "the factorial methods were developed for the study of individual differences among people but the individual differences may be regarded as an avenue of approach to the study of the processes which underlie these differences" (p. 55). Unfortunately, the avenue of approach has had little traffic, perhaps because "it is difficult to see how the available individual difference data can be used even as a starting point for generating a theory as to the process nature of general intelligence or of any other specified ability" (McNemar, 1964, p. 881).

The problem is that factor analysis is capable only of analyzing *inter*item structure in a test, whereas a process analysis would require analysis of *intra*item structure. It would require elucidation of the steps involved in the solution of a single item. Factor analysis "deals only with the end products of human thinking and behavior, and throws little light on how these products come about in individual human beings" (Vernon, 1971, p. 9). Because of this, factorial studies do not "enable us to decide what are the basic components of mental organization" (Vernon, 1970, p. 100).

Interindividual nature of analysis.   The components of intelligence are intra-individual — they exist within individual subjects. Factor analysis, however, is generally interindividual — it analyzes patterns of individual differences across subjects. Since individual differences are meaningless in the context of one individual, it is not clear how factor analysis could enable us to discover what the components within an individual are. While certain modes of factor analysis could be used intraindividually, it has not been shown that they could discover underlying components of intelligence.

The effects of this binding of factor analysis to individual differences can be illustrated with reference to Table 2.1. Five hypothetical mental ability tests require eight hypothetical mental components for their solution. Capitalized letters — A, C, C', E, F, F' — represent components that are sources of individual differences in test performance. Some of these sources of individual differences are very highly correlated with each other, and these correlated sources are represented by primed and unprimed pairs — C' and C, F' and F. Other mental components are not sources of substantial individual differences in the sample of the population to which the tests are given, although they might show individual differences in some other more heterogeneous sample. The sample might be composed of college sophomores taking introductory psychology, although the population of interest is somewhat wider than that. These components (in which there are unsubstantial levels of individual differences) are represented by lower case letters — b, d.

The correlation matrix from the tests is factor analyzed, and the outcome will depend for its interpretation upon the rotation used (if any). However, one idealized, psychologically interpretable outcome would consist of a general factor, a group factor, and specific factors. But these factors will not represent individual components. At best, they will be confounded.

TABLE 2.1
Components in Five Hypothetical Mental Ability Tests

1	2	3	4	5
A	A	A	A	A
b	b	b	b	b
C	C	C		
C'	C'	C'		
d		d	d	
			E	
				F
				F'

There will be just one general factor, that for component A. Component b will not be represented by a general factor, or any factor, because although it is "general," it cannot be identified due to its constant value across subjects. Factors and factor scores are standardized so that any constants are removed.

The group factor will include both components C and C', because although they are separate components, they are highly enough correlated across subjects so as to be inseparable through factor analysis. It should be noted that in spite of this high correlation across subjects, C and C' may be weakly correlated or even uncorrelated across tasks. "Group" component d will not be accounted for at all because of the absence of individual differences.

Component E will emerge as a separate specific factor, but F and F' will be confounded, and if there are 1s in the diagonal of the correlation matrix, error variance will be confounded with systematic specific variance from component E and from components F and F'.

The purpose of this analysis is to show that factors are not representations of the components of intelligence. The analysis is both hypothetical and idealized. With real data, even the confounded components would not emerge so cleanly. Furthermore, even in the ideal situation, the above scheme is only one of an infinite number possible through rotation of axes. Rotation would very likely result in some or all components being split up between factors, so that not only would components be confounded, but they would be fragmented as well. Factor analysis provides no way of isolating the components or assuring that they will remain intact.

SUMMARY

During the first half of the century, factor analysis seemed to provide the keys to unlock the mysteries of intelligence. During the second half of the century, criticism became widespread, and even some prominent factor analysts began to question whether factor analysis was the appropriate method for discovering the structure of intelligence.

There have been two major schools of thought regarding how factor analysis should be used in scientific investigations. One has held that it is useful primarily as a tool in hypothesis formation, while the other has held that it is useful primarily as a means of testing hypotheses. Many investigators have also taken the intermediate position — that factor analysis is of some use in both pursuits.

The fundamental unit of analysis in factor analysis is the factor. There has never been much consensus among factor analysts as to just what a factor is. There have been two major points of view regarding the nature of factors — the descriptive and the causative. The former viewpoint regards factors as describing behavior, while the latter viewpoint regards factors as sources of behavior.

Prior to factor analysis, an investigator must: (1) select tests; (2) select subjects; (3) administer tests to subjects; (4) score the tests; and (5) compute basic statistics, including intercorrelations among the tests. The data are then ready for factor analysis.

Factor analysis represents a variable in terms of several underlying factors, or hypothetical constructs. The input to a factor analysis is usually a correlation matrix, with either 1s, reliabilities, or communalities in the diagonal. The choice of diagonal entries determines the partitioning of variance within each variable.

Variance may be distributed between factors according to either of two basic models: the component model or the factor model. The former requires 1s in the diagonal of the correlation matrix, while the latter requires reliability or communality estimates. Hence, the way in which intravariable variance is partitioned is one ingredient in determining the way in which variance will be distributed across factors.

The output from a factor analysis consists of two matrices: a factor pattern and a factor structure. These matrices are mathematically related, and the relation is such that the two matrices are identical when the factors are all uncorrelated. The two matrices can be used to reproduce the original correlation matrix, although the reproduction will not be perfect unless all components or factors are extracted, in which case no data reduction will have occurred.

The pattern and structure matrices for a given factor analysis are not unique, because any of an infinite number of coordinate reference systems is mathematically permissible.

A number of factor-analytically derived theories of intelligence have been proposed. Among the most well known are Spearman's two-factor theory, Thomson's theory of bonds, Holzinger's bi-factor theory, Thurstone's multiple-factor theory, Guilford's Structure-of-Intellect (SI) model, and the hierarchical models of Burt and Vernon. There are a number of ways in which factor-analytic investigations could support different theories. The three most important are probably selection of tests, method of, and criterion for, rotation; and alternative interpretations of identical results.

The differential approach to intelligence was for many years a most productive one. Through factor analysis, it (1) provided the Zeitgeist for two generations of ability researchers; (2) permitted the investigation of complex psychological constructs; (3) generated theories at a macrotheoretical level; (4) provided a systematic means for studying individual differences; (5) fostered a symbiotic relationship between theories of measurement and intelligence that led to greater sophistication in each; and (6) proved itself relevant to the needs of applied settings. Because of these contributions and because for many years there was no viable alternative to the differential approach, it is not surprising that it thrived for as long as it did.

Factor analysis, like other methods, has been subject to common technical misuses. More serious are four intrinsic limitations that restrict the kinds of interpretations that should be drawn from factor-analytic results. Two of these limitations are statistical, and two are psychological. Because of the statistical limitations, factor analysis lacks inferential power for distinguishing among theories. Because of the psychological limitations, factors cannot be components of intelligence.

First, the machinery of factor analysis rather than the investigator formulates and thus has control over the mathematical theory, resulting in a reduced ability of the investigator to perform theory-comparison operations. Second, solutions are indeterminate because of the infinite number of possible axis rotations. Third, factor analysis is done over items, and hence cannot be used as a means for discovering or explicating the processes that are used in solving individual items. Fourth, intelligence and abilities exist within the individual, but factor analysis is between individuals (except in rare uses).

Factor analysis can be of considerable value in the study of human abilities. Uses of factor analysis in the framework of componential analysis will be discussed in Chapter 4. Factor analysis is not a direct means toward the discovery of the basic underlying components of mental ability. Unfortunately, this has been one of the most common purposes for which factor analysis has been used.

3
The Information-Processing
Approach to Intelligence

Many investigators of intelligence have adopted the view of human abilities as dynamic information-processing capabilities (cf. Resnick, 1976). The information-processing view provides an alternative to the differential view of abilities as static psychological factors. Information-processing psychology, however, was developed not as an alternative to the factor-analytic concepts of differential psychology, but as an alternative to the stimulus-response concepts of behaviorism.

The nature of the opposition between the two schools of thought was well expressed by Miller, Galanter, and Pribram (1960):

> On the one hand are the optimists, who claim to find the dependency [of the organism on what happens around it] simple and straightforward. They model the stimulus-response relations after the classical, physiological pattern of the reflex arc and use Pavlov's discoveries to explain how new reflexes can be formed through experience. This approach is too simple for all but the most extreme optimists. . . . So the model is complicated slightly by incorporating [reinforcing] stimuli that occur after the response in addition to the stimuli that occur before the response.
>
> Arrayed against the reflex theorists are the pessimists, who think that living organisms are complicated, devious, poorly designed for research purposes, and so on. . . . They are quite sure that any correlations between stimulation and response must be mediated by an organized representation of the environment, a system of concepts and relations within which the organism is located. A human being – and probably other animals as well – builds up an internal representation, a model of the universe, a schema, a simulacrum, a cognitive map, an Image. (pp. 6–7)

The research of the "pessimists" took many forms, from the creation of detailed computer programs to the formulation of complex mathematical models. "The common new emphasis was . . . the exploration of complex processes and the acceptance of the need to be explicit about internal, symbolic mechanisms" (Newell & Simon, 1972, p. 4).

One of the earliest tasks of the information-processing psychologists was to overthrow the reflex as the fundamental unit of analysis. The reflex is a concept borrowed from physiology — an extension of the notion of the reflex arc from the purely physiological regularity in behavior to other predictable uniformities in behavior.

The major argument against the reflex (as against other stimulus–response concepts) was that it is a gross oversimplification. Miller and his colleagues argued on the basis of physiological evidence that the neural mechanisms involved even in reflex actions cannot be diagrammed as a simple reflex arc or even as a chain of stimulus–response connections. They noted that the general pattern of reflex action "is to test the input energies against some criteria established in the organism, to respond if the result of the test is to show an incongruity, and to continue to respond until the incongruity vanishes, at which time the reflex is terminated" (p. 26).

THE FUNDAMENTAL UNIT OF ANALYSIS

The Elementary Information Process

The fundamental unit of analysis in information-processing psychology is the *elementary information process* (eip) (Newell & Simon, 1972). It is assumed that all behavior of a human information-processing system is the result of sequences of these elementary processes. They are elementary in the sense that they are not further broken down into simpler processes by the theory under consideration. The level of analysis that is defined as "elementary" will depend upon the type of behavior under consideration, and the aspects of that behavior that are of interest. The processes must be well defined, and the collection of them must be sufficiently general and powerful to compose all macroscopic performances of the human information processing system (Newell & Simon, 1972).

The notion of an elementary information process is a general one. Some investigators have sought to specify further the notion and the way multiple eip's combine to form macroscopic performances. Two further specifications are the TOTE (Miller et al., 1960) and the production (Newell, 1973; Newell & Simon, 1972).

The TOTE

Miller, Galanter, and Pribram (1960) have proposed as the fundamental unit of behavior the TOTE (Test–Operate–Test–Exit). Each unit of behavior begins with a test of a present outcome against a desired outcome. If the result of the test is congruent with the desired outcome (called an *Image*), an exit is made. If not, another operation is performed in order to make the result of the next test conform as closely as possible to the Image. If the result of that next test is

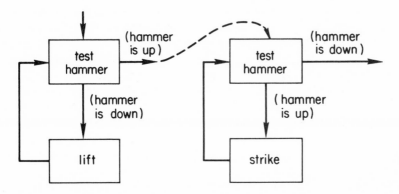

FIGURE 3.1 Example of a Plan. (From *Plans and the structure of behavior*, by George A. Miller, Eugene Galanter, and Karl H. Pribram. Copyright © 1960 by Holt, Rinehart, and Winston, Publishers. Reprinted by permission of Holt, Rinehart, and Winston, Publishers.)

congruent with the Image, an exit is made. Otherwise, still another operation is performed, and so on down the line until a test result corresponds to the Image (which may have been modified along the way in order to make it conform more closely to the demands of reality). An individual TOTE, a hierarchy of TOTEs, or a sequence of TOTEs (which may include hierarchies) executed in order to realize an Image is called a *Plan.*

The concept of a TOTE leads quite naturally to the flow chart as a representation for sequences of TOTEs (Plans). A simple example of TOTEs combining into a Plan expressed as a flow chart is shown in Figure 3.1.

The flow chart shows a Plan for hammering in a nail. The Plan is composed of two higher-order TOTEs, one for testing the nail and one for testing the hammer. Two lower-order TOTEs, one for lifting the hammer and the other for lowering the hammer (to strike the nail), are hierarchically embedded in the more general hammering TOTE. The entire sequence begins by testing the nail to see whether it sticks up or is flush with the surface into which it is being hammered. If it is flush, one is done, and exits. If the nail sticks up, one must then operate with the hammer. One tests the hammer to determine whether it needs to be lifted, and then tests the hammer to determine whether it needs to strike. After lifting and striking, one again tests the nail to determine whether it is flush, and repeats the hammering operation if the nail is not yet flush.

The Production

A production is a condition—action sequence: If a certain condition is met, then a certain action is performed. Sequences of ordered productions are called production systems.

The "executive" for a production system is hypothesized to make its way down the ordered list of productions until one of the conditions is met. The action corresponding to that condition is executed, and control is returned to the top of the list. The executive then makes its way down the list again, trying to satisfy a condition. When it does so, an action is executed, control returns to the top, etc. Hunt and Poltrock (1974) have suggested that the productions may be probabilistically ordered, so that the exact order in which the list is scanned may differ across scannings of the list.

An example of a simple production for crossing the street is the following (Newell & Simon, 1972):

traffic-light red — stop
traffic-light green — move
move and left-foot-on-pavement — step-with-right-foot
move and right-foot-on-pavement — step-with-left-foot

In this production system, one first tests to see whether the light is red. If it is red, one stops, and again tests to see whether the light is red. This sequence will be repeated until the light turns green, at which point one will start moving. If one is moving and one's left foot is on the pavement, one will step with the right foot; or if one is moving and one's right foot is on the pavement, one will step with the left foot.

Newell and Simon's "crossing-the-street" production system is incomplete. There is no production for a light turning amber. And if the light turns red while one is in the middle of the street, one stops dead in his tracks.

The TOTE and the production are related. The test of the former is analogous to the condition of the latter, and the operation of the former is analogous to the action of the latter. The major difference between them is in the control structure that puts together sequences of TOTEs or productions: the Plan versus the production system. While these two control structures are different in nature, Newell (1973), Hunt and Poltrock (1974), and Carpenter and Just (1975) have shown that execution of complex tasks can often be conceptualized as guided by either control structure. It is not clear at present whether they are even distinguishable experimentally.

We have now considered two views of the control structure in information-processing psychology. We turn to a consideration of ways in which control structures and information processes can be studied.

INFORMATION-PROCESSING METHODOLOGY

Artificial Intelligence versus Simulation

The information-processing approach is not a unitary one. Rather, it encompasses a broad range of perspectives and research techniques. The broadest distinction is between artificial intelligence and simulation. Artificial intelligence research is directed toward the creation of models (usually implemented on a computer) that perform complex tasks usually considered to require intelligence. The goal of such research is optimization of performance, with little or no regard to whether the optimal way of performing a task is also the one that humans use. Simulation research is directed toward the creation of models that simulate human performance. Optimization is sought only if humans perform optimally. Otherwise, suboptimal modes of performance are deliberately incorporated into the models.

The two perspectives may be seen as endpoints of a continuum rather than as dichotomous. Information-processing psychologists vary widely in the extent to which they are concerned with the simulation of human behavior. Only the most hardcore artificial intelligence researchers would claim to have no interest in models that in some degree reflect human information processing. Since we are concerned in this volume with human abilities, we shall concentrate upon simulation models of human behavior.

Slow Process versus Fast Process

Within the simulation approach, a further distinction can be drawn between what might be called *slow-process* and *fast-process* research. This distinction is even fuzzier than the first one, and is also continuous rather than discrete. Slow-process research deals with tasks that are usually performed in the order of minutes, and that are somewhat accessible to introspection. The cryptarithmetic, logical proof, and chess tasks studied by Newell and Simon (1972) fall into this domain, as does the hobbits and orcs (missionaries and cannibals) task studied by Greeno (1974) and Thomas (1974). Fast-process research deals with tasks that are usually performed in the order of milliseconds, or at most a few seconds. These are tasks such as the memory-scanning task studied by Saul Sternberg (1969a, 1969b), the sentence–picture comparison task studied by Clark and Chase (1972) and Trabasso, Rollins, and Shaughnessy (1971), and retrieval from semantic memory (Collins & Quillian, 1969). The tasks generally are not readily accessible to introspection.

Slow-process research has made heavy use of protocol analysis and computer simulation as methods for studying behavior. Fast-process research has made heavy use of response-time analysis and mathematical modeling as methods for studying behavior. In these tasks, protocol analysis would be of little use, since subjects perform the tasks so quickly that they are usually unaware of how they proceeded. Reitman (1965), for example, observed that "subjects solve simple analogies so quickly that they can report little but the final result and a few impressions" (p. 227).

The Subtraction Method versus the Additive-Factor Method

Fast-process research involving the modeling of human behavior often proceeds along the lines of either the subtraction method of Donders (1868) or the additive-factor method of Saul Sternberg (1969a). The distinction between these two methods is stated in some detail by Sternberg (1969a) and by Pachella (1974). The methods will be described here only in summary fashion. The subtraction method, which has been the most commonly used,

> ... is applicable when the performance of an experimental task involves the sequential action of a series of discrete mental events. In order to measure the duration of one of these mental events, the reaction time for an experimental task containing the event as a subprocess is compared to that for a comparison task that differs from the experimental task only by the deletion of the process of interest. ... The difference in reaction time for these two conditions will then be equal to the duration of the isolated process. (Pachella, 1974, p. 46)

In actual use, multiple processes will often be of interest, and several tasks may be included in the experimental design that systematically vary the processes required. The critical feature of the method is a set of tasks that, by successive deletions, enables the investigator to estimate the amount of time spent on each component process of interest.

The additive-factor method assumes: (1) that information processing consists of a sequence of independent stages; (2) that each of these stages receives an input from the preceding stage, transforms it, and then passes it along to the next stage; and (3) that the transformation produced in each stage is independent of the duration of any prior stage.

The assumptions about stages have several important implications for the relationship between stage durations and experimental manipulations:

> First, total reaction time is simply the sum of the stage durations. When an experimental manipulation affects the reaction time for a particular information-processing task, it does so by changing the durations of one or more of the constituent stages of processing. Second, if two different experimental manipulations affect two different stages, they will produce independent effects on total reaction time. The effect of one manipulation will be the same, regardless of the level of the other variable. In other words, the effects of the two experimental factors should be additive; they should not interact in a statistical sense. ... Third, if two experimental factors mutually modify each other's effect, that is, if they interact in a statistical sense, they must affect some stage in common. (Pachella, 1974, p. 52)

The additive-factor method is utilized by studying an information-processing task in the context of a multifactor experimental design. The above implications then enable the investigator to make inferences about stages of information processing. Specifically, one examines whether the effects of each pair of experimental factors are additive or interactive. If effects are additive, then plots of response times for successive levels of the pairs of factors will yield parallel lines (see Figure 3.2, left panel). If effects are interactive, then plots of response times will yield nonparallel lines (see Figure 3.2, right panel). Additive factors suggest different stages of processing.

An example of how stages are inferred from additive factors is shown in Figure 3.3 (from Pachella, 1974, and based upon S. Sternberg, 1969a). The effects of

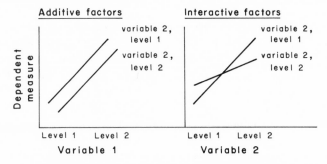

FIGURE 3.2   Effects of additive and interactive factors.

four factors (*F*, *G*, *H*, *I*) on response time are studied in the context of a multifactor experiment. Some of the six possible pairings of factor effects are found to be additive, whereas other pairings are found to be interactive. Factors that add are hypothesized to affect separate stages of processing, whereas interactive factors are hypothesized to affect stages in common. The effects of *F* are found to be additive relative to all other variables, so it is inferred that a particular stage, *a*, is affected only by *F*. *G* and *H* are interactive; *H* and *I* are interactive; but *G* and *I* are additive. Hence, it is inferred that *G* and *H* affect a stage in common; *H* and *I* affect a stage in common; but *G* and *I* do not affect any common stages. Therefore, Stages *b* and *c* may be inferred from the pattern of additivity and interaction. Higher-order interactions should support these inferences.

The classic example of additive-factor logic is that used by Sternberg (1969a, 1969b) in his studies of high-speed memory scanning. A stimulus ensemble is

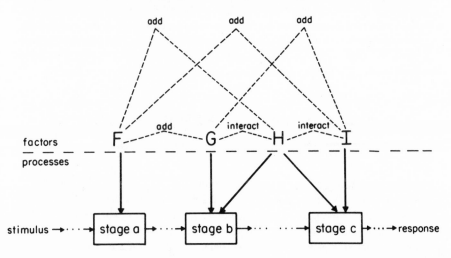

FIGURE 3.3   Effects of factors upon stages. (From Pachella, 1974.)

constructed that consists of all potential test stimuli. From among these stimuli, a set of elements is selected and defined as the *positive set*. These items are presented to subjects for memorization. The remaining items not so presented to subjects become members of the *negative set*. A test stimulus is then presented to a subject, and he must make a positive response if the stimulus is a member of the positive set and a negative response if the stimulus is not a member of the positive set. The dependent variable of primary interest is response latency from the onset of the test stimulus to the indication of a response.

Sternberg varied several independent variables in his studies: (1) stimulus quality; (2) size of positive set; (3) response type (positive or negative); and (4) relative frequency of response type. He tested five of the six possible relationships between pairs of variables and found them all to be additive. He then inferred a four-stage processing algorithm on the basis of these relationships, as well as other considerations. Stimulus quality was assumed to affect a stimulus encoding stage. Size of positive set was assumed to affect a serial-comparison stage. Response type was assumed to affect a binary-decision stage. And relative frequency of response type was assumed to affect a translation and response-organization stage.

It was possible to infer four separate stages only because of the additive relationships between pairs of variables. Had pairs of variables interacted, then it would have been assumed that these pairs were affecting common stages of processing, and a lesser number of separate stages would have been indicated.

The additive-factor method specifies neither the description, duration, nor ordering of the stages. In order for Sternberg (1969a) to formulate a process model from his additive-factor study, it was necessary for him to combine "inferences from the additive-factor method with supplementary arguments and plausible conjectures" (p. 293). A major source of additional information is the nature of the factors. Sternberg inferred, for example, that a stage affected by stimulus quality was likely to be a preprocessing or encoding stage, and that any stage influenced by relative frequency of different response types must follow stimulus encoding (and also serial comparison, another stage in the model).

INFORMATION-PROCESSING THEORIES OF INTELLIGENCE

Overview

Strictly speaking, there are no information-processing theories of intelligence, or at least no theories that even approach the scope of the factor-analytic theories described in the previous chapter. Whereas the theories of differential psychology have tended to emphasize breadth at the expense of depth, information-processing theories have tended to emphasize depth at the expense of breadth. Furthermore, information-processing psychologists studying human intelligence (as distinguished from artificial intelligence) have often been hesitant to refer to their theories as theories of intelligence or its aspects. A few theorists interested in human intelligence, such as Reitman, have speculated on the form that a theory of intelligence might take (Reitman, 1965). But comprehensive theories of intelligence are not to be found. We shall therefore review a sampling of information-processing theories of the sort of task performance often associated with specific mental abilities. Specifically, we will look at theories of tasks involving three of Thurstone's factors: verbal comprehension, spatial visualization, inductive reasoning. These theories, which differ from each other in a number of respects, together present a good picture of the form and content that might be associated with a comprehensive information-processing theory of intelligence. They are representative of some of the best work on intelligence within the information-processing tradition.

Verbal Comprehension

Some of the most interesting research on verbal comprehension has been done in a series of studies by Clark (Clark, 1970, 1971; Clark & Chase, 1972) and by Trabasso (Trabasso, 1970, 1972; Trabasso, Rollins, & Shaughnessy, 1971). Clark and Trabasso independently formulated very similar theories and performed somewhat similar experiments, and so it is not necessary to review both lines of work. We shall describe only a limited aspect of this work, the Clark–Chase theory of the process of comparing sentences against pictures.

In the sentence–picture comparison task, the subject is shown a sentence such as *Star isn't below plus,* and a picture such as $\overset{*}{+}$. The subject has to read the sentence, look at the picture, and indicate as quickly as he can whether the sentence is true of the picture. In the Clark–Chase experiments, there were eight item types (sentence-picture pairs). Items could be either true or false, positive or negative, and use either *above* or *below* as a preposition. While each word (*star* and *plus*) could occur as either subject or as object of the preposition, identical predictions were made for performance in either case, so that the interchange of the two words did not increase the number of distinct item types. The dependent variable in the experiments was response latency, and the nature of the model is to predict response latency from the predictor variables to be described.

Clark and Chase (1972) actually describe two models, *A* and *B,* the former applying when the sentence precedes the picture and the latter applying when the picture precedes the sentence. Since the models are very similar, we shall consider only Model *A*.

Model *A* is divided into four stages. In Stage 1, a subject forms a mental representation of the sentence. It is assumed that sentences are represented in terms of their underlying deep-structure propositions. Thus, *Star is above plus* would be represented (Star above plus)$_{Sen}$ and *Star isn't above plus* would be represented by two propositions, (Star above plus) and (it is false), with the first proposition embedded in the second. It can be seen that encoding of negatives requires formation of an additional embedding proposition.

Above and *below* are antonyms, referring to opposite poles on a verticality dimension. However, the two expressions are not comparable in all respects. Both are indicative of relative height, but height is always measured upward, never downward: The point of reference for height is always at the bottom of whatever is being described. It is suggested, therefore, that *below* is the "abnormal" form used to express relative height. *Below* is called a marked description, and *above* an unmarked description. Previous work (e.g., Clark, 1969) has suggested that the representation of a marked description is more complex than the representation of an unmarked description. In Clark and Chase's coding scheme, *below* is represented as [+Verticality [−Polar]], while *above* is represented as [+Verticality [+Polar]]. It is assumed that the encoding of *below* requires an extra processing step.

The linguistic considerations described above lead to two latency predictions for information processing in Stage 1. One prediction is that encoding of *below* will take longer than encoding of *above*, and the second prediction is that encoding of negatives will take longer than encoding of positives. These latency differences are represented by parameters a and b respectively.

In Stage 2, a subject forms a mental representation of the picture. It is assumed that the picture representation, like the sentence representation, is a propositional encoding, so that a picture of a star above a plus, $\overset{*}{+}$, would be encoded as (Star above plus)$_{Pic}$. It is also assumed that the subject will encode a picture as $(A \text{ above } B)_{Pic}$ if he has just encoded a sentence with an *above* in it, but as $(A \text{ below } B)_{Pic}$ if he has just encoded a sentence with a *below* in it. Although it might be expected that it would take longer to encode *below* than *above* for pictures as well as for sentences, previous empirical work by Clark and Chase suggested that there was no difference in encoding times. Hence, no differential latency predictions were made for Stage 2.

In Stage 3, the sentence is compared to the picture representation. The comparison is based upon Clark's (1969) principle of congruence, which states that two underlying representations can be compared only for identity. If they do not match, additional operations are required. These additional operations take the form of keeping track of a "truth index." It is assumed that the index is initially set at *true,* and changed only if necessary.

The comparison process is hypothesized to consist of two rules:

1. If the embedded strings do not match, change the truth index.
2. If the embedding strings do not match, change the truth index.

The two rules are implemented through two operations. In the first operation, the first noun of the embedded strings of the sentence and picture representations are compared. For example, (*Star*)$_{Sen}$ might be compared to (*Star*)$_{Pic}$. If the nouns match, the second operation is immediately executed. If the nouns do not match, an additional intermediate operation is required in which the current value of the truth index is changed to its opposite. Operation 2 is then executed.

In Operation 2, the embedding strings of the sentence and picture representations are compared to determine whether they match. If neither contains a negative, then execution of Stage 4 begins. If the sentence representation contains a negative, but the picture representation does not, the current value of the truth index is changed to its opposite. Execution of Stage 4 then begins.

Two latency predictions are made in Stage 3. The first is for comparison of embedded strings such as (*Star is above plus*)$_{Sen}$ and the second for comparison of embedding strings, such as (*It is false*). The difference in latency between match and mismatch in the comparison of embedded strings is assigned a parameter c, and the difference in latency between match and mismatch in the comparison of embedding strings is assigned a parameter d.

Stage 4 involves production of a response corresponding to the final state of the truth index (as determined in Stage 3). It is assumed that the amount of time taken by response production is constant across item types, and this constant time is assigned a parameter t_0.

By assuming that the parameters are additive, it becomes possible to test latency predictions of the model. A different prediction is made for each of the eight item types, which differ in the combination of parameters assigned to them. For example, the simplest sentence, *A is above B*, has only the t_0 parameter assigned to it if it is true while the most complex sentence, *A isn't below B*, has all five parameters assigned to it if it is true.

Separate parameter estimates can be made for parameters a, c, and t_0. Since b and d always occur in negative sentences, and never occur in nonnegative sentences, they are inseparable, and it is possible only to estimate the confounded $(b + d)$.

In Experiment I of Clark and Chase (1972), Below Time (a) was estimated as 93 msec, Negation Time $(b + d)$ as 685 msec, falsification time (c) as 187 msec, and base time (t_0) as 1763 msec. The full model accounted for over 99% of the variance in the group means, with 3 df for the treatment and 4 df for the residual. The model therefore provided a very good fit to the data, and analyses of variance determined that all parameters were significantly greater than zero and that the residuals from predicted values for each of the eight item types were not statistically significant.

Both the form and the content of the model are of interest from the standpoint of the theory of intelligence. The parameters of the model correspond to elementary information processes and are combined to form a Plan (model) for solution. The Plan can be represented in the form of a flow chart.

Further experiments in Clark and Chase (1972) found the parameters to be general across variants of the sentence—picture comparison task, and essentially the same parameters have been found to be applicable to the similar tasks studied by Trabasso, Rollins and Shaughnessy (1971). The essential ingredients of the theory would seem to consist of the set of parameters (plus some others relevant to variants of the task described), plus the additive combination rule. Several models are possible under the general theory, and they differ according to the variant of the task they describe.

The Clark–Chase model was not intended to provide a general theory of verbal comprehension. Nevertheless, it seems like an excellent start in this direction. While the sentence–picture comparison task is a highly specialized one, the negation, falsification, and marking parameters would seem potentially applicable to a wide variety of verbal comprehension tasks, and some generality has already been shown. Hunt, Lunneborg, and Lewis (1975) have shown that sentence–picture comparison performance is related to individual differences in general verbal ability. A problem for the Clark–Chase theory is that other equally plausible theories have been shown to provide comparable fits to the Clark–Chase data (e.g., Anderson, 1976; Carpenter & Just, 1975). From an information-processing point of view, a full understanding of verbal comprehension would entail identification of all the component processes involved, and would require distinguishing true components from spurious ones postulated by incorrect theories.

Spatial Visualization

Spatial visualization has been investigated extensively in studies by Shepard and his students (e.g., Cooper & Shepard, 1973; Shepard & Feng, 1973; Shepard & Metzler, 1971). These studies are as much directed toward understanding the form of internal representation for visualized objects as they are toward understanding the mental transformations that are made upon these objects. What makes them of particular interest is their use of tasks similar and in some cases identical to those used in conventional mental ability tests measuring spatial visualization ability.

In a first experiment (Shepard & Metzler, 1971), subjects were required to rotate mentally three-dimensional objects. Subjects were presented with pairs of perspective line drawings of three-dimensional objects (nonsymmetrical arrays of cubes). They were instructed to pull a right-hand lever if the two drawings represented objects of identical three-dimensional shape, regardless of differences in spatial orientation. They were instructed to pull a left-hand lever if the two drawings represented different objects. On half of the trials, the objects were identical and were permitted to differ only in spatial orientation. On the other half of the trials, the pictures were also permitted to differ in spatial orientation, but the objects were reflections of each other in three-dimensional space, and hence could not be rotated into congruence. There were two principal findings:

1. The response time to determine that the two objects were the same increased linearly as a function of the angular difference in portrayed orientation.

2. The intercept and slope of the function relating response time to angular difference was about the same, regardless of whether the difference between the two pictures was produced simply by a rigid rotation of one of the pictures in the picture plane, or by rotation of one of the pictures *in depth* (and thus outside the picture plane).

The results are inconsistent with theories according to which subjects "compute" some sort of rotationally invariant code for each of the two pictures separately, and then compare the two codes, for either a match or a mismatch. This sort of "feature comparison" theory would predict a horizontal rather than a linearly increasing slope for the response-time function. Rather, the results support a theory according to which subjects construct some sort of internal representation of the three-dimensional pattern that permits them to carry out mentally an analogue rotation of the internal representation of the object. This sort of theory is congruent with subjects' introspective claims regarding the way problems of this type are solved. The rate of rotation, estimated from the slope of the response-time function, appeared to be about $60°$ per second.

It should be noted that not all "feature" theories predict a horizontal slope in the mental-rotation task. A feature representation can be constructed in which degree of angular difference does affect stimulus comparison time (e.g., Palmer, 1975), and such a theory predicts a linear increase in response time with degree of angular rotation.

In another experiment, Cooper and Shepard (1973) required subjects to indicate whether an alphanumeric character (*G, J, R, 2, 5, 7*) was in normal or mirror-image form. Characters were presented in six different spatial orientations, and half of the trials involved normal characters while the other half involved mirror images.

Subjects in this experiment were given differential advance information regarding the identity of the character to be seen and the orientation in which it would be seen (but not, of course, whether it was normal or backward). The condition of greatest interest was that in which they were given both advance identity and orientation information sequentially, with the orientation information lasting either 100, 400, 700, or 1000 msec before it disappeared and was replaced by the test stimulus. It was found that with longer duration of the advance information, the effect of angular departure of the test stimulus from the upright position decreased. Subjects thus appeared able to use the advance information to begin a mental rotation of the expected alphanumeric character into the rotated position. The longer the orientation information lasted, the more time subjects had for mental rotation, so that the effect on solution time of angular departure from the upright decreased. With enough time (1000 msec), subjects could complete the mental rotation (even to $180°$), and a horizontal slope was found.

Shepard and Feng (1973) studied mental paper folding of the type required in the Surface Development test of the French Kit of Reference Tests for Cognitive

Factors (French, Ekstrom, & Price, 1963). On each trial, subjects were presented with a two-dimensional pattern of six squares that were attached so that if the squares were physically folded up, they would form the surface of a three-dimensional cube. Subjects were given sufficient information so that they would know which squares to fold into which. On each pattern, an arrow was drawn in the middle of an edge of two different squares. The subjects' task was to determine whether the two arrows would or would not meet at the same edge of the cube if the cube was fully folded. The subjects thus had to use the information given to construct an internal representation of the fully folded cube.

Response times increased approximately linearly with the minimum number and complexity of folds that would be required to determine whether or not the arrows would meet if the two-dimensional patterns were actually folded up in physical space. The results seemed to implicate an analogue process of "mental paper folding."

Taken together, the results of these and other experiments place certain constraints on theories of the internal representation of objects and the way in which these objects are manipulated in space. In particular, it appears that from an information-processing point of view, spatial ability will have to be understood in terms of one or more analogue transformation parameters, each of which maps physical transformations onto mental ones. Subjects may differ in their ability to construct mental representations of objects, or in the speed at which they rotate, fold, or otherwise transform them.

One of the most impressive aspects of the work of Shepard and his students is that the analogue transformation process has been implicated in a wide variety of spatial visualization tasks, only a few of which are cited above. These tasks are not merely minor variants of each other, but represent almost the full range of tasks that have been proposed for studying spatial ability. The analogue theory thus appears to be a general one.

It remains to be determined whether the transformation parameters applied to the various tasks are multiple manifestations of a unitary elementary information process, of several such processes, or of as many processes as there are tasks. Presumably, the second alternative (several eip's) is the most plausible one, but the relationships among the parameters should be further elucidated. Shepard and Cooper are presently conducting experiments designed to elucidate further the nature of the underlying elementary information processes.

Inductive Reasoning

One of the most widely used measures of inductive reasoning ability is the letter series completion task. Subjects are presented with a series of letters, such as *a c e g* _____, and are required to supply the next letter in the series. This task has been investigated by Simon and Kotovsky (1963) and Kotovsky and Simon (1973), who have proposed a theory of how subjects solve these problems.

Simon and Kotovsky's (1963) theory is based upon a language they invented for characterizing serial patterns. The language assumes that subjects have available to them in memory: (1) the English alphabet; and (2) the alphabet backward. Subjects are further assumed to have available the concepts of: (1) *same* or *equal;* and (2) *next* (on a list). Finally, subjects are assumed to be able to: (1) produce a cyclical pattern; and (2) keep track of a small number of symbols in memory.

The characterization of a pattern in the language has two parts, an initialization and a sequence iteration. The initialization indicates how the pattern starts, and the iteration indicates how it proceeds from there.

Consider as an example the series $a\ a\ a\ b\ b\ b\ c\ c\ c\ d\ d$ _____ The initialization takes the form $[M1 = \text{Alph}; a]$. This initialization is interpreted as indicating that variable $M1$ is set equal to a letter of the alphabet, a. The sequence iteration is $[M1, M1, M1, N(M1)]$. This iteration may be interpreted as follows:

$M1$: The first letter in the series is the value of $M1$, a.
$M1$: The second letter in the series is the value of $M1$, a.
$M1$: The third letter in the series is the value of $M1$, a.
$N(M1)$: The letter next in the alphabet after $M1$, b, replaces $M1$, a.

The cycle is then repeated, starting again with $M1$, which is now equal to b. It should be noted that expressions such as $N(M1)$ do not correspond to letters in the series, but rather to operations that generate letters. Thus, the period of this example is just three letters.

Consider as a second example a more complex series, $p\ o\ n\ o\ n\ m\ n\ m\ l\ m\ l\ k$ _____. The initialization is $[M2 = M1 = \text{Balph}; p]$. This is interpreted as indicating that two variables, M2 and M1, are set equal to a letter of the backward alphabet, p. We now know that the progression from p will be backward through the alphabet rather than forward. The iteration is $[M2, N(M2), M2, N(M2), M2, N(M1), E(M2, M1)]$. The iteration is interpreted in the following way:

$M2$: The first letter in the series is the value of $M2$, p.
$N(M2)$: The letter next in the backward alphabet after $M2$ replaces $M2$, o.
$M2$: The second letter in the series is the value of $M2$, o.
$N(M2)$: The letter next in the backward alphabet after $M2$ replaces $M2$, n.
$M2$: The third letter in the series is the value of $M2$, n.
$N(M1)$: The letter next in the backward alphabet after $M1$ replaces $M1$, o.
$E(M2, M1)$: $M2$ is set equal to $M1$, o.

The cycle then repeats, with the fourth letter of the series equal to the value of $M2$, which is now o.

The theory consists of two parts: a *pattern generator* and a *sequence generator*. The pattern generator accepts as input the given series of letters, and infers from it a pattern description, using the language described above. The sequence generator accepts as input the pattern description that is the output of the pattern generator, and extrapolates the series in order to complete it.

In order for the pattern generator to infer the pattern description, it must first discover the periodicity of the series. The pattern generator seeks periodicity by searching for a relation that repeats at regular intervals. For example, in the series *a b c a b c a b c,* the period is easily discovered to be *a b c.* If no relation repeats regularly, then the pattern generator searches for a relation that is interrupted at regular intervals. For example, in the series *a b c m a b c n a b c o,* the *next* relation is interrupted every four letters.

Once the periodicity is discovered, the pattern generator searches for patterns of *same* and *next* between successive symbols within each period and between symbols in corresponding positions between periods. This information enables the pattern generator to form a description of the series in the pattern language described above.

In order for the sequence generator to extrapolate the letter series, the generator must first have available to it the description from the pattern generator. It uses this description to continue the sequence. Consider as an example the series *u r t u s t u t t u* _____. Simon and Kotovsky (1963) suggest the following sequence of events:

1. *Hold* the letter "*r*" on the list named "Alphabet" *in immediate memory.*
2. *Produce* the letter "*u.*"
3. *Produce* the letter that is in immediate memory (initially, this will be "*r*").
4. *Put the next* letter on the list in immediate memory (on the first round, this will move the pointer to "*s*").
5. *Produce* the letter "*t.*"
6. Return to Step 2, and *repeat* the sequence as often as desired. (p. 539)

The theory is embodied in an IPL-V (Information Processing Language Five) computer program that generates the patterns and sequences for letter series completion items. Different variants of the program have been written, some more powerful than others. The variants are intended to simulate individual differences in subjects' abilities to solve the problems.

Several tests of the program are possible. One is a sufficiency test, which is satisfied by the program actually solving problems. Passing this test requires the theory (as embodied in the computer program) to be specified in detail sufficient for problem solution. This test was passed.

A second test is the determination of whether the item difficulties for the program match those for human subjects. First, the computer program should fail to solve only those items that were most difficult for human subjects and should successfully solve the easier items. Second, the amount of time taken by the computer program to solve each item may be highly correlated with the amount of time taken by human subjects (although there will probably be a large constant difference, so that equal times would generally not be expected).

Simon and Kotovsky (1963) found good agreement between computer and human data, using both of these criteria, and Kotovsky and Simon (1973) found that, with minor modifications of the theory, good agreement could be found even with more extensive tests. The theory thus appears to provide a good approximation to the mechanisms used by human subjects in solving the letter series completion problems.

Comparison among Theories

The Simon—Kotovsky theory of letter series completion is similar to the Clark—Chase and Shepard theories in that the fundamental unit of analysis is the elementary information process. In the Simon—Kotovsky theory, the operators *same* and *next* are shown to be remarkably powerful when embedded in a detailed specification of how series completion problems are solved. The theory differs in two major respects from the others, however, in part because, whereas Clark and Chase and Shepard studied relatively fast processes and used the response-time subtraction method that is appropriate under these circumstances, Simon and Kotovsky studied processes of intermediate duration and used the computer simulation method that is more widely used in the study of slow processes.

First, the Clark—Chase and Shepard information-processing theories were made testable by mathematical models, whereas the Simon—Kotovsky theory was made testable by a computer model. Indeed, these authors have taken the position that the computer program *is* the theory.

Second, in the Clark—Chase and Shepard theories, a latency is assigned to each elementary information process. One can therefore estimate the amount of time each process contributes toward overall problem solution. There are no comparable "parameter estimates" in the Simon—Kotovsky theory, although the theory could certainly provide the basis for such estimates in future work.

What are the advantages and disadvantages of theories such as the ones described in this chapter relative to those described in the last chapter? We shall consider both in the next two sections.

ADVANTAGES OF
THE INFORMATION-PROCESSING APPROACH

The information-processing approach suffers from none of the limitations of the factor-analytic methods used in the differential approach:

1. The investigator has control over the mathematical (or computer) model. He can compare multiple models on the same set of data, or he can apply the same model (or a controlled variant of it) to different sets of data.

2. There is no rotation dilemma, because unless confounded, the parameters in a given parameter space are unique.

3. Information-processing theories specify the *processes* that are used in the solution of single items. They "get inside" the solution process.

4. Information-processing theories are intraindividual. They are based either upon the data for a single individual, or upon the data for the average of multiple individuals. Multiple individuals and individual differences are not *required* either for theory formulation or theory testing.

The first two advantages bestow upon information-processing methodology a far greater degree of inferential power than is available through differential methodology. It is possible to make strong inferences regarding the relative superiority of one theory over another and to reject theories that are clearly inappropriate. If a particular experiment does not permit strong inferences, then another experiment can be designed to enable the investigator to select among theories. Since the investigator has control over the mathematical (or computer) model, he can be sure that he is testing the same operational theories. And since the parameters of a given model are uniquely determined, the investigator need not concern himself with the dilemma of which are the "psychologically true" parameters for the identical parameter space.

The second two advantages make information-processing methodology appropriate for studying the "latent traits" that underlie performance in tasks requiring various mental abilities. The elementary information process is a suitable unit for characterizing the latent traits.

Information-processing methodology enables the investigator to study a wide variety of abilities and to specify in considerable detail the elementary processes and accompanying mechanisms that are responsible for task performance. Nevertheless, the methodology does suffer from certain limitations. These are the subject of the next section.

LIMITATIONS OF
INFORMATION-PROCESSING METHODOLOGY

Overview

We shall use the typology of methodologies suggested earlier as the basis for organizing this section. Once again, we shall pass over artificial intelligence work, since we are interested in this volume in *human* abilities. We shall limit ourselves to simulation methodologies. These include the computer simulation methods usually used to study slow processes, and the mathematical methods used to study fast response times. Response times, in turn, have been studied both by the subtraction method and by the additive-factor method.

Computer Simulation

1. *Computer theories are inaccessible to the scientific public.* Computer theories and implementations are difficult for members of the scientific community (other than their creators) both to understand and to test. In practice, such theories have a degree of inaccessibility that may thwart the public nature of scientific enterprise. The increasing sophistication of psychological theory is due at least in part to the opportunities for psychologists to replicate or refute the results of others. But opportunities for progress are diminished when the theories are inaccessible, buried in computer programs that are difficult to acquire and understand.

2. *Computer theories lack parsimony.* Parsimony for its own sake may be of questionable value. But ignoring parsimony can lead to unfortunate results. Computer theories contain many statements, most of them interactive with other statements, so that it becomes difficult to assess what effect each one has, and whether a given statement is really a necessary ingredient of the theory. In other words, it becomes difficult to separate the wheat from the chaff. Simon and Kotovsky (1963) and Kotovsky and Simon (1973), for example, describe the differences in performance among more and less powerful variants of their theory; but they do not make clear what distinguishes one variant from another. With computer programs, simple characterizations are difficult to come by. Lack of parsimony further contributes to the difficulty other members of the scientific community have in testing the theory.

3. *Computer theories do not generally provide process parameter estimates.* One may want to know the degree to which each elementary information process contributes to the latency or difficulty of a given problem. This information is difficult to obtain from a computer-based theory because of the large numbers of interactive variables involved in most computer programs.

Mathematical Models of Response Time

The Subtraction Method

1. *Parameters are often confounded.* Explicit and implicit confoundings of parameters are fairly common in response-time studies using the subtraction method. The study of Clark and Chase (1972) provides an example. Although there are two parameters involved in negation, only one parameter estimate is possible. The parameter b in the model represents the amount of additional time it takes to encode a negative sentence, and the parameter d represents the amount of time it takes to process a mismatch of the embedding strings of sentence and picture representations. Since these two parameters occur in all negative sentences, and only in negative sentences, they are inseparable in this study, yielding a confounded parameter estimate of 685 msec.

There is also at least one implicitly confounded parameter in the Clark–Chase model, the t_0 "base-time" parameter. Missing from the Clark–Chase model are separate parameters for base sentence-encoding (reading) time and for base picture-encoding time. The absence of such parameters puts Clark and Chase in the untenable position of claiming that the amount of time to compare the sentence *Star is above plus* to the picture ⁺ is equal to "base time", t_0. Certainly there are *some* interesting psychological processes involved in this problem. At the very least, parameters are needed for base sentence- and picture-encoding times. Yet, none are provided or could be provided in the Clark–Chase experiments, since these encoding times are always confounded with each other and with response time.

In general, an unreasonably large parameter estimate for a particular process is a good indication of a confounded parameter. There are two examples of such confoundings in the Clark–Chase studies, only one of which is made explicit. At least five parameters are represented as just two.

2. *Alternative models are often indistinguishable.* Alternative models become indistinguishable when the parameters that could distinguish them are confounded. Suppose, for example, one wanted to compare the effects of sentence-first and picture-first encoding of basal sentences such as *Star is above plus* and pictures such as ⁺. One would be unable to do so, because there are no encoding parameters to compare. These parameters are confounded.

3. *Parameter estimates are based upon too few degrees of freedom for residual.* In the Clark–Chase study described, four parameters (one a constant over items) were estimated from eight data points, leaving four degrees of freedom (df) for the residual. The relatively large number of parameters to estimate combined with the relatively small number of data points leaves an undesirably small number of df. Small numbers of df invite both unreliable parameter estimates and inflated estimates of percent variance accounted for. It becomes more difficult to falsify models, because they all do too well in accounting for the data, perhaps because of capitalization upon sampling error. Indeed, Carpenter and Just (1975) have shown how comparable fits to the Clark–Chase data in terms of percent variance accounted for can be obtained with fewer parameters.

The Clark–Chase example is by no means the most extreme. Clark (1971) does several parameter estimations with three parameters (including a constant) and four data points, leaving just 1 df. Glucksberg, Trabasso, and Wald (1973), also in a study of linguistic structure and mental operations, estimate twelve independent parameters to fit fourteen data points. It becomes less surprising that these investigators account for from 98% to almost 100% of the variance in their data.

The degrees of freedom problem has become particularly severe in recent years, as research into more complex thought processes has made it less unfashionable to use large numbers of parameters with few data points. Parameter-estimation techniques (such as multiple regression) are very prone toward capitalization upon error in data. Unfortunately, cross-validation of parameter estimates is rare, although not entirely neglected (e.g., Anderson, 1974). In short, increasing the degrees of freedom for residual (by increasing the number of data points to be predicted) is a responsible way of guarding against spurious "good fit."

The "degrees-of-freedom" problem is of less concern when investigators conduct proper goodness of fit tests for their models. These tests take into account the number of degrees of freedom used in making predictions. Such tests are often not conducted, however, either through negligence or because no satisfactory error term exists against which to test residuals of predicted from observed values. When goodness of fit is not tested, the percent variance accounted for by a given model can be a misleading descriptive statistic unless the statistic is estimated with a large number of degrees of freedom to spare. And these tests do nothing to solve the problem of unstable parameter estimates.

4. *Ordering of parameters is not mathematically specified.* Information-processing models always specify the order in which elementary information processes are executed, but the mathematical realization of these models may have no order constraints. For example, the five parameters of the Clark–Chase model described previously could occur in any of 120 possible permutations, and the mathematical predictions of the model as tested would be identical. Obviously, only a small number of these orders will be psychologically plausible ones, and through indirect inference it is possible to eliminate various orderings. But it would be desirable to build at least some constraints into the mathematical model to distinguish among various possible orderings of information processes.

5. *Results of external validation may be distorted.* Suppose one wants to relate individual differences in parameter values either to each other or to individual differences in other variable values. Correlational patterns will be distorted if there are confounded parameters, and the confounded parameters are not very highly correlated with each other. There is no a priori reason to expect confounded parameters to be highly correlated, and they may even be negatively correlated. So the problem is likely to arise if external validation is attempted and the confounded parameters in combination do not form a unitary source of individual differences.

These are not the criticisms usually made of the subtraction method. There are two criticisms that are frequently made (Pachella, 1974; S. Sternberg, 1969a):

1. "The starting point for the application of the method is a relatively sophisticated one: In order to construct a comparison task, one must already know the sequence of events that transpires between stimulus and response. Such sophisticated knowledge is rarely available. . . . Obviously, the conclusions reached on the basis of the application of the method can then be no stronger than the substantiation of the initial conceptualization of the experimental task" (Pachella, 1974, p. 47).

It is true that the subtraction method requires a strong model. I view this as an advantage rather than a disadvantage, however. First, it is because the method requires a strong model that it is inferentially powerful and thus capable of rejecting the model. Second, a good experiment will often be designed so that it is capable of rejecting models or classes of models other than the investigator's preferred one. Thus, both Clark and Chase in their experiments and Shepard in his show how the results are incompatible with other commonly accepted models. Third, if the investigator's and other a priori models are shown to be inadequate, it is possible to construct a post hoc model after viewing the data. Such a model will certainly have to be cross-validated on other data and under other experimental conditions, but it is not the case, as Pachella (1974) claims, that the conclusions reached "can be no stronger than the substantiation of the initial conceptualization of the experimental task" (p. 47).

The criticism regarding the sophisticated starting point of the subtraction method provided one of the motives behind S. Sternberg's development of the additive-factor method. Yet, it is not clear that in practice there is as great a difference between initial conceptualizations as has been claimed. Haphazard selection of factors for a multifactor experiment cannot be expected to yield enlightening results. The investigator should choose factors that he believes are best able to differentiate stages of processing, and in order to choose them in this way, the investigator must have at least some prior idea of what stages different patterns of additivity and interaction would imply. As Calfee (1976) points out, "The first step in this paradigm is the analysis of the underlying cognitive operations required to perform a task" (p. 24). The investigator should at least have an idea of what the maximal stage model (all effects of factor pairs additive, as found by S. Sternberg, 1969b) will look like, because there is no point to including in the experimental design a factor that could not conceivably be additive with the others. This requirement is comparable to that for an investigator designing an experiment using the subtraction method: He should have an idea of the maximum number of parameters and what they might mean. It is always possible to test alternative models that differ solely in number of parameters, and thereby to discard superfluous parameters.

To summarize the first general criticism, two points should be emphasized. First, the necessity of a strong model is viewed as a strength rather than a weakness of the subtraction method, since it is what gives the subtraction method its inferential power. Second, design of a good additive-factor experiment, like design of a good subtraction-method experiment, requires a relatively well-defined maximal model. However, the additive-factor experiment will return to the investigator less information, as will be shown in the next subsection.

2. "A second general criticism of the Subtraction Method concerns the comparability of the experimental and comparison tasks, or as Sternberg (1969b) has called it, the assumption of pure insertion. This refers to the assumption that it is possible to delete (or insert) completely mental events from an information-processing task without changing the nature of the other constituent mental operations" (Pachella, 1974, p. 48). "Experimental operations. . . which might

be thought of as deleting entire stages without altering the functions of other stages, are probably very rare; they should be considered special cases" (Sternberg, 1969a, p. 280).

While the validity of the assumption of pure insertion has been challenged for some time now (e.g., Külpe, 1895), it seems that the criticism should be properly directed not at the assumption, but at the failure of many users of the assumption to test it. Perhaps it was true in former years that little was known "about how to test the validity of any particular application of the subtraction method" (Sternberg, 1969a, p. 277). But this is no longer the case. Both Clark and Chase in their experiments and Shepard and his students in theirs have demonstrated convincingly the additivity of the various experimental conditions. They have done this by showing that their models provide excellent fits to the experimental data. Their models are additive ones, and nonadditivity across experimental conditions could only be expected to contribute error variance, which would then be variance unaccounted for by any model. If the models had failed to fit the data well, then one could not be certain whether it was because of the inadequacy of the models or because of the failure of the experiments to test them adequately, as, for example, if the assumption of pure insertion were invalid. But if the models fit the data well (and, of course, there are at least some residual degrees of freedom), then one is justified in accepting the assumption.

This criticism of the assumption of pure insertion provided a second motive for the formulation of the additive-factor method. The additive-factor method was designed to make the weaker assumption that factors would change only the duration, but not the inclusion, of various stages. As Pachella (1974) has observed, however, "the manipulation of factor levels may cause a fundamental change in the processing sequence as may happen with the deletion of an entire stage within the Subtraction Method. From a procedural point of view, the difference between the Subtraction Method and the Additive Factor Method can be quite subtle" (p. 57). As Pachella points out, the distinction between methods is a matter of degree rather than kind. It is by no means clear that experimental factors will always affect only duration and not inclusion.

In the subtraction method, it is clear how one can demonstrate the validity of the assumption of pure insertion, if the model is true or close to the true model. It is not clear, however, how the user of the additive-factor method can demonstrate that only duration and not inclusion of stages is affected. If stage inclusion is affected, interpretation of the pattern of factor additivity and interaction will be compromised.

Suppose that in a memory-scanning task, for example, presentation of a degraded stimulus to subjects results in an extra stage being added to processing. Thus, instead of the stimulus-encoding stage being lengthened (as is customarily assumed), stimulus encoding is actually unaffected but a new preencoding process is added that is needed only when the stimulus as presented cannot be encoded and needs to be "cleaned up." Only one experimental factor (degraded versus intact stimulus) affects the "cleaning up" stage, by determining whether or not it will be present. By additive-factor logic, the effect of this factor will therefore be orthogonal to the effects of all other factors, and hence additivity will be inferred. However, the fact that a new stage of processing has been inserted will not be known, unless some new factor is subsequently discovered that affects the stimulus encoding stage, or vice versa. In general, then, the additive-factor method does not readily indicate whether a stage has been added (or deleted) by the manipulation of experimental factors. To summarize, it is not the assumption of pure insertion that deserves criticism, but failure to test the assumption, and the means to test this assumption are available in sophisticated applications of the subtraction method. It is not clear how a given application of the additive-factor method can be shown to dispense with the assumption, nor is it clear how the user of the additive-factor method would interpret the results of a multifactor experiment if addition or deletion of stages occurred.

The Additive Factor Method

1. *The additive-factor method does not reveal stage duration.*
2. *The additive-factor method provides no direct indication of stage order.*
3. *The additive-factor method provides no direct indication of the substantive interpretation of any stage.*
4. *The fundamental assumption regarding the means of identifying separate stages is questionable.* "In situations where stages have some independent definition, it is perfectly conceivable that two factors might affect a single stage in an additive manner or that they might affect different stages and interact" (Pachella, 1974, p. 58). Indeed, the assumption that variables affecting a single stage will interact seems to be highly questionable. In the Clark–Chase model, both the *above–below* and the *positive–negative* difference (assigned parameters a and b, respectively) are assumed to affect processing in Stage 1. Yet, Clark and Chase's Model A states that these variables do not interact. Clark and Chase's data support the model; a significant interaction was not obtained. Hence, additivity may not be a clear indication of separate stages, unless a stage is defined in terms of additivity of effects. In this case, the definition will be circular, since one originally set out to show the existence of separate stages by the additivity demonstration. The assumption of additivity of effects for variables affecting separate stages would be questionable if an experimental factor affected not only the duration of a stage, but also its output. The effect of one stage might then be carried over to a subsequent stage.

Common Limitations

Certain limitations are common to both methods, and to computer simulation methodology as well:

1. *Information-processing methodology does not provide a means for systematically studying correlates of individual differences in performance.* If one

wants to examine either consistencies in patterns of individual differences across different task parameters, or between task parameters and external measures of performance, the correlational methods of differential psychology are needed to accomplish this goal.

2. *Information-processing methodology does not provide a common language across tasks (and investigators).* As information-processing methodology has become more widely used, the list of parameters corresponding to hypothesized elementary information processes has grown, and it will continue to grow. How does one know whether the *a* parameter of one task is the same as or different from the *x* parameter of another task? In most cases, differences will be clear, but identity is difficult to establish. The correlational methods of differential psychology are useful in solving this dilemma. If values of the two parameters are very highly correlated across individuals as well as tasks, then one's confidence that the parameters are equivalent is bolstered, although a high correlation is only a necessary but not sufficient condition for parameter equivalence. If individual differences in the parameters are unrelated or weakly related, the parameters cannot represent the same underlying process.

Differential psychology has also provided a useful way of characterizing constellations of components that in combination form stable patterns of individual differences. Thurstone's primary mental abilities provide one convenient language for this purpose. Even if two elementary information processes are not the same, one has a better understanding of their interrelationship if one can say, for example, that both contribute to individual differences in reasoning, or that one contributes to individual differences in reasoning and the other to individual differences in verbal comprehension.

3. *Information-processing methodology does not prevent overvaluation of task-specific components.* A particular parameter may account for individual differences in performance of a particular task. But if it accounts for individual differences in performance *only* of that task, it is of limited interest. Highly specialized information-processing tasks have been studied extensively, but there have been almost no attempts to show that the parameters that account for individual differences in single specialized tasks are generalizable to other tasks. Correlational methods provide a way of demonstrating generalizability.

SUMMARY

The information-processing view of human abilities as dynamic information-processing capabilities provides an alternative to the differential view of abilities as static psychological factors. The emphasis in information-processing psychology is on the exploration of complex processes and on being explicit about internal mechanisms.

The fundamental unit of analysis in information-processing psychology is the elementary information process. It is assumed that all behavior of a human information processing system is the result of sequences of these elementary processes. Some investigators have sought to specify further the notion of the elementary information process and the way such processes combine to form macroscopic performances. Two further specifications are the TOTE and the production, which combine respectively into Plans and production systems. A Plan is any hierarchical process that can control the order in which a sequence of operations is to be performed. A production system is an ordered set of condition-action sequences. While the notions of Plan and production system lead to different conceptualizations of performance, it is not clear at present whether they are distinguishable experimentally.

The information-processing approach is not unitary: It encompasses a broad range of perspectives and research techniques. The broadest distinction is between artificial intelligence and simulation, which may be viewed as two ends of a continuum. The former seeks optimization of performance, regardless of its similarity to human behavior, while the latter seeks to model human behavior, regardless of whether or not it is optimal.

Within the simulation approach, a further distinction can be drawn between slow-process and fast-process research. The former tends to rely upon protocol analysis and computer modeling, the latter upon response-time analysis and mathematical modeling.

Fast-process research often proceeds along the lines of either the subtraction method of Donders or the additive-factor method of S. Sternberg. The critical feature of the subtraction method is a set of tasks that by successive deletions enables the investigator to estimate the amount of time spent on each component process in interest. The additive-factor method infers stages of processing from the pattern of factor additivity and interaction in a multifactor experimental design.

Strictly speaking, there are no information-processing theories of intelligence, or at least none that approach the scope of the factor-analytic theories. Information-processing theories have tended to emphasize depth rather than breadth, and the relevant theories are of limited aspects of intelligence. Three such theories are the Clark—Chase theory of the process of comparing sentences against pictures, the Shepard theory of mental transformation and internal representation, and the Simon—Kotovsky theory of letter series completion.

The Clark—Chase theory accounts for certain aspects of verbal comprehension. The theory describes the processes by which a subject compares a sentence such as *Star isn't below plus* to a picture such as ⁎. The subject must indicate whether the sentence correctly describes the picture. The theory (Model A) postulates four stages: mental representation of sentences, mental representation of pictures, comparison of sentence and picture representations, response production. Latency predictions are made on the basis of the mental operations that are hypothesized to occur in each stage, and predicted latencies are extremely close to obtained ones.

The Shepard theory accounts for aspects of spatial visualization, such as the way subjects mentally rotate internal representations of objects or mentally fold sides to form a cube. The theory suggests that subjects construct an internal representation of objects that permits an analogue transformation upon the representation. The rates at which transformations are carried out can be estimated by one or more parameters of each task model.

The Simon–Kotovsky theory accounts for completion of letter series problems such as *a c e g* ____. The theory consists of two parts: a pattern generator and a sequence generator. The pattern generator accepts as input the given series of letters and infers from it a pattern description. The sequence generator accepts as input the pattern description that is the output of the pattern generator and extrapolates the series in order to complete it. The theory is fully specified as a computer program that actually solves letter series completion problems.

The information-processing approach suffers from none of the intrinsic limitations of the factor-analytic method: (1) the investigator has control over the mathematical or computer model; (2) there is no rotation dilemma; (3) intraitem processes are specified; (4) the theories are intraindividual. As a result, information-processing methodology can be inferentially powerful and is appropriate for uncovering "latent traits."

Various types of information-processing techniques have different limitations. Computer theories, for example, are: (1) inaccessible to the scientific public; (2) lacking in parsimony and manageability; and (3) generally unable to provide estimates of component latency or difficulty.

In the subtraction method: (1) parameters are often confounded; (2) alternative models are often indistinguishable; (3) parameter estimates are often based upon too few degrees of freedom for residual; (4) ordering of parameters is not mathematically specified; and (5) results of external validation may be distorted. Two other criticisms are often made of the subtraction method: (1) it requires an overly sophisticated initial conceptualization of a processing model; and (2) it makes the assumption of pure insertion – that stages of task performance can be inserted and deleted without changing the nature of the task. These two criticisms are unjustified.

The additive-factor method: (1) provides no indication of stage duration; (2) provides no direct indication of stage order; (3) provides no direct indication of the substantive interpretation of any stage; and (4) makes a questionable assumption regarding the means by which separate stages may be identified.

None of the three methodologies (computer simulation, subtraction method, additive-factor method) (1) provide a means for studying systematically correlates of individual differences in performance; (2) provide a common language across tasks and investigators; or (3) prevent overvaluation of task-specific components.

4
The Componential Approach
to Human Intelligence

In the preceding two chapters, it has been demonstrated that the respective strengths and weaknesses of the differential and information-processing approaches to intelligence are complementary. Each approach is capable of providing useful but incomplete explanations of human behavior.

The differential approach provides powerful psychometric techniques for discovering constellations of mental operations. In combination, these operations generate individual differences in performance across a wide variety of tasks. The approach fails to provide techniques for discovering what the underlying mental operations are. Thus, we have good reason to believe that there are at least several constellations of operations that form consistent patterns of individual differences in performance. Thurstone's primary mental abilities are good examples of such patterns of individual differences. But we have very little information regarding the nature of the operations that in combination generate each of the primary mental abilities.

The information-processing approach provides powerful analytic techniques for "getting inside" problem tasks, for discovering what mental operations underlie composite performance in particular tasks. The approach does not provide techniques for discovering the ways in which these operations combine to form consistent patterns of individual differences in diverse tasks. Thus, we have evidence (Clark & Chase, 1972; Trabasso, Rollins, & Shaughnessy, 1971) that the process of comparing sentences against pictures consists of four stages, each composed of identifiable real-time operations that contribute to response latency. But we do not know which of these operations contribute to individual differences in performance of related tasks; nor do we even know which are interesting sources of individual differences in performance of the sentence–picture comparison task.

Given the complementary strengths and weaknesses of the differential and information-processing approaches, it should be possible, at least in theory, to synthesize an approach that would capitalize upon the strength of each approach, and thereby share the weakness of neither. There have been pleas for investigators to do just that (Cronbach, 1957; Messick, 1973), and in recent years, several syntheses have been made (e.g., Carroll, 1974; Day, 1973; Hunt, Frost, & Lunneborg, 1973). The componential approach described in this chapter continues and draws upon the syntheses developed by Carroll, Day, Hunt, Simon, and others.

PRELIMINARIES

Purpose of Componential Analysis

The overall purpose of componential analysis is to identify the component mental operations underlying a series of related information-processing tasks and to discover the organization of these component operations in terms of their relationships both to each other and to higher-order constellations of mental abilities. From a differential viewpoint, componential analysis may be viewed as a detailed algorithm for construct validation, the effort to elaborate the inferred traits (which, in our case, are mental operations) determining test behavior (Campbell, 1960). From an information-processing viewpoint, componential analysis may be viewed as a set of procedures for discovering the identity and organization of elementary information processes (Newell & Simon, 1972). This volume may be read from either or both points of view.

Fundamental Unit of Analysis

The fundamental unit of analysis in componential analysis is the *component*. A component is an elementary information process that operates upon internal representations of objects or symbols (Newell & Simon, 1972). The component may translate a sensory input into a conceptual representation, transform one conceptual representation into another, or translate a conceptual representation into a motor output. Componential analysis is therefore akin to information-processing analysis in that its elementary unit is a process rather than a construct representing a static source of individual differences.

The component is not necessarily, and usually will not be, the most elementary unit of behavior that might be studied. Operations that are thought to be theoretically unimportant will be specified in the information-processing model of task performance, but will not be identified as separate components. The reason for this selectivity is that complex tasks may require hundreds or even thousands of operations, most of which are theoretically uninteresting. Componential analysis, like all of psychology, is reductionist in that it selects for examination only those aspects of behavior that are thought to be of theoretical import. These aspects of behavior are understood through componential theories and models.

Componential Theories and Models

A componential theory consists of two parts: (1) identification of the components involved in task performance; and (2) specification of the combination rule for these components.

Two theories may differ from each other because they differ in the components theorized to enter performance. Suppose, for example, that Theory 1 specifies three components: a, b, and c. Theory 2 might specify a subset of these components: a and b. Theory 3 might specify a superset of these components: a, b, c, and d. Theory 4 might specify an overlapping set of components: b, c, and d. Finally, Theory 5 might specify a disjoint set of components: d, e, and f.

Two theories may also differ from each other because they differ in the combination rule for components. Suppose, for example, that Theory 1 specifies a fully additive combination rule:

$$\text{Response Time (RT)} = a + b + c.$$

According to this rule, RT is the sum of the times spent on each component. Theory 2 might specify a partially additive combination rule:

$$RT = a + \text{Min}(b, c).$$

According to this rule, component a is always performed, and only the less time-consuming of components b and c is performed. Theory 3 might specify a nonadditive combination rule:

$$RT = \text{Max}(a, b, c).$$

According to this rule, either (1) only the most time-consuming of the three components is executed, or (2) the three components are executed in parallel, with the longest one determining the effect on RT.

A componential theory does not fully account for the information-processing behavior under consideration. For this reason, it is necessary to propose one or more componential models, each of which is consistent with the componential theory. A model further specifies (1) the order of component execution, and (2) the mode of component execution.

Order of component execution refers to how components are sequenced. For example, the components a, b, and c could be executed in any of 3!, or 6 possible orders.

Mode refers to exhaustive versus self-terminating processing, serial versus parallel processing, and holistic versus particularistic processing. *Whereas the combination rule for components indicates how time is summed across components, mode indicates how it is summed within components.* Suppose, for example, that four repetitions of component *a* are guaranteed to solve a problem. Processing may be either exhaustive or self-terminating: Component *a* may be repeated only as many times as are needed to solve the problem (which may be less than four), or component *a* may be repeated four times, even if fewer repetitions could solve the problem. Processing may be either serial or parallel: The component may be executed four times in succession, or four times simultaneously, with the longest time determining overall RT. Processing may be either holistic or particularistic: The stimulus may be segmented, or treated as a whole.

Componential models are expressed in information-processing terms, usually as flow charts. The flow chart should describe fully the processes involved (including ones not designated as components) in task solution. The information-processing model must then be translated into some form that is suitable for empirical test. There are two conventional ways of doing this. The first is by simulating the model on a computer and then determining whether the computer found difficult (or easy) the same items that human subjects found difficult (or easy). A second test requires formulation of a mathematical model of performance, with parameters of the mathematical model corresponding to components of the information-processing model. The model is then validated in terms of its fit to experimental data.

The distinction between the aspects of a componential theory and those of a componential model can be summarized simply: If response time (or error rate) is expressed as a combinatorial function of the total time spent on each component, aspects of the theory change the form of the function but aspects of the model do not. For example, if $RT = X + Y$ (where X equals total time spent on component x and Y equals total time spent on component y), changes in the theory will change the form of the equation, but changes in the model will not. Aspects of the theory are more general and more basic than those of the model.

Table 4.1 summarizes the aspects of performance that distinguish among theories and models. When all four aspects of performance are specified (compo-

TABLE 4.1
Aspects of Theories and Models in Componential Analysis

Theory	Identification of components	Specification of component combination rule
Model	Stipulation of component execution order	Stipulation of component execution mode

nents, combination rule, order of component execution, mode of component execution), the behavior under consideration is well understood.

Individual Differences

In componential analysis, individual differences may derive from five sources. These sources are summarized in Table 4.2. It can be seen readily that four of these sources have already been discussed as providing the bases for distinguishing among theories and models.

At the theory level, individual differences may occur in either the components involved in task performance or the combination rule for components. If individual differences derive from either of these two sources, then one theory is inadequate for explaining the behavior of all subjects.

At the model level, individual differences may occur in either the order of component execution or the mode of component execution. Again, if individual differences derive from either source, then one model is inadequate for explaining the behavior of all subjects.

At the component level, individual differences may occur in component time or difficulty. In other words, some subjects may perform certain operations more quickly or more easily than do other subjects. When individual differences are at the component level only, then one theory and one model are applicable for all subjects.

The five sources of individual differences are hierarchically organized into three levels: theory, model, component. Individual differences at higher levels affect interpretation of individual differences at lower levels. Several examples will help clarify how these effects operate.

First, consider two examples at the theory level. If one subject uses components a, b, and c and another uses components c, d, and e, then it will be possible to compare component orders, modes, and values only for one component, the overlapping c. Suppose instead that both subjects use components a, b, and c, but one subject uses an additive combination rule $(a + b + c)$ and the other subject uses a multiplicative combination rule $(a \times b \times c)$. Component values must then be considered in light of the number of times each component is executed. The first subject, for example, executes component a once, while the second subject executes it bc times.

Now consider two examples at the model level. If one subject executes components a, b, and c in that (forward) order and another subject executes them in the reverse order, component values may be affected by the efficiency of one or the other strategy. In this case, working backward may or may not be efficient, but it is likely to have at least some effect on the amount of time spent on each component. Suppose that, instead, the difference is in mode of execution, such as in self-terminating versus exhaustive search. Faster execution of individual components in the exhaustive search may be more than offset by the

TABLE 4.2

Sources of Individual Differences in Componential Analysis

Level	Source	Explanation	Example
Theory	Components	Some subjects use more components, fewer components, or different components from those used by other subjects	Subject 1 solves problem using components a, b, c; Subject 2 solves problem using components c, d, e.
	Combination rule for components	Some subjects combine components according to one rule, others according to a different rule.	Subject 1 combines components additively: $a + b + c$. Subject 2 combines them multiplicatively: $a \cdot b \cdot c$.
Model	Order of component processing	Some subjects order components in one sequence, others in a different sequence.	Subject 1 orders components a, then b, then c; Subject 2 orders them c, then b, then a.
	Mode of component processing	Some subjects process particular components in one mode, others in another mode.	Subject 1 processes component a in self-terminating mode; Subject 2 processes component a exhaustively.
Component	Component time or power	Some subjects process particular components more quickly or more powerfully than do other subjects.	Subject 1 is quicker in processing component a than is Subject 2.

greater number of times the components must be executed. Thus, although amount of time per component execution may be shorter, total amount of time spent on a given component may be longer (owing to repeated executions of that component).

In general, then, the effects of individual differences in component processes higher in the hierarchy will affect interpretation of individual differences lower in the hierarchy. The reverse may also be true. If, for example, a subject is inept at execution of a particular component, he may look for a processing strategy that minimizes the importance of the component.

The five sources of individual differences described above are for subjects' behavior. There are also individual differences in the predictability of subjects' behavior. For example, the best model may account for 85% of the variance in the most predictable subject's response times, but only for 69% of the variance in the least predictable subject's response times. (This was the actual range for the People Piece Experiment.) Individual subjects' data must be viewed in light of their predictability, particularly in cases where the best model fails to predict well.

Because parameters in componential analysis are estimated separately for individual subjects (as well as for group data), it is possible to make several statements about the predictive accuracy of the best model for each subject. A summary statement may be made in terms of the percent variance accounted for by the best model, or in terms of the standard error of estimate. When linear regression is used to estimate parameters for individual subjects, it is also possible to make a statement about the standard error of each parameter for each subject. Since estimates of error are based upon individual rather than group data, there is no need to be concerned as to whether a group statistic is applicable to any individual subject. While group estimates are also computed, these are applied only to group data, so there should never be any confusion as to the origin of estimates of measurement error.

In summary, componential analysis provides a useful and general framework for investigating individual differences both in subjects' behavior and in the predictability of that behavior. The framework supplies five sources of individual differences at three levels of a hierarchy. At the theory level, differences may be found in the components used and in the combination rule for components. At the model level, differences may be found in the order or mode of component execution. At the component level, differences in component time or difficulty may be found.

Structure of Componential Analysis

In its barest outline (shown in Table 4.3), a componential analysis consists of a series of intensive task analyses that, taken together, form the basis for an extensive task analysis. The goal of an *intensive task analysis* is to understand as

TABLE 4.3
Componential Task Analysis

		Internal validation	External validation
Extensive analysis	Intensive analysis 1		
	Intensive analysis 2		
	.		
	.		
	.		
	Intensive analysis N		

fully as possible the psychology of one particular task. In particular, it is designed to identify and understand the components of performance on that task. The goal of an *extensive task analysis* is to integrate the findings of a series of interrelated intensive analyses. In particular, it is designed to demonstrate the psychological reality and generalizability of the identified components.

Each intensive analysis consists of two parts, internal and external validation. *Internal validation* consists of the attempt to break down composite task performance into underlying components. *External validation* is the attempt to understand how the identified components of task performance generate individual differences in performance on external tasks. One is obliged to show through external validation that patterns of individual differences in components for the particular task under investigation are not specific to that task, but are instead of general interest.

We now turn to a more detailed description of the procedures involved in intensive and extensive task analysis.

INTENSIVE TASK ANALYSIS

Composite Task or Test Score

An investigator administers Task X (it might equally be called Test X) to a group of subjects and then analyzes his data in two ways: He computes a task score for each subject and an index of difficulty (such as proportion correct or response time) for each item or item type. He has previously collected data on Tasks $A, B,$ and C from the same group of subjects, but his primary interest is in Task X. What does he do with his new data?

If the investigator is a differential psychologist, he is likely to use the set of scores as a basis for studying individual differences among subjects. He might first compute basic statistics for Task X (such as the mean and standard deviation), and then compute correlations between scores on Task X and scores on Tasks *A, B,* and *C.* The correlations will enable him to determine the degree to which individual differences in subjects' scores on Task X are related to individual differences in scores on Tasks *A, B,* and *C.* He may then draw certain conclusions regarding the extent to which the tasks are tapping common intellectual functions. The investigator might attempt to understand these intellectual functions more fully by factor analyzing the set of tests, thereby isolating as factors the common intellectual functions tapped by the set of tasks.

If the investigator is an information-processing psychologist, he is likely to concern himself primarily with data for items or item types. He can use the set of item difficulties as a basis for studying differences among items. The information-processing psychologist might then attempt to form an information-processing model of behavior that accounts for the differential difficulty encountered by subjects in answering different types of items. Having formed such a model, he might attempt to simulate it on a computer or else write a set of mathematical equations that accounts for the difficulty pattern across items. In short, the information-processing psychologist is concerned primarily with item or task variance, the differential psychologist with subject variance.

Taking componential analysis as our viewpoint, we will be interested in variance across both subjects and items, but our initial strategy will be different from either of those outlined above. We will think of the composite task score as a measurement of the *manifest trait* of personality theory. The manifest trait represents observable behavior, but our primary interest is not so much in this behavior as in the *latent traits* that underlie this behavior. In order to reach the level of the latent trait, we shall go through an intermediate level between the manifest and latent traits, which are measured by composite task scores and component scores respectively. This intermediate level is the level of the *interval score.*

Interval Scores

Formation. The first step in a componential analysis is to form interval scores from the breakdown of the composite task into a series of subtasks, as was done by Johnson (1960) in his pioneering method of serial analysis. Each of these subtasks requires successively less information processing, and thus the time intervals involved in processing become successively shorter.

Consider as an example a true–false analogical reasoning task, requiring subjects to determine the truth or falsity of analogies presented in the form *A:B::C:D.*[1] In order to break up the task, one might eliminate from considera-

---

[1] In order to motivate the componential analysis described later in this volume, an analogical reasoning task will be used as an example of interval score formation, and also as an example of other procedures described in this chapter. However, other examples could be used instead, because componential analysis is a general method that can be applied to a wide variety of problems. A recently completed study by the author, for example, applies it to deductive reasoning in three-term series problems.

tion successive terms of the analogy. Since the analogy has four terms, four subtasks might be formed. The first would be identical to the composite task, requiring solution of the full analogy. The second subtask would be based upon analogy solution for the last three terms. Subjects might be given as much time as they want to look at the first term of the analogy, and then be given the last three terms of the analogy when they indicated they were ready to look at them. Timing would be done separately for the first and second parts of the trial. A third subtask would be based upon analogy solution for the last two terms. Subjects might be given as long as they want on the first two terms of the analogy, and then timed separately on the last two terms. Finally, a fourth subtask might be based upon analogy solution for the last term. Separate timing would occur for the first three terms and then the single last term.

The general strategy, then, is to give subjects successively greater amounts of prior information (precueing) in the first part of the trial, so that successively less processing is required in the second part of the trial. Subjects are given as long as they need for both parts, so that maximum information processing is encouraged both before termination of precueing and before selection of a response. Subjects are shown just the precueing information in the first part of the trial, and either the whole item or just the second (new) part of the item in the second part of the trial. Only the former procedure — showing the whole item in the second part of the trial — has been used to date.

Types of interval scores. Two types of interval scores are formed from the breakdown of the task, one type for the first part of the trial and one type for the second part of the trial. Both are interval scores in the sense that they represent processing in some time interval during task solution. The interval score for the first part of the trial is called a *cue score* because it is based upon performance in the precueing part of the trial. The cue score represents the time from the onset of precueing until the subject indicates his readiness for the second part of the trial. The interval score for the second part of the trial is called a *solution score* because it is based upon performance during that part of the trial requiring item solution. The solution score represents the time from the onset of the second part of the trial (usually the full problem) until the subject indicates his solution.

It is possible for the solution score to be proportion correct or some variation of it, rather than response time. If this is the case, subjects would be given information needed to solve the problem up to a certain point, and would be expected to continue from that point on their own. The cue score would still be a response time — the amount of time spent viewing the cue information. The solution score would be a proportion correct, or some variation of it.

Assumption of additivity. Only one assumption is made in the breakdown of the composite task and the formation of interval scores. This assumption is additivity — interval scores reflecting lesser amounts of processing are "contained in" interval scores reflecting greater amounts of processing. The interval scores may be viewed as a series of concentric circles, with the composite-task interval score encircling interval scores for all subtasks, and scores for each successive subtask encircling all those that are based upon less processing.

In order for the additivity assumption to be justified, the precueing procedure must not alter the nature of the task. The succession of subtasks must actually represent processing that occurs in successively later intervals of the full task. Additivity is not a foregone conclusion. For example, it is possible that when a subject is given three cues in the analogies task, he uses the cues to form in his mind's eye a mental image of the correct fourth term. When given the fourth term in the second part of the trial, he then compares the full image against the presented term. However, in other cueing conditions, he may never bother to form this mental image, since in no other cueing condition is he given enough information to construct an image of the correct answer. Instead, he may merely check individual features of the fourth term of the analogy, one at a time.

It is important to note one assumption that is *not* made — that interval scores correspond to distinct stages of processing (Sternberg, 1969a). It is possible for multiple stages to occur within one interval, or for a particular stage to occur during several intervals. In short, no assumptions at all are made about stages.

Internal validation: Simplex model. The assumption that interval scores requiring less processing are contained in interval scores requiring more processing is empirically testable. If the assumption is correct, then the succession of interval scores should form a simplex (Guttman, 1954). Internal validation of the interval scores is accomplished by testing this assumption.

Details of tests for simplicial structure are presented in Chapter 7 and will not be mentioned here. One very simple test that can be done by eye will be mentioned, however. It is performed by inspecting the intercorrelation table of solution (or cue) scores with themselves. If correlations generally decrease in magnitude as they move away from the principal diagonal of the intercorrelation table, then the solution (or cue) scores are probably related simplicially.

The scores of primary interest are the solution scores, and these are formed into a simplex model. The model consists of a set of equations in which each solution score is predicted by regression from the immediately adjacent solution scores. Thus, for example, the zero-cue solution score is predicted from the one-cue score (since there is only one adjacent score); the one-cue score is predicted from the zero-cue and two-cue scores; the two-cue score is predicted from the one-cue and three-cue scores, etc. Such a model can be used as a basis for further testing of simplicial structure (see Chapter 7).

In practice, the succession of interval scores will rarely show perfect additivity. There are two reasons for this. First, interval scores will generally be somewhat unreliable, and to the extent that measurement error in one interval score is uncorrelated with measurement error in another interval score, additivity will be lacking. Second, it is likely that the breakdown of the task into subtasks will at least slightly alter the nature of processing in one or more subtasks relative to the full task. Again, additivity will be affected. Experience indicates, however, that the procedures of componential analysis are quite robust in the face of additivity violations, although large violations will obviously compromise results.

External validation. External validation of the interval scores begins by correlating the interval scores with scores from the reference ability tests. One wants to demonstrate both convergent and discriminant validity.

Convergent validity is demonstrated by showing that the interval scores correlate highly with well-established tests or other performance criteria that are hypothesized to measure the same thing as the interval scores. If the task under consideration is analogical reasoning, then tests of inductive reasoning ability would be good choices for use as reference ability tests.

Discriminant validity is demonstrated by showing that the interval scores correlate only trivially with tests measuring abilities hypothesized to be unrelated. Or if there are confoundings of particular concern, then discriminant validity may be shown by holding constant statistically the scores on the confounded test(s). In the case of analogies, one could obviously choose tests that bear only the weakest resemblance to the analogies, for example, pitch discrimination. However, a strong demonstration of discriminant validity would require administration of tests with which the new analogies test is likely to be confounded. If the analogies test uses response time as a dependent variable, standard tests of perceptual speed would be appropriate. Vocabulary or general verbal comprehension would also be appropriate.

Component Scores

Formation. Component scores are parameter estimates for individual subjects. They are hypothesized to measure the durations or difficulties of the components of the information-processing model of task solution. These scores differ in three key ways from composite task scores and interval scores.

First, the scores differ in the level of measured behavior. The composite task score is viewed as measuring the overt or manifest trait. The interval scores are all at intermediate levels, except for the zero-cue score, which is identical to the composite task score. The component scores are viewed as measuring latent traits, the root processes underlying observable behavior.

Second, the scores differ in the purity of measured behavior. The composite task score is, as its name implies, a composite, a measurement of a mixture of various elementary information processes. Interval scores formed from the composite score are also themselves composites. However, successive interval scores (from 0 to N cues, where N is an arbitrary integer) may contain different numbers of elementary information processes. Each component score is hypothesized to be a measure of the duration or difficulty of a single elementary information process. It is a "pure" measure at the level of interest of the investigator.

Third, the scores differ in their dependence upon a theory of measured behavior. The composite task score may be theory-free, with no theory behind it at all. (This has often been the case in the history of differential psychology.) It is for this reason that it has been possible to go into a factor analysis without a theory and to come out of it with a theory: The computation of scores from which the input correlation matrix is calculated may be theory free. The interval score is bound to a theory about the measurement process. The theory is that the succession of interval scores is additive. The theory is mathematically formulated in terms of a simplex model. The component score is bound to a theory about psychological process. The component scores will change if the theory (or specific model) changes. The theory is the component theory together with the specific model under that theory.

Internal validation: Component model. Internal validation of the component scores is by the component model. An estimate of goodness of fit (such as percentage of variance accounted for) or badness of fit (such as RMSD) is calculated for each individual subject under each model. The best fitting model will then usually be used as the basis for computing component scores.

It is worth repeating that no assumptions are made about stages. In some models, certain component operations may be repeated after other component operations intervene, so if some kind of stage representation is used, it is advisable to allow for the possibility that a stage may be reentered after it has been executed.

One must be careful not to label repetitions of the same component process as separate processes. This error is especially likely to occur if other processes intervene. If the investigator is uncertain whether a particular operation is unique or a repetition of a previous operation, analysis of individual differences may help settle the question. Component scores can be calculated as though the two processes are distinct. If the component scores are very highly correlated across subjects (after correction for attenuation), then there is a good chance that the component scores are actually measures of the same component. One cannot be certain, however, since distinct components may be correlated. However, if the component scores are not highly correlated (after correction for attenuation), then they must represent distinct components. Otherwise, they could not represent independent sources of individual differences.

One may study the effects upon the component model and component values of experimental factors using the additive-factor method. The advantage of studying these effects in the componential method is that the effects of the factors on component durations can be quantified. In addition, it is possible to discover whether a particular factor adds or deletes a component. One may do a full additive-factor analysis upon the factors if they are experimentally independent (which they need not be). Hence, componential models can be studied by the additive-factor method, but as will be seen, componential analysis can supply much more information about underlying processes than can an additive-factor analysis alone.

It is possible to form a component model for either solution time, error rate, or both (as is done in Chapter 7–9). The two types of models differ in two fundamental respects.

First, the error model provides component estimates for difficulty rather than duration. The two need not be highly correlated. Componential analysis enables one to investigate relationships between the two types of components, as is done in this volume.

Second, whereas all components must enter into the solution-time model, all components need not enter into the error model. The reason for this is that while all components must take some amount of real time to execute, the execution of one or more components may be error free, or nearly so. If there are any errors in performance, then they should be due to faulty execution of one or more components. However, not all components need lead to errors, and so the error model may contain only a subset of the components involved in the solution-time model.

External validation. Procedures for external validation of the component scores are similar to those for external validation of the interval scores. The component scores are correlated with the reference ability scores and thereby assessed in terms of convergent and discriminant validation.

Reference Ability Scores

Formation. Reference ability scores are based upon conventional tests of mental ability that are selected so as to provide criteria for convergent and discriminant validation of the interval and component scores. When more than one test of each ability is used (as is advisable), a factor score (derived from factor analysis) may be used to summarize the information from the battery of tests.

Two views of reference ability scores. Differential psychology has generally viewed factors as representing latent traits of some kind (see Chapter 2) and, therefore, sees factor scores for reference abilities as measurements of these latent traits. This view is not accepted here. Rather, it is claimed that factors could not possibly represent latent traits because of two intrinsic characteristics described in Chapter 2. First, factor analysis is based upon interitem rather than intraitem analysis. Second, factor analysis is based upon interindividual rather than intraindividual analysis, so that it is impossible to infer directly anything about what takes place inside a single individual.

It simply does not make sense to have factors represent latent traits, and it is fortunate that they do not. If factors represented latent traits, the traits would be nonidentifiable because factor axes may be rotated in any of an infinite number of ways in a factor space. Since all rotations of a given set of axes account for the same proportion of variance in the data, there would be no way of internally validating one orientation of axes as the "true" set of latent traits.

In componential analysis, reference abilities are defined as constellations of components (latent traits) that in combination form stable patterns of individual differences across tasks. Note that in this definition, reference abilities are defined in terms of multiple tasks, individual differences, and constellations of components. These three properties suggest the role factors might play in componential analysis.

Componential view of factors. In componential analysis, factors are mathematical representations of reference abilities, just as parameters are mathematical representations of components. The limitations of factors that make them unsuitable as representations of latent traits cease to be problems when factors are viewed as representations of reference abilities rather than of latent traits.

First, both factors and reference abilities are defined in terms of multiple tasks and individual differences. Their intrinsic properties are therefore congruent, and it is quite appropriate to use factor scores as measures of reference abilities.

Second, both factors and reference abilities may be understood in terms of constellations of components. When they are defined in this way, nonuniqueness ceases to be a problem, because it is simply a manifestation of the many, indeed infinite, number of ways in which components can be combined to form constellations. A single component may enter into many factors and may be of differential importance (weight) in different factors.

While it was not possible to select among axis orientations on the basis of internal validation, it is possible to select on the basis of external validation: Some orientations lead to more interpretable relationships than do others. The orientation of axes one chooses for a particular study is therefore a matter of convenience and illustrative value. Since reference abilities are part of the external validation procedure in componential analysis, it makes perfect sense to identify them (by labeling factors) on the basis of considerations of external validity.

To summarize, factors are not representations of manifest traits. In componential analysis, manifest traits are represented by composite tasks. Manifest traits are therefore constellations of processes. Nor are factors representations of latent traits. In componential analysis, latent traits are components and are represented by parameters. The latent trait is viewed as a process. Rather, factors are representations of reference abilities. The reference abilities are constellations of latent traits (components) that in combination form stable patterns of individual differences in manifest traits.

Relationship between tasks and factors. A major consequence of linking composite task scores to manifest traits and factor scores to reference abilities is that tasks and factors come to be seen as quite similar in one fundamental respect: Both represent constellations of components. Given this similarity, they also differ in one fundamental respect: The components entering into tasks are held together by information-processing constraints – a certain set of components is required to process the task; the components entering into factors are held together by individual-differences constraints – certain sets of components form stable patterns of individual differences.

According to this viewpoint, the manifest trait (measured by composite-task scores) and the reference ability (measured by factor scores) are at the same "depth." Both are constellations of components "glued together" by different sorts of glue. One type of glue – the constraints of individual differences – has been primarily of interest to differential psychologists. The other type of glue – the constraints of information processing – has been primarily of interest to information-processing psychologists. Thus, the differential psychologist has looked at differences across subjects, and the information-processing psychologist has looked at differences across tasks. Either way, however, the psychologist is looking at constellations of components.

By their nature, both tasks and factors are arbitrary. The number of tasks that can be devised requiring different combinations or weightings of components is probably endless, and the fineness with which sources of individual differences can be identified is also probably endless. As new tasks requiring new combinations or weightings of components are devised, new sources of individual differences will be found, if only the distinctions are drawn finely enough. It is for this reason that differential psychology has seen a proliferation of factors. With enough different tests, the possibilities are endless.

Components are nonarbitrary, and their number is finite. Although they can be combined and weighted in an infinite number of ways, and thus appear in many guises, they remain the same. They are the latent traits that account for both task scores and factor scores.

Componential view of factor analysis. It is now possible to turn to the two major uses of factor analysis in componential analysis.

First, factor analysis is used in the attempt to recover the hypothesized reference abilities from the manifest trait data. One has no guarantee that when subjects are given a series of ability tests, the recovered factor structure will correspond to the hypothesized categorization of reference abilities. In the experiments described in this volume, for example, the desired recovery was obtained in the People Piece Analogy Experiment (Chapter 7) but not in the Geometric Analogy Experiment (Chapter 9). One is obliged to show that the observed pattern of individual differences corresponds to the predicted pattern. If it does not, the identities of the reference abilities may have to be reconceptualized.

Second, factor analysis is used to provide summary factor scores for each identified reference ability. It is always advisable to give at least two and preferably more tests of each ability in order to separate the common variance of interest in the tests from specific variance that is not a true part of the reference ability.[2] One could use some a priori weighting of tests to form a

---

[2] Because one is interested in the common and not the specific variance, communalities are used in the diagonal of the correlation matrix to be factored.

composite estimate of performance on the reference ability. The advantage of using a factor score is that it is the statistically optimum estimate of performance on the factor and therefore of performance on the reference ability. Factor scores thus have the dual advantage of being convenient summary scores and, at the same time, optimum estimates of reference ability performance.

Factor analysis plays a role in componential analysis, but it is a much less ambitious role than its role in traditional differential psychology. It is used to identify stable patterns of individual differences and to quantify these patterns by assigning one or more numbers to each subject. When factor analysis is used for these more modest purposes, the problems with its use cited earlier disappear because these problems occur only in the conventional use of factor analysis to uncover the latent structure of human abilities. Factor analysis is simply the wrong technique for this job.

Reference abilities models.   Reference abilities are defined in terms of constellations of components. Given their definition, it should be possible to dissect these abilities into their underlying components. This dissection is attempted through reference abilities models.

In reference ability modeling, one attempts to account for individual differences in subjects' reference ability scores in terms of individual differences in their component scores. Full understanding of a given reference ability would be attained when all the systematic between-subjects variance in the reference ability scores was accounted for by a combination of components.

Reference ability scores can also be modeled in terms of interval scores, although such models will be less revealing than models based upon components. In either case, there is one model for each reference ability.

Integration: Structural Regression Model

Three different types of model have been described so far: the simplex model (for solution scores), the component model, and the reference abilities models. The outcomes of these three different types of model can be integrated through a structural regression model. This model gives an overall account of the interrelationships of individual differences in the various types of scores. The design of a structural regression model (as applied to componential analysis) is shown in Figure 4.1.

A structural regression model is a causal account of interrelationships. In componential analysis, the causal elements are the components. Parameters representing hypothetical component durations or difficulties are shown in the third row of the model in the figure. These components combine to form two types of entities. The first is embodied in the subtasks formed by breaking down the total task. These subtasks are shown in the second row of the model. Arrows are shown leading upward from the parameters to the subtasks. Not all parameters are shown for all subtasks. Parameters are shown only if the corresponding components enter into performance on the subtask. The second type of entity is

Level

Factor

Subtasks

Parameters

Factor

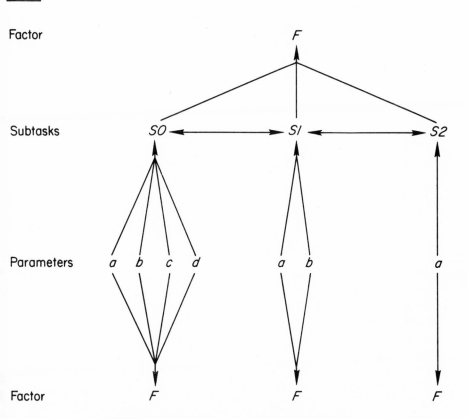

FIGURE 4.1   Design of a structural regression model.

the reference ability. A hypothetical factor is shown in the fourth row of the model (and also the first, for reasons to be described). In Figure 4.1, arrows are shown leading downward from the parameters to the factor representing the reference ability.

The relationship of the reference ability to the components is mediated by the use of subtasks. One is able to get to the reference ability from the components via the subtasks that form the basis for componential modeling. Operationally, therefore, subtasks form a mediate link, and reference ability scores can be accounted for in terms of solution scores, which are themselves accounted for by the component scores. Thus, arrows are drawn from the subtasks to the factor, although it is understood that these subtasks represent only mediating operational links in the chain. From a theoretical vantage point, the solution scores can be dispensed with once the component scores are estimated. In practice, however, they are very useful even after the component scores have been estimated (as will be shown later in this chapter and volume).

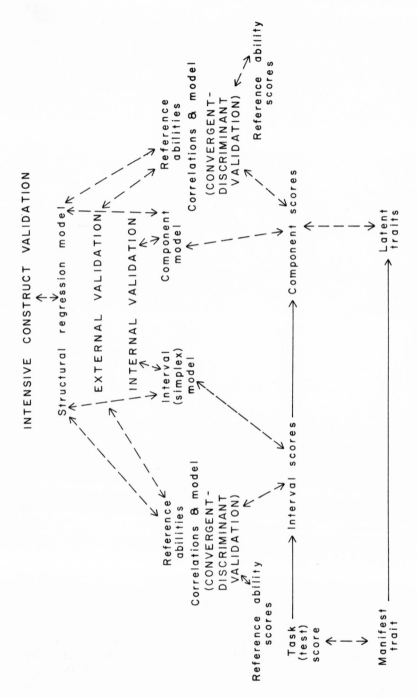

FIGURE 4.2 Componential three-level intensive task analysis.

In an actual structural regression, numerical coefficients will be attached to each arrow leading from one symbol to another. These coefficients are standardized partial regression coefficients and are frequently called path coefficients. Each path coefficient represents the independent contribution of a given predictor variable to the predicted variable, with the other predictors in the set held constant.

The structural regression model summarizes in compact form a large quantity of data from the intensive analysis. It may be seen as forming the basis for construct validation of the system of models and of the task used to validate these models. High construct validity is indicated by a high level of prediction for: (1) interval scores from component scores; (2) reference ability scores from component scores; (3) reference ability scores from interval scores; and (4) interval scores from each other.

Overview

The structure of the entire intensive analysis is shown in Figure 4.2. The composite task score, measuring the manifest trait, is broken up into interval scores. Internal validation of the interval scores is through the simplex model. External validation is through correlations with scores on reference abilities tests and through the reference abilities models. In the correlations, one attempts to show both convergent and discriminant validity. The interval scores are used as a basis for computing component scores, which are hypothesized to measure latent traits. Internal validation of the component scores is through the component model. External validation is through correlations with the reference abilities and through the reference abilities models. Again, one attempts to show both convergent and discriminant validity. The various types of models are combined into a structural regression model, which forms the basis for intensive construct validation of the system of models and of the task used to validate the models.

EXTENSIVE TASK ANALYSIS

An extensive analysis is composed of a series of related intensive analyses. The fundamental purpose of extensive analysis is to show through a sequence of converging operations (Garner, Hake, & Eriksen, 1956) that the components identified in one particular intensive analysis have psychological reality, and that they are generalizable to a variety of related tasks.

Information-processing psychology has been caught in a web of specificity, perhaps because its very nature lends itself to specific theories. Little attempt has been made to show that the parameters that are applicable to one task are applicable to related tasks as well. There have been a few exceptions to this trend. The human associative memory (HAM) model of memory (Anderson &

Bower, 1973), for example, is in part an attempt to demonstrate that a relatively small number of algorithms can account for many of the diverse phenomena that have been discovered in the study of memory. In general, however, the tendency has been toward the identification of very specific parameters for even more specific tasks, with no attempt to show that the hypothesized parameters are of any relevance or interest beyond a given task or even specific task material.

The extensive analysis strategy one follows will depend upon the task domain under study, and so it is necessary to be somewhat specific in showing the course an extensive analysis might take. Table 4.4 summarizes the extensive analysis strategy used in the present series of studies.

In the extensive analysis for the analogies studies, five task variables were systematically varied: dependent variable, response format, type of content, difficulty, and definition of attributes. Three intensive analyses used response time as the primary dependent variable (although error rate was studied as well), while one used proportion correct. In two studies, the response format was true–false; in two, it was forced choice. In two experiments, the content of the analogies was verbal; in two, it was nonverbal. Items across studies ranged from very easy to very difficult. In one study, stimulus attributes were well defined; in two, they were somewhat defined; in one, they were poorly defined. If the same theory can be found to apply across all these different task manipulations, then it can be concluded that the theory is a general one.

WHY COMPONENTIAL ANALYSIS?

Overview

Why use componential analysis, rather than the psychometric techniques of differential psychology or the modeling techniques of information-processing psychology? Componential analysis will generally be more expensive, both in

TABLE 4.4
Overview of Converging Operations in
Analogical Reasoning Extensive Task Analysis:
Extensive Construct Validation

Type of analogy	Dependent variable	Response format	Type of content	Difficulty	Definition of attributes
People Piece analogies	Response time	True–false	Nonverbal	Very easy	Well defined
Verbal analogies	Response time	True–false	Verbal	Fairly easy	Poorly defined
Geometric analogies	Response time	Forced-choice	Nonverbal	Fairly difficult	Somewhat defined
Animal name analogies	Proportion correct	Forced-choice	Verbal	Very difficult	Somewhat defined

TABLE 4.5

Advantages of Interval, Component, and Reference Ability Scores

Interval scores	Component scores	Reference ability scores
1. Separate components which otherwise would have been confounded	Estimate scores by inferentially powerful model controlled by investigator	Identify correlates of individual differences in component performance
2. Compare models which otherwise would have been indistinguishable	Represent scores uniquely within parameter space — no "rotation dilemma"	Prevent overvaluation of components with task-specific individual differences
3. Increase degrees of freedom for residual in prediction	Interpret scores in terms of mental process	Provide a common language across different tasks and researchers
4. Specify precisely temporal ordering and location of components	Provide scores based upon a well-specified theory and model derived from individual behavior	
5. Prevent distortion of results from external validation	Permit systematic study of individual differences at theory, model, and component levels	
6. Provide component-free estimates of performance for nested processing intervals	Pinpoint individual sources of particular strength or weakness for diagnosis and training	
7.	Fit into a systematic framework for understanding intellectual development	
8.	Derive estimates of measurement error from data for individual subjects	

terms of time and money, and one may wonder whether the benefits justify the costs. We now consider 17 advantages associated with the use of interval scores, component scores, and reference ability scores. These advantages are summarized in Table 4.5.

Interval Scores

Interval scores are formed from the breakdown of a composite task into a series of subtasks, each requiring successively less information processing. Studies such as that of Clark and Chase (1972) demonstrate that information processing models can be constructed without breaking down the composite task into subtasks and the composite task score into interval scores. What, then, are the advantages of the breakdown?

1. Interval data enable one to disentangle sources of variance that would otherwise be confounded. Often, for example, multiple sources of variance are dumped into the additive constant of a regression equation. The constant then comes to be called a "wastebasket parameter" (Clark & Chase, 1972) or, in the extreme case, is denied to be a parameter (Carpenter & Just, 1975)!

Consider as an example parameter estimation for latencies in an analogical reasoning task, with analogies of the form $A:B::C:D$. If we were to estimate parameters only for composite task latencies, we generally would be unable to separate from the additive constant the amount of time it takes to encode each term (assuming terms are of comparable complexity), since there are always four terms to be encoded. In other words, encoding time is constant across items and, therefore, is dumped into the "wastebasket parameter," where it does not belong. In certain models of analogical reasoning, inference time (the amount of time it takes to comprehend the relationship between A and B) would also be confounded with application time (the amount of time it takes to apply this transformation from C to D).

Analogies provide only one of many possible examples. In any task requiring multiple encoding operations (which includes most complex reasoning and sentence verification tasks), or requiring separate operations distinguishable only by temporal ordering, interval data enable one to separate the multiple operations from each other.

2. The second advantage derives from the first. Interval data enable one to compare certain models that would otherwise be indistinguishable. The additional model comparison becomes possible if confounded parameters that would distinguish the models become disentangled through interval scoring. In the People Piece Experiment (Chapter 7), for example, models postulating self-terminating encoding are distinguishable from models postulating exhaustive encoding only because of the separation of the encoding parameter from the preparation–response parameter.

3. Interval data can greatly increase the available number of degrees of freedom (df) for residual used in modeling (see Chapter 3 for discussion of df in modeling). Increasing the available df for residual is a responsible way of guarding against spurious "good fit." In the People Piece Experiment, for example, the use of interval breakdown more than quadrupled the number of df for residual, and in the Geometric Analogies Experiment, the number of df was more than doubled.

4. Interval breakdown requires the investigator to specify in what interval(s) of processing each mental operation takes place, and thus requires tighter and more complete specification of the relationship between elementary information processes and mathematical parameters of a given model. In conventional information-processing models, the processes could occur in any order at all, and the mathematical predictions would remain unchanged. In componential analysis, it is no longer sufficient to state only that a particular process occurs at some time during the course of mental events. At a bare minimum, one must specify the interval(s) in which each particular process occurs.

Detailed specification for each process can be quite difficult. In the People Piece and Verbal Analogy Experiments, for example, it was not obvious whether the application component occurred during cueing or during solution of items in the three-cue condition. However, the reward for more detailed specification is an increased understanding of the relationship between the structure of the problem and the course of mental processing as the problem is solved.

5. Interval scoring prevents possible distortion of results from external validation. The reason for this, once again, is that it often becomes possible through interval breakdown to separate sources of variance that would otherwise be confounded. Two component scores may show quite different correlations with an external criterion, but if these components are confounded, then the difference will be washed out. In the extreme case, the correlations may actually be of opposite sign; if the components are confounded, this will never become apparent.

In the People Piece and Verbal Analogy Experiments, two such correlations actually were of opposite sign. The encoding component scores showed positive correlations with a reference ability, while the preparation-response component scores showed negative correlations. If the two components had been confounded, as they would have been if interval data had not been used, then the correlation for the confounded component score would have been a near-zero correlation that obscured the true pattern of relationships.

6. The final benefit of interval scores to be mentioned here is that they provide component-free estimates of performance for a series of nested processing intervals. These estimates will be particularly useful when either (1) one has no component theory of information processing; (2) the theory one has does not fit the data for individual subjects well; or (3) parameter estimates for individual subjects are unreliable. In such cases, component scores will be unavailable or

unusable. Because interval scores represent an intermediate step between the composite task score and component scores, the interval scores will provide more information about mental processing than will a composite task score alone.

Suppose, for example, that component scores had been unavailable in the People Piece Experiment (Chapter 7), for any of the above reasons. One could still discover many interesting patterns in the interval score data, such as an unexpected pattern of correlations that emerged between the sequences of interval scores (both cue and solution scores) and the reasoning factor score. The pattern could be discovered only because of the availability of interval scores. Although it could not be well understood without the component score correlations to explain it, the pattern would nevertheless be in full view and thus available for tentative or future explanation.

These advantages mitigate limitations of the information-processing approach described in Chapter 3. As will be seen in subsequent chapters, the interval scores are quite useful even when component scores *are* available. Their use, therefore, is recommended in conjunction with component scores when the latter are computed.

Component Scores

The component scores estimated in componential analysis provide at least eight benefits. The first four are of particular interest, because they overcome or assuage the four limitations of factor analysis (and hence of factor scores) described in Chapter 2.

1. Component scores are estimated by an inferentially powerful mathematical modeling technique. Scores derived from a model can be no better than the model itself: If the model is inadequate, the scores will be as well. Fortunately, componential models are relatively easy to disconfirm. Moreover, the theorist controls the mathematical model, so that it is possible to estimate comparable component scores for different tasks. Factor analysis is an inferentially weak technique (see Chapter 2), and the theorist does not control the mathematical model. Hence, factor scores are relevant only to a particular stimulus material.

2. Component scores are uniquely defined for a given parameter space. Since the scores are unique, there is no arbitrariness in the selection of a given set of scores: There is no "rotation dilemma." Factor scores, however, are not uniquely defined for a given factor space, because each of the infinite number of possible orientations for factor axes yields a different set of factor scores. Different sets of factors and factor scores may lead to quite disparate interpretations of individual differences.

3. Component scores are based upon intraitem analysis. Hence, it is possible to interpret component scores in terms of mental process. In a typical response-time experiment, it will be possible to interpret a component score in terms of

the amount of time spent on each component. If raw parameters (often regression weights) are used, the scores may be criterion referenced: It may be possible to interpret component scores in terms of the absolute amount of time spent on each component. Attribute-comparison components in the response-time analogy experiments, for example, can be interpreted in terms of seconds (or milliseconds) per attribute value change. Factor scores, on the other hand, are based upon interitem rather than intraitem analysis and therefore are not directly interpretable in terms of mental process. In addition, they are never criterion referenced.

4. Component scores are based upon a well-specified model of behavior that is validated on data for individual subjects. Hence, the calculation of component scores is not dependent upon the availability of data for multiple persons, the existence of individual differences, or the assumption that all subjects — if there are multiple subjects — followed the same model. The calculation of factor scores, on the other hand, is dependent upon all three of these assumptions.

As stated earlier in the chapter, the intrinsic limitations of factors and therefore of factor scores become irrelevant when they are interpreted in the framework of componential analysis. When used to describe performance on reference abilities tests, factor scores supplement component scores in a useful, if modest, way.

5. Componential analysis permits systematic study of individual differences at theory, model, and component levels. Furthermore, the hierarchical nature of the five sources of individual differences described earlier in the chapter makes clear the limiting circumstances under which it makes sense even to study sources of individual differences lower in the hierarchy. For example, it only makes sense to study individual differences in all component values if the theory and model applicable to all individual subjects are identical. If they are not, then only some, or possibly none, of the component-score differences are readily interpretable.

The hierarchical nature of the sources of individual differences is ignored in much traditional individual-differences research. Indeed, all but the last source of individual differences (in score magnitudes) are usually given no attention. Composite task scores, whether expressed as raw scores or as some form of standard score (such as IQ), are usually compared under the assumption that the processes leading to the score are identical or that differences in these processes are of no consequence in the interpretation of differences in the composite score. These assumptions are almost never tested. Their blind acceptance is unfortunate, because the most important sources of individual differences may be at the model or theory levels (see 6 and 7 below).

6. The componential framework for individual differences provides a useful way of pinpointing individual sources of particular strength or weakness. This information may be used for diagnostic purposes, and later for remedial training.

Suppose, for example, that an individual has difficulty in solving analogies relative to other individuals of his age or grade level. It will generally be assumed that he is inferior in reasoning to the others, or at least inferior in analogical reasoning. In exceptional cases, he may be given training in reasoning to bring him up to average age or grade level. This is about the optimal outcome that could be expected in present educational environments, and yet it is unsatisfactory because the source of difficulty has not been located. But this "optimal" outcome is an unlikely one. More likely, teachers' expectations for the student's performance will be lowered, and the student may be relegated to a lower track in school.

In order to provide relevant training for the individual, it is necessary to know the source of his difficulty. For example, it may not be at the component level at all, but at the theory or model level. At the theory level, the individual may be using a component that is inappropriate for analogy solution, or he may be using an inappropriate combination rule for components. At the model level, he may be ordering the components incorrectly, or he may be using an inefficient mode of component processing, such as exhaustive scans where self-terminating scans would do. Finally, the difficulty may be at the component level: He may be slower or have greater difficulty executing one or more components than other individuals to whom he is compared.

The crucial point about the above analysis of possible sources of individual differences is that of the five sources of such differences, the first four are the most easily trainable. They indicate incorrect or inefficient problem-solving strategies, and, through componential modeling, it may be possible to determine quite precisely the nature of the strategy being used and how it differs from the typical or optimal strategy. Although the theory and model level individual differences are easiest to train, since they would tend to indicate a strategy problem rather than an ability problem, these four sources of individual differences are almost uniformly ignored. The source of difficulty is attributed to an ability problem, which in componential analysis would usually be reflected by a component-score value. Certainly the theory and model level sources of individual differences should be ruled out before the most pessimistic assessment, that of a difference at the component level, is made!

Perhaps, though, the problem of our hypothetical student is at the component level. Even in this case, the problem may not be one of reasoning. One of the components in the theory of analogical reasoning to be described is an encoding component, which is hypothesized to be perceptual in nature. It is possible that the student's difficulty is not in reasoning about the terms of the analogy, but in encoding those terms. If the problem is a perceptual one, then training in reasoning will be misdirected. Yet, through ordinary composite score analyses, the true nature of the problem may never come to light, because the perceptual problem depresses overall task performance. Performance will probably be depressed in a variety of tasks, and the student may easily come to be classified as generally "unintelligent."

Finally, it may be found that the student's problem is indeed one of reasoning. The componential analysis will still prove to be of benefit, because it is possible to pinpoint the source of difficulty much more precisely than would be possible with just a composite task score. If the problem is one of application — applying what the student knows — then training that emphasizes inference processes may be a poor use of limited time. Training should instead be directed at the utilization of existing knowledge.

7. The componential framework for individual differences provides a systematic way of understanding intellectual development. A fundamental question of developmental psychology, perhaps *the* fundamental question, is: What does it mean that, as children grow older, they become better at performing a variety of tasks? In componential analysis, the question can be answered in five ways. The first four answers have two parts: acquisition and application.

First, the child can acquire new components, or he can learn to apply components he has already acquired to specific problems in which they are relevant. Second, he can acquire new combination rules for components, or he can learn how combination rules he has acquired can be applied to specific problems in which they are useful. Third, he can acquire new orders for component sequences, or he can learn how a particular order with which he has prior familiarity can be applied to specific problems. Fourth, he can acquire new modes of component processing, or he can learn which mode is most efficient for each component in a given problem. Fifth, he can improve in ease or speed of component execution.

8. Component modeling for individual subjects allows the investigator to derive estimates of measurement error for individual subjects from each subject's individual data. These estimates may be for overall error, measured by indices such as the standard error of measurement, the standard error of estimate, or the root-mean-square deviation (RMSD). Or the estimates may be for particular sources of error. If linear regression modeling is used, it is possible to derive standard errors for each individual component score (which are equal to the standard errors of the raw regression coefficients). It is then possible to assess how much confidence can be placed in each component score for each individual. It is also possible to draw confidence bands around the component scores.

In common psychometric analyses, the standard error of measurement and the standard error of estimate are derived from group data and therefore will be averages. They may not be quite correct for the data of any one individual subject, and, for subjects with extreme scores, they may be quite inaccurate. These measures have different meanings when derived for the individual and for the group. Consequently, it will generally be advisable to compute both individual and group indices. This is easily done if componential analysis is used.

Reference Ability Scores

Reference ability scores as used in componential analysis provide at least three benefits. These benefits are not obtained in customary information-processing analyses, because reference abilities are ignored. In fact, the three benefits overcome or assuage the three limitations of information-processing analyses described in Chapter 3.

1. Reference ability scores enable one to identify correlates of individual differences in component performance. They enable the investigator to determine the patterns of individual differences generated by components. In information-processing research, such determinations have generally been either ignored or taken for granted. Consider two examples.

First, it has been assumed that the animal name analogies used to validate Rumelhart and Abrahamson's (1973) model of analogical reasoning actually measure reasoning. This assumption has not been tested in previously published work. It is tested in this volume.

Second, it might be assumed that in the theory of analogical reasoning presented in this volume, the attribute comparison component scores for inference, mapping, and application measure reasoning, while the other components — encoding and preparation—response — do not. Indeed, these were the predictions made. In fact, these predictions were incorrect.

The general point is that the patterns of individual differences generated by components should be neither ignored nor taken for granted. They can be discovered only by empirical test.

2. Correlating components with reference ability scores prevents overvaluation of components that generate task-specific individual differences. A component may be "real" in a particular task, in the sense that it accounts for a nontrivial proportion of variance in the best model of task performance. However, the component may be of no interest outside the particular task: It may not correlate with anything but itself. Correlating components with reference abilities forces the investigator to show that identified components are of general interest, that they are correlated with variables other than themselves. Given the exotic nature of many information-processing tasks studied in the laboratory, such demonstrations seem essential. A proliferation of trivial components analogous to the proliferation of trivial factors can be prevented if components are shown to be important in accounting for both task performance (correlations across items) and individual differences in performance (correlations across subjects).

3. Finally, reference abilities provide a common language across different tasks and researchers. They relate the components of one experiment to those reference abilities that have been explored in hundreds or even thousands of experiments. When we talk about a two-cue solution score, or a component-c score, we are in unfamiliar terrain. There is no standard language for elementary information processes, and it is possible that one investigator's component c is another investigator's component x. When we say, however, that component c appears to be one of the components that in combination are generally known as reasoning, we are in more familiar terrain. This familiarity can be deceiving,

though. Differential psychologists became so familiar with constellations of latent traits (such as inductive reasoning) that they came to think of the constellations as the latent traits, which they are not.

SUMMARY

The strengths and weaknesses of the differential and information-processing approaches to mental abilities are complementary, and so it should be possible, at least in theory, to synthesize an approach that shares the strengths of each approach and the weaknesses of neither. It is suggested that componential analysis fulfills this goal.

The overall purpose of componential analysis is to identify the component mental operations underlying a series of related information-processing tasks and to discover the organization of these component operations in terms of their relationships both to each other and to higher-order constellations of mental abilities. The fundamental unit of analysis is the component, which is an elementary information process that operates upon internal representations of objects or symbols.

A componential theory consists of two parts: identification of the components involved in task performance and specification of the combination rule for these components. The theory does not fully describe task performance, and so a specific model is needed as well. A componential model further specifies the order of component execution and the mode of component execution (serial versus parallel, exhaustive versus self-terminating, holistic versus particularistic).

In componential analysis, individual differences may derive from five sources. These five sources are hierarchically organized into three levels. At the theory level, individual differences may occur in either the components of task execution or the combination rule for components. At the model level, individual differences may occur in either the order of component execution or the mode of component execution. At the component level, individual differences may occur in speed or ease of component execution.

Componential analysis consists of two basic parts: intensive and extensive analysis. The goal of intensive analysis is to understand as fully as possible the psychology of one particular task. The goal of extensive analysis is to integrate the findings of a series of interrelated intensive analyses. In particular, it is designed to demonstrate the psychological reality and generalizability of the identified components.

Each intensive analysis consists of two parts: internal and external validation. Internal validation consists of the attempt to break down composite task performance into components. External validation is the attempt to understand how the identified components of task performance generate individual differences in performance on external tasks.

The first step in a componential analysis is to form interval scores from the breakdown of the composite task into a series of subtasks. Each of these subtasks requires successively less information processing. Test trials are generally divided into two parts, with precueing in the first part and solution in the second part. The scores for subtasks are of two types. Cue scores are response times for the precueing (first) part of the trial; solution times are response times for the solution (second) part of the trial. Proportion correct or some variation of it may also be used for the solution score. Both types of scores are called "interval scores," because they represent processing in some specified interval of total task performance.

It is assumed that successive interval scores are additive: Interval scores reflecting lesser amounts of processing should be "contained in" interval scores reflecting greater amounts of processing. In order for this assumption to be justified, precueing must not alter the nature of the task. The assumption is tested empirically by the interval score simplex model. This simplex model provides internal validation of the interval scores. External validation of these scores is provided by correlations with reference abilities scores. Both convergent and discriminant validity should be demonstrated. High correlations are predicted with certain reference abilities, but low correlations are predicted with others that are likely sources of confounding.

Component scores are parameter estimates for individual subjects. They are hypothesized to measure durations or difficulties of the components of the information-processing model of task solution. Internal validation of the component scores is through a component model; external validation is through correlations with reference ability scores and through reference ability models.

Reference abilities are defined as constellations of components that in combination form stable patterns of individual differences across tasks. Reference ability scores are based upon conventional tests of mental ability that are selected so as to provide criteria for convergent and discriminant validation of the interval and component scores.

In componential analysis, factors are mathematical representations of reference abilities, just as parameters are mathematical representations of components. Factors are similar to tasks in that both represent constellations of components. In tasks, the components are held together by information-processing constraints. In factors, the components are held together by individual-differences constraints. Both tasks and factors are arbitrary in that an infinite number of tasks or factors could probably be differentiated, each based upon different numbers of components. The components, however, are hypothesized to be nonarbitrary and finite in number.

Factor analysis serves two purposes in componential analysis. The first is an attempt to recover the hypothesized reference abilities from the ability test data. The second is the provision of summary factor scores for each identified reference ability. Factor analysis plays a relatively modest role in componential analysis, but one it is well equipped to handle.

Reference abilities models are an attempt to account for subjects' reference abilities scores in terms of their component scores. Full understanding of a given reference ability would be attained when all the systematic variance in the reference ability score was accounted for by a combination of components.

Integration of the three types of models — simplex, component, and reference ability — is attained through a structural regression model. This model attempts to provide a causal account of the interrelationships among the three types of scores. The underlying causative elements are hypothesized to be the components.

Extensive analysis integrates the results from a series of related intensive analyses. In selecting tasks for extensive analysis, one wants to vary as many task attributes as possible without changing certain fundamental aspects of the task. The same theory should apply in each intensive analysis.

Componential analysis has a number of advantages over differential and information-processing approaches to mental abilities. Seventeen of these advantages are considered, resulting from: (1) the breakdown of the composite task into subtasks and the formation of interval scores; (2) the formation of a component model and component scores; and (3) the use of reference abilities and reference ability scores. By using componential analysis, the limitations of the differential and information processing approaches are largely overcome.

Part III

A COMPONENTIAL ANALYSIS
OF ANALOGICAL REASONING

5
Theories of Analogical Reasoning: A Literature Review

Reasoning by analogy is pervasive in everyday experience and would seem to be an important part of what we commonly refer to as intelligence. We reason analogically whenever we make a decision about something new in our experience by drawing a parallel to something old in our experience. When we buy a new pet hamster because we liked our old one or when we listen to a friend's advice because it was correct once before, we are reasoning analogically. Such decisions are "intelligent" if the parallels to past experience are properly drawn.

Analogical reasoning is of the utmost importance in a variety of intellectual disciplines. The role of analogy in science, for example, can scarcely be overestimated:

> Whether or not we talk of discovery or of invention, analogy is inevitable in human thought, because we come to new things in science with what equipment we have, which is how we have learned to think, and above all how we have learned to think about the relatedness of things. We cannot, coming into something new, deal with it except on the basis of the familiar and the old-fashioned. The conservatism of scientific enquiry is not an arbitrary thing; it is the freight with which we operate; it is the only equipment we have. (Oppenheimer, 1956, pp. 129–130)

Analogical reasoning also plays an important part in the law, where it may be called reasoning by example:

> The basic pattern of legal reasoning is reasoning by example. It is reasoning from case to case. It is a three-step process described by the doctrine of precedent in which a proposition descriptive of the first case is made into a rule of law and then applied to a next similar situation. The steps are these: similarity is seen between cases; next the rule of law inherent in the first case is announced; then the rule of law is made applicable to the second case. This is a method of reasoning necessary for the law, but it has characteristics which under other circumstances might be considered imperfections. (Levi, 1949, pp. 1–2)

Analogical reasoning has been the subject of a relatively small amount of psychological research, perhaps because of its "characteristics which . . . might be considered imperfections." Psychological investigations of reasoning have tended to focus upon deductive reasoning (e.g., Henle, 1962; Wason & Johnson-Laird, 1972; Woodworth & Sells, 1935), in which there is a fairly standard set of logical principles that remain the same from one instance to another. In analogical reasoning (and in its special instance, legal reasoning), however, "the rules change from case to case and are remade with each case" (Levi, 1949, p. 2). This changing of rules is a fundamental property of analogical reasoning. "It occurs because the scope of a rule. . . , and therefore its meaning, depends upon a determination of what facts will be considered similar to those present when the rule was first announced. The finding of similarity or difference is the key step" in analogical reasoning (Levi, 1949, p. 2).

Induction has not been totally neglected, but the theoretical perspective in much research on induction has been that of learning rather than of reasoning. A case in point is found in the voluminous literature on concept formation (e.g., Bower & Trabasso, 1964; Restle, 1962). Many theories of concept formation have been cast in the mold of mathematical learning theory. These theories have been more informative about learning processes than they have been about reasoning processes. There have been a few exceptions fo this generalization, however (e.g., Hunt, 1962; Hunt, Marin, & Stone, 1966).

Because of the small amount of theoretical work that has been done on analogical reasoning, it is possible to review most of that work here.[1] Theories will be described (along with supporting experiments, if available), and the theories will be evaluated on the basis of five criteria:

1. *Completeness.* A complete theory is one that accounts for all processes involved in analogical reasoning, from beginning to end. A complete theory explains analogical reasoning from the time the analogy is first perceived to the time a response is emitted.

2. *Specificity.* A specific theory describes in detail the workings of each process involved in solving analogies. A theory can be complete but not specific if it accounts for all processes, but does not describe the workings of the processes in detail. A theory can also be specific but not complete if it describes in detail a subset of the processes used to solve analogies.

3. *Generality.* A theory is general if it is applicable across a wide range of analogy problems. A fully general theory would be applicable to all analogy problems, regardless of the content or mode of presentation. It is not obvious a priori that a fully general theory is possible; indeed, most previous theories are not very general.

4. *Parsimony.* A theory is parsimonious if it can account for analogical

---

[1] Philosophical work on the concept of analogy is excluded from this review. This work is reviewed by Dawis and Siojo (1972).

reasoning with a relatively small number of parameters and working assumptions. Parsimony is difficult to evaluate, in part, because many theories that appear parsimonious on their surface have hidden assumptions, while other theories that appear less parsimonious can be taken more easily at face value. As might be expected, there is often a tradeoff between parsimony on the one hand and completeness and specificity on the other. A difficult problem facing theorists is to strike a reasonable balance between them.

5. *Plausibility.* A theory is plausible if it is able to account for experimental (or other) data that provide a test of the theory. Plausibility also involves intuitive judgments about the reasonableness of the theory. If one theory seems less reasonable on its face than another theory, skeptics may require more compelling evidence to convince them of the former theory than to convince them of the latter.

The presentation of theories of analogical reasoning will be divided into two major sections. The first, on differential theories of analogical reasoning, will be quite brief. The reason for its brevity is that differential psychologists have studied analogical reasoning almost exclusively as a byproduct of their work on intelligence. Analogy for its own sake has received little attention. A notable exception to this generalization is Spearman. Spearman's early work on analogy, however, is better classified under information-processing approaches than under differential approaches. Only Spearman's correlational and factor-analytic studies of analogy will be classified under the differential approach. We now turn to a review of theories deriving from the differential approach to analogical reasoning.

DIFFERENTIAL THEORIES OF ANALOGICAL REASONING

Overview

Differential theories of analogical reasoning are based on individual differences in subjects' performance on analogical reasoning tests. These theories most commonly take the form of factor loadings on proposed factors of intelligence. Understanding of intelligence is in terms of all its underlying factors, and understanding of analogical reasoning is in terms of the particular factor or factors of intelligence with which analogical reasoning tests are highly correlated. Analogical reasoning tests, therefore, provide a vehicle for measuring one or more of the factors of intelligence.

Spearman

Spearman was interested in analogical reasoning for several reasons (some of which will be discussed in the next section). One of these reasons was its usefulness in the validation of the two-factor theory of intelligence (see Chapter 2). A good way of validating the theory is to show that tests of mental abilities are highly correlated with g. One test of interest measures analogical reasoning, and Spearman (1927) avers that "it is certain that such tests – if properly made and used – have correlations with all that are known to contain g" (p. 181).

Spearman (1927) reported three correlations between analogy tests and the g factor. One was a correlation of .79 (from the work of Otis) after correction for attenuation. A second was a correlation of .84 (also from the work of Otis) for children in grades four to eight. The third was .71 (from the work of Carothers) for "students." A correlation of .68 with the Stanford–Binet, a measure of g, was also reported (from the work of Stockton). These high correlations support Spearman's theory linking analogical reasoning to the g factor.

Probably the most widely studied inductive reasoning test is Raven's (1938) Progressive Matrices. Problems in the test are similar in form to figural analogies, and the test has been described by its author as "a test of a person's present capacity to form comparisons, reason by analogy, and develop a logical method of thinking regardless of previously acquired information" (Raven, 1938, p. 12). An example of a matrix problem is shown in Figure 5.1. The subject must select from the answer options the one that best fits in the blank space.

Raven's notion of intellectual ability was similar to Spearman's. Raven defined it as the "ability to reason by analogy from awareness of relations between experienced characters" (Esher, Raven, & Earl, 1942, cited in Burke, 1958, p. 202). Spearman (1946) regarded the Progressive Matrices as one of the best available tests of g, and Vernon (1947) also regarded the test as almost a pure measure of g. So correlations between Progressive Matrices scores and the g

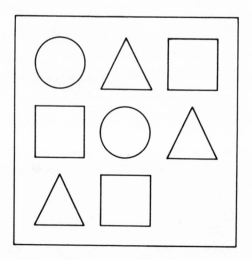

FIGURE 5.1   Example of a matrix problem.

factor serve as a construct validation of both the test and the theory of the general factor.

The evidence on the test, reviewed by Burke (1958), is mixed. The evidence might be summarized by saying that when the Progressive Matrices are factor analyzed along with other tests, the evidence is supportive of a high g loading and relatively small or trivial loadings on other factors. For example, Vernon (1947) found a g loading of .79 and a trivial loading on a practical-mechanical factor. Emmet (1949) found a g loading of .83 and trivial verbal and practical-mechanical loadings. When the Progressive Matrices are factor analyzed by themselves, however, evidence of multiple factors often appears. Banks and Sinha (1951), for example, found that the g factor accounted for only 38% of the variance in the test, and Gabriel (1954) found that a first component accounted for only 60% of the variance in the test. Further components accounted for nontrivial proportions of variance.

Cattell

Cattell (1971) has expanded upon Spearman's theory by splitting g into two separate general factors, g_c and g_f. Crystallized ability, g_c, operates in tasks

> ... of a judgmental, discriminatory, and reasoning nature, ... where the judgments have been taught systematically or experienced before.... Crystallized general mental capacity shows itself heavily in such primary abilities as verbal factor, V; numerical ability, N; reasoning, R or I; mechanical information and skills, Mk; and experiential judgment (in social and other fields). (p. 98)

Fluid ability, g_f, "is an expression of the level of complexity of relationships which an individual can perceive and act upon when he does not have recourse to answers to such complex issues already stored in memory" (Cattell, 1971, p. 99). Fluid ability is measured extremely well by figural analogies, and by verbal analogies in which difficulty is a function of the relations among words rather than of vocabulary. Fluid ability, therefore, is closest to what Spearman had in mind for his g factor.

Thurstone

Thurstone also used analogies as a means to validate his theory of intelligence. Thurstone's theory was that of the primary mental abilities (see Chapter 2).

Thurstone (1938) used verbal analogies and pattern analogies in a large battery of tests. He found loadings of .42 for verbal analogies and .44 for pattern analogies on a factor he labeled perceptual (P). In trying to explain these and other loadings, Thurstone noted that "strictly speaking, all the tests in the battery involve perception, and vision in particular" (p. 80). Certain other tests involving visual perception did not load on the factor, however. Thurstone also suggested that the factor may tap "quick intelligence" as opposed to the "more analytical and reflective aspects" of intelligence, but it is not clear why the tests should tap the former rather than the latter, especially since analogies tests are usually used to measure analytical thinking. Perhaps severe time limits or individual differences in encoding of the analogy terms were responsible for the loadings, which are not all that high in the first place.

Thurstone found a loading of .60 for verbal analogies on a verbal (V) factor, and a trivial loading for pattern analogies. This pattern of loadings is easily interpretable, especially since Thurstone interpreted the V factor as measuring "verbal relations" rather than mere verbal knowledge.

The loading for pattern analogies on factor I (Inductive Reasoning) was .39, but the loading for verbal analogies was trivial. This latter finding is somewhat surprising and suggests either that the relations among words were not difficult enough to generate substantial loadings on this factor, or that the factor is content bound: All of the five high loadings reported by Thurstone for this factor are for figural or symbolic tests.

Guilford

Guilford's Structure-of-Intellect model contains three facets: operations, products, and contents. Analogical reasoning primarily involves two operations — cognition and convergent production — although other operations, such as divergent production, may be involved in special cases. The product of primary importance is the relation, although units may also be involved (see below). The content may be either figural, semantic, symbolic, or behavioral, and we shall discuss each type of content in turn.

"As might be expected, one of the best types of CFR [cognition of figural relations] tests is a figure-analogies form" (Guilford, 1967, p. 86). A Figure Matrix test also provides a good measure of this factor, and as discussed earlier, there is reason to believe that matrix and analogy problems tap similar or identical sources of individual differences.

"We might expect a verbal-analogies test to be one of the best for factor CMR [cognition of semantic relations], and this seems to be the case. In Verbal Analogies I an effort was made to emphasize variance in CMR at the expense of variance in NMR [convergent production of semantic relations] by making the apprehension of the relation between the first pair of words relatively difficult and the satisfaction of the relation in the second pair relatively easy. Verbal Analogies II was constructed with the relative difficulties reversed so as to stress NMR variance" (Guilford, 1967, p. 88). Another NMR test was designed to minimize CMR variance. In the test, Inventive Verbal Relations, subjects are told the relation between the first two words, and then subjects must complete analogies, using the given relation.

Guilford attempted to measure CSR (cognition of symbolic relations) through two types of analogies, Word Relations and Letter Analogies. A typical Word

Relations analogy is the following (Guilford, 1967, p. 88):

on-no   A. art
           B. pat
top-pot   C. rapt
           D. tar
part-——   E. trap

The correct answer is E. The second test, Letter Analogies, was presented in a similar format, except with single letters rather than combinations of letters. The test failed to measure CSR strongly.

Cognition of behavioral relations (CBR) was measured with a Cartoon Analogies Test. In this test, analogies were formed from body parts. The test was moderately successful.

Guilford (1967) also notes that CMU (cognition of semantic units) can be involved in verbal analogy tests in which vocabulary contributes to test difficulty, and it would seem that CFU (cognition of figural units) might be involved in solution of figural analogies in which the figures are more exotic than those usually found in analogy tests (e.g., degraded stimuli such as those used in the Mutilated Words Test, a test of CFU).

Evaluation

The differential theories were formulated as theories of intelligence, not as theories of analogical reasoning, and hence they are less complete than they might have been if the theorists had devoted their attentions to analogical reasoning in particular. Only Guilford's theory fares at all well by the completeness criterion, in part because it is the only differential theory with clear process implications. The theory suggests that at least two processes are involved in analogical reasoning, cognition of relations and convergent production of relations and that, under some circumstances, other processes such as cognition of units and divergent production of relations may be involved as well.

None of the theories are specific in their accounts of analogical reasoning. The differential theories of Spearman, Cattell, and Thurstone do not clearly describe processes, and Guilford's theory, while naming processes, does not specify just what is involved in the execution of each.

Guilford's theory is very general, accounting for performance on verbal, figural, symbolic, and even "behavioral" analogies presented in a wide variety of formats. Guilford's separation of abilities into three general facets gives his theory considerable flexibility in accounting for a wide range of performances. Thurstone's theory does not clearly separate content from process, and it is perhaps because of this lack of clear separation that the pattern of factor loadings presented by Thurstone (1938) is somewhat confusing. Verbal analogies, for example, load on a perceptual factor but not on an inductive reasoning factor. Thurstone used only two types of analogies, with confusing results, and so the generality of Thurstone's theory is questionable even for these two analogy types. Cattell's theory can handle different types of content, but has nothing to say about the different processes used when different item formats are employed. Spearman's theory is best suited to figural analogies or verbal analogies in which vocabulary plays an unimportant part.

The theories are all reasonably parsimonious. Spearman's theory is obviously the most parsimonious, followed by Cattell's, then Thurstone's, and then Guilford's. As stated earlier, there is often a tradeoff between parsimony and completeness, and in the present instance, the theories other than Guilford's appear to have gone too far in the direction of parsimony.

The theories have all been tested on experimental data. Spearman's theory is inadequate in accounting for a wide range of data. Even factor analyses of relatively pure tests of g such as the Progressive Matrices show more than a general factor. Thurstone's theory, as noted above, shows a somewhat confusing pattern of loadings for Thurstone's own tests. Guilford's theory can account for a wide range of data, although the factor loadings presented in Guilford and Hoepfner's (1971) book for analogy tests on the relevant factors are often disappointing.

Overall, Guilford's theory seems to be the best of the differential ones in accounting for analogical reasoning. Some information-processing theories, however, do even better.

INFORMATION-PROCESSING THEORIES
OF ANALOGICAL REASONING

Spearman

In the preceding section, we discussed Spearman's theory of individual differences in analogical reasoning. Spearman is unique in having a process theory as well as a differential theory. The two are treated separately for three reasons. First, there is no necessary connection between them. Either the differential theory or the information-processing theory can be correct even if the other is incorrect. Second, the differential theory is testable through differential methods (correlations across subjects and factor analysis), whereas the information-processing theory is testable through information-processing methods. Third, the information-processing theory was published separately from the differential theory. The information-processing theory was presented primarily in *The Nature of Intelligence and the Principles of Cognition* (Spearman, 1923) while the differential theory was presented primarily in *The Abilities of Man* (Spearman, 1927).

Processes. Spearman (1923) proposed three qualitative principles of cognition.

1. Apprehension of experience: *"Any lived experience tends to evoke immediately a knowing of its characters and experiencer"* (p. 48).
2. Eduction of relations: *"The mentally presenting of any two or more characters (simple or complex) tends to evoke immediately a knowing of relation between them"* (p. 63).
3. Eduction of correlates: *"The presenting of any character together with any relation tends to evoke immediately a knowing of the correlative character"* (p. 91).

The three principles are illustrated diagrammatically in Figure 5.2. Analogy problems require use of all three principles. Consider how they might apply to

Apprehension of experience

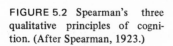

FIGURE 5.2 Spearman's three qualitative principles of cognition. (After Spearman, 1923.)

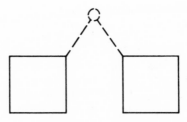

Eduction of relations

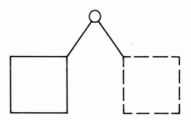

Eduction of correlates

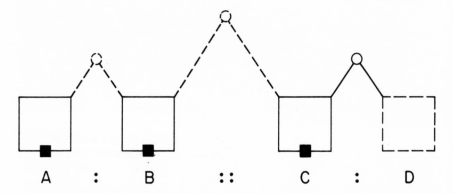

FIGURE 5.3 Spearman's three principles of cognition applied to analogy problems.

the solution of an analogy, $A:B::C:$____. The apprehension of experience corresponds to the encoding of each analogy term. The eduction of relations corresponds to inference of the rule relating the A term to the B term. The eduction of correlates corresponds to the application of the inferred rule to the C term of the analogy to produce an answer, D. The separate principles may be combined into a composite diagram illustrating how analogies are solved. This diagram is presented in Figure 5.3.

Types of relations. Spearman (1923) specified not only the operations involved in analogical reasoning, but the "range of relations" as well. Relations are of two major types, real and ideal. Consider first the real relations.

1. *Attribution:* ". . . the relation of a character to its fundament, as of redness to the thing which is red. Another instance is the relation borne by any relation itself to either of the things related, as that of fatherhood to father" (p. 69).

2. *Identity:* ". . . a fundament can remain identical with what it was before in spite of any of its characters giving place to others" (p. 69).

3. *Time:* "When one period of time occurs subsequently to another, both the relation involved (that of sequence) and also the fundaments are of the temporal class" (p. 70).

4. *Space:* relations of physical position.

5. *Cause:* relations of cause and effect.

6. *Objectivity:* "The simplest of these consists only in the basal relation that holds between any object as mentally presented and the process of mentally presenting it. . . ; between any presented event and the willing that this should actually occur. . . ; the presented items are submitted to the relation of being approved or disapproved" (p. 71).

7. *Constitution:* "X, r, and Y bear to (X, r, Y) a relation which may be called that of constitution" (p. 71), where r is a relation linking X to Y.

Consider next the ideal relations.

1. *Likeness:* This relation includes similarities and differences;
2. *Evidence:* X is recognized to be evidence for the truth of Y;
3. *Conjunction:* the "and" relation;
4. *Intermixture:* any mixture of the preceding ten relations.

Evaluation. We now turn to an evaluation of the theory. It is more nearly complete than any of the differential theories and more nearly complete even than many of the information-processing theories that proceeded it by about 50 years. The theory includes operations of encoding (apprehension of experience), rule inference (eduction of relations), and rule application (eduction of correlates). An examination of Figure 5.3, which is based on Spearman's theory, suggests two processes that may be missing from the theory. One is the process by which the higher-order relation relating the first half of the analogy ($A:B$) to the second half of the analogy ($C:$____) is discovered. This process corresponds to the recognition of the analogical relationship: the discovery of a relation between two relations. The other missing operation is some process by which the subject communicates his answer once it is generated. A criticism of cognitive theories is that they leave the organism "buried in thought." Spearman's theory would seem to have this fault.

The processes of the theory are not well specified. The apprehension and eduction operations are said to be "evoked immediately," but this description is not informative. It does not state what psychological mechanisms lead to immediate evocation.

The theory is quite general. The three general principles of cognition should be applicable to analogies of all types. In addition, Spearman lists the various relations that may be educed. While the list is not likely to be complete (for example, no relation of instrumentality is included), and while some of the choices of relations may be questioned, the list is certainly a first step in the right direction. Even modern semantic theories (e.g., Katz, 1972) are unable to specify all possible relations between pairs of words.

The theory is parsimonious and, as suggested above, is probably too parsimonious. At least two more processes would seem to be needed.

Unfortunately, Spearman (1923) presented no experimental data in support of the theory. Strangely enough, some of the best evidence in support of the theory would appear to be Guilford's factor-analytic results. Guilford's cognition of relations corresponds to Spearman's eduction of relations, and Guilford's convergent production of relations corresponds to Spearman's eduction of correlates. Both these operations and products were implicated in analogical reasoning. Guilford and Hoepfner (1971) reported that "the expectation that an analogies test would represent two different abilities, depending upon the emphasis, whether on *seeing* the relation or on *completing* the relationship by giving the correlate, was fulfilled" (p. 72). Moreover, cognition of units was implicated in solution of at least certain types of analogies, and this operation and product would seem to correspond to Spearman's apprehension of experience. Individual differences in this ability will show up in a factor analysis only when the terms of the analogy present an unusual challenge, as when the words in a verbal analogies test are at a high vocabulary level, or when figures of nonverbal analogies are presented in degraded form.

Spearman's information-processing theory is most impressive. Many subsequent theories, including the one presented in Chapter 6, are merely extensions of Spearman's. We shall now consider one extension of Spearman's theory, the theory of Shalom and Schlesinger (1972).

Shalom and Schlesinger

Nature of analogy. Shalom and Schlesinger (1972) define an analogy item as a relation presenting one or more of the ordered pairs of which the relation is constituted. Consider an example, the relation specifying modes of transportation in its domain and surfaces of conveyance in its range. The relation might look like this: $\{(car, river), (train, road), (boat, tracks)\}$. The Cartesian product consists of all possible sets of ordered pairs. The domain of the relation consists of $\{car, train, boat\}$ and the range consists of $\{river, road, tracks\}$. A relatively easy analogy can be formed by pairing modes of transportation to their corresponding surfaces of conveyance: car : road :: train : tracks. A more difficult analogy could be formed by pairing noncorresponding terms: car : river :: train : road. In this case, the analogy links vehicles to means of conveyance that are not used by the particular vehicle.

Processes. Shalom and Schlesinger (1972) draw a distinction between the selection rule (SR), which is the logical relationship among analogy terms, and the connection formula (CF), which is that particular formula used by the subject to solve an analogy. The CF may be quite different from the selection rule.

Solving an analogy involves two processes: forming a CF and applying the CF. These two processes obviously correspond to Spearman's eduction of relations and eduction of correlates, or to Guilford's cognition of relations and convergent production of relations. The final CF used to solve an analogy is not necessarily the first one. Subjects may try out and then discard a number of CFs before finding the one that permits solution of the analogy.

Internal representation. The authors argue that qualitatively different internal representations are used in verbal versus figural analogies. They consider two alternative internal representations for verbal analogies. The two alternatives derive from different models of semantic structure in the internal lexicon. One model, a componential one,[2] has been proposed by Katz and Postal (1964); the other, a relational one, has been suggested by Quillian (1969). The major distinction between such models, according to Shalom and Schlesinger, is that the semantic markers of a componential theory contain only information that is deemed essential for defining the word in question. The markers do not relate to more general knowledge about the world. In the Quillian model, however, the meaning of a word consists of all the factual information about the word that is stored in memory. Shalom and Schlesinger find the relational model more compatible with their notions about analogical reasoning. When presented with a pair of terms, the subject "traverses" the path in the semantic network that connects the appropriate nodes, and this path corresponds to the CF. The process of finding an initial CF is similar to the process of judging similarities between concepts. In the limiting case, that in which the two terms of a pair are synonymous, the semantic search process will not have to be carried beyond the node at which it starts. In general, the search for an initial CF will take longer and be more likely to fail as the length of the path connecting the nodes in question increases.

Shalom and Schlesinger (1972) suggest a different representation for figural analogies. To find a CF connecting a pair of figures, a subject must search through a list of operations stored in memory, looking for the operation that corresponds to the relation between the A and B analogy terms. "This list is probably of very limited size, but since for each pair of figures more than one operation may be applied . . . the number of possible CFs is very large" (p. 290).

The solution of verbal analogies requires a search process in both the inference and application operations. The solution of figural analogies, however, requires search only in the inference operation. Once the CF has been selected from among the possible CFs stored in the list of operations, the search process is terminated, and all the content required for solution should be contained in the test item itself.

Item difficulty. Shalom and Schlesinger cite five sources of item difficulty, indicating that there are other (unspecified) ones as well. The sources they cite are: (1) distance between the initial and final CFs; (2) salience of relations exemplified; (3) degree of abstractness; (4) degree of indeterminacy; and (5) the associations aroused.

Experimental data. The theoretical analysis of Shalom and Schlesinger (1972) leads to an

. . . important practical conclusion, namely, that the process of inferring CFs cannot be trained. Once it has started, the search procedure (whether through the semantic

---

[2] The term *componential* as used in semantics has a meaning different from that of *componential* as used elsewhere in this volume.

network or through the list of operations) may be assumed to be automatic. If it is desired to train a person, one can do little more than try to increase his motivation to start such a search procedure or to persevere in it; the search itself cannot be directed. One may also concentrate on the second stage of solving analogy items: modifying the CF and applying it. As stated, it is the application of CFs, not their inference, which is customarily required in school performance. (p. 292)

Feuerstein, Schlesinger, Shalom, and Narrol (1972) have presented the results of a rather extensive training program for both verbal and figural analogies. These results and the theory are presented in a single volume. Feuerstein et al. (1972) employed two forms of training: One was task-specific, and the other was more general.

The specific training was devised to help and encourage subjects to use extensive verbal mediation in the formation of CFs. Subjects were presented with verbal matrix problems, such as

House   Hut

_____   Bush

and were given six alternative terms for the blank element. The examiner illustrated the verbal mediation process by making a statement such as "The hut is small and the house is big. So what's bigger than the hut? The house." The subject was then asked to perform the verbal mediation himself and, thereby, to realize that a tree is bigger than a bush. For figural training, the same types of matrices and verbal mediation were employed, except that the problems were figural rather than verbal.

The more general training procedures, which were called "metalearning" procedures, were designed to teach general cognitive skills of importance in analogical and other types of reasoning. Various exercises were employed to help subjects develop systematic classificatory behavior, summing-up behavior, perceptual discrimination, comparative behavior, and divergent thinking. One exercise also instructed subjects in the use of Venn diagrams.

The authors found that their treatment groups all improved more than did the control group. The differential improvement was significant for five of seven figural treatments and for two of seven verbal treatments. The results seemed to indicate the presence of complex aptitude-treatment interactions, none of which would have been readily predictable on an a priori basis.

Evaluation.   The Shalom–Schlesinger theory is among the most detailed. The process model of analogical reasoning would seem to be incomplete, however. Missing from the model is an explicit encoding operation for perceiving analogy terms, some kind of "mapping" operation in which the analogy between A and B terms on the one hand and the C and D terms on the other is recognized, and a response operation by which the solution is communicated.

The authors achieve a considerable degree of specificity by specifying the internal representation upon which the inference and application operations are theorized to act. A relational network has been specified in sufficient detail to be simulated on a computer (Quillian, 1969), and the "list of operations" notion is used by Evans (1968) in his analogy-solving program (discussed later). A logical analysis in terms of Cartesian products did not seem to add much to the specificity or completeness of the theory.

The theory is rather general, applying to both verbal and figural analogies. It is not clear what differences in operations would be involved, if any, for analogies presented in different formats, such as true—false and forced-choice.

The process model is probably too parsimonious, at the expense of missing operations. The structural model requires two different representational structures for verbal and figural items and corresponding differences in the search process for the two types of items. This dual-representational system is a sensible one, but it has yet to be shown that a unitary system is incapable of accounting for data from verbal and figural analogies. Such data are not presently available.

The empirical results of Feuerstein et al. (1972) are of interest in their own right. They bear little relation to the Shalom and Schlesinger (1972) theory, however. Experimental data are needed in particular to: (1) verify the dual-representational system for verbal and figural analogies; (2) show that the inference and application processes are sufficient to account for analogical reasoning, and (3) confirm the suggested sources of item difficulty.

Johnson

Johnson (1962) has suggested that analogical reasoning involves two problem-solving operations: the inductive and the deductive. These two operations correspond to Spearman's eduction of relations and eduction of correlates and to Shalom and Schlesinger's (1972) formation of the connection formula and application of the connection formula.

Johnson (1962) investigated the nature of the two processes by varying their difficulty. Fifty analogies were constructed. In 25 of them, the locus of difficulty was in the inductive operation (for example, feline : canine :: cat : ?), and, in the other 25, the locus of difficulty was in the deductive operation (for example, lose : win :: liability : ?). Analogies were presented to three groups of 20 subjects in three different formats. The first group received a production format, as illustrated in the examples above. The second group received a multiple-choice format, and the third group received a multiple-choice format in which only the initial letter of each answer option was given. Analogies were presented by a method of serial exposure. During a preparatory exposure, subjects saw only the first two terms of the analogy. Subjects manually controlled the duration of the first exposure. When they terminated it, a second exposure commenced immediately, consisting of the remainder of the analogy. Each exposure was timed separately.

There were two main findings in Johnson's experiment. First, the difficulty manipulation was successful. The preparatory period was longer for problems in which induction was difficult than for those in which deduction was difficult, while the second period was longer for problems in which deduction was difficult than for those in which induction was difficult. Second, production analogy problems were more difficult than either of the types of multiple-choice analogy problems, which did not themselves differ significantly in difficulty. As predicted, the longer time for production problems was localized in the second period, that in which production occurs. Preparation times were about the same for all three types of analogies.

Johnson (1960) designed a similar experiment, varying whether exposure of the two parts of the analogy was subject controlled (as in the above experiment) or experimenter controlled. He found better differentiation between the two types of analogies (induction difficult and deduction difficult) in the subject-controlled presentation method.

Rumelhart and Abrahamson

Nature of reasoning. Rumelhart and Abrahamson (1973) define reasoning processes as those thought processes in information retrieval that operate upon the structure, as opposed to the content of organized memory. If information retrieval depends upon specific content stored in memory, we refer to the retrieval as remembering. If, however, it depends upon the form of one or more relationships among words, we refer to the retrieval as reasoning.

Following this definition of reasoning, the authors claim that probably the simplest possible reasoning task is the judgment of the similarity or dissimilarity between concepts. They assume that the degree of similarity between subjects is not directly stored as such, but is instead derived from previously existing memory structures.

According to Rumelhart and Abrahamson (1973), judged similarity between concepts is a simple function of the "psychological distance" between these concepts in the memory structure. The nature of this function and of the memory structure upon which it operates is clarified by their assumptions (after Henley, 1969) that: (1) the memory structure may be represented as a multidimensional Euclidean space and (2) judged similarity is inversely related to distance in this space.

Nature of Analogy. Analogical reasoning may itself be considered a kind of similarity judgment, one in which not only the magnitude of the distance but also the direction is of importance. We would ordinarily read the analogy problem, $A:B::C:X_i$, as stating that A is similar to B in exactly the same way that C is similar to X_i. According to the assumptions outlined above, we might reinterpret this as saying that the directed or vector distance between A and B is exactly the same as the vector distance between C and X_i.

Rumelhart and Abrahamson (1973) formalize the assumptions of their model by stating that given an analogy problem of the form A:B::C:$(X_1, X_2, \ldots, X_n)$, it is assumed that:

A1. Corresponding to each element of the analogy problem there is a point in an m-dimensional space. . . .

A2. For any analogy problem of the form A:B::C:?, there exists a concept I such that A:B::C:I and an ideal analogy point, denoted I such that I is located the same vector distance from C as B is from A. The coordinates of I are given by the ordered sequence $\{c_j + b_j - a_j\}$ $j = 1, m$.

A3. The probability that any given alternative X_i is chosen as the best analogy solution from the set of alternatives $X_1, \ldots, X_n$ is a monotonic decreasing function of the absolute value of the distance between the point X_i and the point I, denoted $|X_i - I|$. (p. 4)

Experimental data. Three experiments were carried out in order to test the model. The authors used, as terms of their analogy items, the set of animal names from Henley's (1969) scaling studies. In her scaling studies, Henley fitted thirty mammal names into a three-dimensional space. The three dimensions were tentatively identified as size, ferocity, and humanness.

The purpose of the first experiment was to determine whether subjects' selections of best answers to analogies such as gorilla : deer :: bear : (cow, pig, tiger, monkey) could be predicted from the assumptions of the model. (The answers in this analogy problem are "correctly" rank ordered from best to worst.) Each of thirty analogy problems had four alternative answers, with the alternatives selected so that the "correct" answer option was extremely close to the ideal point, and distractors were at successively greater distances from that point. Subjects were instructed to choose the term that they believed best completed the analogy, and then to indicate their second, third, and fourth choices. Quantitative choice predictions were made through use of Luce's (1959) choice axiom and the assumption that the monotone decrease in probability of selecting options at successively greater distances from the ideal point followed an exponential decay function.

The correlation between predicted and observed number of subjects ranking each alternative as the best analogy solution was .93. The authors plotted expected versus observed response distributions for first-, second-, third-, and fourth-choice data. The observed patterns of results were extremely close to the predicted patterns.

The second experiment was designed to test the model's prediction that the probability of choosing any particular alternative X_i as the best alternative depends upon the ideal solution point, I, and upon the alternative set, $(X_1, \ldots, X_n)$, but not at all upon the particular terms in the analogy itself.

Thus, all possible analogies with a given ideal solution point, I, and a given alternative set, $(X_1, \ldots, X_n)$, should yield the same distribution of responses over the X_i.

This is a very strong prediction, and the reason for it should be made clear. The Rumelhart–Abrahamson (1973) model requires just one parameter, α, which relates the distance of an alternative from the ideal point to the probability of selecting that alternative. How can the model account for analogical reasoning without at least the inference and application parameters that appear in the preceding two models, and possibly some other parameters as well? It can do this only if the distribution of responses to analogy options is unrelated to these hypothetical parameters. If the rankings are related to ease of inference (perhaps determined by A to B distance) or any other processes related to the analogy stem (A:B::C:), then the Rumelhart–Abrahamson model is incomplete. If there is no relation, however, then the model provides an extremely parsimonious account of the ranking data.

In Experiment II, twelve pairs of analogy problems were constructed in which each pair had the same ideal point within a tolerance of .12 units (roughly the distance between a lion and a tiger), and in which the ith closest alternative for one set was at about the same distance from the ideal point as the ith closest alternative for the other set. There were no overlapping elements, however, in either the analogy stems or in the corresponding pairs of alternative sets. For each ideal point, the alternative sets were paired arbitrarily with the two analogies, and a given subject encountered both members of the analogy pair and both alternative sets, but in only one of the two possible combinations.

The prediction that the response distribution should depend upon the ideal solution point and upon the alternative set, but not upon the particular analogy problem, was tested by computing chi square between the response distributions formed by subjects to the two halves of each analogy pair for each response set. The resulting chi square was larger than would have been expected by chance, although most of the deviation from the null hypothesis was accounted for by a few items. The results were therefore interpreted as supporting the model, "at least to a first order of approximation."

The third experiment used a concept-formation design. Assumption A2 implies that for each statement of the form A:B::C:? there exists some concept I against which alternative responses are compared to find the best alternative. In Experiment III, the point I was given a name in order to determine whether subjects are able to use the newly named concept in the same way that they are able to use concepts they already know.

Three points were chosen in Henley's animal space and labeled bof, dax, and zuk. The points were chosen so as to be fairly remote from each other, with a bof lying between elephant and camel, a dax near chimpanzee, and a zuk between fox and wolf. Subjects were "taught" the concepts by an anticipation method. Subjects were first given an analogy problem of the form A:B:(bof, dax, or zuk): $(X_1, \ldots, X_4)$, and were then asked to guess the best alternative, X_i. Following their guess, subjects were informed of the correct alternative and were also given correct rankings for the remaining alternatives. Subjects were given time to study the rankings, and the process was then repeated. Following training on each of the three concepts, subjects were asked to rate, on a scale from 1 ("very similar") to 10 ("very different"), the dissimilarity of each of the three artificial animals to each of the thirty animals in Henley's animal space and to each other.

Rumelhart and Abrahamson (1973) compared the mean numbers of subjects choosing each of the four alternatives as best, averaging over all anticipation trials after the fifth (the trial at which learning appeared to be complete). The predicted values were very close to those obtained, suggesting that the concepts of bof, dax, and zuk functioned in the analogies in a way similar to the conventional animal names. Mean dissimilarity judgments between each of the three concepts and each of the thirty mammal names were correlated with the corresponding psychological distances (as obtained through multidimensional scaling). The correlations were .95 for bof, .90 for dax, and .92 for zuk. These correlations were of approximately the same magnitude as those obtained using only the conventional animal names, suggesting that the new concepts were treated very similarly to the old concepts, the mammals.

Evaluation. The Rumelhart–Abrahamson (1973) theory is not a process theory, and hence it cannot be evaluated in the same light as the other theories. The results of Experiment II suggest that, contrary to the theory's prediction, aspects of the analogy stem do affect item difficulty. Hence, a one-parameter model is probably incomplete.

The theory specifies in some detail the internal representation of information, although by design it does not specify the processes used in solving analogies, and how they are executed. Presumably vector distances are calculated and compared to each other in the multidimensional space. The generalizability of the theory may be limited. As Rumelhart and Abrahamson (1973) state,

> We are not suggesting that a multidimensional representation is sufficiently rich to encode all types of semantic relationships. Therefore, we are not proposing that this model of analogical reasoning is completely general. It seems rather that the semantic relationships among certain sets of concepts can be represented by a multidimensional structure. (pp. 27–28)

Rumelhart and Abrahamson report that they have generated analogies from the Munsell color space, and have obtained similar results to those obtained with animal names. Rips, Shoben, and Smith (1973) found that scaled distances predict analogy responses when two of the terms are from one semantic space (that of bird names), and two are from another (that of mammal names).

Nevertheless, these domains are still very restricted, and their compatability with the Rumelhart and Abrahamson theory appears to be largely dependent upon their scalability.

The theory is extremely parsimonious in its use of just one parameter to predict rank-order data, and the number of assumptions is relatively small. Even the representational model would seem to be extremely parsimonious, requiring only three dimensions to account for relations among mammals.

No other previous theory of analogical reasoning has as much supporting evidence to back it as the Rumelhart—Abrahamson theory. The experiments testing the theory are ingenious, and provide strong tests of the theory. The theory is also stated explicitly enough to be falsified, so that it provides a sound basis for further investigations.

Computer-Based Theories

Reitman.   Reitman (1965) has proposed a computer-based theory of analogical reasoning, ARGUS, that solves verbal analogies. The theory, like the componential theory presented in Chapter 6, is intended to serve as the beginning of a more general theory of intelligence.

Reitman (1965) describes ARGUS as a reaction to many of the assumptions embodied in Newell, Shaw, and Simon's (1960) General Problem Solver (GPS) program. Reitman appears to have been particularly concerned about two major aspects of GPS's functioning. The first is its "single-mindedness. So total a lack of distractability might perhaps occur in some perfect exemplar of the Pavlovian 'strong nervous system,' but it is by the same token quite atypical of human thinking generally" (Reitman, 1965, p. 205). The second aspect of concern is GPS's strictly sequential, centralized processing.

Reitman notes that several psychological theories avoid the assumptions of current versions of sequential, centralized programs, but that the outstanding one among them is Hebb's (1949) theory. "Hebb never shows how this theory might account for goal-directed thinking . . . ; neither have we been able to imagine any way in which a system consisting entirely of Hebbian cell assemblies might be made to do so" (Reitman, 1965, pp. 207–208). Nor did Hebb specify explicitly how the cell assembly system would work in parallel. The theory nevertheless laid the groundwork for further theorizing that would meet these specifications. Reitman viewed ARGUS as a first step in this direction, positing gradual loss of information, distractability, and active cognitive elements operating in parallel.

The ARGUS progrm was written in IPL-V and was designed to solve analogy problems of the form, $A:B::C:(X_1, \ldots, X_4)$. The main aspects of the program are a sequential executive, a network of active semantic elements that may operate in parallel, and channels of interaction between the executive and the semantic elements.

Activity of the executive program is organized into four levels, which from top down are subject, problem, strategy, and strategy step. The subject is conceptualized as a set of information-processing strategies and rules for their use. The ARGUS experimenter generates an analogy problem, which is presented to the subject. Having comprehended the problem, the subject generates a series of strategies, built of steps, in order to solve the problem.

Changes in the state of the semantic network occur within, but never between, strategy steps. The order in which changes occur within a step is relevant only locally. All such intrastep changes become available to the executive simultaneously, and only after the step in which they occurred has been completed. From the standpoint of the executive program, therefore, the network state transitions that occur within a step take place in parallel. The executive cannot detect intrastep sequences of activity.

The basic units of cognitive structure incorporated into ARGUS are the semantic elements, which correspond in function to Hebb's cell assemblies. Each semantic element is an IPL-V structure consisting of three description lists. Entries on the first list specify the attribute-value pair that relates one semantic element to another. "For example, the relation from the semantic unit corresponding to the sensation of heat to the one representing its opposite, cold, would be given by the pair (opposite, cold) on the first description list of the semantic element named heat" (Reitman, 1965, pp. 212–213). Paired entries on the second list specify the current strength of association for relations between the element being defined and each associated semantic element within the cognitive structure. Entries on the third description list specify the parameters defining the current state of the semantic unit.

The overall process by which an analogy problem is solved is as follows. The system first "fires" a semantic element, A, corresponding to the first analogy term. It then fires a semantic element, B, corresponding to the second analogy term. The system next inquires whether any other semantic element has fired spontaneously. If not, the system exits, and the strategy has failed. Suppose, however, that a semantic element I has fired spontaneously. Then the system finds the relation of I to A. The system next fires the semantic element, C, corresponding to the third analogy term. Then it fires an answer option. If another semantic element fires spontaneously, it finds the relation J to C. If the relation J to C is equal to the relation I to A, the analogy is solved. I and J are analogous relations, and an exit is possible. The last option tested is correct. If no relation J fired when the first option was tested, or if the relation J to C is not equal to the relation I to A, then it is necessary to fire another alternative. The system keeps firing (testing) alternatives until one is found in which the relation I to A is equal to the relation J to C. If no option is found that meets this condition, then the system exits, having failed to solve the analogy.

Evans. Evans' (1968) ANALOGY program solves geometric analogy problems of the type found on many intelligence tests. Indeed, the items used by Evans were taken from examinations of the American Council on Education designed to measure reasoning ability assumed to be prerequisite for college-level work. The analogies are therefore fairly difficult ones, and a program able to solve them can be assumed to operate at a high level of sophistication.

ANALOGY comprises two parts. In the first, input figures are decomposed into subfigures, and various properties of and relations between these subfigures are computed. The resulting decompositions form the basis for a new, higher level description of the geometric figures, and this description is made available to the second part of the program, which attempts to construct a rule that transforms Figure A into Figure B and Figure C into exactly one of five answer figures.

As Evans himself noted, the sharp decomposition of the ANALOGY program into two parts with separate functions and very restricted communication between them was unfortunate. The need for two parts arose from storage limitations imposed by the use of the 7090 LISP system. Independence between program segments

> ... effectively prevented any scheme of program organization in which the rule-finding part controls the application of the facilities of the geometrical-manipulation part according to its needs of the moment. Such a scheme of organization would have considerable advantages in power and efficiency and would parallel in an interesting way the human capability of returning to the figures for further detail, as required. (p. 317)

Since ANALOGY does separate "perceptual" from "conceptual" processes, we shall deal here only with that part of the program that performs the reasoning operations.

The first step of Part 2 requires the matching of objects in the A term of the analogy to those in the B term. The basis for this matching is similarity computed in Part 1 of ANALOGY. The result of the matching is an expression stating which objects must be removed from A, which must be added to A, and which must be paired with objects of B in order to transform the set of objects in A to those in B. Once all possible matchings between A and B have been generated, a rule corresponding to each matching is constructed. Each rule consists of a list of expressions, one corresponding to objects removed from A, one corresponding to objects added to A, and one corresponding to parts of A objects matched to parts of B objects.

After the set of rules relating A to B has been generated, it is necessary to extend each of these rules to the transformation of C into each admissible answer figure. The program does this by determining the set of all correspondences between objects in the Figure A to Figure B transformation and between those in the Figure C to Figure X_i transformation. For each Figure A to Figure B rule, the program generates a new transformation rule by removing from the old rule those particular statements that are not true of the Figure C to Figure X_i transformation. The result is a rule that still takes Figure A into Figure B, but also takes Figure C into Figure X_i. At least one such rule can always be found, although it may be so diluted that all distinguishing features of the analogical relationship have disappeared. ANALOGY possesses a function, *rval*, which assigns to each rule a numerical value intended to correspond to its strength. Roughly, the function *rval* measures the length of the rule. After numerical values have been assigned to each of the competing rules (one for each answer option), the one with the largest value is chosen (except in case of a tie, in which case certain tie-breaking strategies are employed, for example, rating a rotation higher than a reflection).

Evans has tried out his ANALOGY program on a number of analogies taken from American Council on Education examinations, with impressive results. Evans (1968) presents 20 sample problems and solutions: Only one solution obtained by the program differs from the keyed answer. Evans estimates that the program could solve correctly at least 15, and possibly as many as 20, out of the 30 problems on a typical form of the analogy tests. This level of performance can be compared to a mean score of 17 correct for ninth grade pupils, and 20 correct for twelfth grade pupils.

Winston, Kling, Becker, Williams. Winston (1970) have suggested ways in which Evans' basic ideas can be extended to three-dimensional objects. The basic algorithm begins with a comparison of the A and B analogy terms. The resulting "comparison-describing network" is denoted by $d(A:B)$. Similarly, C is compared with each answer figure, generating descriptions of the form $d(C:X)$. Next, the algorithm calls for a comparison of the descriptions $d(A:B)$ with each of the $d(C:X)$ to see which is closest to it. The best match, $\text{Min}[d(d(A:B):d(C:X))]$, minimizes the distance between the descriptions and forms the problem solution.

Kling (1971) has written a program, ZORBA, that uses analogical information in the context of a first-order resolution logic theorem prover. The type of analogical reasoning used by Kling's program is of a general transfer-of-training type, rather than of the more specific type used for conventional analogy problems of the form $A:B::C:D$. The task environment for the program, however, is so abstract and abstruse that the processes employed within it may not have much generality to other, more concrete, task domains. In ZORBA, an analogy is a relation $A^p \times A^c \times A^v$, where

1. A^p is a one–one map between the predicates used in the proof of the proved theorem T and the predicates used in the proof of the unproved theorem T_A.

2. A^c is a one–many mapping between clauses. Each clause used in the proof of T is associated with one or more clauses from the data base D that ZORBA-I expects to use in proving T_A.

3. A^v is a many–many mapping between the variables that appear in the statement of T and those that appear in the statement of T_A. (Kling, 1971, p. 153)

Becker (1969) also presents a theory of analogical reasoning that is in the computer-science tradition, although it is not implemented as a program. In order to introduce Becker's notion of analogy, it is first necessary to define two terms. A Node is simply a concept. A Kernel is an ordered n-tuple of Nodes. "An *Analogy* between two situations is a *motivated correspondence* between the elements of the situations. In essence, an *Analogy* between two Situations S_1 and S_2 is defined to be a one-to-one *mapping* of the Kernels of S_1 onto the Kernels of S_2" (Becker, 1969, p. 659). Becker's notions, like Kling's, are intended to be of the transfer-of-training type.

Williams (1972) has written an operational computer program, the Aptitude Test Taker, which can solve a rather wide range of problems found in inductive reasoning tests. The program is of special interest to ability theorists because it shows how a relatively small number of processes and organizing assumptions can be combined into a powerful problem-solving device. The program uses worked examples of test items to induce the rules for solving the items. The program has been applied to only one type of analogy, letter analogies, with encouraging results. A Kendall coefficient of concordance of .69 was obtained between rank orders of subject and program times on 20 letter analogy items.

Evaluation. In our evaluation, we shall concentrate primarily upon the Reitman and Evans programs. The Winston program is primarily an extension of Evans' program, and thus does not require separate treatment. The Kling program solves problems that probably could be solved only by a small fraction of one percent of the general population (problems in resolution logic), and hence appears to be of too little psychological generalizability to receive detailed consideration. Becker's theory does not yet have clear empirical implications, and Williams' theory has been applied only to letter analogies. These theories also will not be discussed further.

The ARGUS and ANALOGY programs are both complete in the superficial sense that they are implemented as computer programs that solve analogies. The ANALOGY program, however, includes sophisticated perceptual-processing routines (Part 1) that preprocess descriptions of geometric figures so as to make them comprehensible to the reasoning routines (Part 2). ARGUS does not have perceptual routines, and input into this program is preprocessed at a level analogous to the input to Part 2 of ANALOGY. ANALOGY is therefore more complete, although even ANALOGY requires preprocessing of the figures into descriptions that can be read by a LISP program.

Both ARGUS and ANALOGY are well specified enough to be successfully executing computer programs. In ANALOGY, both processes and internal representation are specified in detail. The latter is in terms of elementary features of the stimulus figures. The theory of internal representation is less clear in ARGUS. Although ARGUS solves verbal analogies, there is no clear semantic theory underlying it. Perhaps this is why ARGUS solves more difficult analogies in the same way it solves easier ones.

Neither ARGUS nor ANALOGY is general. ARGUS has a small, fixed vocabulary of words, and it can handle only a very limited number of analogies that employ those specific words. ANALOGY can handle a wide variety of geometric analogy problems (especially when augmented by Winston's program to solve problems with three-dimensional figures). The programming improvements that would be necessary to generalize the performance of ANALOGY within its own content domain are probably much smaller than those that would be necessary to improve the performance of ARGUS, although this maybe in large part a function of the enormous complexity of the semantic lexicon.

Neither theory is parsimonious, at least when compared to the differential and information-processing theories discussed previously. Computer theories in general are not parsimonious: Completeness and specificity are achieved at the expense of parsimony.

Neither computer-based theory has experimental data to support it. Both theories have been shown sufficient to solve problems, but a minimum test of psychological plausibility would require comparison of computer errors with those of human subjects. At the present time, the theories present interesting ideas with no demonstrated psychological validity.

Other Information-Processing Theories

Hunt. Hunt (1974) has proposed two algorithms by which items from Raven's Progressive Matrices may be solved. The first algorithm is called the Gestalt algorithm, and the second, the analytic algorithm.

"The Gestalt algorithm consists of three answer generators and an executive subroutine. The executive applies the answer generators and uses the answer evaluator to accept the results of each generator" (Hunt, 1974, p. 137). The three answer generators are these:

1. *Continuation.* Any visual progression that is interrupted by the blank answer space is continued through the blank answer space.

2. *Superimposition of whole patterns.* "A complete matrix element can be superimposed on another by placing the outer borders of the base element (that is, the trial answer) and some other matrix element in correspondence. In doing so, the algorithm permits distortion of either the *x* or *y* scales *of the base element.* The psychological justification for doing so is that human vision is surprisingly insensitive to distortions of scale" (Hunt, 1974, pp. 138–139).

3. *Superimposition based on point matching.* Point superimposition is defined as "an operation in which the point of maximum curvature of the boundary of a base element is placed on the point of maximum curvature of a matrix element. Changes in the scale of the base element are permitted, if required" (Hunt, 1974, p. 140).

The analytic algorithm consists of a set of operations and a framework for executing them. Consider a matrix of the form

$$X \ Y \ Z$$
$$X' \ Y' \ \_$$

The missing element is correctly identified as Z'. According to Hunt (1974), the operations on matrix elements are these:

1. *Constancy.* "If $X = Y = Z$, then $Y' = Z'$" (p. 146).
2. *Supplement–delete.* "There is an element e_1 present in Y which is not present in X. Determine whether there is also an element present in Z which is not present in Y. If e_1 is present in Y' but not in X', then add e_2 to Y' to produce Z'. The above definition holds for the supplement operation. The delete operation is identical, except that the roles of X and Y, and Y and Z, are interchanged, and e_2 is deleted from Y' " (pp. 146–147).
3. *Expansion–contraction.* "There is a subelement which appears in X and Y, and differs only in the size of its physical dimensions" (p. 147).
4. *Addition–subtraction.* "The operation is similar to expansion/contraction, except that it is applied to a *number* property of a subelement" (p. 147).
5. *Movement.* A matrix element is here assumed to shift systematically to different regions of a matrix element such as X, Y, or Z.
6. *Composition–decomposition.* "Subelements which are present in X are absent in Y and *vice versa*" (p. 147).

The analytic algorithm has been shown by Hunt to be capable of solving correctly all problems in Set I of the Progressive Matrices. The Gestalt algorithm cannot solve all problems and solves some problems incorrectly. The analytic algorithm is clearly closer to the one that would be used by sophisticated problem solvers.

Jacobs and Vandeventer. Jacobs and Vandeventer (1972) have proposed a somewhat different set of relations that they believe is sufficient to classify correctly the vast majority of matrix items. These relations are

1. *Identity:* "repetition with no change."
2. *Shading:* "change may be complete or partial."
3. *Movement in a plane:* "figure moves as if slid along surface."
4. *Reversal:* "two elements exchange some feature, such as size, shading, or position."
5. *Addition:* "the figure in one column (row) is added to that in a second, and the result placed in the third."
6. *Number series:* "arithmetic or geometric series generates successive cells."
7. *Shape:* "complete change of form, or systematic change, as from solid to dotted lines."
8. *Size:* "proportionate change, as in photographic enlargement."
9. *Flip-over:* "figure moves as if lifted up and replaced face down."
10. *Added element:* "a new element is introduced, or an old one removed."
11. *Unique addition:* "unique elements are treated differently from common elements, e.g., they are added while common elements cancel each other out."
12. *Elements of a set:* "each element appears three times in a 3 × 3 matrix." (Jacobs and Vandeventer, 1972, p. 243)

Jacobs and Vandeventer (1972) were primarily interested in this set of relations as a means to increase children's intelligence. If young children could be taught to recognize and use these relations, their test performance and presumably their intelligence would be increased. Jacobs and Vandeventer (1971a, b) conducted training studies using Raven's Colored Progressive Matrices, which are suitable for young children at the primary school level. Jacobs and Vandeventer (1971a) taught first graders to solve matrix problems using rules of color and shape, and found that trained subjects scored significantly higher than controls, on a posttest involving these two dimensions, and also on a transfer test involving new stimulus dimensions, size and shading. Jacobs and Vandeventer (1971b) also found both improved performance on the trained relations and limited transfer to new relations in an experimental group relative to an untrained control group.

Santesson. Santesson (1974) has proposed yet another classification of matrix relations. Subjects were presented with cards containing matrix problems from the Progressive Matrices. Subjects were instructed to sort the cards into groups based on the same principle or rule. They were permitted to use as many categories as they wished, and the task was untimed.

Santesson tabulated the number of times each matrix problem was sorted with every other matrix problem and then performed a hierarchical clustering analysis on the resulting halfmatrix without diagonal. In a hierarchical clustering analysis, a treelike graph is created in which strongly related items are grouped together at low levels of the hierarchy and items with weaker relations are grouped together higher in the hierarchy. Details of the method are presented in Johnson (1967) and Miller (1969).

Santesson found three distinct clusters of items. Items in the first cluster seemed to involve either an increase or decrease of size or number of elements. Items in the second cluster seemed to involve figures that are altered in one or two dimensions. Items in the third cluster involve combined addition and subtraction of parts of figures. These clusters correspond quite closely to Raven's a priori classification of matrix items. Raven (1960) classified items into three groups, corresponding to Sets *C, D,* and *E* of the test. Set *C* contains items with progressive alterations of patterns, and corresponds to the first cluster in eight out of ten items. Set *D* contains items with permutations of figures, and corresponds perfectly to the second cluster. Set *E* contains items with resolution of figures into constituent parts, and corresponds to the third cluster in four of six items. The results of Santesson's analysis therefore support Raven's a priori classification.

Linn. Linn (1973) studied performance of children on the Progressive Matrices. She suggested that there are two basic types of matrix, and that solution processes are different for each. In a P (prediction) matrix there are few plausible answer options and sometimes just one plausible option. In an E (elimination) matrix, there are several plausible distractors. Even if the examinee has a fairly good idea of what to look for in an answer option, he may still have a difficult time singling out the correct one. Linn devised two separate training procedures to improve performance on each type of matrix problem.

In a P matrix training session, Linn taught examinees to avoid two common types of errors. The most common is to select an answer choice that matches a picture already in the matrix. This she calls a matching error. The second most common error is to select a picture that has elements from several pictures in the matrix. Linn calls this a conglomerate error.

In an E matrix training session, Linn taught children three strategies. The first was to eliminate answer choices that were clearly incorrect; the second was to work backward in the elimination of answer choices; the third strategy was to give reasons for the elimination of every answer option except the one that was chosen. This strategy might be called one of verbal mediation.

All subjects were given two pretests and two posttests. The pretests were matrix problems of both the performance and elimination varieties, plus Nonverbal Form 3a of the Lorge–Thorndike Intelligence Test. The posttests were alternate forms of these tests. Subjects were assigned to either experimental or control groups by a stratified random procedure that matched groups for pretest scores. The experimental group received the training described above while the control group received no training on matrix problems.

Linn found that the training procedures improved the performance of experimental relative to control subjects who received no training. In particular, experimental subjects showed smaller proportions of matching and conglomerate errors than did control subjects. The relative improvement did not generalize, however, to the Lorge–Thorndike Intelligence Test, and there was thus no evidence of transfer from the matrix test.

Linn reported correlations between P and E scales for control and experimental subjects. Most interesting was the correlation between the posttest P and E scales of .55 for control subjects, but of only .13 for experimental subjects. The difference must be interpreted cautiously. The reliabilities of the short P and E scales were low: .69 and .26 respectively for control subjects, and .48 on both scales for experimental subjects. Although Linn corrected interscale correlations for attenuation due to low scale reliabilities, the reliabilities of the scales were so low that one may be hesitant to place much confidence in the corrected interscale correlations.

Whitely and Dawis. Whitely and Dawis, like Hunt, Jacobs and Vandeventer, and Santesson, were interested in the relations used to solve analogical problems, except that they studied relations for verbal analogies.

Whitely (1973) asked subjects to sort analogies into groups on the basis of similarity of analogical relations. Whitely used latent partition analysis (Wiley, 1967) to identify subjects' implicit categories of relations. Eight categories were named and defined by inspecting item loadings on the categories. The eight categories, as reported in Whitely and Dawis (1973a), were these:

1. *Similarity:* "The relationship between two words is a similarity when the words have the same or nearly the same meaning" (p. 6).
2. *Opposites:* "The relationship between two words is opposites if they have opposite meanings" (p. 7).
3. *Word Pattern:* "A word pattern relationship does not depend on the meaning of the word, but on other things such as spelling, sound and number of letters in the word" (p. 8).
4. *Class Membership:* "The relationship between two words is class membership if the objects named by the words both belong to some group or have some common characteristic" (p. 11).
5. *Class Naming:* "The relationship between two words is class naming if one word names some group or characteristic of the object" (p. 12).
6. *Change Into:* "The relationship between two words is change into if one thing will be changed to the other over time or by some process" (p. 13).
7. *Functional:* "The relationship between two words is functional if one thing performs some activity on or for the other" (p. 16).
8. *Quantity:* "The relationship between two words is quantity when the objects differ in size or amount" (p. 17).

Whitely and Dawis (1973a) described a "cognitive intervention for improving the estimate of latent ability measured from analogy items," and Whitely and Dawis (1973b) tested this and other interventions on high school students. There were five interventions and a control condition. The control condition consisted of a filler task, and the experimental conditions were designed to improve solving of analogies. Two interventions consisted of practice in solving analogies, but no instruction. In one condition, subjects were given feedback on the correct answer after completing each problem, and in a second condition they were given no feedback. In the other three interventions, subjects were taught the categories for analogies described above. In a third condition, subjects were given feedback on performance after each item, but were not told the correct category into which each item fell. In a fourth condition, subjects were given limited category information, but were not given feedback. In a fifth condition, subjects were both told the correct category and given feedback.

The practice groups did not perform better than controls, but the instruction groups did perform better. Experimental groups receiving feedback did not perform better than groups not receiving it, but the group receiving category information in addition to feedback performed significantly better than the comparable group not receiving category information. These and other results suggested that the category information was critical to improved performance.

In an unrelated study, Ace and Dawis (1973) examined the effect of item structure on the difficulty of verbal analogies. They varied the position of the missing analogy term (*A, B, C,* or *D*) and the position of the correct answer option (1, 2, 3, 4, or 5). Ace and Dawis (1973) found four major results:

1. Blank position alone does not appear to be a significant factor influencing the item difficulty of verbal analogy items. (p. 147)

2. However, correct response position is probably a significant determinant of item difficulty; . . . placing the correct response in the fifth (last) response position tended to result in the most difficult item, followed by placement in the third (middle) position. (pp. 147–148)
3. Interaction between blank and correct response position is probably a significant factor in difficulty level of analogy items. (p. 148)
4. There is some suggestion in the results of this experiment that changes in item difficulty as a result of changes in blank and correct response position tend to occur for easier than for [sic] more difficult items. (p. 148)

In still another study, Tinsley and Dawis (1972) compared difficulties of semantic and figural versions of the "same" items. The correlation between scores on the two test forms was .86. Means and standard deviations did not differ significantly. In 27 out of 30 items, the proportion of corresponding responses on verbal and figural versions of the "same" item was greater than chance.

Willner. Willner (1964) describes analogical reasoning as consisting of "the extraction of a relationship in one realm, construction of a closely equivalent relationship in a different realm, and a careful inspection to see that both relationships are closely matched" (p. 481). Willner (1964) suggests four variables that may contribute to the difficulty of analogy problems:

1. "the distance between the realms characteristic of the first and second pair of words" (p. 482)
2. the type of relationship required for analogy solution
3. "a precise matching process requiring a very fine tuning where S must search among similar alternatives to find the correct answer" (p. 482)
4. "set-shift, e.g., cases where a less obvious relationship must be extracted from a pair of words, in the presence of another more obvious relationship" (p. 482)

Willner was particularly interested in the extent to which analogies can be solved by word association. Past evidence seemed to implicate word association. Zirkle (1941) discovered that more subjects solve an analogy when the correct answer has a high association to the third (C) analogy term. He further found more of an improvement for "duller" subjects than for "brighter" ones. And, Scheerer, Rothman, and Goldstein (1945) suggested that an idiot savant may solve many analogy problems by word association.

A first experiment investigated whether Miller Analogies Test items can be solved by word association. Subjects received 88 items from a Miller form, with 12 items excluded because they were not based upon semantic relationships. The test was given as a word association test. In the Miller Analogies Test, the missing term may be either the A, B, C, or D term. Willner removed the intact word pair from each item (A and B or C and D), so that the items could not possibly be solved on the basis of analogical reasoning. The subjects selected the option that was most highly associated to a single analogy term, unaware that the terms were from an analogies test. Willner found that 25% of the items were "solved" correctly more often than would be expected by chance ($p < .05$).

In a second experiment, Willner studied a larger number of verbal analogy items taken from a wide variety of analogy tests. A word-association test was again constructed with the intact pair of analogy terms removed. Both multiple-choice items and open-ended items were solved at better than a chance level ($p <$ .05). (The procedure used to estimate the chance baseline for open-ended items is described in the report.)

A third experiment was conducted to test the hypothesis that subjects "who do not correctly solve analogy items use word association" (Willner, 1964, p. 486). Analogies were constructed in which the correct answer could not be reached by the technique of word association. Analogies were scored by a standard "correct answer key," and by a separate "association foil key" that listed the most commonly given answer when the analogy is solved by word association. In 74% of the items, the most frequent incorrect answer was the association foil. In 68 of 101 analogy items, the association foil was chosen significantly more often than any other incorrect answer ($p <$ .05). The results therefore supported the initial hypothesis.

Achenbach.   Achenbach (1970) was also interested in the role of word association in solving verbal analogies. Over 300 fifth graders took Achenbach's Children's Associative Responding Test (*CART*), which was designed to identify children who rely on free association rather than reasoning processes in the solution of multiple-choice verbal analogies. Two experiments replicated previous findings of Achenbach's that correlations between school performance and ability measures are lower for children who rely heavily upon free association in solving analogies. These results support Willner's conclusion that word association can be an important process in solving verbal analogies, and the results further show that subjects' use of word association reduces analogy test validity.

Gentile.   Gentile, Kessler, and Gentile (1969) have made even stronger claims than Willner and Achenbach. They argue that "the process that Ss use in solving analogy items is primarily an associative process' (p. 501). This conclusion somewhat overstates their results. The authors found that "associative relatedness among the words in the analogy items (as measured by the Word Relatedness Rating Scale) appears to account for from 28% to 50% of the variance in the analogy solutions" (Gentile, Kessler, and Gentile, 1969, p. 501). The authors used an unusual method of measuring word association (described in their report), and the method probably inflated the proportion of variance accounted for by word association. The results nevertheless indicate once again the importance of associative processes in the solution of verbal analogies.

Verbrugge.   Verbrugge (1974) has studied analogy through the comprehension and recall of similes such as "A dictator's treatment of people is like a heavy boot dealing with a ladybug on the driveway" and "An empty prison cell is like a Venus flytrap, waiting for its next victim to enter." Most of the experiments used prompted recall in the context of a two-factor design: Acquisition lists were crossed with prompts for recall that were either relevant or not relevant to the lists. The prediction was that there would be an interaction between prompts and lists: Prompts would improve performance on the lists for which they were relevant but not on the lists for which they were not relevant. This prediction was confirmed in numerous studies using different materials and types of prompts.

Verbrugge enumerates a number of implications of his results for theories of memory and comprehension. Three of Verbrugge's (1974) implications are of particular interest here:

1. When dealing with the topics and vehicles of analogic sentences, it is very doubtful that words are central to subjects' 'encodings' of the acquisition items. . . . Integral to the memory of an analogic sentence is an inferred abstract relation among the elements of the topic and vehicle domains. (pp. 223, 224)

2. The structure of the 'memory trace' cannot be a multidimensional set of elementary attributes, features, properties, labels, images, or other specific entities (cf. Bower, 1967; Underwood, 1971; Katz, 1971). The memory for analogies essentially involves an abstract relation among *variables* which can be filled by any number of specific entities. (p. 225) [Verbrugge's view is thus inconsistent with the attribute representation used in this volume.]

3. An analogic sentence involves a *predication* on a topic, not simply an association of two phrases or domains. (p. 227) [Verbrugge's point of view is thus also inconsistent with the association theories described above.]

Evaluation. The theories described in this section are less fully developed than the major theories described in earlier sections and therefore have been described in less detail. The only theory that fares well by the completeness and specificity criteria is Hunt's, which presumably could be developed into a computer simulation. None of the theories are very general. All are limited either to verbal analogies or figural matrix problems. The word association theories are particularly parsimonious, but might be seen as alternatives to theories of analogical reasoning rather than as such theories themselves, claiming that subjects may solve analogies by word association rather than by analogical reasoning. There is clear evidence that word association can play a part in solving verbal analogies, but the data do not support the notion that word association is used to the exclusion of reasoning processes.

ISSUES CONFRONTING RESEARCH
ON ANALOGICAL REASONING

1. *Empirical support for theories.* There is a remarkably low ratio of data to theory in research on analogical reasoning. Of the large number of theories discussed, only the Rumelhart—Abrahamson theory can be said to have a minimally satisfactory data base supporting it, and that data base consists of three experiments reported in one article (Rumelhart & Abrahamson, 1973) and

a separate experiment reported by Rips, Shoben, and Smith (1973). While other researchers have conducted experiments, there is a pronounced tendency for the experiments to be only weakly related to the theories proposed. The experiments on word association are tied fairly closely to the theories about word association, but these theories have nothing to say about analogical reasoning per se. They suggest an alternate way by which some verbal analogies can be solved.

2. *Theory completeness.* The only theory that can make any strong claim to completeness is the Evans theory as embodied in the ANALOGY program. Other theories account for only limited aspects of the analogical reasoning process. The ANALOGY program, however, is only complete in that it is sufficient to solve analogies from beginning to end. It has not been shown to give a complete account of the way *humans* solve geometric analogy problems, and it is unlikely that the theory does indeed provide such an account.

3. *Generality.* None of the theories discussed are completely general. The theory that comes closest is probably Guilford's. This theory can account for differences in item format as well as a wide range of item content. Shalom and Schlesinger (1972) achieve some generality (of content) at a considerable cost to parsimony. They propose qualitatively different solution processes for verbal and figural items.

4. *Individual differences in information processing.* None of the theories provide a satisfactory account of individual differences in information processing. Spearman provides both differential and information-processing theories, but the differential theory has been shown to be inadequate. Guilford's theory has implications for individual differences in information processing, but Guilford has not presented a full information-processing theory of analogical reasoning.

SUMMARY

Differential and information-processing theories of analogical reasoning were summarized and evaluated. The theories were evaluated according to their fulfillment of five criteria: completeness, specificity, generality, parsimony, and plausibility.

Four differential theories were reviewed, those of Spearman, Cattell, Thurstone, and Guilford. According to Spearman's theory, performance on analogy tests is almost a pure measure of g. Cattell views analogy performance as an excellent measure of fluid ability (g_f), unless the test relies upon vocabulary or general information. In Thurstone's theory, one would expect analogical reasoning to load primarily on the inductive reasoning factor. Only figural analogies loaded significantly on this factor, however. Both figural and verbal analogies loaded on a perceptual factor, and verbal analogies loaded on the verbal factor as well. In Guilford's theory, analogy tests measure cognition of relations and convergent production of relations. Under certain circumstances, they may also measure cognition of units.

The information-processing theories considered in most detail were Spearman's, Shalom and Schlesinger's, and Rumelhart and Abrahamson's. Spearman's theory is based upon three qualitative principles of cognition: apprehension of experience, eduction of relations, and eduction of correlates. Spearman also suggested 11 relations that may be found in analogies: attribution, identity, time, space, cause, objectivity, constitution, likeness, evidence, conjunction, and intermixture.

According to Shalom and Schlesinger, solving an analogy involves two processes, forming a connection formula and applying the connection formula. These authors suggest that two quite different internal representations are used in verbal as opposed to figural analogies. In verbal analogies, processes operate in a relational network. In figural analogies, a list of operations stored in memory is searched for the appropriate operation, and the operation is used in analogy solution.

In the Rumelhart-Abrahamson theory, analogical reasoning is viewed as a set of operations in a semantic space. Vectors are constructed in which the psychological distance between A and B is the same as the psychological distance between C and I, the ideal solution. An analogy is viewed as a parallelogram in semantic space.

Two computer-based theories are considered in some detail, those of Reitman and Evans. In Reitman's ARGUS program, verbal analogies are solved through a network of active semantic elements. The semantic elements in the network correspond to Hebb's cell assemblies. Changes in the state of the semantic network occur in parallel. In Evans' ANALOGY program, geometric analogies are solved in two parts. In the first part, the analogy figures are decomposed into primitive descriptions. In the second part, these descriptions are used as the basis for inferring the relation between A and B, and then applying it from C to each answer option. The program selects the best answer option on the basis of the resemblance between the C to D_i rule and the A to B rule.

Winston has shown how Evans' theory can be extended to three-dimensional objects. Kling has written a computer program that uses analogical information in the context of a resolution-logic theorem prover. Becker has proposed information-processing algorithms by which verbal analogies can be solved. Williams has written an Aptitude Test Taker program that solves letter analogies and other induction problems.

Hunt has proposed two algorithms that can be used in the solution of matrix problems, a Gestalt algorithm and an analytic algorithm. The Gestalt algorithm consists of three answer generators and an executive subroutine. The three answer generators are continuation, superimposition of whole patterns, and superimposition based on point matching. The analytic algorithm consists of six basic operations: constancy, supplement–delete, expansion–contraction, addition–subtraction, movement, and composition–decomposition.

Jacobs and Vandeventer have proposed twelve relations that they believe are sufficient to classify the vast majority of matrix items. The relations are identity, shading, movement in a plane, reversal, addition, number series, shape, size, flipover, added element, unique addition, and elements of a set.

Santesson has suggested yet another classification of matrix relations. Using hierarchical clustering, she found three major clusters of items: items involving an increase or decrease of size or number of elements, items involving figures that are altered in one or two dimensions, and items involving combined addition and subtraction of parts of figures. These three clusters of items correspond closely to a priori clusters suggested by Raven for the Progressive Matrices.

Linn classified matrix items into two types: P matrices, in which there are few plausible answer options, or even just one plausible option, and E matrices, in which there are several plausible distractors. In the latter type of item, finding a correct answer may be difficult even if the subject has a fairly good idea of what to look for in an answer option.

Whitely and Dawis have suggested eight categories of implicit relations used by subjects in solving verbal analogies. The categories were determined by a latent partition analysis performed by Whitely. The categories are similarity, opposites, word pattern, class membership, class naming, change into, functional, and quantity.

Willner has described analogical reasoning as involving extraction of a relationship in one realm, construction of a closely equivalent relationship in a different realm, and inspection to make certain the relationships are closely matched. Willner found that subjects rely fairly extensively on word association in solving verbal analogies. Gentile confirmed this finding, and Achenbach extended this finding to children.

Verbrugge has studied comprehension of analogy in similes.

Four major issues confront research on analogical reasoning. The first is lack of empirical support for theories. Many of the experiments conducted have been only weakly related to theory, and none of the theories have much empirical backing. The second issue is theory completeness. Most theories are very incomplete, accounting for only aspects of analogical reasoning. The third issue is generality. None of the theories are completely general, and many are quite narrow. The fourth issue is the inability of most theories to account for individual differences in information processing.

6
A Componential Theory
of Analogical Reasoning

In this chapter, I will present a componential theory of analogical reasoning and four alternative basic models that fall under the theory. These models take slightly different forms, depending on whether analogies are true—false or forced-choice. For forced-choice analogies, the models again take slightly different forms, depending upon the conceptualization of the option-scanning process.

NATURE OF ANALOGY

An analogy is a hierarchy of relations taking the form A is to B as C is to D' ($A:B::C:D'$). An analogy exists when there is a higher-order relation of equivalence or near-equivalence between two lower-order relations (A is to B and C is to D'). In the terminology of this volume, an analogy exists when there is a rule, Y, that maps a domain rule, X, into a range rule, Z.[1]

The domain refers to the A and B terms of the analogy. It is in the domain of the analogy that the first lower-order relation X is discovered. The range refers to the C and D' terms of the analogy. It is to the range of the analogy that the X relationship is mapped through the formation of an isomorphic relation Z. The essence of analogy is in the higher-order relation, Y, that maps the domain into the range of the analogy. It is therefore surprising that this higher-order mapping relation is absent in many other theories of analogical reasoning (see Chapter 5)!

---

[1] The terms *domain* and *range* are used here in a way different from that of the Shalom and Schlesinger theory (see Chapter 5).

THE COMPONENTIAL THEORY

Overview

The componential theory of analogical reasoning contains six information-processing components, five of them mandatory and one of them optional.
The components are of three general types; attribute identification, attribute
comparison, and control. The combination rule for the components is one of
additivity. The structure of the theory is summarized in Table 6.1, and the
functions of the five mandatory components are shown schematically in Figure
6.1 for a true—false analogy.

Components

Attribute identification.   There is one attribute-identification component, *encoding*. In encoding, the stimulus is translated into an internal representation
upon which further mental operations can be performed. The internal representation is stored in working memory and is assumed to consist of an attribute-

TABLE 6.1
Componential Theory of Analogical Reasoning

Component process	Latency parameter	Description
		I. Components of Analogical Reasoning
		A. Attribute Identification
Encoding	(*a*)	Identify attributes and values of each term of the problem.
		B. Attribute Comparison
Inference	(*x*)	Discover rule relating *A* to *B*. *Domain.*
Mapping	(*y*)	Discover rule relating *A* to *C. Domain to range.*
Application	(*z*)	Generate rule to form *D'* and evaluate *D. Range.*
Justification	(*t*)	*Optional.* Test validity of operations as performed. *Domain. Range.*
		C. Control
Preparation— response	(*c*)	Prepare for analogy solution. Monitor solution process. Translate solution into response.
		II. Combination Rule
Additive		Solution time = encoding time + inference time + mapping time + application time + (justification time) + preparation— response time
		Solution difficulty = encoding difficulty + inference difficulty + mapping difficulty + application difficulty + (justification difficulty) + preparation—response difficulty

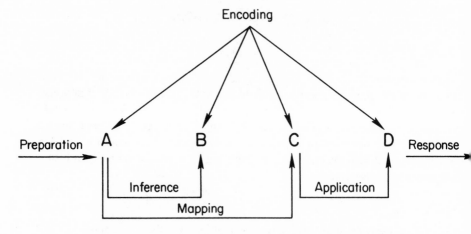

FIGURE 6.1   Schematic representation of analogical reasoning theory.

value list. Consider an example analogy: red:stop::green:go. In encoding, each of the four analogy terms is comprehended and stored in memory.

Attribute comparison.   There are three mandatory attribute-comparison components and one optional one.

Inference is the process by which a rule, X, is discovered that relates the A term of the analogy to the B term. Inference thus occurs in the domain of the analogy, and the outcome is stored in working memory. In the example analogy, inference is the discovery of the relation between *red* and *stop*.

Mapping is the process by which a higher-order rule, Y, is discovered that maps the domain of the analogy into the range. Mapping requires discovery of a rule that relates A (the first term of the domain) to C (the first term of the range). The rule is stored in working memory. In the example analogy, mapping is the discovery of the relation between *red* and *green*.

Application is the process by which a rule, Z, is generated that forms D' (an image of the correct answer) and evaluates D. Application thus occurs in the range of the analogy, and the outcome is stored in working memory. In the example analogy, application is the formation of an analogous rule that enables the subject to decide that *go* correctly completes the analogy.

Justification, an optional component, is the process by which one of several answer options that are nonidentical to D' is justified as closest to D'. The process is required only in forced-choice analogies in which none of the presented answers conforms to the visualized answer, D'. In the analogy red:stop: :green:(a. going, b. caution), *going* is initially rejected because it is the wrong part of speech, but is justified as correct because it is semantically near-correct and better than the alternative answer.

Control.   There is one control component in the theory. This component includes the processes by which subjects prepare for solving the analogy, monitor the solution process, and translate the solution into a response. The component, *preparation–response,* contains those operations that were not thought worthy of separate components, but were thought to be suitably represented in combination.

Combination Rule

Response time is hypothesized to equal the sum of the amounts of time spent on each component operation. Hence, a simple linear model predicts response time as the sum across the different component operations of the number of times each component operation is performed (as an independent variable) multiplied by the duration of that component operation (as an estimated parameter). Corresponding to each component operation, then, is a parameter representing its duration. These parameters are shown in Table 6.1.

Proportion of response errors (item difficulty) is hypothesized to equal the (appropriately scaled) sum of the difficulties encountered in executing each component operation. A simple linear model predicts proportion of errors as the sum across the different component operations of the number of times each component operation is performed (as an independent variable) multiplied by the difficulty of that component operation (as an estimated parameter). This additive combination rule is based upon the assumption that each subject has a limit on processing capacity (or space, see Osherson, 1974). Each execution of an operation uses up capacity. Until the limit is exceeded, performance is flawless except for constant sources of error (such as motor confusion, carelessness, momentary distraction). Once the limit is exceeded, performance is at a chance level.

In the response-time models (with solution latency as a dependent variable), all component operations must contribute significantly to solution latency, since by definition each execution of an operation consumes some amount of time. In the response-error models (error rate as dependent variable), however, all component operations need not contribute significantly to proportion of errors because some operations may be so easy that no matter how many times they are executed, they contribute only trivially to prediction of errors.

COMPONENTIAL MODELS OF ANALOGICAL REASONING

Four Basic Models

Overview.   Four alternative models of analogical reasoning processes are proposed. The models share the same information-processing components and combination rule, but differ in the way the components are organized into a strategy

TABLE 6.2
Attribute-Value List for Analogy Example
Washington:1::Lincoln: (a. 10, b. 5)

Encoding
  Washington. [(president (first)), (portrait on currency (dollar)), (war hero
    (Revolutionary))]
  1. [(counting number (one)), (ordinal position (first)), (amount (one unit))]
  Lincoln. [(president (sixteenth)), (portrait on currency (five dollars)), (war hero (Civil))]
  10. [(counting number (ten)), (ordinal position (tenth)), (amount (ten units))]
  5. [(counting number (five)), (ordinal position (fifth)), (amount (five units))]

Inference
  Washington → 1. [(president (ordinal position (first))), (portrait on currency (amount
    (dollar))), (∅))]

Mapping
  Washington → Lincoln. [(presidents (first, sixteenth)), (portraits on currency (dollar, five
    dollars)), (war heroes (Revolutionary, Civil))]

Application
  Lincoln → 10. [(∅), (∅), (∅)]
  Lincoln → 5. [(∅), (portrait on currency (amount (five dollars))), (∅)]

---

for solving analogy problems. The models are discussed in terms of an attribute-value list representation for information, but could be mapped into other representations as well. An example analogy, Washington:1::Lincoln:(a. 10, b. 5), will be used to illustrate the models. The results of operations upon this analogy are shown in Table 6.2 and described below.

Model I. A schematic flow chart for Model I is presented in Figure 6.2. (Detailed flow charts for the models are presented in the appendix to this chapter.) Names of operations are inside the boxes of the flow chart, and the latency parameters assigned to those operations are to the right of the boxes.

The subject begins analogy solution by encoding the first analogy term, *Washington,* and then the second analogy term, 1. In the example, the subject stores in working memory the facts that Washington was the first president, a portrait on a dollar bill, and a Revolutionary War hero. For the numeral 1, possibly relevant facts are that it can represent the first counting number, the first ordinal position, or a unitary amount.

Next the subject infers the relation between the first two analogy terms. In the example, two of the three attributes encoded for *Washington* can be used to relate that analogy term to the second term, 1. The inferred relation states that Washington was the first president and is the portrait on a dollar bill. No relation to 1 could be found for the third attribute-value pair identifying Washington as a Revolutionary War hero, and so that attribute-value pair is assigned a null value, ∅, in the inference relation.

The subject then encodes the third analogy term, *Lincoln,* enabling him to map the relation between the first and third terms. In the example, the subject recognizes that both Washington and Lincoln (a) were presidents, (b) are portraits on currency, and (c) were war heroes.

The final required encodings are of the answer options, *10* and *5.* Once these terms are encoded, the subject attempts to apply from *Lincoln* to each answer option a relation analogous to the one previously inferred. An attempt to construct an analogous relation from *Lincoln* to *10* results in a null relation, because no analogy can be found: Lincoln was neither the tenth president nor is he the portrait on a 10-dollar bill. An analogous relation can be constructed from *Lincoln* to *5,* however, because Lincoln's portrait appears on a 5-dollar bill.

The analogy is now solved. All that remains is for the subject to communicate the solution. The subject responds with option *b,* completing the analogy problem.

Note that in Model I, inference, mapping, and application – the attribute-comparison operations – are all exhaustive processes. All attributes are compared in each type of operation. This characteristic does not hold true for the subsequent models to be described.

Model II. The schematic flow chart for Model II, shown in Figure 6.3, is identical to that for Model I through the encoding of D (including D_1 and D_2).

FIGURE 6.2   Schematic flow
chart for Model I.

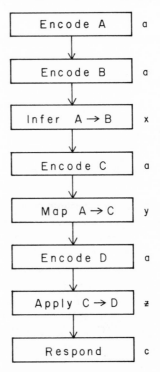

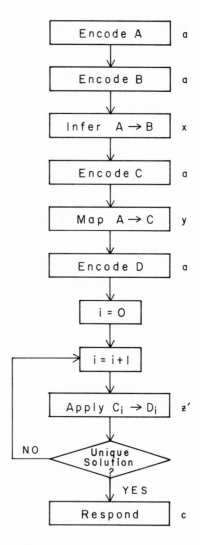

FIGURE 6.3   Schematic flow chart for Model II.

At this point, an "attribute counter" is set equal to zero and then incremented by one. Only one attribute is applied. This attribute, that Lincoln was the sixteenth president, fails to distinguish between answer options. So the subject returns to the attribute counter, and again increments it by one. The subject now applies the second attribute. In doing so, the subject recognizes that 5 refers to the amounts of the bill on which Lincoln appears. Since the second option leads to an analogous rule, the subject responds *b*.

Note that in Model II, inference and mapping are exhaustive, but application is self-terminating. Latencies of self-terminating components are represented in the flow charts by primed parameters. Whereas, in Model I, all attributes were applied, in Model II, only as many attributes are applied as are needed to reach a unique solution. The subject never reaches the third attribute-value pair identifying Lincoln as a Civil War hero, because the second attribute permitted a unique solution.

Model III. The schematic flow chart for Model III, shown in Figure 6.4, is identical to that for Model II through the encoding of the third analogy term. At

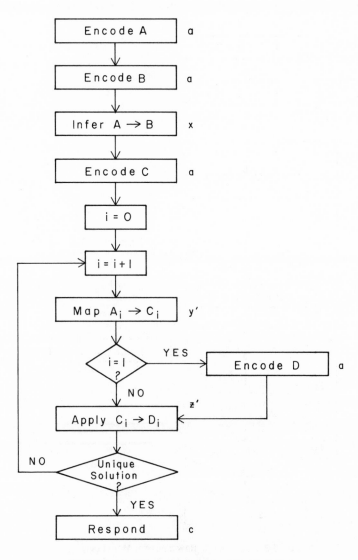

FIGURE 6.4   Schematic flow chart for Model III.

this point, the subject enters the attribute-testing loop that in Model II includes only application. The subject maps one attribute, recognizing that Washington and Lincoln were both presidents, the first and sixteenth respectively. Since $i = 1$ (the subject is traveling through the loop for the first time), the subject encodes D. He will not reencode D should subsequent iterations through the loop be

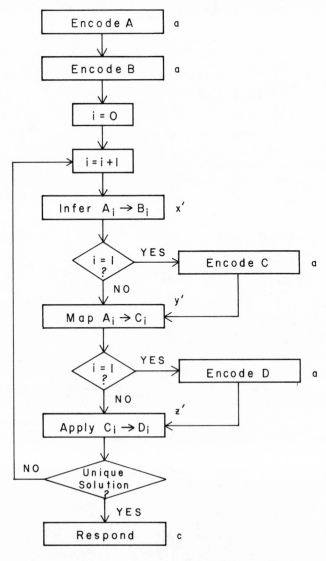

FIGURE 6.5   Schematic flow chart for Model IV.

necessary, since, in subsequent iterations, i ≠ 1. Next the subject applies the first attribute, that Lincoln was the sixteenth president. This application fails to yield a unique solution, so the subject returns to the beginning of the loop. As in Model II, the second trip through the loop does yield a unique answer.

Note that in Model III, inference is exhaustive, but mapping and application are self-terminating. Whereas Model II required mapping of all three attributes to solve the analogy, Model III requires mapping of only two attributes.

Model IV. The schematic flow chart for Model IV, shown in Figure 6.5, is the same as that for Model III through the encoding of the second analogy term. At this point, the subject sets $i = 0$, and then enters the attribute-testing loop. Once again, the loop is arranged so that analogy terms are encoded only on the first trip through the loop. The subject infers, maps, and then applies an attribute, trying to select a unique answer. If he cannot, he returns to the beginning of the loop, and infers, maps, and applies another attribute, continuing the iterative process until the analogy is solved.

Note that in Model IV, inference, mapping, and application are all self-terminating. Whereas Model III required inference of all three attributes to solve the analogy, Model IV requires only two inferences.

Two Basic Strategies in Application

In applying the analogous rule from C to D, two basic strategies may be followed. The essential aspects of the two strategies are presented schematically in Figure 6.6.

Sequential option scanning. In one strategy, scanning of presented answer options is sequential. The subject applies attributes onto one option before applying any attributes onto another option. It is assumed that as a safeguard against premature decisions, the subject checks all options.

Consider the example in Table 6.2. The subject initiates application by applying the first attribute-value pair for *Lincoln,* (president (sixteenth)), onto *10.* This fails to yield a match, as do subsequent applications onto *10.* Next, the subject applies each of the attribute-value pairs onto *5,* finding a match for (portrait on currency (five dollars)).

Alternating option scanning. In a second strategy, scanning of presented answer options is alternating. The subject applies an attribute onto each option before applying any further attributes. Again, the subject is assumed to check all options.

In the example, the subject initiates application by applying (president (sixteenth)) first onto *10,* then onto *5.* This fails to yield a match. The subject then applies (portrait on currency (five dollars)) onto *10,* and then *5,* obtaining a

SEQUENTIAL   OPTION   SCANNING

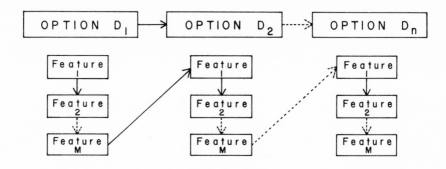

ALTERNATING   OPTION   SCANNING

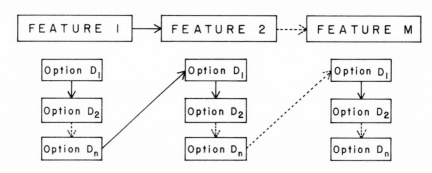

FIGURE 6.6   Schematic representations of two types of forced-choice models.

match. Note that whereas sequential option scanning required application of all attributes onto the first answer option, alternating option scanning required application of only two attributes onto this answer option.

Scope of the Models

Analogy format. The models are applicable to analogies presented in either forced-choice or true–false format. Application for force-choice analogies proceeds as described above and may be extended to analogies with more than two answer options. In true–false analogies, the subject proceeds through the analogy and tries to determine whether a relation can be constructed from C to D that is analogous to the relation from A to B. If such a relation can be constructed, the analogy is true; otherwise, it is false. The distinction between sequential and alternating option scanning becomes irrelevant, because there is only one answer option.

Analogy content. The models can be applied to a wide variety of analogy content, using the same encoding scheme. The example of Table 6.2 is a verbal analogy. Another type of analogy used in the present series of experiments is the People Piece analogy. People Pieces are schematic drawings of people varying on four binary attributes. A tall, fat, blue male, for example, could be represented as [(height (tall)), (girth (fat)), (color (blue)), (sex (male))]. Still another type of analogy to be considered is the geometric one. A black square inside a white circle might be represented as [((shape (square)), (position (surrounded)), (color (black))), ((shape (circle)), (position (surrounding)), (color (white)))]. The animal name analogies used by Rumelhart and Abrahamson (1973) might also be represented in this formalism: [(Size (X)), (Ferocity (Y)), (Humanness (Z))], where X, Y, and Z are coordinate values in a multidimensional semantic space. The present representation appears to be isomorphic to the spatial one employed by Rumelhart and Abrahamson (1973).

Analogy processes. While the models specify in some detail alternative ways in which attribute information can be combined to arrive at a solution for analogy problems, the models do not specify what the possible attributes are for different types of analogies, nor do they specify how subjects discover these attributes in the first place. A complete theory of analogical reasoning would have to specify this further information, something that has not yet been done.

EVALUATION OF COMPONENTIAL THEORY

How well does the componential theory of analogical reasoning satisfy the criteria by which other theories were evaluted in Chapter 5? Let us consider each criterion.

Completeness

The theory does quite well by the completeness criterion: The analogical reasoning process is described by detailed models from beginning to end. Each model falling under the theory can be represented fully in flow chart form, with all necessary processes explicitly stated and shown in their relations to each other. (See the appendix to this chapter for detailed descriptions of the models.)

Specificity

The theory is quite specific in describing the details of the three mandatory attribute-comparison operations. It is less specific in describing the details of the encoding process. The theory describes many minute bookkeeping (monitoring) operations, although the internal mechanisms behind "preparation" and "response" remain a mystery.

Generality

The theory is very general. It is applied to Chapters 7, 8, 9, and 10 to four different types of analogies: People Piece analogies, verbal analogies, geometric analogies, and animal name analogies.

Parsimony

The theory achieves a considerable degree of parsimony by specifying all operations, but assigning separate information-processing components only to psychologically significant operations. The theory thus manages to be complete while at the same time retaining parsimony. The major aspects of analogical reasoning are accounted for in five mandatory and one optional component. But the minor aspects are represented in the flow charts, and in most cases, are absorbed into the c component.

Plausibility

Chapter 7, 8, 9, and 10 are devoted to tests of the theory and models. The results will show that the theory accounts for the data very well. Consider some alternative theories.

One theory (class of models) stipulates inference and application but not mapping as component operations in analogical reasoning. The former two operations have gone under different guises. Spearman (1923) refers to the eduction of relations and the eduction of correlates, Shalom and Schlesinger (1972) to the formation of the connection formula and the application of the connection formula, and Johnson (1962) to the inductive operation and the deductive operation. In each of these models, the subject infers the relation from A to B, and then applies it from C to D. None of these models contain the equivalent of the mapping component.

Is mapping necessary? The experimental data to be presented suggest that it is. The mathematical parameter made a statistically and practically significant contribution to the prediction of solution latencies and error rates in all three experiments. In the People Piece and Geometric Analogy Experiments, more time was spent on mapping than on any other attribute-comparison component. Moreover, the operation might be viewed as logically necessary, since it is in mapping that the higher-order relationship constituting the analogy is recognized. Somehow, the two halves of the problem (A and B, C and D) must be recognized as analogous.

An alternative class of models stipulates inference and mapping, but not application, as component operations in analogical reasoning. The computer-program theories of Evans (1968) and Winston (1970) are examples of such models. In these programs, the relation between A and B is computed by what we have called inference. The relation between C and each answer option D_i is also computed by inference. Then the description of the A to B relation is compared to the description of each C to D_i relation (mapping) to determine which pair of relations forms the best analogy.

Is a separate application operation necessary, or is application really a repeated inference operation? The Evans and Winston models show that the distinction is logically unnecessary, but the data to be presented suggest that it is psychologically sound. First, the durations of single inference and application operations differed, with inference taking longer than application in all three experiments. Second, individual parameter estimates for the inference and application operations were not significantly correlated across subjects in any of the experiments. Were both parameters measuring durations of the same operation, one would expect them to show highly similar patterns of individual differences.

On balance, the componential theory does quite well by the five criteria. In the next chapters we shall consider explicit tests of the theory and models.

SUMMARY

An analogy exists when there is a higher-order relation of equivalence or near equivalence between two lower-order relations. The hierarchy of relations takes the form A is to B as C is to D' $(A:B::C:D')$.

Analogy problems may be of several types. Two types of analogies considered here are true—false and forced-choice analogies.

The componential theory of analogical reasoning consists of six components, five of which are mandatory and one of which is optional. The components are of three general types: attribute identification, attribute comparison, and control.

There is one attribute-identification component, encoding. In encoding, the subject identifies the attributes of each analogy term.

There are three mandatory attribute-comparison components: inference, mapping, and application. In inference, the subject discovers the rule relating A to B. In mapping, the subject discovers the higher-order rule relating A to C. In application, the subject generates the rule to form D' and evaluate D.

An optional attribute-comparison component is justification. In justification, the subject checks the validity of operations as performed. This component is used only in forced-choice analogies in which (1) both presented answers can be viewed as correct; (2) neither presented answer is correct; or (3) the subject has made an error.

There is one control component, preparation-response. This component includes processes by which the subject prepares for analogy solution, monitors the solution process, and translates the solution into a response. The component was intended to absorb information processes that were not deemed of sufficient psychological interest to be represented as separate information-processing components.

The combination rule for the componential theory is additive. It is assumed that solution time is equal to the sum of the times spent on each of the separate components and that error rate is equal to the sum of the difficulties encountered in executing each component.

All mandatory components must enter into each solution-time model, since components are executed in real time, and therefore must have a latency. All components need not appear in models for error rates. Since error components are not real-time components, they may have zero values when execution of a component is error-free.

Four basic componential models of analogical reasoning are proposed. All models fall under the identical componential theory, since the identities of the components and the combination rule are the same. The models are distinguished in terms of the mode and order of component processing.

In Model I, all three mandatory attribute-comparison components are exhaustive. First, the subject infers all possible value changes; then he maps all possible value changes; then he applies all possible value changes.

In Model II, inference and mapping are exhaustive, but application is self-terminating. First, the subject infers all possible value changes; then he maps all possible value changes. He only applies as many attributes as are needed to disconfirm incorrect answer options.

In Model III, inference is exhaustive, but mapping and application are self-terminating. The subject first infers all possible value changes. He then maps and applies only the attributes needed to disconfirm incorrect options.

In Model IV, inference, mapping, and application are all self-terminating. The subject infers, maps, and applies only those attributes needed to disconfirm incorrect options. In this model, the subject takes an attribute at a time and carries it through each operation, returning to consider an additional attribute only if falsification was impossible on the basis of the original attribute.

Two classes of forced-choice models are considered, models with sequential option scanning and models with alternating option scanning. In the former, all attributes of one option are tested before any attributes of another option are tested. In the latter, a single attribute is tested on all options before the subject proceeds to test another attribute. Models I, II, III, and IV are applicable to either class of models, although the processing assumptions differ for each model class.

The componential theory fares quite well according to the five criteria used to evaluate theories in Chapter 5. It is probably weakest in meeting the specificity criterion and strongest in meeting the criteria of generality and plausibility in accounting for experimental data (as will be shown in subsequent chapters). The theory is also quite parsimonious, assigning separate components to only the six processes deemed of particular psychological importance, and is complete in accounting for the solution process from beginning to end.

APPENDIX:
DETAILED SPECIFICATIONS
OF COMPONENTIAL MODELS

Overview

This section describes in detail the componential models for true—false and forced-choice analogies. Readers may wish to refer to the earlier example analogy in Table 6.2 as they follow the flow charts of the models.

True—False Models

Model I. The flow chart for componential Model I is shown in Figure 6.7. Analogy solution begins with the setting of a truth index, T, equal to 0. The analogy is true if $T = 0$ and false otherwise. This means that the analogy will be assumed true unless falsified by a subsequent increment in the value of T. The initial predisposition is toward a true response. Since this initialization always occurs once in each analogical solution process, it is "constant" over items and is incorporated into the c parameter. Many other bookkeeping operations of this type (represented by small rectangles) also occur a constant number of times across items, and hence are absorbed into the c parameter. Henceforth, this fact will not be mentioned explicitly in the discussion of bookeeping operations.

Truth value initialization is followed by encoding of the A and B terms of the analogy. Each encoding is assumed to take an amount of time equal to a, the encoding parameter. After these two terms are encoded, a counter i is set equal to 0. The subject then enters an inference loop.

The inference loop begins by the incrementing of the counter i by 1. This counter will count attributes, and can range from 0 to N, where N is the number of attributes to be examined in the inference loop. The value of N is available from the encoding operations, as are the identities of the specific attributes.

After incrementing the counter, the subject sets the ith value in a transformation vector X equal to nullity. This means that the subject has a predisposition toward null transformations (as in the Clark—Chase sentence—picture comparison theory). What is the advantage of the null predisposition, or any predisposition at all? The advantage is that nonbranching bookkeeping operations are assumed to be performed extremely rapidly, whereas branching attribute-

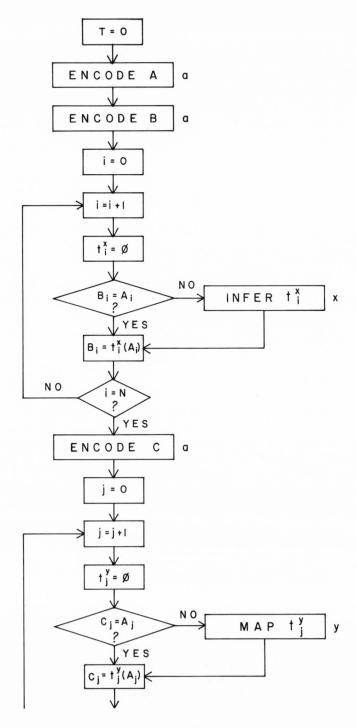

FIGURE 6.7A   Model I_{TF}.

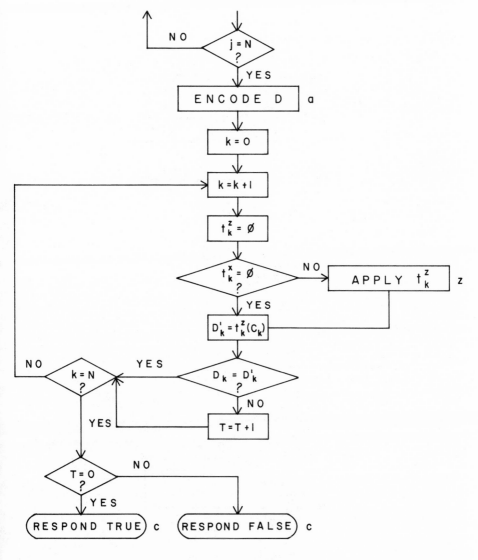

FIGURE 6.7B   Model I_{TF}.

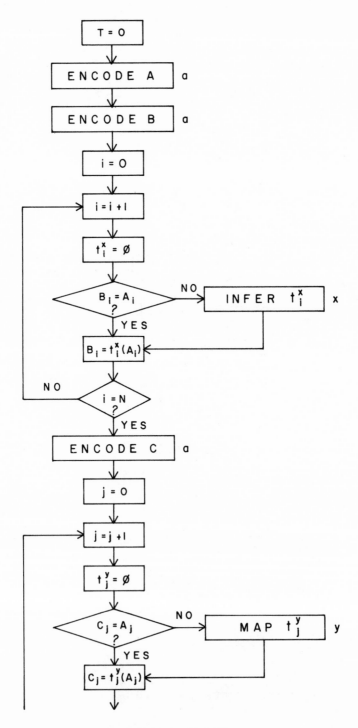

FIGURE 6.8A Model II$_{\text{TF}}$.

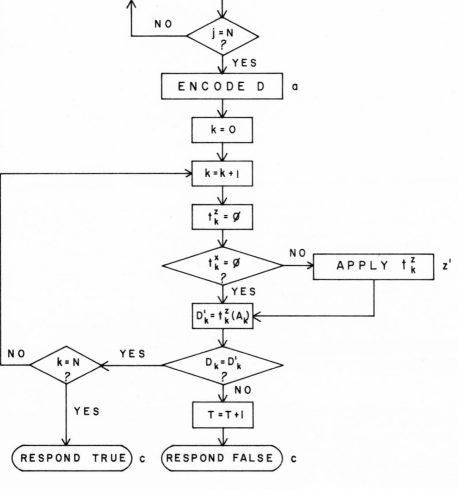

FIGURE 6.8B Model II$_{TF}$.

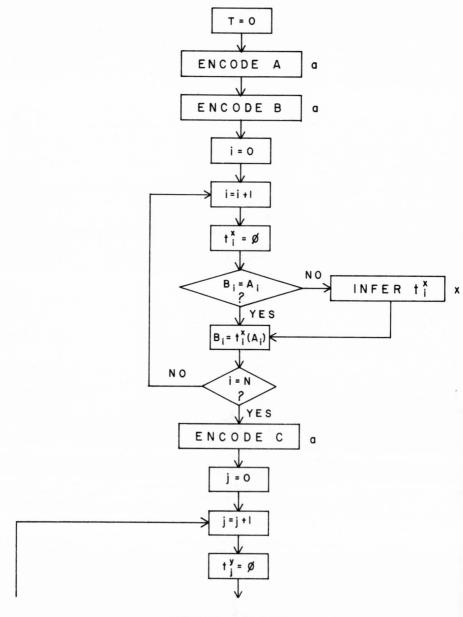

FIGURE 6.9A   Model III$_{\text{TF}}$.

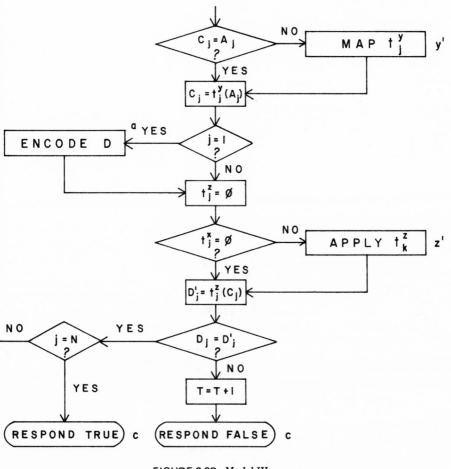

FIGURE 6.9B   Model III$_{\text{TF}}$.

155

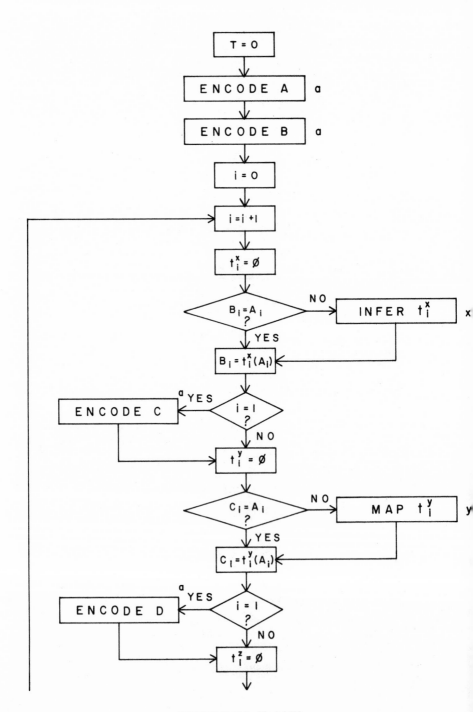

FIGURE 6.10A   Model IV$_{TF}$.

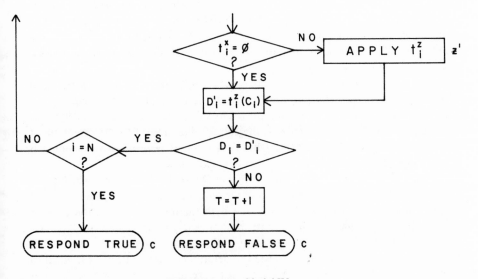

FIGURE 6.10B   Model IV_{TF}.

comparison operations are assumed to be time consuming. If the branching attribute-comparison operation can be avoided, a considerable amount of time and processing effort can be conserved, even though there will be cases in which the null value of the transformation vector will have to be replaced by a nonnull value.

After the value of the ith attribute in the X transformation vector is set equal to nullity, the subject investigates whether the ith attribute of B has the same value as the ith attribute of A. If it does, no further transformation operations are necessary, since the value was previously set equal to nullity. If it does not, the nature of the transformation from A to B must be inferred. Inferring this transformation takes an amount of time represented by the x parameter.

Once the nature of the ith transformation is determined, the value of the ith attribute of B must be set equal to the value of the ith attribute in the t^X transformation vector. B_i is thus understood in terms of its relation to A_i, rather than just in terms of itself. The value of B_i will be identical to that of A_i if t_i^X remained null, or will equal some other value if t_i^X did not remain null.

Having related B_i to A_i, the subject is prepared to query whether the inference loop is completed. It will be completed if the counter i is equal to N, the number of attributes. If i does not yet equal N, the subject returns to the beginning of the inference loop, once again incrementing i by 1. If i equals N, exhaustive inference is completed, and an exit is made from the inference loop.

The next process is the encoding of C, which takes time a. After C is encoded, a counter j is initialized to 0, and then a mapping loop is entered.

The mapping loop begins and proceeds in the same way as the inference loop. The j counter is incremented by 1, after which the value of the jth attribute in a second transformation vector t^Y is set equal to nullity. The subject queries whether C_j equals A_j, and if it does, further transformation operations are unnecessary. If it does not, then it is necessary to map A into C, replacing the null value of t_j^Y with an appropriate nonnull value. This mapping operation takes an amount of time y.

After attribute comparison is completed, the value of attribute C_j is set equal to the value of the jth attribute in the t^Y transformation vector. C is thus understood in terms of its relation to A. The subject is then ready to query as to whether j equals N. If it does not, the subject must return to the beginning of the mapping loop, incrementing j by 1. If j equals N, exhaustive mapping is completed, and the subject proceeds to the next operation.

The next operation is the encoding of the D term of the analogy, which takes time a. After D is encoded, a counter k is initialized to 0, and then an application loop is entered. Entry begins with the incrementing of the counter by 1. Next, the value of the kth attribute in a transformation vector t^Z is set equal to nullity. Then the kth attribute in the t^X transformation vector, which was formed during inference, is tested to determine whether its value is equal to nullity. If it is, no further operations on t^Z are required. If, however, the kth attribute of t^X was subject to a nonnull transformation during inference, then a corresponding transformation must be entered into the t^Z vector. The transformation is entered through the application process and is assumed to take an amount of time, z. Once the value of the transformation is determined, the subject sets D'_k equal to the value of the kth attribute in the t^Z transformation vector. D'_k thus becomes a single constructed attribute of the correct answer, D'.

Having constructed D'_k, the subject inquires whether the value of D_k, the kth attribute of the presented answer, is equal to the value of D'_k, the kth attribute of the correct answer. If it is, the subject proceeds to inquire whether all N attributes have been exhaustively carried through the application loop. If the value of D_k does not equal the value of D'_k, then the truth index T is incremented by 1, falsifying the analogy. The subject then inquires whether k equals N, and if it does not, he returns to the beginning of the application loop, incrementing k by 1. If k does equal N, application is complete, and the subject responds "true." Otherwise, the subject responds "false."

Note that in this model (and others), the subject stores the results of attribute-comparison operations in attribute-transformation vectors X, Y, and Z. These vectors enable the subject to keep his place in the solution process. Once an entry has been placed in a given "slot" of the vector, the subject does not return to the attribute comparison corresponding to that slot, since the existence of an entry in the slot shows that a comparison has already been made. The contents of the vectors therefore help the subject keep track of where he is in the analogy solution process.

Model IV. Let us skip over Models II and III for the moment, and consider Model IV, the other "extreme" model. In this model, all attribute-comparison operations are self-terminating. Let us see how processing proceeds. Consider Figure 6.10.

The solution process begins with the setting of the truth index T to 0, just as in Model I. Next, the A and B terms of the analogy are encoded, with each encoding taking time a. Then the counter i is set equal to 0. Having done this, the subject enters a large loop that will include mapping and application as well as inference.

The first operation in the loop is the incrementing of the i counter by 1. Next, the subject sets the value of the ith attribute in the t^X transformation vector equal to nullity, and then inquires whether the value of the ith attribute of B equals the value of the ith attribute of A. If it does not, he must infer the nature of the ith transformation, which takes an amount of time, x'. (A notational convention is used whereby self-terminating parameters are primed and exhaustive ones are not.) The subject then sets the value of the ith attribute of B equal to the value of the ith attribute in the t^X transformation vector. B_i is thereby understood in terms of its relation to A_i.

The subject now asks whether i equals 1. If it does, the subject is going through the big loop for the first time, and must encode the C term of the analogy, which takes time a. If i does not equal 1, then the subject has been through the loop before, and it is unnecessary to encode C, since it was encoded in a previous excursion through the loop.

Once encoding, if needed, is completed, the subject sets the value of the ith attribute in the t^Y transformation vector equal to nullity. Note that he has now left operations associated with inference. Rather than inferring all possible changes, he has examined just one attribute and is now carrying this attribute through to mapping operations. The subject inquires whether the value of the ith attribute of C equals the value of the ith attribute of A. If it does, mapping of a nonnull transformation is unnecessary. If the two are not equal, however, the subject must determine the nature of the transformation that maps A_i into C_i, and enter this value into the t^Y transformation vector. This mapping operation takes time y'. Having completed it, the subject sets C_i equal to the value of the ith attribute in the t^Y transformation vector. C_i is thereby understood in terms of its relation to A_i.

The subject continues through the loop, again querying whether it is the first time through the loop ($i = 1$). If the answer is yes, the subject encodes D, which takes time a. If the answer is no, the subject proceeds directly to the next operation, setting the value of the ith attribute in the t^Z transformation vector equal to nullity. Note that the subject has now left operations associated with mapping and is carrying over to application the single attribute that he selected for inference. The subject inquires whether the value of the ith attribute in the t^X transformation vector, formed during inference, is null. If it is not, the subject must apply the transformation, and enter it into the t^Z vector. This operation takes time z'. The subject is then able to construct D_i', a single attribute of the correct answer (as he conceives it). D_i' is the ith attribute in the t^Z transformation vector.

The subject next queries whether the value of the ith attribute of D is equal to the value of the ith attribute of D'. If the answer is no, the analogy must be false. The subject increments the truth index T by 1 and immediately responds "false." Response is incorporated into the c parameter. If D_i does equal D_i', the subject cannot falsify the analogy on the basis of this attribute. The subject inquires whether i equals N. If it does, all attributes have been tested, and since the analogy has not been falsified, it must be a true analogy. The subject responds "true." If i does not equal N, the other attributes remain to be examined, and it is necessary to return to the beginning of the big loop, incrementing i by 1 and selecting another attribute to examine.

In this and the other self-terminating models, some bookkeeping operations are not absorbed into any one component. An additional component could be included to absorb them, but empirical tests revealed that the additional component always accounted for trivial proportions of variance. This is to be expected, since the bookkeeping operations are assumed to be executed in negligible amounts of time.

Model II. We shall consider Model II in less detail, because it is a mixture of Models I and IV, and therefore may be understood in terms of either of these two models. Model II is in fact identical to Model I, except for one important difference. This difference is in the way the application loop terminates. The subject does not necessarily apply all attributes. Instead, he terminates processing as soon as the analogy is falsified.

Model II is shown in Figure 6.8. Near the end of the application loop, the subject queries whether the value of the kth attribute of the presented answer, D, equals the value at the kth attribute of the constructed correct answer, D'. If it does, the subject inquires as to whether all attributes have been tested. If they have not, he returns to the beginning of the application loop. However, if the value of the kth attribute of D does not equal the value of the kth attribute of D', the analogy must be false. The subject increments the truth index T by 1, and responds false. Only if the subject has tested all N attributes of the analogy and not been able to falsify any of them does he respond "true." In short, application is self-terminating, but inference and mapping remain exhaustive.

Model III. Model III shall also be considered in less detail, since it is a mixed model. Model III is shown in Figure 6.9.

In Model III, inference is exhaustive as in Models I and II, but mapping and application are self-terminating, as in Model IV. The "big loop" referred to in Model IV begins with the incrementing of the j counter for mapping rather than the i counter for inference.

In this model, the subject exhaustively infers all value changes. He then selects an attribute, j, which he proceeds to map and then apply. If D_j does not equal D_j', the subject increments the T counter by 1, and responds "false." If D_j does equal D_j', the subject cannot falsify the analogy on the basis of the attribute. He inquires whether j equals N. If it does, all attributes have been tested, and the subject responds "true." If j does not equal N, the subject must return to the beginning of the big loop, which is at the point the j counter is incremented by 1. He then maps another attribute, applies it, and again tries to falsify the analogy. This process continues until either the analogy has been falsified, or all attributes have been tested.

Forced-Choice Models

Alternating option scanning. We shall consider in some detail two alternating option scanning models, Models I and III. Flow charts for these models are shown in Figures 6.11 and 6.12. The processing assumptions of Models II and IV can be readily inferred from these two descriptions, and they will be discussed only briefly. We shall consider only the case in which two alternative

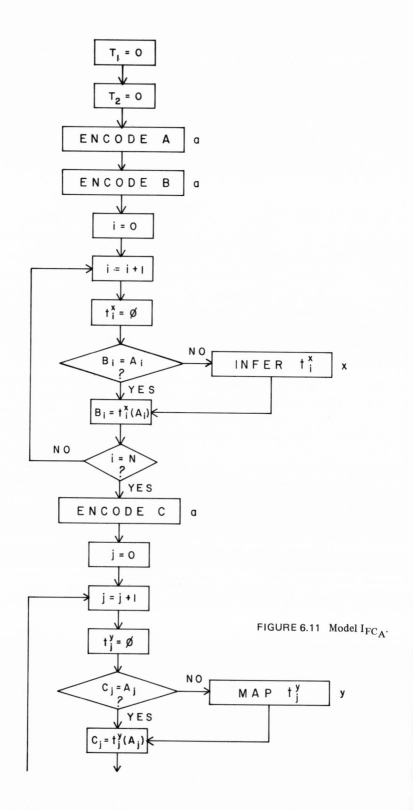

FIGURE 6.11   Model I_{FC_A}.

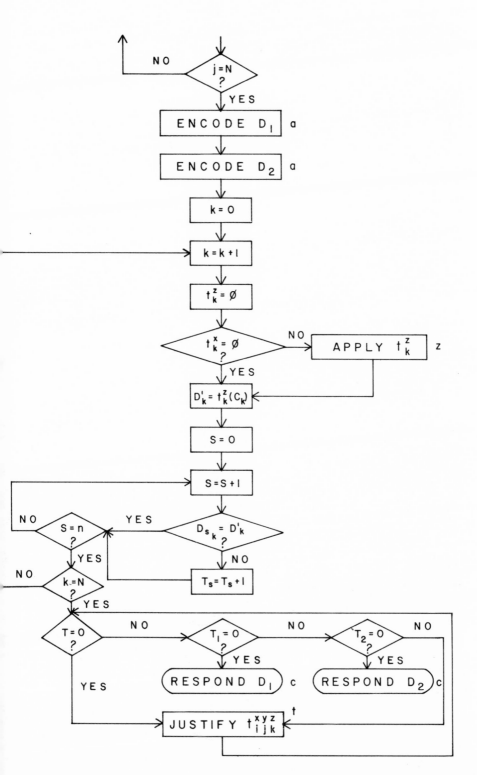

163

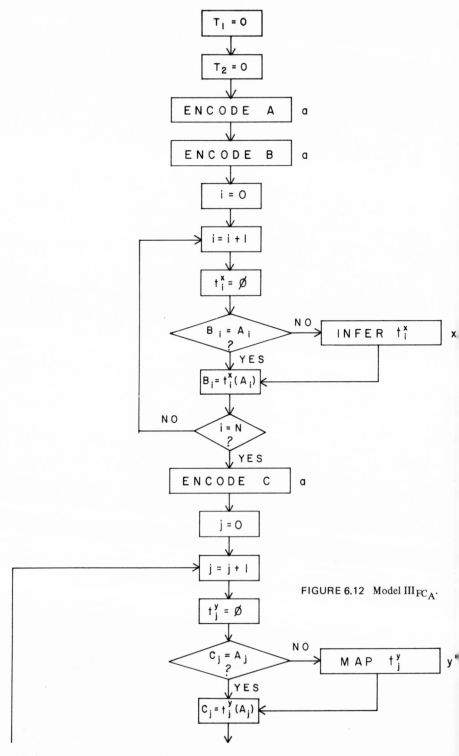

FIGURE 6.12   Model III_{FC_A}.

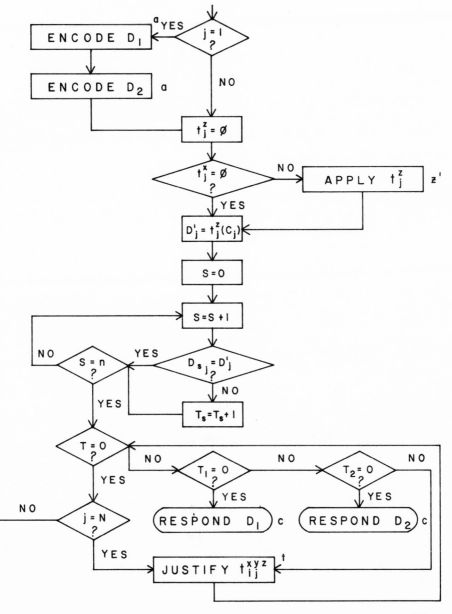

answer options are presented. The extension of each model to cases with larger numbers of options is straightforward.

In Model I (Figure 6.8), solution processing begins with the subject setting two truth indices, T_1 and T_2, equal to 0. The subject therefore has a predisposition toward each option being true. Solution processing then proceeds as in true– false Model I, until the completion of mapping operations. We shall begin our detailed description after mapping operations are completed.

Once mapping is completed, the subject encodes D_1 and D_2, the two presented answer options. Each encoding takes time a. The subject then sets a counter k equal to 0 and enters an application loop.

The first operation of the application loop increments the counter, k, by 1. Then the value of the kth attribute in t^Z is set equal to nullity. Next, the subject queries whether the value of the kth attribute in t^X is null. If it is not, the corresponding transformation must be applied to C_k, and the result of this transformation is entered into t^Z. The time to apply the transformation is equal to z. Once application is completed, D'_k is set equal to the value of the kth attribute in the t^Z vector. An attribute of the correct answer has thereby been constructed.

A new counter, s, is set equal to 0, and then incremented by 1. This counter is an option counter, counting the number of the option that is currently being examined. Once it is incremented, the subject queries whether the value of the kth attribute of the option D_s is equal to the value of the kth attribute of D'. If it is not, T_s, the truth index corresponding to option s, is incremented by 1. The subject then asks whether s equals n, the number of options. If it does not, s is again incremented, and the next option is tested for the attribute currently being examined. When s does equal n, the subject proceeds to ask whether k equals N, the number of attributes. If it does not, the subject returns to the beginning of the application loop, and increments k by 1. He then processes the next attribute. When k does equal N, the subject exits from the application loop and queries whether all values of the truth index T are equal to 0. If they are, the subject is in trouble, because he has been able to falsify neither option. He proceeds to justification. If they are not all equal to 0, he then tests each value of T separately.

If T_1 is equal to 0, the subject knows that D_1 is the correct option, and responds appropriately. The response process is absorbed into the c parameter. If T_1 does not equal 0, the subject tests T_2, the truth index for the second option. If it is equal to 0, the subject responds D_2. If it also does not equal 0, the subject is in trouble, because he has falsified both options. He must then proceed to justification.

In justification, entries in the attribute transformation vectors are evaluated against the problem as encoded to determine whether one of them is erroneous, or whether a necessary entry is missing. The encoding itself may also be checked against the physical stimulus. The purpose of the operation is to justify some answer option as correct. Once justification is completed, the subject returns to the query asking whether all values of T are equal to zero. He once again tries to select one or the other option by then testing T_1 and T_2.

Need for justification can arise in three general ways. The first is an ambiguous item in which both presented answer options can be viewed as correct or equally close to the correct answer. The second is an item in which neither presented answer is quite correct, but one answer is better than the other. The third is subject error: The subject has generated a D'_k that is erroneous.

In Model III (Figure 6.12), processing also begins with the setting of two counters, T_1 and T_2, to 0. Processing then proceeds as in true–false Model III until mapping is completed. If the subject is on his first cycle through the big loop (which began when j was incremented by 1), he must encode two presented answer options, D_1 and D_2. He then sets the value of the jth attribute in the t^Z transformation vector equal to nullity. Next, he queries whether this value in the t^X transformation is null. If not, he must apply the relation Z and place the result in the jth position of the t^Z vector. This application process takes time z'. The subject then constructs the jth attribute of D', which is equal to the value of the jth attribute in t^Z.

The subject is now ready for option scanning. He sets the counter, s, equal to 0 and then increments it by 1. This counter keeps track of which option is being scanned. Next, he asks whether the value of the jth attribute of option D_s is equal to the value of the jth attribute of D'. If it is not, the truth index for that option is incremented by 1. After incrementing (if required), the subject asks whether he has tested attribute j on all n options. If he has (s equals n), then the subject proceeds to test the truth indices. If, however, there are more options left, he increments s by 1 again and tests attribute j on remaining options. When attribute j has been tested on all options, the subject asks whether all values of T equal 0. If they do, no falsification has occurred. The subject next asks whether all N features have been tested. If they have, the subject is in trouble, because he has completed attribute testing without falsifying either option. He must then justify an option. If all attributes have not been tested, the subject returns to the beginning of the big loop. In Model III, the big loop starts at the beginning of mapping operations (j is incremented by 1). In Model II, the loop would have started at the beginning of application operations, and in Model IV, it would have started at the beginning of inference operations.

Suppose that when all values of T are tested, at least one does not equal 0. Then the subject has falsified one or the other option and is prepared to test each value of T individually. First he asks whether T_1 equals 0. If it does, D_1 must be the correct answer, and the subject responds D_1. Response time is absorbed into the c parameter. If T_1 does not equal 0, the subject asks whether T_2 equals 0. If it does, D_2 must be correct, and the subject so responds. If T_2 does not equal 0, the subject has falsified both answers, and is in trouble. He must then justify one or the other answer (which takes time t).

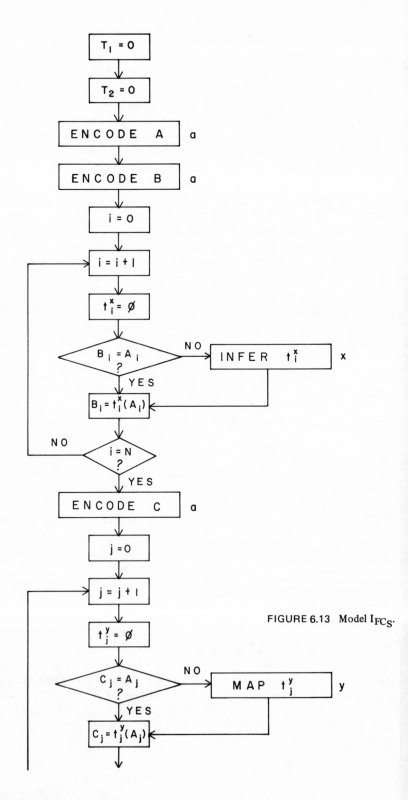

FIGURE 6.13   Model I_{FCS}.

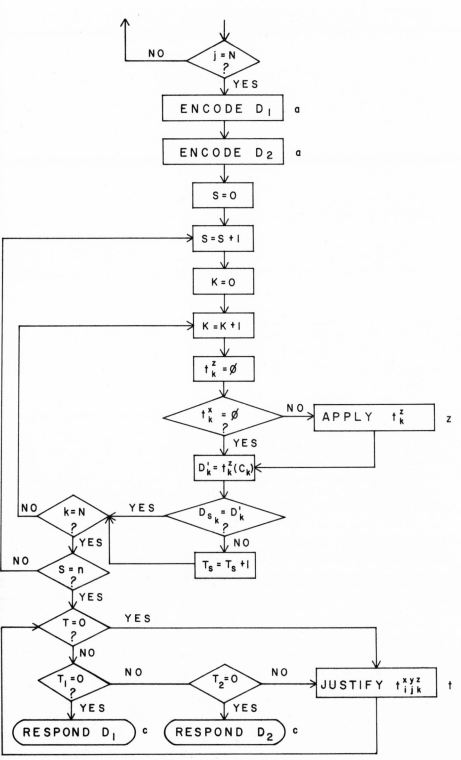

With two options, falsification of one option is tantamount to verification of the other (unless justification is needed). When items have more than two options, falsification of all but one option is tantamount to verification of that option. The models could be extended to cases in which more than two answer options are presented.

To summarize, alternating option scanning involves testing a single attribute on all options, then testing a second attribute on all options, and continuing until falsification. In Model I, option scanning is done after all inference, mapping, and application have been completed. In Models II, III, and IV, inability to select an option after a cycle results in a return to either application (Model II), mapping (Model III), or inference (Model IV).

Sequential option scanning. In sequential option scanning, all attributes of one option are scanned before any attributes of another option are scanned. Only the flow chart for Model I is presented (see Figure 6.13). The flow charts for the other models can be easily inferred from this one.

Model I for sequential scanning is the same as that for alternating option scanning through the encoding of D_2. After D_2 is encoded, the subject sets the s counter equal to 0, and then increments it by 1. This counter keeps track of which option is being scanned. The subject next sets the k counter equal to 0 and proceeds to increment that counter by 1. This counter keeps track of which attribute is being tested. The subject sets the value of the kth attribute in the t^Z transformation vector equal to nullity, and then tests whether this value in the t^X transformation vector was null. If not, then the corresponding value change is computed and entered into the t^Z vector. Application takes time z. The value of the kth attribute of D' is then set equal to the value of the kth attribute in the t^Z transformation vector.

The subject is now prepared to ask whether the value of the kth attribute of option D_s is equal to the value of D'_k. If it is not, the truth index for option s, T_s, is incremented by 1. The subject then inquires whether all attributes have been tested. If not, he returns to the beginning of the application loop, incrementing k by 1. If all attributes have been tested, the subject asks whether all options have been tested. If not, the subject returns to the point at which s is incremented by 1, and thereby prepares for testing the next option.

If all attributes of both options have been tested, the subject is prepared to respond. He first inquires whether all values of T equal 0. If so, he is in trouble, since no option has been falsified. He must then justify one option over the other. If at least one value of T is nonzero, then the subject proceeds to further testing of the truth indices. If T_1 equals 0, then D_1 is the correct answer. If T_2 equals 0, the subject has falsified both answers and must justify one or the other option.

In Models II, III, and IV, k need not equal N before testing of the truth indices occurs. The subject will attempt to falsify a single option as soon as possible and when this is done, he proceeds to the next option. He tests attributes only until one disconfirms the option, and then moves on to the next option. In these models, self-terminating operations are performed separately onto each option. In Model II, the subject applies transformations onto D_1, then onto D_2. In Model III, the subject maps and applies transformations onto D_1, then D_2. In Model IV, the subject infers, maps, and then applies transformations onto D_1, and then onto D_2.

To summarize, sequential option scanning differs from alternating option scanning in that all attributes of a given option are tested before the subject proceeds to the next option. In models with self-terminating attribute-comparison operations, only as many attributes of an option are tested as are needed to falsify that option.

Option Selection and Option Ranking Models

The analogy task of primary interest in this volume is option selection: The subject solves the analogy by selecting the best answer option. An alternative task, studied by Rumelhart and Abrahamson (1973) and Rips, Shoben, and Smith (1973) (see Chapters 5 and 10 for further details) requires ranking of alternatives in terms of their goodness of fit as answer options. At first thought, the ranking task would seem to be a simple extension of the selection task, but more careful examination of task requirements reveals that this is not the case. Use of a ranking task may well change a subject's solution strategy.

A model that is sufficient for option selection may not be sufficient for option ranking, although a model sufficient for option ranking will always be sufficient for option selection. In the componential theory, the "truth index" T_s for a given option D_s is incremented by 1 every time an attribute of D_s is falsified. Thus, a value of 0 indicates that the option is correct, and a value greater than 0 indicates that it is incorrect. In Model I, processing of all D_s is exhaustive, and hence the final value of T_s for each answer option D_s will equal the number of attributes by which D_s differs from the ideal answer, D'. These values of T_s may be used as a basis for ordering the options. Options are ranked in order of T_s, with higher values of T_s corresponding to higher ranks.

If application is self-terminating, as it is in Models II, III, and IV, then an option will be falsified as soon as T_s is equal to 1 (hence is false, because T_s exceeds 0). This falsification strategy can be quite efficient when the task is to select the best option, since processing time is not wasted on options that have already been falsified. The strategy does not provide a good basis for ranking alternatives, however, since all false answers will have a T_s value of 1. The ranking task, therefore, almost forces subjects to use the fully exhaustive Model I or a variant thereof. It is not a simple extension of the option selection task unless option selection proceeds via Model I.

A model for ranking will be complex unless (1) no errors are made; or (2) errors that are made are attributable to the c_e component alone. If either of these contingencies applies, then ranking of options depends only upon the value of T_s and therefore depends only upon the distance of each option from the ideal D'. This qualitative prediction is in agreement with the Rumelhart-Abrahamson theory. (A quantitative prediction would require adoption of a choice rule, such as the Luce Choice Axiom adopted by Rumelhart & Abrahamson, 1973.) Neither of these two contingencies applies, however, to any of the four experiments in this volume, including the Animal Name Analogy Experiment. In each experiment, error rates, no matter how small, differ significantly from 0 and derive from sources other than the c_e component. This means that rankings of options would be determined jointly by the distance of each option from D' and by errors made in the execution of analogy components.

7
The People Piece
Analogy Experiment

The first experiment in the series was the People Piece Analogy Experiment.[1] The experimental stimuli were People Pieces, schematic pictures of people varying on four binary attributes. The major dependent variable was solution time in solving the People Piece analogies. Subjects viewed each analogy in a tachistoscopic field and pressed the appropriate button on a button panel indicating whether the analogy was true or false. The analogy was true if the last term of the analogy was correct in all four attributes; otherwise it was false. The major independent variable, item difficulty, was manipulated by varying the number of values transformed between pairs of analogy terms, and by varying the amounts of precueing information.

In addition to solving People Piece analogies, subjects were asked to complete a number of pencil-and-paper ability tests. These were of three general types: reasoning, perceptual speed, and vocabulary.

Internal validation was accomplished by predicting solution times and error rates from indices of item difficulty. Four process models were then tested in their ability to account for the relationship. External validation was accomplished by correlating analogy solution times and process components with ability test scores.

METHOD

Materials

The experimental stimuli were Elementary Science Study (ESS) People Pieces, drawings of people varying on four binary attributes: height, girth, color, and

[1] I am grateful to Mary V. McGuire for serving as coexperimenter, and for her valuable help in many phases of the experiment.

FIGURE 7.1   Stimuli in the People Piece Experiment.

sex. The People Pieces are usually found in the form of plastic tiles, which elementary school children use in logic games. In the present experiment, the pictures were drawn on mimeograph stencil, reproduced, colored, and then pasted on 6 × 9-inch tachistoscope cards. The complete set of stimuli is presented in Figure 7.1. (The color of each piece, red or blue, is represented in the figure as white or black, respectively.)

Procedure

Pretesting. The experiment began with ability testing of an entire winter-quarter introductory psychology class at Stanford University. The class, Psychology 1, contained 268 students the day of the testing.

The ability tests were specially constructed for use in this experiment, although the item types used were similar and in some cases identical to those used by Thurstone (1938) in his studies of the primary mental abilities. Sample items from the tests are shown in Table 7.1.

In the first test, Word Grouping, subjects were presented with 25 rows of 5 words to a row and were given 2 min to draw a circle around the word in each row that did not belong with the others. In the second test, Same–Different Comparisons, subjects were given 70 sec to mark each of 48 pairs of numbers as same (S) or different (D). In the third test, Letter Series Completion, subjects were allowed 2 min, 45 sec, to complete 20 rows of series of letters that formed patterns. In the fourth test, Letter Identification, subjects had 70 sec to draw a slash through each *l* and a dot inside each *o* in 25 rows containing various letters of the alphabet.

A composite Reasoning score was formed by doubling the Letter Series score and adding to it the Word Grouping score. A composite Perceptual Speed score was formed by summing scores from the Same–Different Comparison and Letter Identification tests.

Subject selection. A computer printout was obtained for subjects falling into each of four groups: (1) subjects scoring above the 80th percentile on both Reasoning and Perceptual Speed (Hi–Hi); (2) subjects scoring above the 80th percentile on Reasoning and between the 10th and 30th percentiles on Percep-

TABLE 7.1
Items from the Subject Selection Tests

I. Word Grouping (reasoning): 25 items, 2 min
    19. (1) hammer   (2) wrench   (3) screwdriver   (4) nail   (5) drill
    21. (1) shoes   (2) dresses   (3) mittens   (4) stockings   (5) gloves

II. Same–Different Comparison (perceptual speed): 48 items, 70 sec
    11. 295699_____295699
    12. 372081_____342081

III. Letter Series (reasoning): 20 items, 2 min 45 sec
    3. d f h j (1) k (2) l (3) m (4) n
    14. c d c f g f i j (1) i (2) j (3) k (4) l

IV. Letter Identification (perceptual speed); 25 lines, 70 sec
    7. n t v l c k d f b n u o y p l v g b h p
    10. k o p e d n c l o v c w t r v n a l c h

tual Speed (Hi–Lo); (3) subjects scoring between the 10th and 30th percentiles on Reasoning and above the 80th percentile on Perceptual Speed (Lo–Hi); and (4) subjects scoring between the 10th and 30th percentiles on both Reasoning and Perceptual Speed (Lo–Lo). Subjects scoring below the 10th percentile on either test were excluded to eliminate those who willfully did poorly. Since the median proportion of shared variance, r^2, between reasoning and perceptual speed tests was only .046 in the subject pool, $N = 268$, the "pseudo-orthogonal" design probably had little effect on interpretation of correlational data to be reported.

Introductory session (Session 1). The introductory session began with a brief description of the 9-hr experiment and some remarks as to why it is important to understand how people solve analogies. Subjects were reminded that they could receive various combinations of pay ($2 per hour) and Psychology 1 experiment-participation credit. A bonus was paid for error rates under 5%.

Next, subjects were introduced to the People Pieces by means of two sorting tasks. Subjects were asked first to sort the pieces four times, once by each attribute. Then subjects were asked to sort the pieces six times, once for each pair of attributes.

Having completed the sorting task, subjects were retested on an alternate form of the ability test battery that had been given in class. After the retest, the People Piece analogy task was explained to each subject, and he was given 48 practice trials.

People Piece analogy testing (Sessions 2 to 5). People Piece analogy testing began during the second session, and continued through the fifth session. Testing sessions lasted an average of one hour and fifteen minutes each.

During People Piece analogy testing, subjects were seated in front of an Iconix 6137 three-field tachistoscope. Each of the 1152 test trials consisted of two parts, both initiated by the experimenter. The first part of the trial consisted of precueing, while the second part consisted of the full analogy.

The first part of the trial began with the appearance of a fixation point. This point was located at the spot where the first term of the analogy would appear. After 1000 msec, the fixation point vanished and a certain number of cues appeared on the screen. The number of cues could be either 0, 1, 2, or 3. In the zero-cue condition, a lighted but blank field appeared. In the one-cue condition, the first term of the analogy appeared; in the two-cue condition, the first two terms of the analogy appeared; and in the three-cue condition, the first three terms appeared. Subjects were given as long as they wanted to view whatever cues appeared, but were told that they would be timed on the cueing as well as the solution part of the analogy, so that they should take only as much time as they really needed. After a subject felt ready to continue, he pressed a red button in the center of a three-button response panel. The experimenter immediately initiated the second part of the trial.

The second part of the trial, like the first, began with the 1000-msec appearance of a fixation point. This point appeared immediately to the right of the last visible cue. The point was intended to guide subjects' eyes to the next term of the analogy that they would see, and to discourage looking back at terms that had been viewed during precueing. After the fixation point disappeared, the full analogy appeared on the viewing field. Analogies were in a true—false format, and subjects pressed either the left or the right button to indicate whether each analogy was true or false. Buttons were counterbalanced across subjects and groups so that two subjects in each ability group used their preferred hand, and two subjects their nonpreferred hand to designate a true response.

All testing sessions were conducted by two experimenters. One experimenter — the same person throughout the experiment — carried out the physical manipulation of the cards. She inserted the analogy card into the appropriate tachistoscope channel and also a cue-card overlay that covered up all but the cued terms of the analogy. The subject's pressing of the red center button on the response panel served as the signal to the experimenter to remove the cue-card overlay and then to start the second part of the trial. On each trial, the other experimenter recorded latency and error data.

Presentation of test items was divided into four blocks per testing session. Each block consisted of a different cueing condition, so that every cueing condition was presented during every session. Cueing conditions were ordered in a Latin square arrangement both between and within sessions. Items always occurred in a Latin square permutation of the cue order 0–1–2–3. One-fourth of the subjects, one in each ability group, began each session with each cueing condition.

Subjects received the same set of 288 items in each of the four testing sessions (for a total of 1152 trials), each time receiving a given item in a different cueing condition. The 288 test items were divided into four forms, matched item-by-item so as to be quasi-parallel. Form order remained the same for a given subject throughout the four sessions, although order of items within a given form was rerandomized each time the form was presented in a given test block. The forms were also arranged into a Latin square, but only across subjects, so that one subject in each ability group received each of the form orders 1–2–3–4, 2–3–4–1, 3–4–1–2, 4–1–2–3.

The four different cue presentation orders crossed with the four different form presentation orders permitted sixteen possible cue-form sequences. Each sequence was received by one of the 16 subjects. Thus, full counterbalancing of cue order with test form order occurred just once across all subjects and groups.

Further ability testing (Session 6). After analogy testing, each subject returned for a sixth session devoted to ability testing and debriefing. The order of testing was the same for each subject.

The first test was Finding As, Test P-1 in the French Kit of Reference Tests for

Cognitive Factors (French, Ekstrom, & Price, 1963). The test was in two parts, each timed for 2 min. The task was to scan columns of words and to cross out the five words in each column that had the letter *a* in them. The next test was Form A of the Cattell Culture-Fair Test of *g* (Cattell & Cattell, 1963), a difficult test of nonverbal reasoning. Total test time for the four subtests (excluding time for directions and practice items) was 12.5 min. The third test was Number Comparison, Test P-2 in the French Kit. This test (like the Same–Different Comparisons described earlier) required subjects to scan pairs of numbers, and to decide whether or not they were the same. If the numbers were the same, the subject was instructed to ignore the pair. If they were different, he was instructed to put an *X* on the line between them. The test was in two parts, each timed for 1.5 min. After completing the two parts, each subject was given a short rest period.

The fourth test in the series was Form B of the Cattell Culture-Fair Test of *g*. Like Form A, it consisted of four subtests timed for a total of 12.5 min. After completing the test, subjects were given Test P-3 in the French Kit, the Identical Pictures Test. The subject's task was to look at a picture of an object on the left and then choose one of five pictured objects on the right that exactly matched the object on the left. There were two parts to the test, each timed for 1.5 min. After the two parts were completed, subjects finished the testing by taking three vocabulary tests, Tests V-3, V-4, and V-5 in the French Kit. All were administered without time limit. Before leaving, subjects were asked to describe in as much detail as they could the procedures they had used in solving People Piece analogies. They were then debriefed about the experiment.

Final session (Session 7). The final session took place from two to five weeks after the ability testing session. Some of the tasks completed in this session are discussed in later chapters. One task is of interest here. This task called for People Piece Perceptual Similarity Ratings. There are 120 pairs of nonidentical People Pieces, and these pairs were printed in booklets of 12 pages each, 10 pairs to a page, with pages ordered in a Latin square. Subjects were asked to rate, on a nine-point scale (1 = extremely dissimilar; 9 = extremely similar), the "perceptual similarity" of each pair of pictures.

Similarity ratings for naive subjects. Seventy-two Psychology 1 subjects, otherwise uninvolved in the People Piece Analogy Experiment, also provided People Piece Perceptual Similarity Ratings. Administration was given in small groups immediately following subjects' participation in an unrelated experiment.

Subjects

The High Reasoning–High Perceptual Speed (Hi–Hi) group consisted of four men, all but one of whom were right-handed. The Hi–Lo group consisted of three right-handed men and one left-handed woman. The Lo—Hi and Lo—Lo groups were each composed of two men and two women, all right-handed.

Design

The four precueing conditions were crossed with 75 item types. Items differed in the number of attribute values changed from the A to B terms of the analogy ($A{:}B{:}{:}C{:}D$), in the number of values changed from the A to C terms of the analogy, and in the number of values by which the D term of the analogy differed from the correct answer, which will be labeled D'.

The number of values changed from A to B and from A to C were not independent. This nonindependence can be traced to item construction stipulations: (1) only *unidirectional* analogies were permissible; and (2) analogy falsification could not be accomplished without processing of the D term.

A unidirectional analogy is one in which the direction of the transformation matters. If, for example, color changed from red to blue in the A to B transformation, color had to change from red to blue in the C to D transformation in order for the analogy to be correct. It could not change from blue to red. If color did change from red to blue in the A to B transformation, then the C term of the analogy had to be red. Otherwise, subjects would have been able to falsify the analogy without even looking at the D term. If color did not change from A to B, then it might or might not change from A to C. The relationship between the A to B and A to C transformations can be summarized by the statement that the sum of the number of values changed from A to B and from A to C could not exceed 4.

The number of values changed from D to D' was independent of the number changed from A to B and from A to C. The number changed from D to D' was the number of values by which the analogy was incorrect. Thus, if this number was 0, the analogy was a true one. If the number was between 1 and 4, the analogy was false. Half the items were true and half were false, with equal numbers of analogies incorrect by 1, 2, 3, and 4 features.

In all, there were 15 possible combinations of A to B and A to C value changes. These were crossed with the 5 possible D to D' changes, for a total of 75 different item types in each cueing condition, of which 15 types were true items and 60 types were false items. Sample items of various types are shown in Figure 7.2. Red pieces are represented as white, blue pieces as black.

There were three kinds of items: degenerate, semidegenerate, and nondegenerate. The first pictured item is a degenerate one, or one in which the number of values changed both from A to B and from A to C is zero. These analogies are of the form, $A{:}A{:}{:}A{:}A;$ the fourth term of a true analogy will always match all the other terms. The pictured item is a true one.

The second pictured item is an example of a semidegenerate one, or one in which the number of values changed either from A to B, or from A to C (but not

FIGURE 7.2 Sample items from the People Piece Experiment.

both) is zero. These analogies are of the form, $A:A::B:B$, or $A:B::A:B$. The pictured item is of the latter form; it is, however, a false item, since the fourth term does not match the second. In general, the fourth term of a true semidegenerate analogy will always match either the second or the third analogy term.

The third and fourth pictured examples are nondegenerate analogies of the standard form, $A:B::C:D$. In true nondegenerate analogies, the fourth term will not match any other term of the analogy. The third pictured item is true, and the fourth item is false. There were 16 degenerate analogies, 128 semidegenerate analogies, and 144 nondegenerate analogies, with equal numbers of true and false analogies in each category.

INTERNAL VALIDATION

Interval Scores

Terminology. Interval scores are mean response times for subjects in individual cueing conditions. They are of two kinds. Cue scores (or times) are mean response times for the first part of the analogy trial, from the onset of the cue to the pressing by the subject of the "ready" button that blanks out the cues. Solution scores (or times) are mean response times for the second part of the analogy trial, from the onset of the full analogy to the indication by the subject of either a true or false response. The symbols $C0$, $C1$, $C2$, and $C3$ refer to cue times in the zero-, one-, two-, and three-cue conditions. Similarly, the symbols $S0$, $S1$, $S2$, and $S3$ refer to solution times in the zero-, one-, two-, and three-cue conditions. The expressions *cue time* and *cue score,* or *solution time* and *solution score,* are used interchangeably.

Basic statistics. Table 7.2 presents means and standard deviations for each of the cue and solution times (scores), both overall and for the first and last sessions. The number of observations in this and subsequent tables is the number of data points (subjects × items) on which each mean is based. For example, the overall cue and solution scores were each based upon 4608 observations – 16 subjects × 288 items.

As expected, cue times increased and solution times decreased with more cues. Cue and solution time variabilities varied directly with means: higher mean response times were paired with higher standard deviations, and vice versa. Response times (for both cue and solution scores) decreased from the first to the last session. The amount of the decrease was greater for higher response times, which presumably reflected larger numbers of component operations.

Reliabilities. The split-halves reliabilities of the interval scores were calculated by correlating separate scores for odd and even numbered items and then correcting the resulting correlations by the Spearman–Brown formula. Reliabil-

TABLE 7.2
Basic Statistics for Scores in People Piece Experiment:
Interval Scores[2] (N = 16)

	Mean	Standard deviation	Number of observations
Cue scores			
Overall			
$C0$	530	131	4608
$C1$	755	187	4608
$C2$	952	261	4608
$C3$	1147	363	4608
Session 1			
$C0$	635	200	1152
$C1$	990	417	1152
$C2$	1352	554	1152
$C3$	1540	844	1152
Session 4			
$C0$	460	129	1152
$C1$	574	154	1152
$C2$	731	235	1152
$C3$	917	303	1152
Solution scores			
Overall			
$S0$	1423	235	4608
$S1$	1328	222	4608
$S2$	947	193	4608
$S3$	681	170	4608
Session 1			
$S0$	1646	319	1152
$S1$	1587	288	1152
$S2$	1173	251	1152
$S3$	820	205	1152
Session 4			
$S0$	1277	245	1152
$S1$	1153	195	1152
$S2$	820	187	1152
$S3$	618	181	1152

[2] Response times are expressed in milliseconds.

ities were extremely high, ranging from .98 to .99+. These high reliabilities indicate that there was very little error in the interval scores, so that one can have confidence in subsequent analyses based upon these scores. The interval-score simplex model is such an analysis.

Simplex model. An assumption of componential analysis is that interval scores are additive. The assumption works in opposite directions for cue and solution scores. Thus, it is assumed that $C1$ contains all the processes contained in $C0$ plus additional processes; $C2$ contains all the processes contained in $C1$ plus additional processes; and $C3$ contains all the processes contained in $C2$ plus additional processes. In other words, $C3$ contains $C2$, which contains $C1$, which contains $C0$. Conversely, it is assumed that $S0$ contains $S1$, which contains $S2$, which contains $S3$. Cue scores for higher cue conditions contain more processes, but solution scores for higher cue conditions contain fewer processes. We consider only the scores of primary interest, the solution scores.

The additivity assumption holds if the cueing conditions truly capture successive intervals of processing — if they break up the whole task into overlapping chunks. The additivity assumption fails if the cueing conditions somehow change the task — if the presentation of cues alters the way subjects go about solving the problems. Since subsequent analyses will assume additivity, it is important to demonstrate at the outset that the additivity assumption is a viable one.

TABLE 7.3
People Piece Solution Score Simplex Model

I. Correlations

Predicted variable	Predictor variable			
	$S0$	$S1$	$S2$	$S3$
$S0$	1.00	.95	.80	.72
$S1$	–	1.00	.91	.80
$S2$	–	–	1.00	.88
$S3$	–	–	–	1.00

II. F values for standardized regression coefficients

Predicted variable	Predictor variable				R^2
	$S0$	$S1$	$S2$	$S3$	
$S0$	–	53.0**	3.5	0.2	.93
$S1$	53.0**	–	11.4**	0.2	.97
$S2$	3.5	11.4**	–	6.7*	.91
$S3$	0.2	0.2	6.7*	–	.78

III. Raw regression coefficients for simplex model

Predicted variable	Predictor variable				Constant	R^2
	$S0$	$S1$	$S2$	$S3$		
$S0$	–	1.01	–	–	81.34	.91
$S1$	.60	–	0.46	–	40.17	.97
$S2$	–	0.48	–	0.50	–30.38	.89
$S3$	–	–	0.78	–	–56.26	.78

*$p < .05$.   **$p < .01$.

If the additivity assumption holds, then the succession of solution scores should form a simplex (see Chapter 4). If the scores form a simplex, then the intercorrelation matrices for solution scores should show a certain property: Correlations near the principal diagonal of a matrix should be high, and they should taper off monotonically as entries move further away from the principal diagonal. It is possible to verify this prediction for the People Piece interval scores by examining Panel I of Table 7.3. The correlation matrices for solution times all show simplicial structure, with no breakdowns at all. Correlations decrease as they move away from the principal diagonal.

Because of the overlapping nature of interval scores, a second prediction can be made. If each interval score is predicted from every other interval score, then only predictor interval scores immediately adjacent to the predicted interval score will contribute significant variance to the prediction. The reason for this prediction is that since nonadjacent interval scores either contain or are contained in adjacent interval scores, any variance contained in the nonadjacent scores that is not also contained in the adjacent ones should be uncorrelated with the predicted variable. This prediction may be tested in two ways.

The first test requires that only standardized partial regression coefficients (β weights) for variables adjacent to the predicted variable should be statistically significant. An examination of the F values in Table 7.3 reveals that this prediction is confirmed (see Panel II). Only adjacent variables yielded statistically significant β weights; other β weights were trivial.

The second test of the prediction requires that values of R^2 (the squared multiple correlation coefficient) computed from variables adjacent to the predicted variable should be equal to or trivially less than values of R^2 predicted from nonadjacent as well as adjacent variables. A comparison of the values of R^2 in Panels II and III of Table 7.13 reveals that this was the case. The values of R^2 in Panel III (based upon adjacent variables only) were in all cases equal to or trivially less than values of R^2 in Panel II (based upon nonadjacent as well as adjacent variables). Both tests of the second prediction show that nonadjacent variables contributed only trivial prediction to each successive solution score, again confirming the simplicial structure of the solution scores.

Panel III of the table displays the solution-score simplex model. The table indicates, for example, that using regression estimates, $S1 = (0.60)S0 + (0.46)S2 + 40.17$, where $S0$, $S1$, $S2$, and the additive constant are expressed in milliseconds. The regression weights must be interpreted cautiously, because the predictor variables are highly intercorrelated. However, they do quite well. This equation accounts for 97% of the variance in $S1$. Overall, the simplex model is successful in predicting the solution scores.

Error Rates

Error rates were very low in the People Piece Experiment, ranging from .5% to 2.6%, with a mean of 1.4%. These very low error rates were probably attributable in part to the easiness of the items, and in part to the instructions, which encouraged very low error rates and offered a bonus for them. As expected, error rates decreased with greater amounts of precueing, and decreased across sessions, with the major drop occurring between Sessions 1 and 2.

Correlations across subjects between error rates and solution scores show a clear speed–accuracy tradeoff. These correlations ranged from −.53 to −.70, with a median of −.62. Across item types, however, there was a positive correlation of .64 between solution latencies and error rates: Harder items took longer to solve.

Component Scores

Mathematical formulation of the models. The mathematical modeling to be described was done by linear multiple regression. Solution times for 300 data points were used as the criterion to be predicted. Each of the 300 data points represented a different item type (15 value-change possibilities from A to B and A to $C \times 5$ value-change possibilities from D to D' $\times$ 4 cueing conditions). Since there were at least two items of each type, each of the 300 data points is an average of solution times for at least two items (and as many as twelve items). In the regressions, each of the 300 points was weighted by the number of observations that went into it. The predictors were numbers of terms to be encoded and functions of numbers of value changes, and the parameters of the models were the estimated unstandardized regression coefficients.

Table 7.4 shows the basic equations for Models I, II, III, and IV. All parameters of each model enter into analogy processing in the zero-cue condition. The subjects must encode all four terms of the analogy, as well as perform the inference, mapping, application, and preparation–response processes. The one-cue condition differs only slightly, requiring the encoding of just three analogy terms rather than all four. The first term is presented during precueing, and it is assumed that it is encoded at that time. In the two-cue condition, there is yet one less term to encode, and the inference parameter drops out as well. Since the A and B terms of the analogy are precued, it is assumed that inference occurs during precueing. In the three-cue condition, there is only one term left to encode, and the mapping parameter drops out. Since the A and C terms are available during precueing, it is assumed that mapping occurs at that time. In general, the successive cueing conditions are characterized by the successive dropout of model parameters.

Although they are not shown in the figure, parameter dropouts also occurred through null transformations in which zero values were changed from A to B and/or from A to C. These dropouts occurred in the degenerate and semidegenerate analogies. (Indeed, these types of analogies involving zero value changes were originally included for the purpose of providing a zero baseline for parameter estimation.) For example, in the zero-cue condition, the inference and application parameters drop out when zero values are changed from A to B, and

TABLE 7.4
Basic Equations for the Models
of Analogical Reasoning

Model I

0 cues	$ST_0 = 4a +$	$fx +$	$gy +$	$fz + c$
1 cue	$ST_1 = 3a +$	$fx +$	$gy +$	$fz + c$
2 cues	$ST_2 = 2a +$		$gy +$	$fz + c$
3 cues	$ST_3 = a +$			$fz + c$

Model II

0 cues	$ST_0 = 4a +$	$fx +$	$gy +$	$f'z' + c$
1 cue	$ST_1 = 3a +$	$fx +$	$gy +$	$f'z' + c$
2 cues	$ST_2 = 2a +$		$gy +$	$f'z' + c$
3 cues	$ST_3 = a +$			$f'z' + c$

Model III

0 cues	$ST_0 = 4a +$	$fx +$	$g'y' +$	$f'z' + c$
1 cue	$ST_1 = 3a +$	$fx +$	$g'y' +$	$f'z' + c$
2 cues	$ST_2 = 2a +$		$g'y' +$	$f'z' + c$
3 cues	$ST_3 = a +$			$f'z' + c$

Model IV

0 cues	$ST_0 = 4a +$	$f'x' +$	$g'y' +$	$f'z' + c$
1 cue	$ST_1 = 3a +$	$f'x' +$	$g'y' +$	$f'z' + c$
2 cues	$ST_2 = 2a +$		$g'y' +$	$f'z' + c$
3 cues	$ST_3 = a +$			$f'z' + c$

Symbol Definitions

ST_i = solution time i

a = exhaustive figure scanning and encoding time

x = exhaustive inference time

y = exhaustive mapping time

z = exhaustive application time

x' = self-terminating inference time

y' = self-terminating mapping time

z' = self-terminating application time

c = constant preparation and response time

N = total number of features

T = truth index (0 = true; 1 = false)

f = number of features changed from A to B

g = number of features changed from A to C

h = number of D features correctly matched to D'

f' = $[(N + T)/(N - h + 1)] \times (f)/(N)$

g' = $[(N + T)/(N - h + 1)] \times (g)/(N)$

the mapping parameter drops out when zero values are changed from A to C. The same type of selective dropout occurs in all four cueing conditions, so that multiple estimates of all parameters can be obtained.

The models as formulated make separate attribute-comparison "time charges" only for value transformations. Value identities are not separately charged. Recognizing them is assumed to require trivial amounts of time, and they are generally absorbed into the base time parameter (c). This type of "difference" parameter is used throughout the experiments and has been used by others as well (e.g., Clark & Chase, 1972). The rationale underlying it is that subjects are preset to expect "sames." This initial state is altered for a value transformation, and the attribute-comparison parameters measure the amount of time required for alteration of the initial state.

Reliability.   The internal consistency (split-halves) reliability of the data was .972.

Experimental data.   Figures 7.3 and 7.4 show the data for item types in each cueing condition. Figure 7.3 shows solution times for true items in each cue condition, and Figure 7.4 shows solution times as a function of truth or degree of falsity (D to D' value changes).

Solution times for nondegenerate items, shown by filled circles, conform to four major qualitative predictions of the self-terminating models (II, III, IV): (1) slopes across numbers of value changes decrease with higher numbers of cues, since fewer processes per value change are involved in solution as attribute-comparison operations drop out; (2) curves are displaced downward with higher numbers of cues, since less encoding is required as picture encodings drop out; (3) true solution times are slower than false solution times, since in self-terminating models true items require more attribute comparisons, on the average, than do false items; (4) solution time decreases with increasing degree of falsity (Figure 7.4): The more incorrect the analogy, the more quickly it is solved. With regard to this last prediction, Figure 7.4 shows that even the acceleration of the curve across D to D' value changes is as predicted by the self-terminating models. The data for the nondegenerate items, therefore, are in good qualitative agreement with the predictions of the self-terminating models.

The semidegenerate analogies, shown by white circles, reveal an unexpected pattern. Solution times for the semidegenerate analogies show no slope across value changes whatsoever! If zero values are changed from A to B, then it does not matter how many values are changed from A to C: Solution times do not increase across value changes, regardless of the truth or falsity of the item, or of the cueing condition in which the item was solved. Similarly, if zero values are changed from A to C, then it does not matter how many values are changed from A to B: Solution times again do not increase across value changes, regardless of truth or falsity or of cueing condition. A final unexpected pattern of data is found in Figure 7.4. Solution times for false items decrease with

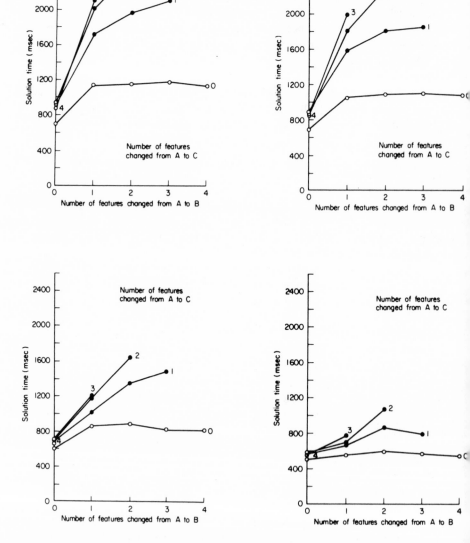

FIGURE 7.3   Solution times for feature changes: true analogies.

increasing degree of falsity, but solution times for true items are lower than for any of the false item types except that in which all four values are incorrect! In general, then, true items are faster than false ones, a reversal of the predicted pattern and the pattern found for nondegenerate items. Error data for different item types in each of the four cueing conditions show the same patterns of results. First, error rates are higher for nondegenerate analogies than for degenerate and semidegenerate ones. Second, for nondegenerate items, true error rates are higher than false error rates, whereas, for degenerate and semidegenerate items, the pattern is clearly reversed. Third, for nondegenerate items, error rates tend to increase with increasing item complexity (as measured by greater numbers of value changes). For semidegenerate items, however, there is no such pattern. Error rates are approximately constant across item complexities.

What kind of model or models would account for data such as those presented above? Subjects' introspective comments suggest the outlines that a model would have to take:

S2: Special instances applicable were when all figures were the same, and I could perceive it then true. . . . Special instances (a) 2 figures same – look for 2 same, (b) one incongruent figure.

S3: . . . if the relationship was simple (i.e., equality), I just saw if the last two had it.

S4: Look to see if just two are same – then second [two] must be same, etc.

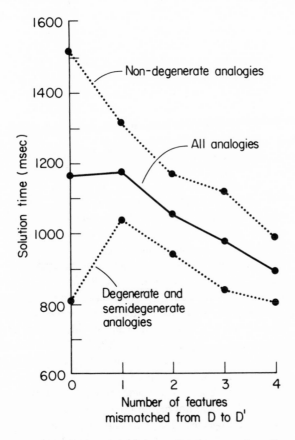

FIGURE 7.4   Solution times for feature mismatches: all cues.

S5: I began looking for obvious dissimilarity (i.e., 3 red, 1 blue). . . . Also I would notice for very obvious similarities (all four alike), (2 + 2 alike).

S7: I usually make a preliminary scan. . . . I just looked at the figures quickly and pushed *true* if it 'felt' right. . . . Again, if my preliminary 'scan' didn't solve the analogy, then I was forced to 'solve' it.

S11: I looked for simple match-ups . . . between pix 1 + 3. If they were similar, I continued checking 1 + 2 with 3 + 4 to see if other matchups occurred.

S12: First of all, I would look to see if there was any obvious incongruity between the 4 people. . . . At the same time I would look to see if they were all the same or 2 and 2 of the same. If I still couldn't tell, I'd figure out the first analogy and compare it to the second.

S16: I scanned for obvious difference; 1 different height or 1 different color. Also looked for identical pairs and knew 2nd pair must be matching too. That all happened quickly without thought.

Dual processing.　Comments such as these strongly suggest that subjects solved the analogies in two stages. In the first stage, holistic processing, subjects quickly scanned the terms of the analogy for identities between two or more terms (and possibly for glaring incongruities in the fourth term). In the second stage, subjects performed the types of attribute-processing described by the models as formulated in Chapter 6.

The data suggest that the holistic scan and attribute comparison occur in parallel, as in Bamber's (1969) model. The holistic scan does not seem to add any amount of time to nondegenerate analogy latencies. Thus, holistic and attribute processing are assumed to start simultaneously. Holistic processing either reaches or fails to reach a solution before attribute processing is completed. If holistic processing is successful, an answer is chosen and attribute processing is terminated. Otherwise, attribute processing continues until a solution is reached.

Dual-processing component models.　Incorporation of dual processing into the analogical reasoning component models might be accomplished in two ways: (1) by adding one or more new parameters to the models, thereby creating separate parameters for same—different and attribute-processing operations; (2) by reconceptualizing the existing parameters so that the same parameters account for both same—different and attribute-processing operations. The latter course of action was taken here: It is simpler and it proved to be adequate.

In reconceptualizing the existing parameters, it was necessary to introduce only two new assumptions: (1) in degenerate and semidegenerate analogies, all attribute comparison is same—different; (2) "different" transformations take longer than "same" (null) ones. In nondegenerate analogies, attributes are processed as hypothesized by the original models.

There are two major implications of the new assumptions. First, if zero values are changed from A to B, it does not matter how many values are changed from A to C, if any values are changed at all. Similarly, if zero values are changed from A to C, it does not matter how many values are changed from A to B, if any values are changed at all. If the number of values changed from both A to B and from A to C is nonzero, then numbers of both A to B and A to C value changes do affect predicted processing times.

Second, a "same" match from D to D' is assumed to be faster than a "different" mismatch. Whereas, in nondegenerate analogies, subjects attempt to falsify the D term on an attribute-by-attribute basis, in semidegenerate and degenerate analogies, subjects attempt to match the D term to either the B or the C term. Thus, for semidegenerate and degenerate analogies, true responses are predicted to be faster than false responses, whereas the reverse is true for nondegenerate analogies.

Consider as examples the first two items in Figure 7.2. Holistic processing reveals that at least two terms match. In the first term, the subject can match D against either B or C. The match is successful; therefore the item is true. In the second item, D must be matched against B. The match is unsuccessful; therefore the item is false. Consideration of individual attributes is unnecessary, since solution can be accomplished through picture matching.

Mathematically, the identical equations are used for both types of processing. The only difference in attribute values is that for semidegenerate and degenerate analogies. In these analogies, a match is treated identically to zero value changes, and a mismatch is treated identically to one value change. Thus, the number of "values changed" is always zero (match) or one (mismatch).

How well do the dual-processing models fit the data? Model I accounts for 75.5% of the variance in the data, Model II for 84.7% of the variance in the data, Model III for 91.8% of the variance in the data, and Model IV for 90.8% of the variance in the data. (These percentages compare to 55.5%, 59.7%, 62.1%, and 61.9% without dual processing.) Model I can be discounted as providing a much poorer fit than any of the competing models. Model II also provides a poorer fit than the best models. The results do not enable one to distinguish well between Models III and IV, and indeed, no data obtained in this experiment permitted an unequivocal decision. The usual pattern was for Model III to be just slightly better than Model IV.

Variants of the four models were also considered. These variants make different processing assumptions about the way in which analogies are solved, but leave most of the fundamental features of the dual-processing models intact.

Dual processing in application only.   One variant assumes that dual processing occurs during application only, rather than during inference, mapping, and application. In other words, a global comparison is made only when the subject attempts to accept or reject the D term of the analogy. At this point, he uses a match–mismatch process rather than a process of successive attempts to falsify the D term. Although such a variant of the models is considerably better than the original models, it is worse than the models allowing dual processing throughout the solution process. All fits are reduced by from 3% (Models II and IV) to 20% (Model I).

Self-terminating encoding. A second variant assumes self-terminating encoding. In all the models discussed so far, it has been assumed that encoding of each term is exhaustive, occurring all at once. The rationale underlying such an assumption is that subjects are likely to treat analogy terms as wholes, encoding all attributes of the terms at once. The possible disadvantage of such an encoding scheme is that one may encode attributes that have no relevance to solution of the analogy. With self-terminating encoding, it would be possible to check for relevance, one attribute at a time.

In the self-terminating encoding variant models, it was assumed that exhaustive encoding was used for analogy terms processed by exhaustive attribute-comparison operations and self-terminating encoding was used for terms processed by self-terminating comparison operations. This assumption was necessary because self-terminating encoding cannot be used prior to exhaustive attribute-comparison operations, since all attributes are compared in exhaustive comparisons. In Model I, all attribute comparisons were exhaustive, and so all encodings were. The model was therefore identical to the standard dual-processing Model I. In Model II, application was self-terminating, and so self-terminating encoding began with the D term. In Model III, mapping was also self-terminating, and self-terminating encoding began with the C term. In Model IV, inference was also self-terminating, so self-terminating encoding began with the B term. All models provided slightly poorer fits under this assumption (except Model I, which was identical to the standard dual-processing Model I) than under the assumption of exhaustive encoding. Reductions in fit ranged from 1% for Model III to 10% for Model IV. There is thus no evidence to support an assumption of self-terminating encoding from the point at which self-terminating attribute comparison begins.

No mapping. A major distinction between the proposed componential theory of analogical reasoning and many previous ones is the inclusion of a mapping component. On the basis of the experimental evidence for People Piece analogies, the existence of a mapping component is strongly supported. In fact, it proves to be the most time-consuming attribute-comparison operation in all four of the standard dual-processing models. However, the question arises as to whether it would make much difference if the component were omitted from the models. The predictive power of the models is considerably reduced when the mapping component is omitted, with reductions in fit of from 10% (Models I and IV) to 13% (Model III). The component thus appears to be a necessary one.

Solution comparison. All of the models described so far assume that in the application process, subjects apply the analogous relation from C to D. It is possible, however, to split application into two smaller processes. In the first, the subject applies the analogous rule from C to D', forming an image of the correct answer. In the second process, he compares D' to the given answer. This model separates solution comparison, w', which is assumed to be self-terminating, from a more limited form of application, z. It has been assumed up to now that in the three-cue condition, application occurs during the second part of the trial. In this new model, it is assumed that application (of the more limited sort) occurs during the first part of the trial: During the cueing, subjects form an image of the correct answer, D'. Solution comparison is assumed to occur during the second part of the trial: Subjects compare the attribute values of the image (D') to the values of the given answer (D), attempting to falsify the given answer. Since application is split up, the model has six parameters: a, x, y, z, w', c. The model accounts for 88% of the variance in the data. Even with the additional parameter, the model is not as good as Model III.

Weighted attribute models. In the models described so far, it has been assumed that comparisons of all pairs of attributes are equally difficult. This assumption is not necessarily correct, and weighting of value changes on attributes might improve prediction.

A major purpose for collecting the People Piece Perceptual Similarity Ratings, both from naive and from analogy subjects, was to supply weights for use in solution-time modeling. Weighted models were compared using both raw and multidimensionally scaled ratings of both naive and analogy subjects. Since subjects had not been asked to provide ratings for identical pieces, regression estimates were used for null value-change relations.

It was necessary to test the models on the full set of 1152 data points (288 items X 4 cue conditions), since under the weighted models, no two predicted points were identical: Although multiple items had the same *numbers* of values changed from A to B, A to C, and D to D', no two items had the *identical values* changed.

In order to provide a baseline against which to compare the weighted models, the unweighted models were also tested using the full set of data points. Because there were 1147 degrees of freedom for residual (compared to 295 in the earlier tests), the predictive power of the models dropped by about 9%. The drop in predictive power of the unweighted models was almost uniform across models. They retained the same rank ordering of predictive power as they had demonstrated for testing based upon the reduced set of 300 points.

The results of the weighted model comparison can be summarized rather simply. First, the scaled ratings provided better prediction than did the raw ones. Second, ratings of analogy subjects were slightly more predictive of the data than were ratings of naive subjects. Third, the scaled ratings provided about the same level of prediction as the unweighted distances, while the raw ratings provided poorer prediction.

Taken as a whole, the comparison between the weighted and unweighted models shows that there is no loss in predictive power when unweighted models are used. Since these models are simpler than the weighted ones, the unweighted ones are preferred.

First and last sessions. To this point, we have compared models on the basis of data collected over the full four sessions of analogy testing. However, it is not obvious that the same model fitting data from early test trials should fit data from later ones. Indeed, within-subjects experiments are often criticized on just these sorts of grounds (e.g., Poulton, 1973). It is therefore advisable to compare model fits for earlier and later sessions.

The dual-processing models were applied to data taken from the first session only and from the last session only. Experimental variables were not fully counterbalanced over single sessions, so that the reduction in fit is difficult to interpret when compared to that for the full set of data. However, it is reasonable to compare performance of the models for the two individual sessions, and they performed almost identically well in each session. Moreover, Models III and IV are again clearly superior to Models I and II, although Models III and IV are once again virtually indistinguishable. The respective percentages of variance accounted for by Models I to IV were 48.2, 67.7, 77.0, and 77.6%, respectively, for Session 1, and 47.2, 65.8, 77.1, and 78.5%, respectively, for Session 4.

Parameter estimates changed from the first to the last session. All models showed sizable decreases in the values of all parameters except the inference parameter, which showed a small increase. The small increase was probably due to chance.

Final component model. On the basis of the entire set of data, the preferred analogical reasoning model for the People Piece Experiment is the unweighted form of Model III that incorporates dual processing. Detailed statistics describing the model are presented in Table 7.5. Parameter estimates were highly reliable. Each regression parameter is equal to at least 10 times its standard error, and as a result, the regression Fs for the parameters are highly significant.

The stepwise multiple-regression data are shown in the bottom part of the table. The first variable to enter into the stepwise equation was y', and the last variable to enter in was z'. The increments in the squared multiple correlation of the predicted with observed solution times show that each parameter made a substantial practical contribution as well as a statistically significant one, and the simple correlations show that each parameter predicts quite well singly as well as in combination with the others.

One reassuring and relatively unusual aspect of the data is that the regression F for the entire set of parameters is larger than the regression F for any of the previous subsets. This result lends further credence to the hypothesis that all parameters are needed in order to model the analogical reasoning process adequately. Overall, Model III accounted for 92% of the variance in the data, with a root-mean-square deviation of 130 msec.

The parameter estimates for attribute-comparison components reflect the amount of time taken per value change. However, the average number of

TABLE 7.5

Final People Piece Component Model III

Parameter	Time (msec)	Standard error	β	F_{Reg}	df
a	140	9	0.34	227	1, 295
x	130	13	0.23	95	1, 295
y'	324	15	0.46	478	1, 295
z'	154	13	0.27	148	1, 295
c	452				

Stepwise Multiple Regression

Parameter	Cumulative R^2	r	Cumulative F_{Reg}	Cumulative df
y'	.66	.81	569	1, 298
x	.84	.74	805	2, 297
a	.88	.64	706	3, 296
z'	.92	.58	829	4, 295

Standard error of estimate: 131 msec
Root-mean-square deviation: 130 msec

F_{Res}: .77   295, 852 df

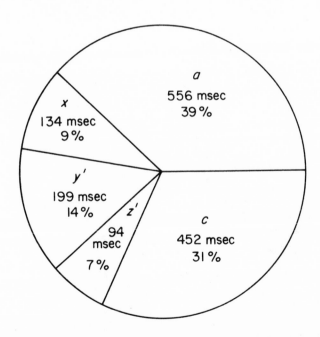

FIGURE 7.5 Distribution of component time on a typical People Piece analogy.

attributes processed by each comparison component was not the same. In general, more attributes will be processed by an exhaustive component, such as x, than by a self-terminating one, such as y' or z'. Figure 7.5 partitions the amount of time spent on a typical analogy into the amount of time spent on each of the five components. The figure shows that 70% of total processing time was taken up by encoding (a) and preparation and response processes (c). Only 30% of total time was spent on attribute-comparison processing, with the most time spent on mapping (y') and the least time spent on application (z'). The total amount of time spent on this average analogy was 1435 msec.

Figure 7.6 shows a scatterplot of predicted (abscissa) versus observed (ordinate) solution times for Model III. The times on the axes are in milliseconds. Mean solution times for the 300-item types ranged from 511 msec to 2461 msec, a range of almost 2 sec. Mean solution time for the 300 data points was 1095 msec, with a standard deviation of 455 msec. The scatterplot is reasonably homoscedastic: Points tend to cluster at a fairly uniform distance from the regression line, and there are no points that are grossly mispredicted. The quality of prediction is high throughout the entire 2-sec range of solution times.

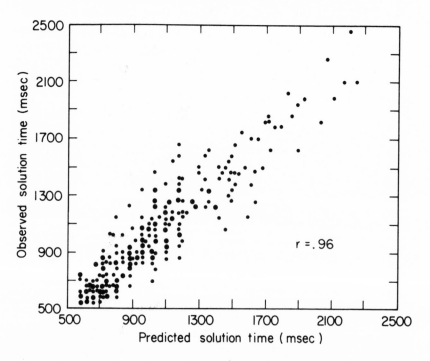

FIGURE 7.6   Scatter plot of predicted versus observed solution times for Model III in the People Piece Experiment.

Final model for full analogies only. What would have happened if modeling was done solely on the basis of the full analogy task, the zero-cue solution scores? We already know that one result would have been confounded parameter estimates. However, Model III is one of the least confounded. Only the encoding and preparation–response components are indistinguishable in the zero-cue condition. Parameter estimates for the other components should be comparable in the zero-cue condition to those for the four conditions considered together. The confounded parameter in the zero-cue condition should be equal to $4a + c$, since the preparation–response component remains constant in each cueing condition, and since it is necessary to encode all four terms of the analogy in the zero-cue condition.

In the zero-cue condition (considered in isolation), Model III accounted for 89% of the variance in the data, with $(3, 71)$ degrees of freedom. This percentage reflects a reduction of only 3% from the 92% figure obtained with the full data set. The value of the confounded $(4a + c)$ component was 982 msec, which differed by just 3% from the value that would have been predicted on the basis of the parameter estimates for the full set of data. The value of x was 119 msec, which differed by 8% from the estimate for all the data; the value of y' was 327 msec, which differed by 1%; the value of z' was 189 msec, which differed by 23%. The only sizable discrepancy, then, was in the estimate of the z' parameter, and even this difference of 39 msec has little if any practical significance. The z' parameter estimate is still somewhat larger than those for the a and x' parameters, and still much smaller than those for the y' and c parameters. The overall character of the model is unchanged.

Would Model III still have been the preferred model if only full analogies (zero cues) were used in the experiment? It is more difficult to compare models in the zero-cue condition alone than across conditions, because of confoundings in parameters. In Models I and IV, it was possible to estimate three parameters, only one of which (mapping) was unconfounded. In Models II and III, it was possible to estimate four parameters, with inference, mapping, and application all unconfounded. The respective fits of Models I–IV were 65, 82, 89, and 88%. Models III and IV are again clearly superior to Models I and II, but the comparison between III and IV is indecisive.

Final model for nondegenerate analogies only. Since most "analogy tests" do not include semidegenerate and degenerate analogies, one might wonder how the models would have fared if only nondegenerate analogies were included in the People Piece Experiment.

The conclusions drawn regarding the relative fits of the models would have been identical. Models III and IV are still indistinguishable, both accounting for 93% of the variance in the data. Model II appears worse, accounting for 85% of the variance in the data. Model I remains the worst model, accounting for 71%

of the variance in the data. All percentage estimates are based upon (4, 115) degrees of freedom.

Parameter estimates for Model III are 174 msec for a, 84 msec for x, 317 msec for y', 163 msec for z', and 396 msec for c. These parameter estimates are generally in the same ranges as the estimates for the full set of analogies, with only one sizable discrepancy, that for x. Again, however, the discrepancy does not substantially affect interpretation of the model.

Component models for error rates. The component models described so far have all been for solution time data. However, the componential theory is claimed to be applicable to errors as well.

Because there were so few errors (fewer than 1.5% of responses), the data base for modeling error rates is much less substantial than that for solution times. Error rates may be modeled nevertheless, simply substituting error probability for solution time as the dependent variable. (Actually, number of errors was used, although since number of errors and error probability are perfectly correlated, either measure could be used with essentially identical results.)

Models were compared with the number of errors as the dependent variable, but with the identical independent variables as those for solution times. Degenerate and semidegenerate analogies were excluded, because almost no errors were made on such items. The analyses were also performed with degenerate and semidegenerate items included, and the results were comparable except for some reductions (about 10%) in percent of variance accounted for. Excluding all items on which no errors were made resulted in comparable reductions in fit.

Model III does quite well, accounting for 59% of the variance in the error data. This percentage is remarkable in view of the small number of errors made. Model

TABLE 7.6
Final People Piece Component Model III for Errors

Parameter	Raw regression coefficient	Standard error	β	F_{Reg}	df
y'_e	.56	.06	.52	93	1, 147
z'_e	.50	.06	.48	80	1, 147
c_e	.77				

Stepwise Multiple Regression

Parameter	Cumulative R^2	r	Cumulative F_{Reg}	Cumulative df
y'_e	.36	.60	83	1, 148
z'_e	.59	.57	104	2, 147

Rejected

a_e	.59	.25	70	3, 146
x_e	.59	.24	52	4, 145

IV, as usual, is almost indistinguishable from Model III, accounting for 60% of the variance in the data. Model II is noticeably worse, accounting for 48% of the variance, and Model I accounts for just 12% of the variance in the data! These results dispense with Model I, are unfavorable for Model II, and do not distinguish well between Models III and IV. We shall accept Model III over Model IV, simply to provide uniformity with the solution time model.

The final model is shown in Table 7.6. It can be seen that mapping and application, the two self-terminating attribute-comparison parameters, contribute about equally to prediction. The encoding and inference parameters are excluded from the model, because they contributed only trivially to prediction of the error data. Thus, it appears that the major sources of errors were in self-terminating attribute-comparison operations. The one exhaustive attribute-comparison operation shows only a small correlation with error rate, as does encoding. Apparently, the gain in time that can be achieved by self-terminating attribute-comparison operations is offset by an increase in error rate due to mistaken comparisons or failure to make all necessary comparisons.

Multivariate component model. It has been shown that the component theory and Model III can account separately for both solution times and error rates. Can the componential theory and model account for both solution times and error rates simultaneously? In other words, is it possible to model solution time and error rate jointly? It is possible, through the powerful statistical technique of canonical correlation. This technique is described in detail in Cooley and Lohnes (1971) and Tatsuoka (1971). It is possible to give only a summary description here.

Canonical correlation was developed by Hotelling (1935), the same person who developed principal-components analysis (see Chapter 2). Tatsuoka (1971) calls canonical correlation a "double-barreled principal-components analysis," and it combines features of principal-components analysis with those of multiple regression. It identifies the linear combination (component) of one set of variables that is most highly correlated with an identified linear combination (component) of another set of variables. Rather than having just one dependent variable, as in multiple regression, it is possible to have multiple dependent as well as independent variables.

Consider the nature of the extension from simple correlation to canonical correlation. In simple correlation, a dependent variable is correlated with an independent variable. The corresponding regression equation is $Y = aX + b$, where the values of a and b are chosen to maximize the linear fit between the dependent variable Y and the independent variable X. In multiple correlation, a dependent variable is correlated with several independent variables. The corresponding regression equation is

$$Y = a_1 X_1 + a_2 X_2 + \cdots + a_n X_n + b.$$

The values of a_1 to a_n and b are chosen to maximize the linear fit between the dependent variable Y and the independent variables X_1 to X_n. In canonical correlation, several dependent variables are correlated with several independent variables. The corresponding regression equation is

$$c_1 Y_1 + c_2 Y_2 + \cdots + c_m Y_m + d = a_1 X_1 + a_2 X_2 + \cdots + a_n X_n + b.$$

The values of c_1 to c_m, d, a_1 to a_n, and b are chosen to maximize the linear fit between the two sets of variables, Y_1 to Y_m and X_1 to X_n.

Because the various variables may be expressed in widely differing units, usually only the standardized coefficients are of interest. For example, solution time and error rate are expressed in unrelated units, and therefore the raw coefficients of the regression equations would not be interpretable. The standardized coefficients are called canonical coefficients.

So far we have presented canonical correlation analysis as an extension of regression analysis. Canonical correlation analysis may also be viewed as an extension of factor analysis (with the component model) in which the linear fit between two sets of factors is maximized. Canonical correlation analysis is also like factor analysis but unlike regression analysis in that it is possible to have more than one "factor," or canonical variate.

The canonical correlation algorithm first finds a set of weights for dependent and independent variables that maximizes the correlation between them. After this is done, the analysis may be able to discover one or more subsequent sets of weights that are orthogonal to previous sets of weights and, at the same time, describe other aspects of the relationship between the dependent and independent variables.

Canonical correlation is like principal-components analysis in that the first canonical variate is always the one that accounts for the most variance in the data, and successive canonical variates always account for successively less variance in the data. As in factor analysis, one reaches a point at which the canonical variates become of trivial importance, and these canonical variates are disregarded.

Table 7.7 presents the multivariate component Model III for People Piece analogies. As in the error analysis, only nondegenerate analogies were used in this analysis because of the small number of errors on degenerate and semidegenerate analogies. The multivariate model for the full set of analogies, however, is extremely similar in all major respects to the model presented.

The first canonical variate was statistically significant (as tested by χ^2), and accounted for 93% of the variance in the data. This percentage must be greater than or equal to the percentage of variance accounted for in either dependent variable by the independent variables in a multiple regression, since canonical correlation analysis selects the linear combination of the dependent variables that maximizes the correlation with the independent variables. If an additional dependent variable adds nothing over a single one, then the additional dependent

TABLE 7.7
Multivariate Component Model III for People Piece Analogies:
Nondegenerate Items

Model Performance

Canonical variate	Canonical correlation	Variance (%)	Wilks' lambda	χ^2	Degrees of freedom
1	.963	92.7	0.04	457.6***	8
2	.632	39.9	0.60	74.6***	3

Canonical Coefficients

	Dependent Variables	
	Variate 1	Variate 2
Solution time	1.05	−0.79
Error rate	−0.07	1.31

	Independent Variables	
	Variate 1	Variate 2
a	.44	−.67
x	.18	−.22
y'	.48	.59
z'	.24	.66

***$p < .001$.

variable will receive a weight of zero. In fact, this hypothetical situation is close to the actual situation for these data. Canonical coefficients are shown in the middle and at the bottom of the table. These coefficients are analogous to the β weights of multiple regression. The canonical coefficients for Variate 1 of the dependent variables show a striking asymmetry. Solution time receives a substantial weight, whereas error rate receives a trivial weight. Apparently, error rate made only a trivial contribution to prediction over that made by solution time, and in fact, the canonical correlation for solution time and error rate combined is only minutely higher than that for solution time alone.

The canonical coefficients for the first variate of the independent variables are shown at the bottom of the table. The coefficients are very similar to the standardized regression coefficients for Model III (nondegenerate items only) when just solution time is used as the dependent variable. Thus, it is clear that the first canonical variate corresponds closely to the relationship discovered in the modeling of solution time.

The second canonical variate is also statistically significant (as indicated by χ^2), and accounts for 40% of the variance in the data. This variate is orthogonal to the first, and therefore indicates that a full accounting of the relationships between the dependent and independent variables is not expressed by just one equation.

Both solution time and error rate receive weights of large magnitude in Variate 2. The weights for the independent variables are of greater interest. The a and x parameters receive negative weights, while the y' and z' parameters receive positive weights. Thus, the two exhaustive components are weighted in one direction and the two self-terminating ones in the other. It will be recalled that the self-terminating components are the ones that accounted for almost all the variance in the error rate data; therefore, this canonical variate would seem related to this pattern.

The canonical variates can be more fully interpreted by considering the correlations of the dependent and independent variables with the canonical variate scores for the dependent and independent variables. These canonical variate scores are analogous to factor scores. They are obtained by multiplying the variables (in standardized form) by the canonical coefficients. For example, the canonical variate score for the dependent variables on Variate 1 is equal to 1.05 (Standardized Solution Time) + −0.07 (Standardized Error Rate), while the canonical variate score for the independent variables on Variate 1 is equal to .44 (Standardized a) + .18 (Standardized x) + .48 (Standardized y') + .24 (Standardized z').

The correlations with canonical variate scores are presented in Table 7.8 and, in conjunction with the information presented in the previous table, enable us to understand the interrelationships among the variables of interest.

The correlations reveal a general variate followed by a bipolar one. Both dependent variables, solution time and error rate, are highly correlated with the canonical Variate 1 scores for both dependent and independent variables. We know from the canonical coefficients for the dependent variables (see pre-

TABLE 7.8
Correlations of Variables with Canonical Variate Scores

	Dependent variables		Independent variables	
	Variate 1	Variate 2	Variate 1	Variate 2
Dependent variables				
Solution time	.99+***	.06	.96***	.04
Error rate	.60***	.80***	.58***	.50***
Independent variables				
a	.83***	−.31***	.86***	−.49***
x	.71***	−.23**	.73***	−.36***
y'	.81***	.14	.84***	.23**
z'	.36***	.44***	.37***	.70***

$**p < .01.$ $***p < .001$

ceding table) that Variate 1 is almost identical to solution time. This is shown here by the nearly perfect correlation between solution time and the dependent Variate 1 scores, and the very high correlation between solution time and the independent Variate 1 scores. Error rate is also very highly correlated with this variate. Its canonical coefficient was near zero because error rate makes no contribution to the prediction of Variate 1 over and above that of solution time. In other words, its contribution with solution time held constant (which is indicated by the canonical coefficient) is near zero but it is nevertheless highly related to Variate 1. The same pattern of correlations appears with the independent variable scores. The correlations are lower, as would be expected, since solution time and error rate do not directly contribute to the composite of the independent variables.

The pattern of correlations for Variate 2 is totally different. Error rate is highly correlated with scores on this variate, but solution time is uncorrelated with them. Again, the correlations are lower with the independent variables, because error rate and solution time do not contribute directly to these composite scores.

The correlations of the independent variables with the canonical variate scores further elucidate the nature of the canonical variates. All of the independent variables are positively correlated with the first canonical variate, and the correlations are practically identical to those with solution time only. The correlations with the second canonical variate show a different pattern. The exhaustive components are negatively correlated with it, while the self-terminating components are positively correlated with it (although the correlation of y' with the dependent variate scores does not reach significance). The two types of components therefore seem to be fundamentally different in some respect, and we know from previous analyses that self-terminating components, but not exhaustive components, are responsible for most of the errors that subjects make in solving analogies.

To summarize, solution time and error rate are both highly correlated with the first canonical variate. However, error rate makes no contribution over that of solution time and, therefore, receives a trivial weight in forming the variate. On the other hand, error rate but not solution time is quite highly correlated with the second canonical variate. There are thus two aspects to error rate: one that is shared with solution time, and one that is not. A univariate analysis does not show its full complexity. As Cooley and Lohnes (1971) point out, "The canonical correlation model appears at first to be a complicated way of expressing the relationship between two measurement batteries. In fact, it is the simplest analytic model that can begin to do justice to this difficult problem of scientific generalization" (p. 176).

One may well wonder whether such a complex set of interrelationships is replicable. It is. A very similar pattern of results will be shown in the Geometric Analogy Experiment.

Individual differences. Individual data are of interest primarily for determining whether there were individual differences in the models that subjects used in solving the analogies. There are no clear indications of such individual differences. Model III best described the data of 12 subjects, and Model IV best described the data of 4 subjects. Models I and II were never best. There was no systematic trend insofar as which model predicted best for which subjects. In the four cases in which Model IV was superior to Model III, the average superiority was less than .4%. The mean of the individual percentages of variance accounted for was 80.0% for Model III, 79.0% for Model IV, 74.0% for Model II, and 66.0% for Model I. The difference between the predictive power of Models III and IV for the four cases in which the fit of Model IV was better than that of Model III is not sufficient to support the hypothesis that these subjects solved the analogies in a qualitatively different way from the remaining subjects. The data suggest that subjects probably all used the same model or indistinguishable ones and that Models III and IV are extremely close in their predictions. Model III will be accepted as an approximation to the true model.

Tables 7.9 and 7.10 are concerned with individual differences within a given model, namely, Model III. Table 7.9 shows means and standard deviations of the parameter estimates (component scores) for the 16 subjects. The data show that standard deviations of the parameters are quite large relative to their means, indicating positive skewness.

Table 7.10 shows intercorrelations among parameters for the 16 subjects. Internal consistency reliability coefficients (split-halves), corrected by the Spearman–Brown formula, are shown in the diagonal. All parameters are highly reliable. With one exception (a and c) the parameters are uncorrelated, indicating the patterns of individual differences tend not to be consistent across parameters. It had been expected that at least the three attribute-comparison parameters $-x$, y', z' $-$ would be intercorrelated. Their independence is further evi-

TABLE 7.9
Basic Statistics for Scores in People Piece Experiment:
Model III Component Scores[a] (N = 16)

Component score	Mean	Standard deviation	Number of observations
a (Encoding)	140	34	18,432
x (Inference)	130	63	18,432
y' (Mapping)	324	119	18,432
z' (Application)	154	75	18,432
c (Preparation and Response)	452	162	18,432

[a]Times represented by component scores are expressed in milliseconds.

TABLE 7.10
Model III Component Score Intercorrelations

	a	x	y'	z'	c
a	.84***	.10	.16	.11	−.60*
x		.91***	.22	−.36	.10
y'			.95***	.27	.30
z'				.85***	.37
c					.97***

$^*p < .05.$ $^{***}p < .001$

dence that they are indeed distinct processes, and not repetitions of identical processes.

Relations between component and interval scores.   Table 7.11 shows correlations between component and interval scores. Consider first the component that is prominent in all interval scores, preparation–response (c). This component contributes the largest proportion of variance to the $S3$ score, since, according to the formulation for Model III in Table 7.4, only c and z' enter the $S3$ solution score. The component contributes successively less variance proportionally to $S2$, $S1$ and $S0$, as additional components enter into these solution scores. The proportional contribution of c is smallest in $S0$, because $4a$, x, y', and z' also

TABLE 7.11
Correlations of Component Scores with Interval Scores

	Component score				
	a	x	y'	z'	c
Solution score					
$S0$	.29	.47	.70**	.46	.53*
$S1$	.11	.35	.75**	.58*	.66**
$S2$	−.14	.02	.68**	.62**	.82***
$S3$	−.29	.10	.33	.64**	.91***
Cue score					
$C0$	−.17	.03	.42	.12	.63**
$C1$	.17	.13	.40	.20	.43
$C2$	.41	.24	.53*	.16	.26
$C3$	.49	.28	.64**	.11	.12

$*p < .05.$ $**p < .01.$ $***p < .001.$

enter into this solution score. It is also the c component that probably contributes the most variance in the zero-cue score, since there is not much more for subjects to do in zero-cueing other than to prepare and then respond by pressing the red button. In short, the effect of adding components other than c to the interval score was to reduce the correlation with reasoning.

The correlation of the z' (application) component score with solution scores also follows the predicted pattern, increasing with more cues. This component is present in all cueing conditions, but it is relatively more important in those cueing conditions in which there are fewer additional components.

The correlation of the y' (mapping) component score with solution scores is approximately constant across the zero-, one-, and two-cue conditions, and then drops off sharply in the three-cue condition, where it no longer contributes to the solution process. The correlation with solution time for the full analogy ($S0$) is very high $-$ .70. Individual differences in the x (inference) and a (encoding) component scores contributed least to individual differences in the solution scores, perhaps in part because the x and a component scores had the least variance to contribute (see Table 7.9).

The correlations between component and cue scores are shown at the bottom of the table. There is some evidence that a may contribute successively more variance to individual differences in the higher cue conditions. The y' component score also contributes more variance in the higher cue conditions. Note that c correlates .63 with $C0$, which measures preparation time when there are no cues.

EXTERNAL VALIDATION

Reference Ability Tests

Basic statistics. Means and standard deviations of the reference ability tests are displayed in Table 7.12. The French Finding As Test has been excluded from this and subsequent analyses. Performance on this test was found to be unrelated to performance on any other test or on the analogies task.

The results of the Cattell Culture-Fair Test of g, Level III, are of special interest because the scores can be compared to those of the general population. When the mean raw score is converted to an IQ equivalent (population mean = 100, standard deviation = 16), it represents an IQ of 126, while the standard deviation represents an IQ spread of about 12 points. These results show, as would be expected, that the Stanford freshman–sophomore sample that participated in the experiment was higher and less variable in IQ than the general population.

Intercorrelations and reliabilities. The intercorrelations between tests and the reliability of each test are shown in Table 7.13. The intercorrelational structure

TABLE 7.12
Basic Statistics for Scores in People Piece Experiment:
Reference Ability Test Scores (N = 16)

	Mean	Standard deviation	Number of observations
Reasoning			
Word grouping	32	6	16
Letter series	26	6	16
Cattell culture-fair level III	64[a]	7[b]	16
Perceptual speed			
Same–different	59	11	16
Letter identification	72	11	16
French number comparison	28	5	16
French identical pictures	80	14	16
Verbal			
French vocabulary scales 3, 4, 5	68	17	16

[a]This means represents an IQ of 126 ($\bar{X}$ = 100 for normative population).
[b]This standard deviation represents a range of approximately 12 IQ points (SD = 16 for normative population).

of the tests is as desired. Each test intercorrelates more highly with all other tests of the same type (reasoning or perceptual speed) than it does with any test of the other type. The tests used to measure each of the two reference abilities therefore appear to be fairly cohesive.

Reliabilities of the tests ranged from .57 to .99. Each test was given in two parts, and reliability was computed by intercorrelating the two parts and correcting the obtained correlation by the Spearman–Brown formula.

The reliabilities of all tests except Word Grouping were quite high, especially since all the tests except the Cattell took five minutes or less time. The reliability

TABLE 7.13
Ability Test Intercorrelations

Reasoning tests	WG	LS	CR	SD	LI	FNC	FIP	Reliability
Word grouping	1.00	.65	.71	−.05	.12	−.06	.15	.57
Letter series		1.00	.70	.03	.26	.03	.41	.80
Cattell reasoning			1.00	.16	.33	.30	.42	.75
Perceptual speed tests								
Same–Different				1.00	.84	.62	.60	.86
Letter identification					1.00	.48	.74	.94
French number comparison						1.00	.55	.94
French identical pictures							1.00	.99[a]

[a]Reliability spuriously inflated by unsatisfactory time limit.

TABLE 7.14
Ability Test Factor Analysis

	Principal-factor solution		Varimax rotated solution		
	I	II	I	II	Communality
Reasoning tests					
Word grouping	.41	.71	−.05	.82	.67
Letter series	.55	.62	.11	.82	.68
Cattell reasoning	.68	.56	.25	.84	.77
Perceptual speed tests					
Same/different	.72	−.57	.92	−.07	.84
Letter identification	.82	−.34	.87	.18	.79
French number comparison	.56	−.34	.65	.03	.43
French identical pictures	.80	−.17	.75	.31	.66
Eigenvalue:	3.08	1.77	3.08	1.77	

Total variance (%): 77.5

of the French Identical Pictures Test (.99) is spurious. The time limit for this test was too generous, resulting in a few subjects receiving perfect (and therefore identical) scores on both parts of the test.

Factor analysis.   Results of a factor analysis of the tests are shown in Table 7.14. The factor analysis was carried out using successive communality estimates in the correlation matrix diagonal. Extraction of factors was carried out to a termination criterion setting the minimum Eigenvalue of each factor equal to one.

The factorial structure of the tests revealed in a varimax rotation of a principal-factor solution very well recovers the division of the tests into reasoning and perceptual speed groups. All perceptual speed tests show high loadings on the first factor, but no reasoning tests show high loadings. All reasoning tests show high loadings on the second factor, but no perceptual speed tests show high loadings. The choice of Thurstonian-type simple structure as revealed by a varimax rotation is a choice of convenience. No claim is made that this is the *true* solution.

The factor analysis has served the two purposes it is supposed to serve in componential analysis. The first is to determine whether it is possible to recover the desired breakdown of reference abilities. The desired breakdown into reasoning and perceptual speed factors was recovered in this study. The second purpose is to obtain for each subject a factor score on each of the relevant factors. These factor scores conveniently summarize the test data.

Error Rates

None of the correlations between error rates and reference ability test scores is statistically significant; therefore, they will be considered no further.

Interval Scores

Cue scores. Cue score correlations with reference ability scores are shown in Table 7.15. Correlations of the cue scores with vocabulary are presented for the purpose of discriminant validation – to show that high correlations with either of the specific reference abilities are not matched by a correlation with general verbal ability. Significance tests in this and subsequent tables are *two tailed*.

Three points in Table 7.15 merit comment. First, the $C1$, $C2$, and $C3$ cue scores appear to tap individual differences in perceptual speed. (Correlations are negative because superior performance is indicated by lower response times, but higher reference ability scores.) Second, individual differences in vocabulary do not seem to be measured well by cue scores. Third, $C0$ and $C1$ appear to tap individual differences in reasoning, and the correlations of $C0$ to $C3$ with reasoning scores show a declining trend with more cues. This result is somewhat puzzling, and if anything, the opposite result might be expected. As more cues are given to subjects, more reasoning would seem to be involved in precue processing. In the $C0$ condition, there are no cues at all to process, and so it is

TABLE 7.15
Correlations of Cue Scores with Ability Test Scores

	$C0$	$C1$	$C2$	$C3$
Reasoning				
Word grouping	−.53*	−.56*	−.41	−.33
Letter series	−.42	−.40	−.31	−.22
Cattell reasoning	−.69**	−.56*	−.44	−.39
Perceptual speed				
Same–different	−.17	−.47	−.48	−.47
Letter identification	−.45	−.76***	−.79***	−.74***
French number comparison	.09	−.12	−.21	−.21
French identical pictures	−.30	−.60*	−.56*	−.45
Vocabulary				
French vocabulary (Levels 3, 4, 5)	−.25	−.45	−.49	−.46
Factor I (Perceptual speed)	−.30	−.61*	−.58*	−.49
Factor II (Reasoning)	−.62**	−.54*	−.40	−.32

$*p < .05.$ $**p < .01.$ $***p < .001.$

unclear why reasoning ability would play a part. Further results will help illuminate this finding.

Solution scores. Correlations of the solution scores with the perceptual speed and vocabulary tests are not shown, because fewer than 5% of these correlations are significant. The solution scores do not appear to be related to individual differences in perceptual speed or vocabulary. Whatever correlations are obtained with reasoning, therefore, are not artifactual in being confounded with perceptual speed or vocabulary.

Table 7.16 shows correlations of the solution scores with overall, Session 1, and Session 4 reasoning scores. These results are much more interesting. We will begin by examining the correlations in the first four numerical columns.

First, consider correlations between overall solution scores and reference ability test scores. It is clear that certain scores on the People Piece analogies are related to individual differences in reasoning ability. Significant correlations between overall solution scores and reasoning scores were obtained in three of four cueing conditions, with correlations reaching $-.67$. At least one significant correlation was obtained for each reasoning test (of four possible), and three of four factor-score correlations were significant.

TABLE 7.16
Correlations between Solution Scores and Reasoning Scores

	Word grouping	Letter series	Cattell reasoning	FACTOR II reasoning
Solution scores				
Overall				
S0	−.45	−.33	−.48	−.49
S1	−.52*	−.33	−.48	−.52*
S2	−.62*	−.46	−.54*	−.61*
S3	−.55*	−.53*	−.62*	−.67**
Session 1				
S0	−.43	−.35	−.40	−.43
S1	−.45	−.16	−.43	−.39
S2	−.39	−.09	−.28	−.27
S3	−.33	−.35	−.40	−.43
Solution Scores				
Session 4				
S0	−.46	−.27	−.50*	−.47
S1	−.49	−.39	−.49	−.55*
S2	−.73***	−.65**	−.69**	−.80***
S3	−.73***	−.68**	−.64**	−.80***

$*p < .05.$ $**p < .01.$ $***p < .001.$

Second, there were substantial differences between correlational patterns in the first versus the last sessions. The possibility of such a difference was suggested by the relatively low stability coefficients between interval scores for the first and last sessions. In the first session, none of the correlations with any reasoning test were significant, although they were all in the expected direction. In the last session, three of four correlations with Factor II (Reasoning) were significant, and most of the correlations for individual tests were also significant. In this last session, correlations between solution scores and reasoning test scores were of substantial magnitude, reaching −.80 for two factor-score correlations.

The difference in the pattern of correlations between the first and last sessions is related to previous findings. Noble, Noble, and Alcock (1958) used tests from the Thurstone Primary Mental Abilities battery to predict individual differences in trial-and-error learning and found that prediction was higher for total correct scores than for initial correct scores, suggesting that the higher correlation came from performance in later trials. Fleishman and Hempel (1955) and Fleishman (1965) also found that the percentage of variance accounted for in motor tasks by traditional psychometric tests increases with practice. Results such as these have led Glaser (1967) to conclude that "the usual psychometric variables are correlated to a lesser degree with initial acquisition performance" (p. 12).

Vygotsky (1962) noted that mental testing is usually based upon performance in tasks for which no explicit training has been given. He suggested that it might be more appropriate to measure performance after training and practice rather than before, at the upper rather than the lower threshold of performance, if only because "instruction must be oriented toward the future, not the past" (p. 104). The correlations in Table 7.16 are consistent with Vygotsky's hypothesis: Performance at asymptote does appear to be the more meaningful measure of intellectual performance. The correlations are also consistent with Ferguson's (1954) notion of ability as "performance at some crude limit of learning. This applies to the abilities of the Thurstone system and to whatever is subsumed under the term 'intelligence' " (p. 110).

There is a third feature of Table 7.16 that is worthy of mention. This feature is the increase in correlations between solution scores and reasoning scores with greater numbers of cues — the opposite of what would be predicted. In fact, this pattern, seen for overall and for Session 4 solution scores, mirrors that for the cue scores. The cue score pattern was also opposite to the predicted one. It would be expected that with more attribute-comparison processing, the correlation would increase, but instead it decreases. In order to understand this pattern, we must turn to the component scores.

Component scores. The above statements regarding the predicted patterns of correlations imply a set of predictions for the correlations between component scores and reasoning scores. These predictions derive from plausibility considerations, not from the theory itself. This set of predictions is made explicit in Table 7.17.

Encoding, represented by parameter a, is a perceptual process and would seem likely to generate individual differences in perceptual speed, but not in reasoning. Inference (x), mapping (y'), and application (z'), the three attribute-comparison operations, would seem to be the "reasoning" components in analogical reasoning; therefore, they would be expected to correlate with reasoning scores. There is no reason to expect them to correlate with perceptual speed scores. Preparation–response (c) would seem to involve elements of attention, motivation, and motor speed, and so there is no reason to expect a correlation with reasoning. To the extent that motor speed is involved, however, a correlation with perceptual speed scores might be predicted. Since this prediction is questionable, a question mark is placed in the table.

Table 7.18 shows the actual correlations of the component scores with the reference abilities. The data lend little support to the first prediction. Letter Identification is the only test score significantly correlated with encoding component scores. The data fail to support the second set of predictions. The inference (x), mapping (y'), and application (z') component scores are not significantly correlated with any of the reasoning scores, although all but one of the correlations is in the expected direction. None of these scores is significantly correlated with perceptual speed either. The third prediction, of a possible correlation between preparation–response (c) and perceptual speed scores, is not confirmed. The c component score is, however, highly correlated with all reasoning scores!

Two aspects of these data need to be explained. First, why *didn't* the x, y', and z' component scores correlate with reasoning? Second, why *did* the c component score correlate with reasoning?

Four possibilities ought to be considered as to why the inference, mapping, and application scores did not correlate with reasoning: speed–accuracy trade-

TABLE 7.17
Predicted Pattern of Correlations
Between Components and Reference Abilities

Component	Reference ability	
	Perceptual speed	Reasoning
Encoding (a)	+	0
Inference (x)	0	+
Mapping (y')	0	+
Application (z')	0	+
Preparation and response (c)	0 + (?)	0

TABLE 7.18
Model III Component Score Correlations with Reference Ability Scores

	a	x	y'	z'	c
Reasoning					
Word grouping	.25	−.08	−.41	−.26	−.59*
Letter series	.24	.01	−.13	−.09	−.58*
Cattell reasoning	.31	−.18	−.33	−.16	−.64**
Perceptual speed					
Same−different	−.33	.13	−.12	−.04	.15
Letter identification	−.51*	−.01	−.24	−.16	−.04
French number comparison	−.21	−.27	−.03	−.07	.13
French identical pictures	−.16	−.20	.12	−.20	−.29
Vocabulary					
French vocabulary (Levels 3, 4, 5)	−.02	−.25	−.32	−.12	−.32
FACTOR I (Perceptual Speed)	−.22	−.16	.08	−.19	−.22
FACTOR II (Reasoning)	.32	−.13	−.31	−.19	−.71**

*$p < .05.$ **$p < .01.$

off, variance specificity, easiness of analogies, and fixedness of analogy attributes.

The *speed–accuracy tradeoff* explanation suggests that the speed–accuracy tradeoff was different for the reasoning tests versus the People Piece analogies, and that individual differences in the tradeoffs for the two tasks were uncorrelated. This explanation is plausible, since in the People Piece analogies, but not the reasoning tests, subjects were instructed to minimize errors and were paid a bonus for low error rates.

There are two ways in which this hypothesis might be tested. One test of the hypothesis would require an experiment in which the People Piece analogies were administered under conditions that systematically varied in their speed–accuracy tradeoff instructions (macrotradeoff). By comparing correlations with reasoning across conditions, it would be possible to determine whether the magnitudes of the correlations are dependent upon speed–accuracy tradeoff condition. For example, it might be found that the low correlation is limited to situations in which accuracy is stressed (as in the present experiment).

A second test of the hypothesis can be made by correlating the reasoning score with both component (or interval) scores and individual error rates taken together. If speed–accuracy tradeoff is responsible for the low correlations within a given condition (microtradeoff), then the multiple correlation of reasoning with response time and error rate should be higher than the simple correlation of reasoning with response time alone. These multiple correlations were computed, both for component scores and interval scores. The correlations remained practically unchanged: Error rates made practically no contribution to the prediction of reasoning scores. The speed–accuracy tradeoff explanation was therefore not supported by this test.

The *variance specificity* explanation suggests that the x, y', and z' component scores may have actually measured individual differences in reasoning ability, but that the aspects of reasoning they measured are specific to analogical reasoning. A more extreme form of this hypothesis holds that these aspects are specific to People Piece Analogies. This explanation would be borne out if it were shown that values of the x, y', and z' component scores were correlated across analogy tasks (or for the extreme form of the hypothesis, across performances on People Piece Analogies), but were uncorrelated with any other type of reasoning score. If the explanation is correct, then x, y', and z' are relatively uninteresting from an individual-differences point of view. This explanation will be examined in Chapter 8, where scores of the same subjects on the response-time verbal analogies will be compared to their reasoning scores and also to their People Piece Analogy scores.

The *analogy easiness* explanation is that the People Piece analogies were too easy for the subject population to measure individual differences in reasoning ability. That the analogies were quite easy is beyond dispute. Mean solution times even for the most difficult items were just under 2.5 sec, and for the easiest items, the mean solution time was just about .5 sec. Furthermore, the mean error rate for the analogies was less than 1.5%.

There are two ways of testing this explanation. A strong test would require an experiment in which the People Piece analogies are given to subject populations for whom they are differentially difficult. For example, one might include groups of college students, early secondary school students, and early elementary school students. If the easiness explanation is correct, then the correlations of the x, y', and z' components with reasoning should decrease with age.

A weaker test of this explanation will be carried out on the basis of the data that have been collected in the present series of experiments. The verbal analogies were more difficult than the People Piece analogies and the geometric analogies were more difficult yet. If stronger correlations are obtained for either of these other types of analogy, it might be for any of a number of reasons (including the one to be discussed in the next paragraph). But if trivial correlations are again obtained, then it is unlikely that mere item easiness was responsible for the absence of significant correlations, since trivial correlations would have been obtained even with much more difficult items.

The *attribute fixedness* explanation is in many ways the most interesting one. According to this explanation, the failure to obtain significant correlations of reasoning with x, y', and z' component scores was due to the fact that the same attributes – height, girth, sex, color – were relevant to analogy solution on every trial. The x, y', and z' component scores may measure time to *test* attribute relevance, but in the present experiment at least, they do not measure time to *discover* relevant attributes. It is possible that the primary source of individual differences in reasoning is in the discovery process rather than in the testing process, and that because the People Piece analogies did not involve any but the most trivial discovery process, they did not measure individual differences in discovery.

This explanation can be examined by comparing correlations in the present experiment with those in the subsequent two experiments. If the explanation is correct, then high correlations should be obtained in both the Verbal and Geometric Analogy Experiments, because in these experiments, the relevant analogy attributes changed from trial to trial. Indeed, the relevant attributes were never the same in any two items, and in many items they were widely discrepant. Hence, the attribute fixedness explanation can be tested on the basis of existing data, although there might be other reasons for obtaining higher correlations in these other two experiments.

We have considered four alternative explanations as to why the three attribute-comparison component scores, x, y', and z', did not correlate with reasoning. We now turn to a consideration of why the c score did correlate with reasoning. Five explanations will be briefly considered: motivation, attention, decision, bookkeeping, and planning.

One possible explanation is *motivation.* Subjects who were higher in reasoning may have been more motivated to do the task (and similar intellectual tasks), and thus have pushed themselves to respond more quickly.

A second possibility has been suggested by Paul Matthews (personal communication). Subjects who scored higher in reasoning may have paid more *attention* to the task and may have been less likely to let their attention wander. They thus would have tended to respond more quickly.

Robert Abelson (personal communication) has suggested a third possibility. *Decision* time may have been the key intervening variable. On all trials, subjects had to decide whether the analogy was true or false. Whereas higher reasoning subjects may have made quick decisions as to which button to press, lower reasoning subjects may have hesitated longer, and thus exhibited higher solution times throughout.

A fourth explanation, suggested by Edward Shoben (personal communication), was that the *bookkeeping* operations specified in the information-processing models, but not assigned separate components or mathematical parameters, may have been responsible for the correlation. These operations were not assigned separate components because they were believed to be unimportant. However, it may be that superior efficiency in "mental bookkeeping" is what separates high reasoners from low reasoners. The mental bookkeeping operations have to performed very frequently, and individual differences in the speed with which they are performed could be of considerable importance.

The fifth possibility, suggested by Walter Reitman (personal communication), is that executive *planning* operations required for the solution of each item may have been the source of the correlation between the c component scores and reasoning scores. Such operations would make the c component score the most complex rather than the simplest of the five component scores, and might well lead to the high correlation obtained with reasoning.

These explanations have in common their attribution of the high correlation to processes that are hypothesized to occur in approximately equal amounts in the solution of each analogy. This property is a prerequisite for an explanation, because the c component score was estimated as the constant in each individual subject's regression equation: The amount of time spent on the c component was constant across all item types for a given subject. The explanations differ in whether they place the intervening variable at the beginning of analogy solution (planning), in the middle of analogy solution (bookkeeping), at the end of analogy solution (decision), or throughout analogy solution (motivation, attention).

Although the correlation between c and the reasoning factor score was very high, and statistically significant at the 1% level, the possibility of a chance occurrence cannot be ruled out, especially since the result was unexpected and is not readily interpretable. Other evidence supports the finding, however.

Hunt, Lunneborg, and Lewis (1975) found "small, though not statistically significant differences, between high and low verbal subjects on the base task [containing an element of choice] as well as upon the added component" (p. 224). Lunneborg (1974) has reported correlations between choice reaction time and measures of both numerical and verbal reasoning. The correlations of $-.50$ and $-.30$ were significant, the first at the 1% level and the second at the 5% level. The correlations for simple motor reaction time and the two reasoning measures were almost as high: $-.40$ ($p < .01$) and $-.27$ ($p < .05$). In addition, Lunneborg found that the intercept from the Sternberg memory-scanning task correlated significantly with numerical reasoning, whereas the slope did not. In the People Pieces Experiment, c was estimated as an intercept: x, y', and z' were estimated as slopes.

A related finding was that of Hoving, Morin, and Konick (1970), who found that children as young as eight years of age produce memory-scanning functions with higher intercepts, but comparable slopes, to those of adults. This result suggests that intercept decreases with intellectual development, but slope does not (at least from age eight). Again, the result is consistent with both the high c correlation and the low x, y', and z' correlations with reasoning.

The correlation of c with reasoning is therefore accepted, at least tentatively, as a "real" finding. The experiment was not designed to distinguish among alternative explanations of the finding; indeed, the result that needs explanation was unexpected. One other result, however, that might be interpreted as arguing in favor of either the motivational or attentional explanation over the other ones is the high correlation obtained between cue time for the zero-cue condition and reasoning, $r = -.62$, $p < .01$. Performance during the zero-cueing period would seem to be a measure of c, and the data support this interpretation, since the correlation between cue scores for the zero-cue condition and c was $.63$, $p < .01$.

The dependent variable in the cue score is simple rather than choice reaction time, so no decision between alternative buttons was required (athough a decision was required to press any button at all). There would seem to be little if anything required in the way of bookkeeping operations, because no stimulus for which "to keep the books" has yet been presented. Similarly, it is difficult to see how sophisticated planning operations might occur before any aspect of the analogy is even presented, although some kind of preparatory work might take place.

Of course, the correlation of $C0$ with reasoning might be due to some component other than c. However, when c is held constant statistically in the correlation between $C0$ and reasoning, the correlation drops from $-.62$ to a nonsignificant $-.32$. The c component, therefore, would seem to be the essential one.

Because of the $C0$ correlation with reasoning, my preferred explanation for the correlation between the c component score and reasoning remains the first (motivational) or possibly the second (attentional) one, but further data would obviously be needed before any reasonably firm conclusion could be drawn.

Reference ability models. The final aspect of the external validation to be considered is the formulation of reference ability models. As stated in Chapter 4, a major goal of componential analysis is to account for the reference abilities in terms of their underlying components. A "true" understanding of a particular reference ability will be obtained when all components necessary to predict performance on tests of that reference ability have been isolated. In such a case, the multiple correlation of the component scores with the reference ability score will be equal to the score's reliability. The model predicting reference ability test scores from a set of component scores is called a reference ability model. Such a model can also be formed using interval rather than component scores, although the insight to be gained using interval scores rather than component scores is diminished, since interval scores consist of combinations of components.

With component scores as predictors, it is possible to obtain significant prediction for reasoning. The c component accounts for 50% of the variance in the reasoning factor score. (Additional variables failed to make statistically significant contributions to the level of prediction.)

INTEGRATION

To this point, several different models have been presented that attempt to account for different aspects of the experimental results: the simplex model for solution scores, the component model for component scores, the reference ability models for reference ability scores. The structural regression model integrates these different models into one overall account of the interrelations among the different types of scores (see Chapter 4). The model is shown in Figure 7.7.

In the structural regression model, the solution scores are horizontally interrelated to each other and upward-vertically related to the reference ability (or abilities) of interest, represented here by reasoning. The solution scores are downward-vertically related to the components that constitute them — measured here by a, x, y', z', c scores — and these components are in turn related downward-vertically to the reference ability (or abilities), here reasoning.

The numerals along the arrows represent path coefficients — standardized partial regression (β) weights. Each indicates the predictive contribution to the criterion of the variable initiating its path. The bold face numerals at each of the

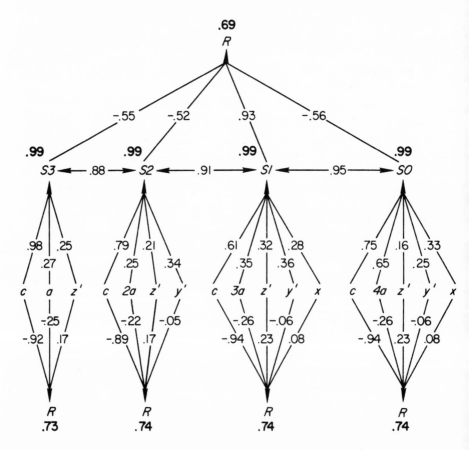

FIGURE 7.7 Structural regression relating component scores, interval scores, and reasoning reference ability.

three levels of converging paths are multiple correlation coefficients, indicating the level of multiple prediction that the converging paths provide.

Starting at the top of the figure, we see that the multiple correlation of the solution scores with reasoning was .69. Because of the simplicial structure and collinearity (high intercorrelations) of the solution scores, the path coefficients are somwhat difficult to interpret. Overall, however, the three-cue, two-cue, and zero-cue solution scores made about equal contributions, and the one-cue solution score served as a strong suppressor variable.

The successive solution scores were highly intercorrelated, although the magnitude of these correlations decreased with successively more cues. This decrease is consistent with the mathematical formulation of Model III. $S0$ and $S1$ differed from each other only by a, one encoding. $S1$ and $S2$ differed from each other by $a + fx$, and $S2$ and $S3$ differed from each other by $a + g'y'$. Thus, $S0$ is "closer" to $S1$ than $S2$ is to $S1$ or $S3$ is to $S2$.

The solution scores were almost perfectly predicted by the component scores, indicating that from an individual-differences point of view, the components hypothesized to enter each solution score in combination gave a full account of the solution score. No more components are required. In all cases, the c component made the largest contribution, although its proportional contribution decreased as more components were added.

Moving downward, we see that the c component score also made by far the largest contribution to the prediction of the reasoning scores; indeed, the magnitude of the c component path coefficient was about the same no matter what other components were added in. This pattern of coefficients provides further evidence that the successively increasing correlations of the solution scores with reasoning were due to the proportionately larger contributions of c, although the absolute amount of its contribution remained the same.

The contributions of components other than c to the prediction of the reasoning score were trivial. Nevertheless, the magnitudes of the correlations (all over .7) were impressive for the ability test data. The multiple correlation between the components constituting each solution score and reasoning remained approximately constant across cue conditions. Again, this constancy indicated that once c was placed into the multiple regression equation, the other components mattered little.

SUMMARY

Sixteen subjects were selected from a large introductory psychology class on the basis of their scores on reference ability tests of reasoning and perceptual speed. Selected subjects solved 288 different People Piece analogies in each of four precueing conditions and also received an intensive battery of reference ability and analogy tests designed to test certain predictions. These subjects also supplied ratings in a People Piece Perceptual Similarities task, as did 72 other subjects otherwise uninvolved in the experiment.

A simplex regression model was formed for the solution scores from each cue condition. The tests of the model generally confirmed the assumption of additivity across solution scores.

Four basic component models were tested for fit against the solution-time data, and all proved to be unsatisfactory. Inspection of solution-time data, error-rate data, and subjects' introspective comments suggested the need for a dual-processing scheme. The first type of processing involved a holistic figure identity scan, and the second type involved individual attribute comparisons.

Modified versions of the four basic models and several variants of them were tested against the solution-time data. The group data overwhelmingly rejected one model, quite clearly rejected a second model, but were equivocal with respect to the other two models. The entire set of results considered as a whole suggested the probable superiority of one of these models, one with exhaustive encoding and inference components but with self-terminating mapping and application components. This final model, Model III, accounted for 92% of the variance in the group data, with five parameters and 294 residual degrees of freedom. The model provided the best fit for the data of 12 of 16 individual subjects, and provided a very good fit even for the other 4 subjects.

The component models were applied to error rates as well as solution time. The number of errors was small, and because almost no errors were made on degenerate and semidegenerate items, only nondegenerate items were used in the analyses displayed. Comparable analyses for the full data set yielded similar results. Model IV accounted for 60% of the variance in the data, Model III for 59% of the variance in the data, Model II for 48% of the variance in the data, and Model I for just 12% of the variance in the data. Although indistinguishable from Model IV, Model III was accepted to provide uniformity with the solution-time model. It was found that the two self-terminating parameters made substantial contributions to the model, but the two exhaustive parameters made trivial contributions. Errors thus appear to be associated with self-terminating operations.

A multivariate component model was constructed through the use of canonical correlation. Both solution time and error rate served simultaneously as dependent variables, while the same attribute-change and precueing variables served as independent variables. Two significant canonical variates were obtained. Solution time and error rate are both highly correlated with the first canonical variate. However, error rate makes no contribution over that of solution time, and hence receives a trivial weight in forming the variate. On the other hand, error rate but not solution time is highly correlated with the second canonical variate. There are thus two aspects to error rate, one that is shared with solution time, and one that is not. A univariate analysis does not show the full complexity of error rate as a dependent variable.

Cue scores were correlated with reference ability test scores. Cue scores for the one-cue, two-cue, and three-cue conditions appeared to tap individual differences in perceptual speed. Surprisingly, cue scores for the zero-cue condition appeared to tap individual differences in reasoning, and the correlations with reasoning scores declined as more cues were added. The opposite pattern had been expected, since more attribute-comparison operations were presumably involved in processing greater number of cues, and these operations were thought to involve reasoning ability.

The pattern of correlations for solution scores was also the reverse of what had been expected. Correlations with reasoning scores increased with greater numbers of cues (and therefore less attribute-comparison processing). Correlations were higher for the last session than for the first session.

Component scores were correlated with reference ability scores and showed that the pattern of correlations for the interval scores could be understood in terms of the unexpected high correlation of the preparation—response component score with reasoning, coupled with the trivial correlations of the other component scores with reasoning. Several alternative explanations were considered for the high correlation between c and reasoning, and the low correlations between x, y', z' and reasoning. Some data bearing on these explanations were presented, but stronger tests are needed and ways in which they could be carried out were suggested.

Reference ability models were presented that attempted to account for the reference ability scores in terms of combinations of solution scores and then components. While the models provided only partial understanding of the components constituting each reference ability, the results were an encouraging first step toward understanding the underlying components that in combination form reasoning.

The results of the various models were summarized in an overall structural regression. The patterns of path coefficients were analyzed, and the interrelations among the various types of scores were further elucidated.

8
The Verbal Analogy Experiment

The second experiment in the series was the Verbal Analogy Experiment.[1] Experimental stimuli were verbal analogies using common words drawn from everyday vocabulary. The major dependent variable was again solution time. Subjects viewed each analogy in a tachistoscopic field and pressed the appropriate button indicating whether the analogy was true or false. An analogy was true if the relationship between the last two terms paralleled that between the first two terms, and false otherwise. The major independent variable was item difficulty, which was again manipulated by varying numbers of value changes (in a way to be described) and by giving varying amounts of precueing information.

METHOD

Materials

The experimental stimuli were verbal analogies typed in large capital letters (IBM Orator typeface) on 6 X 9-inch tachistoscope cards. There were a total of 168 analogies, 84 true and 84 false. Among these analogies were 8 degenerate analogies of the form A:A::A:A, 8 semidegenerate analogies of the form A:A::B:B, and 8 semidegenerate analogies of the form A:B::A:B. These 24 degenerate and semidegenerate analogies, like the 144 nondegenerate ones, were equally divided among trues and falses. In the false analogies, the fourth term did not match any other term.

A representative sample of verbal analogies is shown in Table 8.1. The first digit of the number preceding each analogy indicates whether it is true (0) or

[1] I am grateful to Mary V. McGuire for serving as coexperimenter, and for her valuable help in many phases of the experiment.

TABLE 8.1
Typical Verbal Analogies

006	HAND:FOOT::FINGER:TOE
009	MERCHANT:SELL::CUSTOMER:BUY
010	DIME:10::NICKEL:5
014	ATTORNEY:LAW::DOCTOR:MEDICINE
019	PISTOL:BOW::BULLET:ARROW
025	WORD:LETTER::PARAGRAPH:SENTENCE
045	YOUR:MY::YOURS:MINE
047	HEAR:SEE::DEAF:BLIND
071	COWARDICE:ENVY::YELLOW:GREEN

103	LEOPARD:TIGER::SPOTS:SOUP	(stripes)
108	AUTOMOBILE:ROAD::TRAIN:CABOOSE	(track)
117	LIME:LEMON::GREEN:ANIMAL	(yellow)
119	THUNDER:LIGHTNING::HEAR:TASTE	(see)
126	TRAIN:ENGINEER:PLANE:NOISE	(pilot)
127	SILENCE:DARKNESS::SOUND:MOON	(light)
130	REFRIGERATOR:FOOD::WALLET:PATIENCE	(money)
132	BOTH:EITHER::AND:CONJUNCTION	(or)
144	THEN:NOW::PAST:KIND	(present)

073	ARTIST:ARTIST::ARTIST:ARTIST
078	HAMMER:HAMMER::NAIL:NAIL
084	TREE:FOREST::TREE:FOREST

175	MACHINE:MACHINE::MACHINE:GRASS	(machine)
177	CLOUD:CLOUD::RAIN:SECTION	(rain)
183	WINTER:SEASON::WINTER:MONTH	(season)

false (1). The correct answer to false items is shown in parentheses proceeding the last analogy term, although of course these answers were not shown to subjects. Degenerate and semidegenerate analogies are shown at the bottom of the table, and are numbered between 73 and 84 in their last two digits.

Procedure

Analogy selection. Twenty-four subjects were presented with 190 open-ended nondegenerate analogies, and were instructed to "complete these analogies by filling in the blank following the first three terms of each analogy. Completed analogies should be of the form $A:B::C:D$, where D is your own response. There is not necessarily a unique response; just choose the one you feel is best." Analogies were eliminated from the item pool if: (1) fewer than 21 of the 24 subjects filled in the same last term; or (2) fewer than 23 of the 24 subjects filled in any last term at all. Additional analogies were discarded that seemed to rely primarily on vocabulary or general information for successful solution. Of the remaining 156 analogies, 12 were used for practice items and 144 for test items.

True analogies were constructed by using the consensually validated "best" answer as the fourth analogy term. False analogies were constructed by using some other answer as a fourth term. For half the false analogies, an attempt was made to select fourth terms that were highly related associatively to the correct answer. For the other half, an attempt was made to select fourth terms that were of very low or no relation.

Degenerate and semidegenerate analogies were not pretested, since the semantic content of the analogies was irrelevant.

Relatedness ratings. Twenty-eight new subjects were presented with 860 pairs of words (distributed over two one-hour sessions) and were asked to judge the relatedness of each pair. Included in the list were all possible nonidentical pairs between A and B, A and C, B and D, and C and D. For false items, three additional pairs were included: B and D', C and D', and D and D' (where D was the presented answer and D' the correct answer; for true analogies, these two terms were identical). The 860 pairs of words were presented in a different random order to each subject.

Subjects were instructed that their task in the experiment was to rate the "associative relatedness" of each pair of items. "What this means is that you are to look at each pair of items and decide how closely associated they are in your mind. The two items may be related in any of a number of different ways, and it is up to you to decide in what way they are related." Subjects were particularly warned that " 'associative relatedness' does not mean the same thing as 'similarity of meaning,' or some such similar expression. Two words may mean very different things (opposites, for example) and yet be very highly related." Ratings were made on a nine-point scale, with nine indicating an extremely strong relation and one an extremely weak relation. Subjects were asked to use the whole scale and to work quickly: "First impressions are fine, and you are discouraged from spending too much time puzzling over any pair of items."

A subset of the rating data was used as the basis for assigning items to four quasi-parallel forms. Both true and false items were grouped into quartets closely matched in terms of certain ratings. For true items, matching was done on the basis of A to B, A to C, and C to D ratings. (As would be expected, A to B and C to D distances were very highly correlated.) For false items, matching was done on the basis of A to B, A to C, C to D', and D to D' ratings. One item from each quartet was randomly assigned to each of the four forms.

Underlying this assignment procedure were the assumptions that: (1) the ratings represented an implicit scale of latent "value transformations"; and (2) these value transformations form the basis of item difficulty (see Rips, Shoben, & Smith, 1973, for a similar set of assumptions).

Analogy testing. The verbal analogy subjects were the same as the People Piece subjects. Verbal analogy testing took place between two and five weeks after People Piece analogy testing. The testing procedure was identical to that for the People Piece Experiment, with the following exceptions.

Subjects were given 12 practice items prior to administration of the test items. Three items were presented in each of the four cueing conditions. Presentation of test items was divided into eight blocks. Each block consisted of a different cueing condition. Cueing conditions were ordered in a Latin square arrangement, so that items always occurred in one of four permutations: $0-1-2-3-0-1-2-3$; $1-2-3-0-1-2-3-0$; $2-3-0-1-2-3-0-1$; $3-0-1-2-3-0-1-2$. The particular permutation used for each subject was based on his starting point in the People Piece Experiment. If he had begun the People Piece Analogy Experiment with zero cues, he began the Verbal Analogy Experiment with two cues. The same ordered relationship held for one and three cues, two and zero cues, and three and one cues.

Items were presented in one of four possible form orders: $1-2-3-4-1-2-3-4$; $2-3-4-1-2-3-4-1$; $3-4-1-2-3-4-1-2$; $4-1-2-3-4-1-2-3$. One subject in each group received each of the form orders. Items were randomized within each form before presentation to a new subject, and half the items in a given form were presented in each block.

In the People Piece Experiment, it was feasible to present each item four times, once in each cueing condition, because subjects did not remember particular items. In the Verbal Analogy Experiment, subjects did remember items, so it was not feasible to repeat them. Items were presented just once in a single cueing condition. Thus, while all subjects received the full set of 168 items, only four subjects, one from each group, received the same items in the identical cueing condition. For example, the analogy hear:see::deaf:blind was received by four subjects in the zero-cue condition, four in the one-cue condition, four in the two-cue condition, and four in the three-cue condition.

Pairing of hands with true and false responses was identical to that in the People Piece Experiment. Thus, the same button always indicated a true (or false) response for a single subject, but pairing of buttons with hands was counterbalanced across subjects.

Because subjects remembered analogies, it was not possible to replace error response times with correct times by repeating trials, as had been done in the previous experiment. Instead, all response times, including both correct and error times, were used in subsequent analyses.

Subjects

The 16 subjects in the Verbal Analogy Experiment were the same as in the People Piece Experiment. Subjects in the analogy completion task were undergraduates who participated for course credit or pay ($2 per hour), and also graduate students who participated as a favor to the experimenter. Only undergraduates participating for credit or pay were involved in the ratings task. The three sets of subjects were nonoverlapping.

Design

The four precueing conditions were crossed with value changes. As mentioned previously, the same three types of items were used as in the People Piece Experiment: degenerate, semidegenerate, and nondegenerate. No two nondegenerate items were identical in numbers of values changed between all possible pairs of analogy terms, since it was impossible to equate nondegenerate items exactly.

INTERNAL VALIDATION

Interval Scores

Basic statistics. As in all componential experiments, it is predicted that cue times will increase with increasing numbers of cues, and solution times will decrease. If either function behaves differently, then either subjects are failing to use the cues, or else they are using the cues in a way that impedes rather than facilitates performance.

Table 8.2 presents means and standard deviations for cue and solution times, as well as the numbers of observations upon which each mean and standard deviation is based. Since each of 16 subjects received 42 trials in each cue condition, the number of observations is always 672.

TABLE 8.2
Basic Statistics for Scores in Verbal Analogy Experiment:
Interval Scores ($N = 16$)

	Mean	Standard deviation	Number of observations
Cue scores			
$C0$	547	183	672
$C1$	766	194	672
$C2$	1010	274	672
$C3$	1487	406	672
Solution scores			
$S0$	2418	463	672
$S1$	2053	433	672
$S2$	1496	482	672
$S3$	901	350	672

[a]Interval scores are expressed in milliseconds.

The table shows that the basic predictions were upheld: Cue times increased and solution times decreased with more cues. Base cue time for the zero-cue condition is about the same as in the preceding experiment, as would be expected. In general, however, both cue and solution times are longer for verbal than for People Piece analogies. The magnitude of the difference increases with greater amounts of information processing (more cues for cue times, fewer cues for solution times). On the average, a full analogy took one second longer to solve in the Verbal Analogy Experiment than in the People Piece Analogy Experiment, an increase in time of about 70%.

Reliabilities. Internal-consistency reliabilities ranged from .94 to .96 for cue scores, and from .89 to .94 for solution scores. These reliabilities are high, although they do not reach the near-ceiling levels obtained in the People Piece Experiment. The lower reliabilities are to be expected, since each interval score is based upon only about 15% as many observations. Generalizability coefficients for the interval scores across experiments ranged from .71 to .82 for cue scores, and from .74 to .85 for solution scores, indicating consistent individual differences across experiments.

Simplex model. The simplex model makes three predictions: (1) correlations near the principal diagonal of a correlation matrix should be high, and they should taper off monotonically as entries move further away from the principal diagonal; (2) only predictor interval scores immediately adjacent to the predicted interval score will contribute significant variance to the prediction; and (3) values of R^2 computed from variables adjacent to the predicted variable should be equal to or trivially less than values of R^2 computed from nonadjacent as well as adjacent variables.

The first prediction may be tested by examining Table 8.3. The solution score intercorrelations in Panel I show generally simplicial structure, with one inversion: The correlation between $S0$ and $S2$ is higher than the correlation between $S0$ and $S1$. The difference between the two correlations is trivial and of no consequence.

The results of the second test do not strongly support the simplex model, although part of the problem can be traced to the small inversion described above. As we already know, $S2$ is a better predictor of $S0$ than is $S1$, so that in predicting $S0$, $S2$ shows a significant regression coefficient while $S1$ does not. In predicting $S1$, only $S2$ shows a significant regression coefficient, although $S0$ would be expected to as well. In predicting $S2$, it would be expected that $S1$ and $S3$ would show significant regression coefficients, but instead $S0$ and $S1$ do. Finally, none of the regression weights in predicting $S3$ are significant, although the weight for $S2$ would have been significant if $S0$ and $S1$ were not in the regression equation.

The third test is generally supportive of the simplex model. In the zero-cue condition, there is some loss of prediction if $S2$ is omitted, again because of the

TABLE 8.3
Verbal Analogy Solution Score Simplex Model

I. Correlations

	Predictor variable			
	$S0$	$S1$	$S2$	$S3$
Predicted variable				
$S0$	1.00	.90	.93	.76
$S1$	–	1.00	.95	.82
$S2$	–	–	1.00	.85
$S3$	–	–	–	1.00

II. F values for standardized regression coefficients

	Predictor variable				
	$S0$	$S1$	$S2$	$S3$	R^2
Predicted variable					
$S0$	–	.4	5.1*	.4	.87
$S1$	.4	–	6.5*	0.0	.91
$S2$	5.1*	6.5*	–	3.2	.94
$S3$	.4	0.0	3.2	–	.74

III. Raw regression coefficients for simplex model

	Predictor variable					
	$S0$	$S1$	$S2$	$S3$	Constant	R^2
Predicted variable						
$S0$	–	.97	–	–	435.99	.82
$S1$	.14	–	.73	–	623.03	.91
$S2$	–	.84	–	.33	–526.88	.92
$S3$	–	–	0.62	–	–27.19	.73

*$p < .05$

inversion described above. The losses in prediction are trivial in the other three cueing conditions.

Overall, the solution scores appear to be generally but not fully simplicial. Subsequent component analyses will therefore provide some indication of the robustness of componential analysis.

Error Rates

Individual error rates ranged from .6% to 7.1%, with an overall mean of 4.2% and a standard deviation of 1.6%. Error rates were thus generally higher than in the People Piece Experiment, although they were still low. In this experiment as in the People Piece Experiment, error rates showed the expected monotonic decline from the zero-cue (5.5%) to the three-cue (2.7%) condition.

Subjects' introspective reports following participation in the Verbal Analogy Experiment made it clear that in addition to the usual motor errors and errors caused by attempting to solve problems too rapidly, there were also errors caused by subjects simply not knowing the answers to particular problems.

Correlations across subjects between cue times and error rates ranged from −.12 to .05. Correlations between solution times and error rates ranged from −.06 to −.29. These correlations indicate only a slight speed–accuracy tradeoff. The correlation between error rate and solution time across item types, but collapsed over cueing conditions, was .59.

Component Scores

Application of the component theory and models to verbal analogies. Application of the component theory and models to verbal analogies was identical to that in the People Piece Experiment, with three exceptions. First, rated distances on a scale from zero to eight, rather than objective distances (as measured by numbers of value changes), were used in mathematical modeling. The distances were converted similarities obtained by subtracting each rated similarity from nine. Second, averaging of items to obtain data points for use in mathematical modeling was done differently from in the People Piece Experiment. Third, the scale value for true analogies was reset from 8.00 to 5.68. Each of these differences merits explanation.

In the People Piece Experiment, it was possible to measure value changes both objectively and subjectively. In the Verbal Analogy Experiment, there was no apparent basis for "objectively" measuring value changes. While there have been efforts to identify the attributes (or markers) underlying words (e.g., Katz, 1972; Shoben, 1974), these efforts are only in the earliest stages, and do not provide a suitable metric for the general vocabulary of the English language. Subjective ratings of the kind widely used in semantic memory experiments were therefore used. It is possible to test at least to some degree the assumption that these ratings provide valid measures of semantic distance. If the mathematical models all fail to predict solution times, then one does not know whether it is due to a failure of the models or a failure of the assumption that the ratings provide a valid measure of distance. On the other hand, if at least one model predicts solution times accurately, then it seems reasonable to suppose that the ratings on which the model is based are performing the function they are supposed to perform.

In the People Piece Analogy Experiment, there were at least two and as many as twelve items that had identical value-change specifications (according to the unweighted models). In the Verbal Analogy Experiment, no two nondegenerate items had identical value-change specifications. However, it was necessary in predicting the group data to average over items, because each of the 672 data points (168 items X 4 cue conditions) was based upon observations from just 4 of 16 subjects. Averaging was possible because of the procedure by which items were assigned to forms. Items were assigned in groups of four (quartets), with each of the four closely parallel to the others in the value-change specifications relevant to the theory of analogical reasoning. Since one item from each quartet appeared in each of the four forms, averaging over items in the quartet resulted in solution times for a "composite" form. It had 16 observations, one for each subject, for each of 168 (672/4) data points. In predicting individual solution times, it was not necessary to average. Thus, 168 data points, one for each trial, were predicted for individual as well as group data.

In the People Piece Analogy Experiment, analogies were "analogue" in the sense that a relationship was mapped from the domain (first half) of the analogy to the range (second half) of the analogy. They were digital, however, in the sense that according to the rules of the experiment, there was a uniquely defined answer. This was the answer that required the identical value transformations from C to D as from A to B.

In the Verbal Analogy Experiment, an attempt was made to choose verbal analogies that would be almost "digital." Items were selected only if there was widespread agreement (21/24 or more) as to the correct completion. Several lines of evidence suggest that the attempt to make the analogies digital failed.

First, high-error-rate items were ones for which "false" fourth terms were so close to the correct answer (and to some subjects, indistinguishable) that the "true" answer as defined by the ratings task was not much better (if at all) than the "false" distractor. A smaller number of items were "true" ones in which the fourth term did not quite fit.

Second, some items were revealed to be ambiguous. An example of such an item was Honolulu:Hawaii::Chicago:Illinois. A subject pointed out that the analogy is ambiguous, because if it is based upon the city—state relationship, it is true, but if it is based upon the state capital—state relationship, it is false (since while Honolulu is the capital of Hawaii, Springfield, not Chicago, is the capital of Illinois). It was subsequently pointed out that if Hawaii is interpreted as the island rather than the state, then Honolulu is not even on that island.

Third, it became evident that when true items were scaled as eight on the transformed zero to eight distance scale, there was an inordinately large distance between the true and false items relative to differences in response time. The mean transformed false rating was 3.16, and the highest transformed false rating (with higher ratings signifying distractors closer to the "true" answer) was 5.67. The problem was dealt with by placing given "true" answers at 5.68 on the rating scale. Subjects are assumed to set a criterion for "true" answers at 5.68. The assumption of a uniform scale value for all "true" items is an oversimplification, and is dispensed with in subsequent experiments.

Mathematical formulation of the models. Mathematical modeling paralleled that described in Chapter 7 for the People Piece Experiment. Mathematical modeling was done by linear multiple regression. Solution times for the 168 data points were used as the primary criterion to be predicted. The predictors were numbers of terms to be encoded and functions of numbers of value changes. As in the previous experiment, dual processing was incorporated into the models. "Same" judgments were treated as involving zero value changes, and "different" judgments were treated as involving one value change, regardless of the degree of difference.

Reliability of data. It was not possible to determine the reliability of the data because there were no replications of items having identical value-change properties.

Dual-processing models. The percentages of variance accounted for by Models I–IV, respectively, were 83.2, 84.7, 85.6, and 84.8%. While the results support the componential theory of analogical reasoning, they do not distinguish well among the models falling under the theory. The ordering of models is the same as in the People Piece Experiment, but the differences in percentage of variance accounted for are too small to be interpretable. Thus, these data can only be interpreted as showing that the theory is applicable to verbal as well as People Piece analogies, and that the rating procedure used to validate the theory was successful.

Dual-processing models with zero cues only. Because the interval scores did not exhibit fully simplicial structure, one should be particularly sensitive to the possibility that the inclusion of the one-, two-, and three-cue conditions may have somehow distorted the account of mental process. As in the People Piece Experiment, therefore, it is important to compare the fits of the models for full analogies only, using data from just the zero-cue condition.

The result of major interest in these data is that the fits of the models to the experimental data become somewhat more distinguishable. Model III remains best, accounting for 62% of the variance in the data. Model IV is a fairly close second, accounting for 59% of the variance in the data, and Model II is third, accounting for 58% of the variance in the data. Model I is clearly in last place, accounting for 50% of the variance in the data. This ordering is identical to that obtained in the People Piece Experiment and provides further support for Model III as the preferred model under the componential theory, even when verbal content with poorly defined attributes is used rather than pictorial content with well-defined features. Absolute levels of fit are reduced because of the confounding in the zero-cue condition between encoding and preparation–response.

If Model III is accepted as the preferred model, to what extent do parameter estimates for the full set of cueing conditions correspond to those for the zero-cue condition only? The $(4a + c)$ confounded parameter may be estimated for the full data and is estimated as 1698 msec, a discrepancy of just 5% from the confounded parameter estimate of the 0-cue data. The estimate of x is discrepant by 19%; that of y' is discrepant by 16%; that of z' is discrepant by 18%. These differences have no effect on the substantive interpretation of the parameters.

Dual-processing models for other selected item subsets. Other item subsets beside the zero-cue subset are of particular interest. One such subset is that of false items only. As was stated previously, the assumption that "true" completions of analogies were uniformly satisfactory was an oversimplification. How do the models fare when these "true" items are deleted?

Models II, III, and IV do slightly better, accounting for 88–89% of the variance in the data, while Model I does worse, accounting for 81% of the variance in the data. Once again, the data disconfirm Model I relative to the other models.

For nondegenerate items only, fits are about 1% worse than when all analogies are included. Thus, as in the People Piece Experiment (where fits were about 1% better without degenerate and semidegenerate items), the theory accounts for performance on standard analogies very well.

Variants of the dual-processing models. Variants of the dual-processing models can be compared. The first variant is one with no mapping component. The mapping component does not appear in most other theories of analogical reasoning, and thus it is of particular interest to determine whether inclusion of the component in the theory is justified. The fit of the models is reduced in every case, as would be expected when a parameter is dropped. The fit of Model III is reduced from 85.6 to 81.1%. The F for regression decreases slightly (from 242 to 235) when the parameter is dropped, despite the decrease in the number of parameters. The evidence thus once again supports inclusion in the theory of a mapping component (as will further evidence to be described).

In the second variant, the encoding component becomes self-terminating when attribute-comparison processing does. Instead of encoding occurring exhaustively and all at once, these models assume that attributes are encoded only as they are needed for attribute comparison (see Chapter 7 for further explanation). As with People Piece analogies, the fits are slightly poorer under the assumption of self-terminating encoding, particularly for Model IV. The data therefore support a "unitary" encoding process in which each term of the analogy is fully encoded, rather than encoded in "bits and pieces" only as attributes are needed for comparison.

In order to understand the third variant, consider the analogy snow : blood :: white : red (#002 in the experiment). The analogy may be solved in the usual fashion, A is to B as C is to D. However, it would seem more natural to infer the relationship between A and C, to map this relationship onto B, and then to apply it from B to D. Analogies can be solved either in the sequence A is to B as

C is to D or A is to C as B is to D, and training manuals for students about to take difficult tests emphasize this choice of strategies (e.g., Sternberg, 1974), since its use may improve test scores.

It would seem possible that in the Verbal Analogy Experiment, subjects may have used this knowledge to improve their efficiency in solving analogies. Specifically, they may have inferred the lesser of the $[(A, B), (A, C)]$ distances, mapped the greater one, and then applied the lesser of the $[(C, D), (B, D)]$ distances. Fits of the models to the data generally increase by about 1%. Parameter estimates were therefore computed for subjects individually on the basis of this processing variant, as well as for the standard models.

The pattern of results was the same for the various models, and so only the results for one model, III, will be discussed, since it generally provided the best fits to the data. The standard model provided better fits than this variant model for 12 out of 16 subjects, and there were a substantial number of negative parameter estimates for the variant model. The variant was therefore disregarded.

A final variant involves a sixth, solution comparison component. Execution of the inference, mapping, and application components is assumed to be exhaustive. The application component is conceived of somewhat differently from the way it is conceived of in the standard models. In application, the subject forms an image of the correct answer, but does not compare this image directly. Rather, solution comparison occurs through a separate component (w') that compares attributes of the image to those of the given answer. The solution comparison process stops as soon as the given solution is disconfirmed, or when it cannot be disconfirmed. Application is assumed to be completed during cueing of the three-cue condition, and solution comparison occurs in the solution part of the trial.

The variant model with solution comparison accounted for 85.9% of the variance in the data, making it difficult to distinguish from the other models. The value of c, 66 msec, was implausibly small, although the model cannot be rejected on this basis. Rather, the model will receive no further consideration because the sixth parameter seems to buy the theorist nothing.

Final component model. The data from this experiment support the theory of analogical reasoning but do not distinguish well among models. Taken together, the data (and especially the zero-cue data) are most consistent with Model III. The results of the People Piece Experiment corroborate this choice, since Model III was also the preferred model in that experiment. Model III will therefore be accepted as the final model.

Table 8.4 presents detailed statistics for Model III. All parameter estimates were at least 4.5 times their standard errors, and their F_{Reg} values were all significant beyond the 1% level. It is particularly noteworthy that the value of y' was more than seven times as large as its standard error, and its F_{Reg} value was

TABLE 8.4

Final Verbal Analogy Component Model III

Parameter	Parameter estimate	Standard error	Beta	F_{Reg}	df
a	323	31	0.53	112	1, 163
x	121	22	0.27	30	1, 163
y'	277	39	0.25	50	1, 163
z'	216	47	0.16	21	1, 163
c	406				

Stepwise multiple regression

Parameter	Cumulative R^2	r	Cumulative F_{Reg}	Cumulative df
a	.70	.84	383	1, 166
z'	.79	.31	315	2, 165
y'	.83	.63	265	3, 164
x	.86	.78	242	4, 163

Standard error of estimate: 264 msec

Root-mean-square deviation: 261 msec

the highest of the attribute-comparison parameters. The existence of a mapping component is thus strongly supported by these data.

The progress of the stepwise multiple regression used to estimate parameters is shown at the bottom of the table. Each parameter shows a simple correlation with solution time that is significant at well beyond the 1% level. These correlations can be interpreted more meaningfully when considered in conjunction with scatterplots shown in Figures 8.1–8.3. Plotted are the relationships in the zero-cue condition (full analogies) between solution time and numbers of values changed from A to B (on which the x and z' parameters are partially based), from A to C (on which the y' parameter is partially based), and from D to D' (on which the y' and z' parameters are partially based). Numbers of value changes reflect incorporation of dual processing and of the setting "true" analogies at 5.68 on the value-change scale.

Overall, Model III accounted for 86% of the variance in the data, with a root-mean-square deviation of 261 msec.

As in the People Piece Experiment, the parameter estimates for attribute-comparison components reflect the amount of time taken per "value change." However, the average number of attributes processed by each comparison component was not the same, since in general, more attributes will be processed by an exhaustive component (such as x) than by a self-terminating one (such as y' and z'). Figure 8.4 partitions the amount of time spent on a typical analogy into the amount of time spent on each of the five components. These partitions are invariant under linear transformation of the zero to eight value-change scale, because they represent total time spent on each operation rather than time per value change. It is thus possible to interpret partitions for attribute-comparison components, as well as for the other components, in terms of the absolute amount and the proportion of time spent on each component.

The most striking feature of the distribution is that more than half the amount of time spent on solving analogies was spent in encoding, a clear increase from the People Piece Experiment. As previously mentioned, this suggests that encoding of words takes longer than encoding of People Pieces. The amount of time spent on preparation—response is about the same as in the People Piece Experiment, but since total solution times were longer, the percentage of time is decreased. The amount of time spent on the attribute-comparison components is also greater for verbal than for People Piece analogies, reflecting the greater difficulty of the relationships among analogy terms. The proportion of time spent on the attribute-comparison components, however, was about 30% in both experiments. For two types of analogies, most of a subject's time is spent in preparation—response and in encoding, rather than in attribute comparison.

Figure 8.5 presents a scatterplot of predicted versus observed data points for Model III. Solution times for the 168 data points ranged from 535 to 3534 msec, with a mean of 1717 msec and a standard deviation of 686 msec. The plot

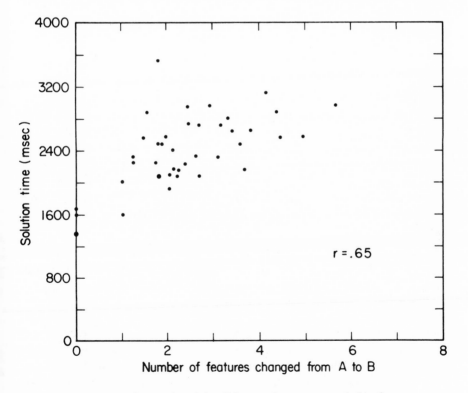

FIGURE 8.1   Scatter plot of A to B feature changes versus solution time.

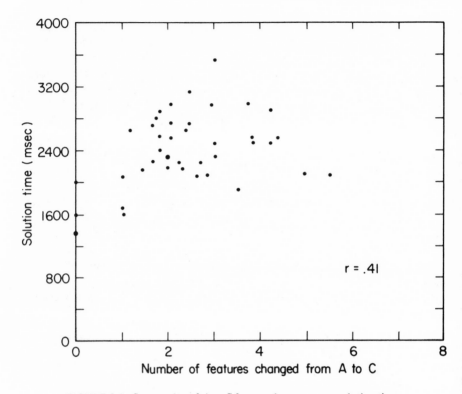

FIGURE 8.2   Scatter plot of A to C feature changes versus solution time.

is relatively homoscedastic. However, there are some systematic mispredictions. One point, in the upper right portion of the plot, was seriously mispredicted. In general, there was a tendency to overpredict solution times on very easy items (particularly degenerate items in the three-cue condition) and to underpredict solution times on very hard items (such as difficult items in the zero-cue condition). These results suggest that a nonlinear transformation of one or more scales used in forming independent variables might have improved fit to some extent.

Component models for error data.   As in the People Piece Experiment, it is possible to model error rates in the same way as solution times. The componential theory should predict error rates as well as solution times.

Respective fits for Models I to IV were 10.0%, 11.4%, 12.2%, and 13.8%. Although these values differ significantly from zero, they are obviously very low, much lower than in the preceding experiment. The low fits may be due to the idiosyncratic knowledge gaps that resulted in many of the errors. Such gaps are not a problem in People Piece or geometric analogies, where indeed, the fits are much better. Whatever the reason for these results, they are clearly unsatisfactory.

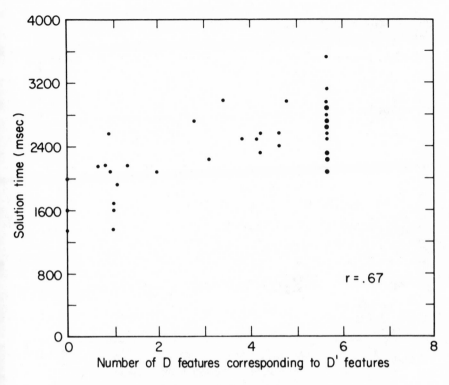

FIGURE 8.3 Scatter plot of *D* to *D'* feature changes versus solution time.

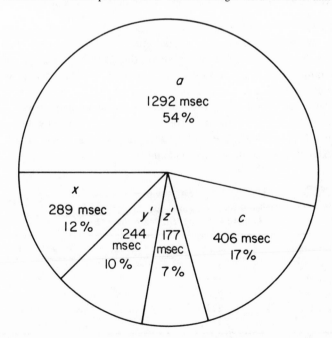

FIGURE 8.4 Distribution of component time on a typical verbal analogy (Model III).

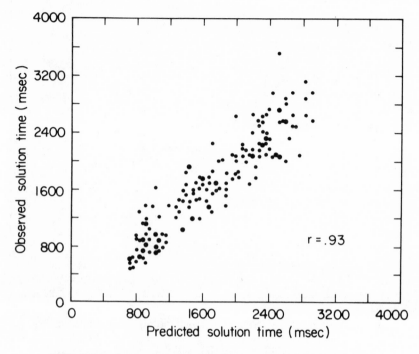

FIGURE 8.5   Scatter plot of predicted versus observed solution time.

Individual differences. Individual model fits were much poorer than in the People Piece Experiment, reflecting perhaps the fact that each fit was based upon 168 rather than 1152 observations per subject. The models were not distinguishable. Models I to IV accounted for an average of 46.2, 47.4, 47.8, and 47.6% of the variance in the data respectively. Subsequent analyses will be based upon Model III parameter estimates (component scores) for individual subjects. There were substantial individual differences in how well Model III accounted for individual data, and these are discussed later.

TABLE 8.5

Basic Statistics for Scores in Verbal Analogy Experiment:
Model III Component Scores ($N = 16$)

Component score	Mean	Standard deviation	Number of observations
a (Encoding)	343	94	2,688
x (Inference)	112	42	2,688
y' (Mapping)	220	151	2,688
z' (Application)	225	138	2,688
c (Preparation and Response)	339	287	2,688

TABLE 8.6
Model III Component Score Intercorrelations

	a	x	y'	z'	c
a	.45	−.56*	−.12	.43	−.48
x		.35	.30	−.44	.29
y'			.54*	.27	.47
z'				.26	.20
c					.82***

*$p < .05$.   ***$p < .001$.

Table 8.5 displays means and standard deviations across subjects for each of the component scores. There was most variance in the c component score, and least variance in the x component score.

Table 8.6 shows intercorrelations among component scores. Internal consistency reliability coefficients (split halves), corrected by the Spearman–Brown formula, are shown in the diagonal. Component score reliabilities are lower than in the People Piece Experiment, reflecting the instability of regression coefficients estimated for individuals on the basis of a small amount of data. Only the c component score is highly reliable.

Only two component scores were significantly correlated, a and x, and this correlation was negative. The corresponding correlation was not significant in the People Piece Experiment. The one negative correlation that was significant in the People Piece Experiment, that between a and c, just misses significance in this experiment.

Table 8.7 displays correlations between component scores from the People Piece and Verbal Analogy Experiments. These correlations must be interpreted

TABLE 8.7
Intercorrelations of Components from People Piece and
Verbal Analogy Experiments ($N = 16$)

People Piece components	Verbal analogy components				
	a	x	y'	z'	c
a	.25	.20	−.08	.06	−.30
x	−.02	.46	.18	−.15	.08
y'	−.40	.57*	57*	−.14	.11
z'	.20	−.11	.35	.59*	.33
c	−.46	.16	.54*	.16	.79***

*p < .05.   ***p< .001.

in light of the fact that all component scores were highly reliable in the People Piece Analogy Experiment, but only c was highly reliable in the Verbal Analogy Experiment. The y', z', and c component scores were significantly correlated across experiments. The correlation for c was particularly high, as would be expected both from its high reliability and from the fact that it is conceived to be unaffected by item content. The x component scores were not quite significantly correlated, although the correlation between them becomes highly significant when corrected for attenuation. The correlation between a component scores was not significant, nor was it significant after correction for attenuation. These data suggest, therefore, that mapping, application, preparation—response, and probably inference form stable sources of individual differences.

EXTERNAL VALIDATION

Reference Ability Tests

The reference ability test data used in this experiment were identical to those used in the People Piece Experiment. Hence, the analyses described in Chapter 7 are relevant here as well.

Interval Scores

Cue scores. Correlations of cue scores with ability test scores and factor scores are displayed in Table 8.8. The correlations are similar in several ways to those in the People Piece Experiment. All significance tests are two-tailed in this and subsequent analyses.

Once again, the cue scores $C0$ and $C1$, but not $C2$ and $C3$, show strong correlations with the reasoning factor scores. Correlations increase with more cues. The replication of the significant correlation for $C0$ is particularly striking, since $C0$ involves no processing of stimulus material.

A second replicated pattern is the significant correlations of $C1$, $C2$, and $C3$, but not $C0$, with perceptual-speed factor scores and certain tests. Rapid cue utilization thus seems to be in large part a perceptual phenomenon.

Solution scores. Correlations of solution scores with ability test scores and factor scores are shown in Table 8.9. There are several noteworthy patterns in the data. First, solution scores (unlike cue scores) do not appear to tap individual differences in perceptual speed. This result was also found in the People Piece Experiment. Second, solution scores do tap individual differences in reasoning. Correlations between solution scores and the reasoning factor score are significant for $S1$, $S2$, and $S3$, reaching $-.75$ for $S3$. The high correlations are exhibited for two of the three individual tests. Third, correlations *increase* with

TABLE 8.8
Correlations of Cue Scores with Ability Test Scores

	$C0$	$C1$	$C2$	$C3$
Reasoning				
Word grouping	−.27	−.39	−.29	−.25
Letter series	−.68**	−.69**	−.41	−.39
Cattell reasoning	−.67**	−.57*	−.34	−.34
Perceptual speed				
Same–different	−.23	−.42	−.59*	−.64**
Letter identification	−.29	−.32	−.43	−.36
French number comparison	−.08	−.12	−.28	−.37
French identical pictures	−.35	−.67**	−.63**	−.68**
Vocabulary				
French vocabulary (Levels 3, 4, 5)	−.33	−.59*	−.54*	−.52*
Factor I (perceptual speed)	−.32	−.53*	−.64*	−.68**
Factor II (reasoning)	−.63**	−.57*	−.28	−.24

$*p < .05.$ $**p < .01.$

TABLE 8.9
Correlations of Solution Scores with Ability Test Scores

	$S0$	$S1$	$S2$	$S3$
Reasoning				
Word grouping	−.17	−.27	−.30	−.38
Letter series	−.65**	−.73***	−.75***	−.80***
Cattell Reasoning	−.46	−.52*	−.51*	−.76***
Perceptual speed				
Same–different	−.27	−.24	−.11	−.24
Letter identification	.02	−.04	.00	−.20
French number comparison	−.29	−.12	−.04	−.22
French identical pictures	−.42	−.31	−.28	−.38
Vocabulary				
French vocabulary (Levels 3, 4, 5)	−.56*	−.57*	−.54*	−.51*
Factor I (perceptual speed)	−.31	−.26	−.15	−.32
Factor II (reasoning)	−.42	−.52*	−.57*	−.72**

$*p < .05.$ $**p < .01.$ $***p < .001.$

additional cues. This result was also found in the People Piece Experiment. It was shown to be attributable to the increasing importance of the c component in solution scores for more cues, and the same interpretation (which will be checked shortly) would seem reasonable here. Fourth, correlations of the solution scores with vocabulary are all significant, and higher than in the People Piece Experiment. The difference is consistent with the fact that the stimulus material was verbal in this experiment, but pictorial in the preceding experiment.

Component scores. The correlations of the interval scores with reference ability scores can be understood in terms of the correlations of the component scores with the ability test scores. These correlations are displayed in Table 8.10.

Consider first the pattern of correlations for a, the encoding score. In this experiment, it appears to be unrelated to perceptual speed as measured by any of the four tests. However, it shows a significant positive correlation with one of the three reasoning tests. The correlations with the factor score and the Thurstone reasoning composite (Word Grouping + 2(Letter Series)) are also significant. The trend appeared in the People Piece data, but did not reach significance. The positive correlation indicates that those who encoded items more slowly attained higher reasoning scores. A possible interpretation of this result will appear shortly, after correlations for the other parameters are discussed.

TABLE 8.10
Model III Component Score Correlations with Reference Ability Scores

	a	x	y'	z'	c
Reasoning					
Word grouping	.58*	−.50*	−.34	.08	−.54*
Letter series	.43	−.48	−.54*	−.23	−.78***
Cattell reasoning	.47	−.40	−.23	−.18	−.59*
Perceptual speed					
Same−different	−.14	−.14	.04	−.12	.13
Letter identification	.25	−.10	.06	−.09	.08
French number comparison	−.31	.04	.20	−.38	.18
French identical pictures	−.13	−.07	−.05	−.31	−.31
Vocabulary					
French vocabulary (Levels 3, 4, 5)	.19	−.45	−.54*	−.17	−.52
Factor I (perceptual speed)	−.10	−.11	.04	−.21	.01
Factor II (reasoning)	.63**	−.48	−.40	−.14	−.77***
(Thurstone reasoning composite)	.55*	−.56*	−.54*	−.14	−.80***

*$p < .05$.   **$p < .01$.   ***$p < .001$.

Next consider the pattern of correlations for x, the inference component score. Only the correlation with Word Grouping is significant, but the other two correlations are close ($p < .10$). The correlation with the factor score ($p < .10$) falls just short of significance, but the correlation with the Thurstone reasoning composite is significant ($p < .05$). These results indicate that subjects who were faster in inference received higher reasoning test scores.

The y' component score shows a significant correlation with one of the three reasoning tests. Neither of the other correlations is significant. The correlation with the Thurstone reasoning composite is significant, however. There is thus evidence indicating that subjects who were faster in mapping were superior in at least some aspects of reasoning.

None of the correlations of z' with reasoning scores are significant. As in the People Piece Experiment, there is no evidence that application is a source of individual differences in reasoning.

None of the attribute-comparison component scores shows significant correlations with perceptual-speed scores. Only mapping shows a significant correlation with the vocabulary score.

The pattern of correlations for c is familiar from the People Piece Experiment. The c component score is highly and significantly correlated with all three reasoning test scores, as well as with the reasoning factor score and the Thurstone reasoning composite. The correlations are comparable in magnitude to those in the People Piece Experiment, as they should be, since preparation–response is theoretically unaffected by item content. The c component score is also significantly correlated with vocabulary, but with none of the perceptual-speed scores.

What conclusions can be drawn when these correlations are considered in conjunction with those obtained in the People Piece Experiment?

First, the strongest conclusion is that preparation–response (c) is a source of individual differences in reasoning. This result appeared very clearly in both experiments, and as discussed in Chapter 7, has also appeared in various forms elsewhere in the experimental literature.

Second, there is evidence that at least two of the three attribute-comparison components, inference (x) and mapping (y'), are sources of individual differences in reasoning. These results support either the item easiness or attribute fixedness interpretation of the failure of x and y' to correlate with reasoning scores in the People Piece Experiment. According to this latter interpretation, the low correlations are due to the use of the same obvious attributes in each analogy. The results are obviously inconsistent with the speed–accuracy tradeoff explanation, since the speed–accuracy tradeoff instructions and even the subjects interpreting them were identical in both experiments. The results are also inconsistent with a strong form of the variance specificity hypothesis, which maintains that inference and mapping are operations specific to analogy solution. It remains to be determined whether there are circumstances under which the application component score, z', can be shown to measure reasoning ability. (It is shown in Chapter 9 that such circumstances exist.)

As mentioned in Chapter 7, a way of choosing between the attribute fixedness and item easiness explanations would be to conduct the People Piece Experiment with children (for whom the analogies are much more difficult) and determine whether any of the attribute-comparison component scores then correlate with reasoning. If so, the item easiness explanation is supported, and if not, the attribute fixedness explanation is favored.

A third result that requires explanation is the positive correlation between encoding time and reasoning scores. The result appeared strongly in this experiment, and was suggested by the People Piece data. It is unusual in the differential psychology literature to find that subjects who have more of one talent have less of another, although the obtained results might be interpreted as indicating something of this kind. An alternate and more satisfying explanation attributes the correlation to strategy differences.

There may be a tradeoff between encoding speed and the speed at which subsequent operations (requiring reasoning) are performed, as suggested by the negative correlation between encoding and inference scores. Slower and more thorough encoding may pay off in increased ability to compare attributes rapidly. An analogy can be drawn to results from one of S. Sternberg's (1969b) memory-scanning experiments. Sternberg used a degraded stimulus in order to lengthen the duration of the encoding stage. Initially, slope as well as intercept was affected by the experimental manipulation, indicating the comparison as well as the encoding stage was being affected. Subjects were not only taking longer to encode the degraded stimulus, but also appeared to be comparing a still partially degraded stimulus to the items in the memory set. Perhaps they were not taking enough additional time in encoding the degraded stimulus. After the first session, only intercept was affected, indicating that subjects had learned to "clean up" the stimulus during encoding. It was therefore possible to compare a clean stimulus to the elements of the memory set. In the Verbal Analogy Experiment, it may be that superior subjects encode the terms of the analogy more fully in order to facilitate inference of the relationship that underlies the analogy. A less efficient strategy used by other subjects would be to encode the stimulus more quickly, resulting in inference between two less than fully encoded stimuli. The encodings are degraded in the sense that they do not fully describe the attributes of each word, and therefore are less suited to the (apparently exhaustive) attribute comparison that takes place during inference. As with S. Sternberg's subjects, this is a less efficient strategy, and one likely to lead to an inferior outcome both in the present analogy task and in reasoning operations in general.

The other possibility (that might occur jointly with the above) is that slower encoding permits more efficient and therefore faster bookkeeping operations in problem solution. These operations enter into the c component. An analogy might be drawn to a lending library. By more careful initial cataloging of the contents of the library, it will become possible later to perform more efficiently the numerous bookkeeping operations that are required in a lending library (checking out books, recording returned books, inventorying books, etc.). The initial time savings acquired by sloppy cataloging will be more than dissipated later on. Similarly, slower and more careful encoding may permit more rapid later bookkeeping in analogy solution. In the analogy models, the bookkeeping operations are those that are part of the information-processing models but are not assigned separate components. Examples of such operations are initializing counters to zero, incrementing them by one, keeping track of value identities and changes, etc. Even the solution of a single analogy requires a very large number of such operations, and more efficient performance of them could easily offset increased encoding time.

The above explanations of the high positive correlation between encoding time and reasoning scores attribute the correlation to strategy differences between higher and lower reasoning subjects, not to ability differences. However, it is possible that subjects who are lower in reasoning simply are able to encode words more quickly. How can a strategy explanation be disentangled empirically from an ability explanation?

According to the strategy interpretation, the underlying source of the correlation between encoding and reasoning is not the absolute amount of time spent in encoding, but the amount of time relative to that spent on other processes: Encoding occupies a larger proportion of the higher reasoning subject's time, whereas subjects lower in reasoning spend proportionately less time in encoding, and proportionately more time in other processes. According to the ability interpretation, the underlying source of the correlation between encoding and reasoning is the absolute time difference. High-reasoning subjects are not able to encode stimuli as quickly as low-reasoning subjects. The two interpretations thus differ in their attribution of the source of the correlation between encoding and reasoning.

The two interpretations are empirically distinguishable. According to the strategy explanation, the high positive correlation between the encoding and reasoning scores should remain high, or even become higher, when encoding is scored ipsatively, that is, standardized separately for each subject, since individual differences between subjects are not considered. According to the ability explanation, the high positive correlation should be reduced or altogether eliminated if encoding is scored ipsatively.

The standardized regression coefficient (beta weight) for the encoding component is an ipsative score. Whereas the unstandardized regression coefficient, which is used as a component score, represents absolute time, the standardized regression coefficient represents relative time. Since it is standardized separately for each subject, variance in beta weights across subjects cannot be due to ability differences.

The correlations of the beta weights for encoding with the reasoning scores are .63 with Word Grouping ($p < .01$), .71 with Letter Series ($p < .01$), .54 with Cattell Reasoning ($p < .05$), and .72 with the reasoning factor score ($p < .01$). Each correlation is higher than its corresponding correlation for the unstandardized regression coefficients (component scores), and each is significant. The results therefore support the strategy explanation of the correlation between encoding and reasoning.

If this explanation is correct, then the correlations of encoding beta weights and reasoning scores ought also be examined for the People Piece Experiment. The correlations are .13 with Word Grouping ($p > .05$), .52 with Letter Series ($p < .05$), .54 with Cattell Reasoning ($p < .05$) and .54 with the reasoning factor score ($p < .05$). Each correlation is higher than its corresponding component score correlation, and two of the three individual test correlations and the factor score correlation are significant. This result further supports the strategy explanation and also reveals a strong relationship between encoding and reasoning that was concealed by the use of unstandardized coefficients.

It is of further interest that the correlation between the beta weights for the encoding and preparation–response component scores is $-.78$ for the People Piece Experiment ($p < .001$), and $-.70$ for the Verbal Analogy Experiment ($p < .01$). These correlations are higher than those for the corresponding component scores and show even more strongly the negative relationship between encoding and preparation–response time. The respective correlations with the inference (x), mapping (y'), and application (z') scores are $-.31$ ($p > .05$), $-.53$ ($p < .05$), and $-.34$ ($p > .05$) in the People Piece Analogy Experiment, and $-.68$ ($p < .01$), $-.70$ ($p < .01$), and $-.03$ ($p > .05$) in the Verbal Analogy Experiment. There is thus strong evidence of an inverse relationship between standardized encoding time and mapping time, at least some evidence of an inverse relationship between standardized encoding time and inference time, and no evidence of any relationship between standardized encoding time and application time. These results support the notion that a greater proportionate amount of time spent in encoding can lead to a reduction in the amount of time needed for other processes.

One might want to entertain the notion that other component score correlations with reasoning scores are also due to strategy differences. The data do not support this notion. Correlations of beta weights for x, y', and z' with reasoning scores are generally lower than those for the unstandardized component scores (no beta weight is available for c, since it is estimated as the constant in the regression equation). Only the difference in encoding time appears to be a difference in strategy.

The third result that requires explanation is the failure of the encoding component score (a) to correlate with perceptual speed scores. In the People Piece Experiment, there was just one significant correlation (with Letter Identification), suggesting that the encoding component as measured by the People Piece task might be the source of just a limited aspect of perceptual speed.

The perceptual speed tests reward somewhat superficial encoding – encoding that is just detailed enough to register a small number of essential attributes needed for a same–different or similar superficial judgment. One does not have to reason with the products of the encodings. This superficial encoding is adaptive for perceptual-speed tests, but not for reasoning tests: Quick and superficial encoding was associated with slower overall response times and with lower reasoning scores.

Relation between component and interval scores.   It is now possible to understand the interval score correlations with reference ability tests in terms of the component correlations with the tests. Correlations between component scores and interval scores are shown in Table 8.11. Patterns of correlations are almost identical to those in the People Piece Experiment. Once again, encoding and inference account for only trivial proportions of individual difference variance in the interval scores. Application accounts for significant proportions of variance in $S0$ and $S2$. As in the People Piece Experiment, mapping and preparation–response account for the bulk of the individual difference variance (lending further support to the psychological reality of the mapping component, since a nonexistent component cannot be a source of individual-differences variance, any more than it can be a source of variance across items).

The correlations of the interval scores with reasoning scores are seen to be attributable primarily to preparation–response variance and secondarily to mapping variance. The increasing correlation of c with successive solution scores explains once again the increasing correlation of the successive solution scores with reasoning scores. The significant correlation of preparation–response with $C0$ and $C1$, but not $C2$ and $C3$, also explains the correlation of $C0$ and $C1$, but not $C2$ and $C3$, with reasoning scores. The contributions of mapping are not

TABLE 8.11
Correlations of Component Scores with Interval Scores

	Component score				
	a	x	y'	z'	c
Solution score					
$S0$	.12	.22	.77***	.62*	.55*
$S1$	−.16	.41	.85***	.38	.58*
$S2$	−.17	.28	.86***	.51*	.69**
$S3$	−.46	.33	.58*	.39	.77***
Cue score					
$C0$	−.42	.10	.43	.48	.68**
$C1$	−.25	.20	.59*	.36	.71**
$C2$	−.09	.20	.49	.47	.45
$C3$	.07	.27	.50*	.46	.33

$*p < .05.$ $**p < .01.$ $***p < .001.$

strong enough, and its correlations with reasoning scores probably not powerful enough, to change this pattern of correlations.

Percentage of variance accounted for by parameters in individual data. One substantial source of individual differences that has been discussed little is the fits of Model III (and of the theory in general, since the models were not well distinguished in this experiment) to individual data. Are these individual differences systematic, and if so, how?

One might conjecture that subjects who are higher in reasoning are more systematic in their solution of analogy and other problems, and hence the data of better reasoners might be more reliable than those of poorer reasoners. If the componential theory in general and Model III in particular were the true theory and model, then one might expect better model fits to be associated with higher reasoning scores. Such a conjecture is speculative, but is in fact supported by the data shown in Table 8.12.

Table 8.12 shows the correlations between percent variance accounted for by Model III in the Verbal Analogy Experiment and scores used in the People Piece and Verbal Analogy Experiments.

There seems to be little that these percentages are not correlated with: Perceptual-speed measures and certain component scores appear to be the only exceptions. Of particular interest are the very substantial correlations with two of the three reasoning tests and with the reasoning factor score and the Thurstone reasoning composite. The percent-variance-accounted-for statistic is significantly correlated with all but one of the interval scores in the two experiments (the one exception just missing significance), and with the mapping and preparation—response components in both experiments.

These correlations are supportive of the componential theory. Unless the theory were actually capturing the major aspects of performance in the analogical reasoning task, it is difficult to see how these correlations could have been obtained. The correlations further suggest that even the degree to which the model fits data from the Verbal Analogy Experiment is a significant variable in its own right. More able subjects tend to be more systematic in their solution of the analogy problems, and the system they use appears to be that specified by the theory.

One further result of interest is the trivial correlation between the percent variance accounted for in this experiment and that same statistic in the People Piece Experiment (−.05). The statistic in that experiment appears to have a very different meaning. If an analogous table were presented for the statistic in the People Piece Experiment, only one significant correlation would be shown, and that would obviously be best attributable to chance. (It is with the x component score for the People Piece Experiment.) Why should the statistic mean such different things in the two experiments? One simple explanation is that the statistic was reliable in the Verbal Analogy Experiment, but unreliable in the People Piece Analogy Experiment, and therefore incapable of correlating with

TABLE 8.12
Correlations of Verbal Analogy Model III:
Percentage of Variance Accounted for and other Measures

Interval scores		Reference ability scores	
People Piece Experiment		Reasoning	
C0	−.51*	Word grouping	.44
C1	−.53*	Letter series	.71**
C2	−.53*	Cattell reasoning	.56*
C3	−.48		
S0	−.72**		
S1	−.81***		
S2	−.85***		
S3	−.66**	Perceptual speed	
		Same−different	.23
Verbal Analogy Experiment		Letter identification	.23
C0	−.78***	French number comparison	.03
C1	−.73***	French identical pictures	.20
C2	−.68**		
C3	−.57*		
S0	−.73***		
S1	−.90***		
S2	−.87**		
S3	−.88***	Vocabulary	
		French vocabulary	
Component Scores		(Levels 3, 4, 5)	.51*
People Piece Experiment			
a	−.06		
x	.00	FACTOR I (perceptual speed)	.24
y'	−.70**		
z'	−.47	FACTOR II (reasoning)	.61*
c	−.59*	(Thurstone reasoning	
Verbal Analogy Experiment		composite)	.71**
a	.48		
x	−.47		
y'	−.76***	People Piece Model III (%)	
z'	−.27	variance accounted for	−.05
c	−.61*		

*$p < .05$.   **$p < .01$.   ***$p < .001$.

anything. However, the reliability of the statistic was .74 in the People Piece Analogy Experiment, and .69 in the Verbal Analogy Experiment, so that if anything, the difference was in the wrong direction. A more plausible explanation relates to attribute fixedness and task definition.

In the People Piece Experiment, analogy items seemed to invite a systematic attribute-comparison strategy, at least in adult subjects: Attributes and attribute values were well defined, were constant over items, and could be sequentially sampled with a trivial attribute-discovery process. In the Verbal Analogy Experiment, neither attributes nor attribute values were well defined, and they changed from item to item. The subject must *discover* attributes, as well as *test* specific values of them. This discovery process, rather than the test process, may be the core of reasoning. It may explain the correlation of inference and mapping with reasoning in this experiment coupled with the absence of such a correlation in the People Piece Experiment. It may also explain the differential function of the percentage of variance accounted for statistic in the two experiments. The correlations may appear only when definition of task-attribute structure is nontrivial and places a burden upon the subjects in addition to that of merely working within the attribute structure once it is defined. This interpretation would seem to be related to findings of DeGroot (1965) and of Chase and Simon (1973) in their studies of the locus of chess-playing skill. The difference between better and worse players appeared to be in their ability to structure meaningfully the patterns on the chess board. The ability to impose a meaningful organization on an ill-defined stimulus would appear to be crucial in complex reasoning tasks.

Reference ability models. Reference ability models are considered in conjunction with the structural regression model about to be described.

INTEGRATION

The findings of the interval score, component, and reference ability models are integrated through the structural regression model, which is shown in Figure 8.6. Coefficients along paths are standardized regression coefficients, and bold face numerals are multiple correlations.

The multiple correlation of the solution scores with the reasoning factor score (R) was .76. The path coefficients are difficult to interpret because of the simplicial structure of the variables. $S3$ and $S2$ make strong contributions, while $S0$ serves as a suppressor variable. (The same type of pattern was found in the People Piece Experiment.)

The multiple correlation of the full set of component scores with the reasoning factor score was .87. This correlation is higher than that for the interval scores, because the components are not bound together by task constraints: They are separated and therefore able to make contributions independent of each other. This high correlation indicates that in combination, the components give a good account of individual differences in reasoning. The c and a components account for most of the individual difference variance. The coefficients are of opposite sign, as would be expected from the negative correlation of c but the positive correlation of a with reasoning. The component scores also provide a good account of individual difference variance in the solution scores, with multiple correlations ranging from .87 for S3 to .96 for $S2$ and $S0$. Individual differences

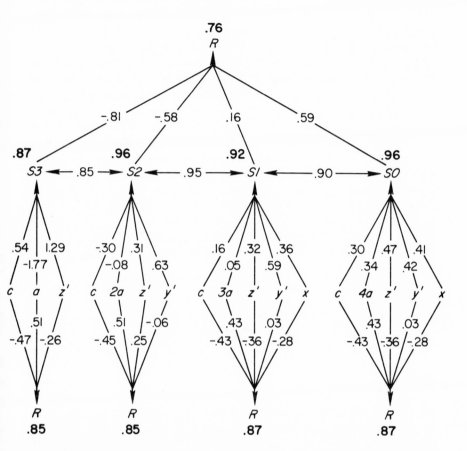

FIGURE 8.6   Structural regression relating component scores, interval scores, and reasoning reference ability.

in overall analogical reasoning latency can thus be accounted for by individual differences in component latencies.

SUMMARY

The 16 subjects from the People Piece Experiment participated in a second experiment requiring solution of 168 true-false verbal analogies, such as hand:foot::finger:toe. Half the analogies were keyed as true and half as false. Included within each group were degenerate, semidegenerate, and nondegenerate items.

Analogies were selected and keyed by having 24 subjects otherwise uninvolved in the experiment complete 190 open-ended analogies. Analogies were eliminated from the item pool if there was not a strong consensus regarding the best completion. A few other analogies appearing to depend upon advanced vocabulary or general information were also eliminated. Of the items remaining, half were used as true analogies and half as false analogies. The false analogies were falsified by choosing a distractor for the fourth term rather than the correct answer. Half the distractors were chosen to be highly associated with the correct answer, and half to be of low association.

Twenty-eight different subjects were presented with 860 pairs of words (spread out over two sessions), and were asked to judge the relatedness of each pair. Included in the list were all possible nonidentical pairs between A and B, A and C, B and D, and C and D. For false items, three additional pairs were included: B and D', C and D', and D and D' (where D was the presented answer and D' the correct answer). Subjects were instructed to rate the "associative relatedness" of each pair of items, and these ratings were later used as the basis for value change distances.

As expected, cue times increased and solution times decreased with more cues. Both cue and solution scores were highly reliable. Solution scores exhibited generally simplicial structure, although there was a slight breakdown among solution scores. There was no evidence in any subsequent data analysis that the slight breakdown had any nontrivial effect upon interpretation of results.

Individual error rates ranged from .6% to 7.1%, averaging 4.2%. Error rates decreased with more cues. There was evidence of only a very slight speed—accuracy tradeoff. Solution latencies were highly correlated with error rates across items.

Application of the component theory and models to verbal analogies was identical to that in the People Piece Experiment, with three exceptions. First, subjective (rated) distances rather than objective distances were used. Second, item solution times were averaged together according to a different criterion. Third, true items were rescaled. Dual processing was incorporated into all four basic models and their variants.

The dual-processing models all accounted for the data quite well, supporting the theory but making it difficult to select a best model. Data for the zero-cue condition alone, however, were somewhat more consistent with Model III than with other models. This was also the preferred model in the People Piece Experiment. Overall, Model III accounted for 86% of the variance in the data, compared with 92% in the People Piece Experiment. All parameters, including the mapping one, appeared to be necessary elements of the model.

An analysis of the distribution of component time on a typical verbal analogy revealed that as in the People Piece Experiment, attribute-comparison operations occupied about 29% of the time spent in analogy solution. Encoding appears to have occupied about 54% of the time, and preparation—response processes 17%.

There was no evidence of substantial differences in which model subjects used, although there did appear to be substantial individual differences in the extent to which subjects used any of the models at all.

Only the a and x component scores were significantly correlated (negatively). The inference, mapping, application, and preparation-response components, but not the encoding component, were sources of consistent individual differences across experiments.

As in the People Piece experiment, $C0$ and $C1$ tapped individual differences in reasoning, but $C1$, $C2$, and $C3$ tapped individual differences in perceptual speed. $S1$, $S2$, and $S3$ correlated significantly with reasoning. The correlations of the solution scores with reasoning increased with more cues. No significant correlations were obtained between solution scores and perceptual speed.

Understanding of the pattern of interval score correlations with reference ability test scores was sought through analysis of the correlations of component scores with ability test scores. The encoding, inference, mapping, and preparation—response components were all shown to be sources of individual differences in reasoning. In the case of encoding, more rapid encoding was associated with lower reasoning scores. Application was unrelated to reasoning. None of the components was a source of individual differences in the perceptual speed tests.

The correlation of the preparation—response score with the reasoning factor score and tests replicated the result obtained in the People Piece Experiment (with the same subjects). The additional correlations for inference and mapping suggested that the failure to obtain significant correlations in the People Piece Experiment may have been due either to item easiness or attribute fixedness. The speed—accuracy tradeoff hypothesis and a strong form of the variance specificity hypothesis were not supported, since these hypotheses could not account for the fact that the correlations were significant in this experiment but not in the other.

The positive correlation between encoding time and reasoning scores was interpreted as evidence that slower and more thorough encoding may pay off in increased ability to compare attributes rapidly or to perform efficiently the numerous bookkeeping operations involved in problem solution. The failure of encoding time to correlate significantly with perceptual speed measures may be due to the different task requirements in reasoning versus perceptual-speed tasks. The former reward complete and careful encoding, whereas the latter reward quick and possibly incomplete encoding.

It had been found in an earlier analysis that there were substantial individual differences in how well the componential theory and Model III accounted for data of individual subjects. External validation revealed these differences to be strikingly systematic. Percent variance accounted for in the Verbal Analogy Experiment was highly correlated with measures of reasoning ability, as well as with interval scores and the y' and c component scores. The statistic was not significantly correlated with perceptual speed. These correlations suggested that subjects higher in reasoning ability tend to be more systematic in their solution of analogy problems and the system they use is that specified by the componential theory.

The comparable percent variance statistic obtained in the People Piece Experiment was not correlated with the verbal analogy statistic; furthermore, it was uncorrelated with all but one of the many measures used in the two experiments. The discrepancy was tentatively attributed to a fundamental difference between People Piece and verbal analogies. Subjects solving verbal analogies must discover relevant attributes as well as test values of these attributes. The discovery process in the People Piece analogies is trivial, since the same well-specified attributes are applicable to every analogy. The correlations may appear only when definition of task-attribute structure is a nontrivial task.

9
The Geometric Analogy Experiment

The third experiment in the series was the Geometric Analogy Experiment.[1] Experimental stimuli were geometric forms such as squares, triangles, circles, and combinations of these and similar forms. The dependent variables were solution time and error rate. Subjects viewed each analogy in a tachistoscopic field and pressed the appropriate button to indicate their choice of either of two presented answer options. The major independent variable was item difficulty, which was manipulated by varying numbers of value changes, complexities of geometric figures, and amount of precueing information.

METHOD

Materials

The experimental stimuli were 90 forced-choice geometric analogies. Analogies were selected from the analogies subtests of the 1934, 1941, 1946, and 1947 editions of the American Council on Education Psychological Examination for College Freshmen.[2]

All items selected for use in the experiment were modified in two ways:

1. The number of answer options was reduced from five to two. Included were the keyed option and a randomly selected option.

2. Items were drawn by an artist in enlarged form on 6 X 9-inch cards suitable for insertion into a tachistoscope.

[1] I am grateful to Michael Gardner for serving as coexperimenter, and for his valuable assistance in various aspects of the experiment.
[2] I am grateful to Rex Jackson of Educational Testing Service for making available to me the ACE analogies.

In addition, 36 of the 90 items (40%) were converted into degenerate or semidegenerate form. Twelve of the analogies appeared in the form $A{:}A{:}{:}A{:}D_1,D_2$; another 12 appeared in the form $A{:}A{:}{:}B{:}D_1,D_2$; and the third group of 12 appeared in the form $A{:}B{:}{:}A{:}D_1,D_2$. For both these analogies and the 54 nondegenerate analogies, the correct answer was D_1 for half the items and D_2 for the other half.

The agreement permitting use of the test items prohibited reproduction of the items in this volume. Some actual items are reproduced, however, in Evans (1968). Figure 9.1 displays items similar to those used in the experiment. As in the actual items, a single vertical line separates the item stem ($A{:}B{:}{:}C{:}$) from the two answer options (D_1, D_2). Whereas the geometric figures were centered on the card, the vertical line was drawn the full length of the card so that it would not be viewed as part of the item.

The first seven items are nondegenerate. It can be seen that they range in difficulty from quite easy to very difficult. The eighth and ninth items are semidegenerate, and the tenth is degenerate. The degenerate items varied somewhat in difficulty, with difficulty depending upon the complexity of the geometric form.

Procedure

Pretesting. The experiment began with ability testing of an entire autumn quarter introductory psychology class at Stanford University. The class, Psychology 1, contained 441 students the day of testing.

Subjects were instructed to enter their name, campus address, and telephone number on the cover of the test booklet. They were then asked to read the directions for the first of two tests, Word Grouping. This test was an expanded (40-item) version of the test described in Chapter 7 and was timed for 3 min.

The second test was the Card Rotations Test (Test S-1) from the French Kit of Reference Tests for Cognitive Factors (French, Ekstrom, & Price, 1963). This test requires mental rotation of geometric forms. Subjects were presented with a target stimulus at the left of a row, followed by a series of figures that were the *same* or *different*. *Same* figures were rotated versions of the figure appearing at the left. *Different* figures were both rotated and reflected to form a mirror image. Therefore, the *different* figures could not be rotated in two dimensions into congruence with the target figure at the left. The test was divided into two parts, with 14 rows of figures in each part. Subjects were permitted 2 min to work on each part.

Subject selection. Although both tests were used in external validation, only the first test (Word Grouping) was used in subject selection, since selection was desired on reasoning but not spatial visualization. (The Card Rotations Test was used in conjunction with the Word Grouping Test for selection of subjects to participate in a different experiment not described in this volume. There was no overlap of subjects between experiments.)

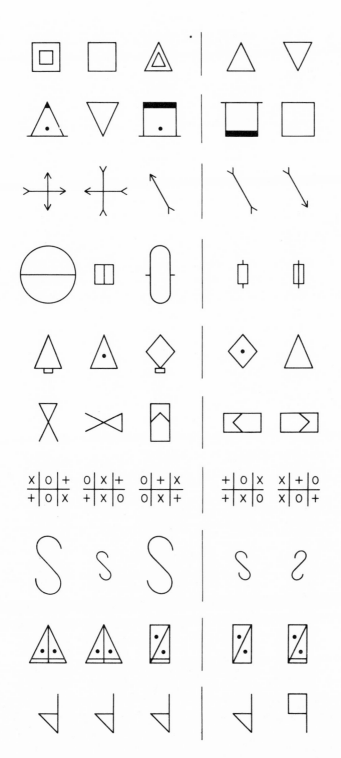

FIGURE 9.1 Types of items used in the Geometric Analogy Experiment.

257

A computer printout was obtained for subjects falling into each of two groups: (1) subjects scoring between the 75th and 95th percentiles on the Word Grouping test; (2) subjects scoring between the 5th and 25th percentiles on the Word Grouping test. Twenty-four subjects, 12 in each group, participated in the experiment.

Session 1.   When the subjects arrived, they were seated in front of a tachisto-scope, and then were oriented to the experiment. Testing procedures were somewhat different from those in the first two experiments. The three major differences in procedure were: (1) subjects were prepared for forced-choice rather than true—false analogies, (2) only the zero-cue and two-cue conditions were used, and (3) a footpedal rather than a button was used to terminate precueing. Solution responses, however, were still indicated by buttons.

As in the preceding two experiments, two experimenters were involved in testing. One manipulated tachistoscope cards; the other recorded response times.

Item presentation order was randomized for each subject. Presentation of items was divided into four blocks. The first two blocks consisted of 15 items per block. The second two blocks consisted of 30 items per block. Each block contained items in a single cueing condition. Two cue orders were used: 0–2–0–2; 2–0–2–0. Half the subjects in each group received each cue order. Subjects received all items in both cue conditions.

After geometric analogy testing was completed, subjects were given further ability tests, including a Letter Series Test, Form A of the Cattell Culture-Fair Test of *g*, and the Extended Range Vocabulary Test (Test V-3) from the French Kit. The test was administered without time limit.

Session 2.   The second session took place on the average two months after the first session. Subjects were reoriented to the experiment with the same instructions, given the 12 practice trials, and then tested on the geometric analogies. Subjects who had received the cue order 0–2–0–2 in the first session received the cue order 2–0–2–0 in the second session, and vice versa. Subjects who had received Form 1 items in the zero-cue condition and Form 2 items in the two-cue condition received the opposite pairing of forms and cues, and vice versa. Therefore, after the second session, all subjects had received all items in both cue conditions, and cue orders had been counterbalanced.

Subjects were asked whether they remembered any specific items from the first session. Most subjects reported that some items looked vaguely familiar, but recollection of specific items seemed to play little if any part in item solution.

After geometric analogy testing, all subjects were given three additional ability tests. The first was the Figure Classification Test (Test I-3) from the French Kit. In each problem on the test there are either two or three groups, each consisting of three figures. Subjects must discover what rule the figures in each group have in common that excludes the figures from the other groups, and then identify the group in which each of a collection of test figures belongs. The next two tests were of spatial visualization ability. The second test was Form MA of the

Minnesota Paper Form Board, requiring subjects to visualize what fragmented forms would look like if their parts were assembled. The third test was the Cube Comparison Test (Test S-2) from the French Kit, requiring subjects to decide whether different views of two cubes *can* be the same, or *must* be different.

The fourth test, administered as an afterthought, was given only to the last 15 subjects. Since subjects were called in a random order, no selection effect was expected, and analyses comparing performances of these 15 subjects to those of the other 9 subjects reveal that no selection effect did occur. The test was Analogies from the Lorge–Thorndike Intelligence Test (1954 edition), Level 5. The test consists of geometric analogies similar to those on the ACE tests from which the experimental stimuli were taken. Items are of the form, $A:B::C:D_1$, D_2, D_3, D_4, D_5.

Value transformation ratings. Forty-eight subjects were presented with geometric analogy items as they appeared in the American Council on Education (ACE) examination, but were not told the items were analogies. Instead, they were told that the items contained geometric forms, and that their task was "to rate the complexity of the transformation which maps the first of the numbered pieces into the second."

Transformations to be rated were those from the A to B analogy terms, the A to C terms, and the D_1 to D_2 terms. Null transformations (used in degenerate and semidegenerate analogies) were not rated. The task took about 40 min.

Figure complexity ratings. A second group of 48 subjects received the same booklets, but were asked to rate the complexity of each figure. Subjects used a one-to-nine scale, where one indicated an extremely simple geometric form, and nine indicated an extremely complex form. Figures to be rated corresponded to the A, B, C, D_1, and D_2 terms of all analogies, including degenerate and semidegenerate ones. The task took about 45 min.

Ratings of distance from given answer to correct answer. Thirty new subjects were given the geometric analogies in open-ended form, and told to visualize the correct answer. They were then instructed to rate on a zero-to-nine scale the distance from their visualized answer to a presented answer. A rating of zero indicated the answers were identical, while a rating of nine indicated they were extremely different. Every subject received each item twice, once with the keyed answer, and once with the nonkeyed answer. Ratings were thus obtained from the same subjects for the distance from the visualized answer to both the incorrect and correct answers. The task took about 1.5 hr, and was divided into two sessions.

Ratings of distance from third term to correct answer. This task was similar to that above, except that only the first three terms of the analogy (the item stem) appeared on each of 90 cards. Thirty new subjects were asked to rate the distance from the third (C) term of the analogy to a visualized answer. The task took about 40 min.

Subjects

Six subjects in each group were male and six were female. All were freshmen or sophomores in Psychology 1, participating for pay and/or credit.

Design

Two precueing conditions (zero and two cues) were crossed with value changes and figure complexities as determined by ratings. Items were of three general types: degenerate, semidegenerate, and nondegenerate.

INTERNAL VALIDATION

Interval Scores

Basic statistics. Table 9.1 presents means and standard deviations for cue and solution times, as well as the numbers of observations upon which each statistic is based. Since each of 24 subjects received 90 trials in each cue condition, the overall number of observations is 2160 for each condition.

As expected, cue times increased and solution times decreased with more cues. Mean response times are much longer than in the People Piece and Verbal Analogy Experiments. The mean overall solution time for full analogies ($S0$) is 4.6 times as long as in the People Piece Analogy Experiment, a difference of 5.16 sec. Mean overall $S0$ time is 2.7 times as long as in the Verbal Analogy Experiment, a difference of 4.16 sec. Differences in cue time are not readily interpretable, because a footpedal was used for cue offset in this experiment, whereas a button was used for cue offset in the preceding two experiments.

Decreases in response time across sessions were moderately small, as would be expected when about two months intervene between sessions. Since this analysis and subsequent ones indicated only a trivial practice effect, most of the analyses will be reported only for combined sessions.

Reliabilities. Internal consistency reliabilities ranged from .91 to .96.

Simplex model. Because there were only two cueing conditions in the experiment, it is not possible to test for simplicial structure across interval scores. It will be possible to check for additivity in component scores, however, by comparing parameter estimates for both cueing conditions to those obtained for the zero-cue condition only.

Error Rates

Individual error rates ranged from 1.1 to 9.4% with a mean of 4.6%. As expected, error rate decreased across cue conditions. Correlations with solution

TABLE 9.1
Basic Statistics for Scores in Geometric Analogy Experiment:
Interval Scores[a] (N = 24)

	Mean	Standard deviation	Number of observations
Cue scores			
Overall			
$C0$	.95	.31	2,160
$C2$	3.83	1.25	2,160
Session 1			
$C0$	.99	.32	1,080
$C2$	4.21	1.61	1,080
Session 2			
$C0$	.94	.33	1,080
$C2$	3.46	1.21	1,080
Solution scores			
Overall			
$S0$	6.58	1.81	2,160
$S2$	4.78	1.67	2,160
Session 1			
$S0$	6.69	2.09	1,080
$S2$	4.92	1.60	1,080
Session 2			
$S0$	6.47	1.93	1,080
$S2$	4.63	1.98	1,080

[a]Response times are expressed in seconds.

scores (−.41 and −.50) showed evidence of a speed–accuracy tradeoff, but correlations with cue scores (.05 and .04) did not. The correlation of error rate with solution latency across item types was .71. As would be expected, item difficulty was reflected both in longer solution latencies and higher error rates.

Component Scores

Mathematical formulation of the models. Mathematical modeling proceeded along the lines described in the previous chapters. Solution times for the 180 data points were used as the primary criterion to be predicted. The predictors were numbers of terms to be encoded and functions of numbers of attribute value changes. Equations were almost identical to those displayed in Table 7.4, except that there were five terms rather than four to be encoded. In this experiment, it was not adequate to estimate amount of encoding by the number of new stimulus figures presented in the second part of the trial, because some stimulus figures were much more complex than others and, therefore, presumably required more encoding. Amount of encoding was instead assumed to depend upon figure complexities.

The modeling process was simplified by the use of just two answer options, but similar principles hold for any number of options. The number of exhaustive attribute-comparison operations required is a function of the number of value changes. The number of self-terminating attribute-comparison operations required depends upon the number of attributes changed from A to B, A to C, C to D', and D_1 to D_2 (assuming that one answer option is correct and the other incorrect). The maximum number of operations required will be determined by the distractor that is closest to the correct answer.

In mathematical modeling, all data, including both correct and error solution times, were used. Dual processing was not assumed, and appears to be used only when the stimuli are highly overlearned.

Reliability of data. The correlation across items of Session 1 and Session 2 solution times was .89. While this correlation is based upon the full set of data points, only half the subjects (12 of 24) contributed to a given data point in either session. Thus, this figure may be interpreted as a lower bound to the true reliability.

Addition of justification component. In forced-choice analogies, there need be no perfectly true answer, since the task requires selection of the better option (or if there are more than two options, the best option). Justification is required when either all options have been falsified or when multiple options have been found to be correct.

Was justification needed? The data suggest that it was. The mean and standard deviation of the distance from D' to D_F, (D', D_F), where D_F is the nonkeyed answer, are 4.86 and 1.85 respectively. The mean and standard deviation of the distance from D' to D_T, (D', D_T), where D_T is the *keyed* true answer, are .41 and .51, respectively. As would be expected, the distributions are quite far apart. What is of particular interest, however, is that the mean for (D', D_T) differs significantly from 0, $t(179) = 10.84$, $(p < .001)$. Individual values of (D', D_T) range from 0.00 $(D' = D_T)$ to 2.03, and of course the distribution is highly skewed (skewness = 1.68). It is clear, however, that keyed D_T answers cannot be assumed to equal or even closely approximate ideal D' answers.

There was no evidence that justification was ever needed because both presented answers were determined to be true. Rather, it appears to have been needed because both presented answers were determined to be false.

Component models with alternating option scanning. Models I–IV accounted for 73.8, 79.7, 80.4, and 80.0%, respectively, of the variance in the data. The rank order of the models is the familiar one – III, IV, II, I – although the models are not well distinguishable. Only the performance of Model I is clearly differentiated from the performance of the other models. The fit of Model III increased from 67.4% to 80.4% with the addition of justification. Since the justification parameter is both statistically and practically significant, the data support the addition of the justification parameter. They also indicate that the theory fits the data quite well.

Component models with zero cues only. It was not possible to test the succession of interval scores for simplicial structure, and so it is particularly important to test the component models for the zero-cue condition only. One is thereby able to compare results for the combined cueing conditions with those for full analogies only. Because the encoding parameter was estimated on the basis of figure complexity as well as number of terms to be encoded, it was possible for the first time to separate a and c in the zero-cue condition: Encoding was no longer constant across all items in this cueing condition.

Results of modeling for zero cues only are almost identical to those for the full data set. Model III, for example, now accounts for 80.3% of the variance in the data, rather than 80.4%. The stability of parameter estimates can also be assessed. The regression parameters are quite stable. Using the zero-cue parameter estimates as the criterion, we find that the percent error for a, x, y', z', t in Model III are 6, 5, 8, 12, and 13% respectively. However, the percent error for c is 307%. The value for the full set of data, .43 sec, is plausible (based upon past estimates in the preceding two experiments), but that for the zero-cue data, .14 sec, is not.

Component models for nondegenerate items only. Model fits for nondegenerate items only are about 10% worse, although still quite respectable. Model III accounts for 70% of the variance in the data (as does Model IV). Once again, the regression parameter estimates are fairly stable except for the value of c, here increasing to .73.

Individual sessions. All models except Model I perform better in Session 2 than in Session 1 (5% increase in fit). There is no evidence, however, that a different model is appropriate for each session: Model I is worst in both sessions, and the other models perform about equally well.

Component models without mapping parameter. The performance of the component models without the mapping parameter is reduced about 2.5%. This is the smallest reduction in any of the three experiments, providing the least support for the mapping parameter. It will therefore be of particular interest to determine whether the contribution of mapping in the final model is statistically significant.

Component models without effect of complexity upon encoding. In the modeling described so far, the multiplier for the encoding parameter has been determined by the mean of the complexity ratings. Does complexity actually have any effect upon solution time, however, over and above that of the number of figures that need to be encoded? Complexities were not used in the previous two experiments, and the results were quite satisfactory. Moreover, Cooper (1973) found no effect of stimulus complexity upon rate of mental rotation. This surprising result suggested the possibility that rates of other types of mental transformations may be independent of the complexity of the figures on which they are performed.

The percentage of variance accounted for by Model III (the best model) is reduced by 3.8%. However, the consequences of not using the complexity ratings are perhaps more serious than this decrease suggests. The simple correlation of amount to be encoded with solution time decreases from .49 to .24, and the standardized regression coefficient (beta weight) in the regression equation decreases from .24 to .10. The contribution of encoding is statistically significant when complexity ratings are used, but becomes trivial when only number of figures to be encoded is used. Since the number of parameters (and therefore regression df) is not increased by using the complexity ratings, and since they appear to be important to the model, they will be retained in subsequent analyses.

Component models with sequential option scanning. Four different variants of the sequential scanning strategy may be considered. The first employs exhaustive scanning on both D_1 and D_2. Only Model I is consonant with this strategy, since it involves exclusively exhaustive scanning. This model accounts for 73.8% of the variance in the data.

In a second variant, the first option is scanned exhaustively, and the second option is scanned in self-terminating fashion. In a third variant, the order of exhaustive and self-terminating scanning is reversed. One would expect the two variants to be about equally powerful, since there is no a priori reason to expect that exhaustive scanning of the first option followed by self-terminating scanning of the second option should be more plausible than self-terminating scanning of the first option followed by exhaustive scanning of the second option, or vice versa. Only Models II, III, and IV are consonant with either mixed strategy, since at least one scan is self-terminating. Model fits are almost identical under the two variants, and they account for the data less well than does the fully exhaustive Model I. In fact, the more self-terminating operations there are, the poorer the fit of the model. Models II, III, and IV account for 71.6, 67.8, and 64.1% of the variance in the data.

A fourth variant assumes self-terminating scanning of both options. One is assumed to scan each option until it is falsified, completing scanning only if the option is the correct option. In order to maximize fit, self-terminating scans onto each answer option were estimated as separate parameters. Thus, z' was estimated separately for Options 1 and 2 in all three models; y' was estimated separately for Options 1 and 2 in Models III and IV; and x' was estimated separately for Options 1 and 2 in Model IV. This parameter estimation procedure resulted in increased regression degrees of freedom for these models, but should have improved fit if the models explain what subjects do in solving analogies. However, fits are only comparable to those for the mixed models, and still worse than the fit for the fully exhaustive Model I.

Other variants of the sequential option scanning strategy were also tested, including ones in which scanning of the second option was never started if the first option was falsified. The performance of the other models was in no case better than the performance of the models considered above.

These results distinguish well between the alternating and sequential scanning strategies, supporting the alternating strategy. Even the best sequential scanning model (Model I for exhaustive scanning) is only equivalent to the worst of the alternating scanning models (also Model I).

What pattern in the data leads to the large difference between the two types of models? The crucial difference is in the correlation of (D', D_F) with solution time versus the correlations of (D', D_1) and (D', D_2) with solution time, where D_F represents the false answer option, and D_1 and D_2 the first and second answer options.

In the alternating scan models with self-terminating operations, the crucial correlation is that of the first distance: (D', D_F). Termination of scanning occurs when either option is falsified, and since scanning alternates between options, it does not matter which option is falsified. The correlation of the (D', D_F) distance with solution time was $-.53$, indicating that the greater the distance, the more quickly the analogy was solved.

In the sequential scan models with self-terminating operations, the crucial correlations are those for the second two distances: (D', D_1) and (D', D_2). Termination of scanning for a given option occurs when that particular option is falsified. The amount of time spent scanning the first option, for example, is independent of the amount of time spent scanning the second option (unlike in the alternating models). All that determines when scanning of that first option will terminate is the (D', D_1) distance. The same applies for scanning of the second option. The correlation of the (D', D_1) distance with solution time was $-.10$. The correlation of the (D', D_2) distance with solution time was $-.14$. These distances, therefore, do not influence solution time.

In other variants of the sequential strategy that were tested, the crucial pattern of correlations is more complex, because the second option is tested only if the first option is falsified, or is never tested at all. As previously stated, such models were no more successful than the ones for which results are displayed. An important point, however, is that strategies that do not *always* call for at least some testing of both options are bound to be maladaptive to the task, because D_T is frequently not identical to D'. Such strategies would lead to very high error rates due to the falsification of the better (although not perfectly correct) option. Thus, unless the correct option is digitally correct, as in the People Piece Experiment, at least some testing of both options is advisable.

Experimental data. The patterns in the experimental data can be better understood by inspection of scatterplots relating figure complexities and value changes to solution time. These scatterplots are shown for the zero-cue condition (full analogies) in Figures 9.2–9.6.

Figure 9.2 shows relationships between figure complexity and solution time. Solution time is plotted against A to B value changes in Figure 9.3, A to C feature changes in Figure 9.4, D' to D_F feature changes in Figure 9.5, and D' to D_T feature changes in Figure 9.6. The distance from D' to D_T is the single most powerful predictor of overall solution time. This result is especially astonishing in view of the very small range in values for this distance. Whereas other distances ranged in value almost over their full scale, (D', D_T) distances ranged only from 0.00 to 2.03. The full possible range was from 0.00 to 9.00. Apparently, even small discrepancies of the best answer from the ideal answer can result in large increases in solution latency.

Another pattern of interest is the curvilinear relationship between (D', D_F) and solution time. This curvilinear relationship is exactly as predicted by the self-terminating models. The variable h', the number of attributes actually

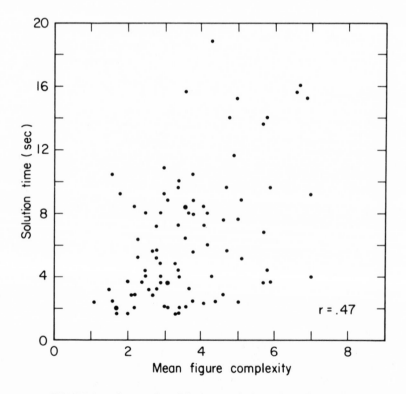

FIGURE 9.2   Scatter plot of figure complexity versus solution time.

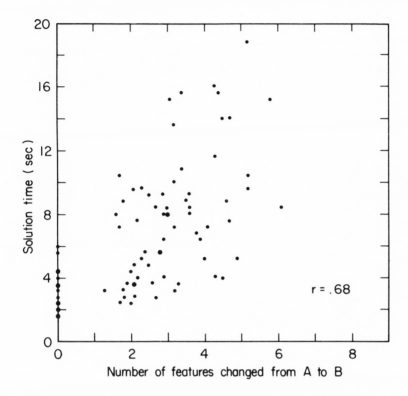

FIGURE 9.3   Scatter plot of A to B feature changes versus solution time.

examined in self-terminating search, is equal to $(N)/(N - h + 1)$, where N is the total number of possible attributes (equal to nine in the arbitrary scale used in this experiment), and h is the number of D_F features correctly matched to D'. (See Table 7.4 and discussion of it for further details.). Thus, the curvilinear relationship is a reciprocal function of (D', D_F). The curve is "straightened out" in the transformation from h to h'.

Final component model. The experimental data are consistent with the component theory of analogical reasoning. More specifically, they strongly support the alternating option scanning models over the sequential scanning models. The data discriminate less well among the models within the alternating scan class. Model I is clearly worse than the other models, but no single model is clearly better. Since Model III was the model of choice in the preceding two experiments, it will be adopted here.

Table 9.2 displays full statistics for component Model III. Parameter estimates are shown in the second column at the top. Only the parameter estimate for c is nonarbitrary, since others depend on the value transformation and complexity scales. The value of c, .43 seconds, is consistent with the values of c in the preceding experiments, but this parameter estimate is known from previous analyses to be unstable.

Each parameter is at least 3.9 times as large as its standard error, and F_{Reg} for each parameter is statistically significant at well beyond the 1% level. All parameters, therefore, merit inclusion in the full model. The contribution of the justification parameter is especially noteworthy, since it appears optionally only when given answer responses in forced-choice analogies are not identical to ideal answers.

The results of the stepwise multiple regression used in parameter estimation are shown at the bottom of the page. The first variable to enter the regression was t, and the last was x. The full model accounts for 80% of the variance in the data, with a root-mean-square deviation of 1.68 sec.

Predicted versus observed solution times are shown in Figure 9.7. Solution times for individual items (in either cue condition) ranged from 1.08 to 19.12 sec with a mean of 5.68 and a standard deviation of 3.78 sec. The model was thus required to predict over quite a wide range of solution times. The scatter plot is heteroscedastic: Prediction was not equally good at all points over the

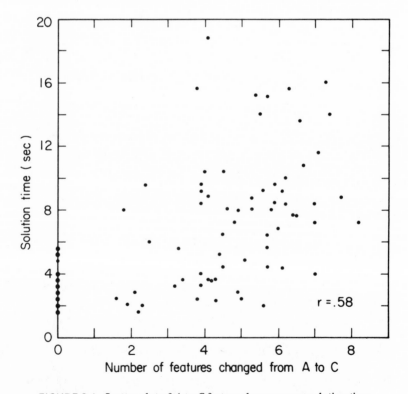

FIGURE 9.4   Scatter plot of A to C feature changes versus solution time.

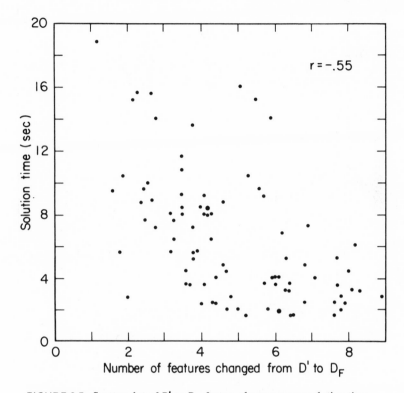

FIGURE 9.5 Scatter plot of D' to D_F feature changes versus solution time.

range of times. Prediction was relatively good in the lower and middle ranges of item solution times, and underprediction was about as likely as overprediction. Certain items tended to be systematically mispredicted, and these same items tended to be mispredicted both in the zero-cue and two-cue conditions.[3] Thus, lack of fit was attributable more to particularly poor prediction for a few items than to relatively small mispredictions for large numbers of items.

Figure 9.8 shows amounts and proportions of time spent on each component operation. There are several striking similarities to the distributions for the preceding experiments, but there are also some equally striking differences.

As in the preceding two experiments, encoding accounts for the largest amount and proportion of time. The proportion is almost identical to that in the People Piece Experiment, although, of course, the amount of time is much greater, 2.41 versus .56 sec. The amount of time spent on preparation—response

[3] There was a clear trend toward misprediction of items requiring spatial visualization (usually in the form of mental rotation). Value-transformation ratings tended to underestimate the difficulties of these items. Santesson (1974) also reported underestimation by subjects of difficulties of (figure matrix) items involving spatial transformations.

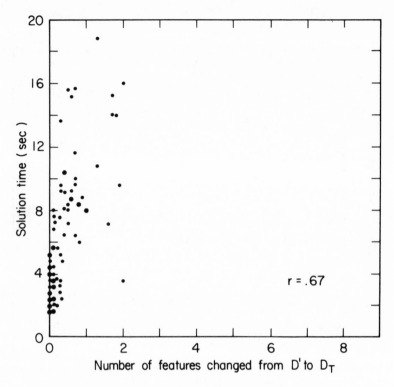

FIGURE 9.6   Scatter plot of D' to D_T feature changes versus solution time.

TABLE 9.2
Final Geometric Analogy Component Model III

Parameter	Parameter estimate	Standard error	β	F_{Reg}	df
a	0.66	0.11	0.24	38	1, 174
x	0.39	0.09	0.17	18	1, 174
y'	1.10	0.23	0.24	22	1, 174
z'	1.29	0.33	0.22	15	1, 174
t	5.47	0.58	0.38	90	1, 174
c	0.43				

Stepwise multiple regression

Parameter	Cumulative R^2	r	Cumulative F_{Reg}	Cumulative df
t	.52	.72	190	1, 178
z'	.67	.71	179	2, 177
a	.76	.49	189	3, 176
y'	.78	.67	158	4, 175
x	.80	.54	143	5, 174

Standard error of estimate: 1.70 sec

Root-mean-square deviation: 1.68 sec

270

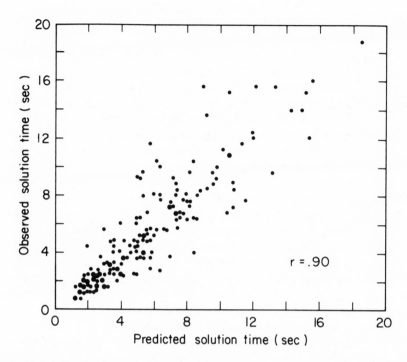

FIGURE 9.7 Predicted versus observed solution times in the geometric analogy experiment.

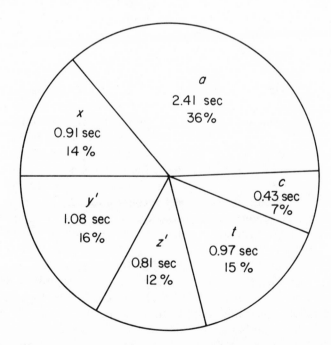

FIGURE 9.8 Distribution of component time on a typical geometric analogy.

271

is quite close to that in the preceding two experiments, but the proportion of time is much smaller. This result is consistent with expectations: Amount of time spent on preparation—response should be fairly constant across different types of analogies, but proportion of time should decrease as the analogies become more difficult and hence total solution time increases.

The striking difference between this distribution and the other two is in amount of time spent on attribute-comparison operations. In the other two experiments, about 30% of solution time was spent on attribute-comparison operations (x, y', z'). In this experiment, 57% of solution time is spent on attribute-comparison operations (x, y', z', t), an increase of close to 100%. Even if justification is excluded, the total proportion for x, y', and z' is 42%, a sizable increase over that for the preceding two experiments. This result is also consistent with expectations. In the People Piece Analogy Experiment, attribute comparison is relatively trivial: The same well-defined attributes are used on every trial, and hence it is not necessary to discover what the relevant attributes are. They are obvious. In the Verbal Analogy Experiment, word encoding becomes a particularly important operation and a source of important individual differences. The analogies were still relatively simple and, as a perusal of the sample analogies in Table 8.1 will show, determining relationships was not particularly difficult. In the Geometric Analogy Experiment, many of the relationships were quite difficult to determine, and once a relationship was inferred, it was often difficult to map or apply it. There are several analogies in which mapping was particularly difficult: It was not obvious how the attributes of the A analogy term related to those of C. In sum, much more of the difficulty of the geometric analogies was due to difficulty of the attribute-comparison operations.

Component model for error data. How well do the component models predict error data? It will be recalled that in the People Piece Analogy Experiment, the component models predicted error data very well (Model III accounted for 59% of the variance in the data), while in the Verbal Analogy Experiment, prediction of error data was unsuccessful (Model III accounted for 12% of the variance in the data). Prediction of error data in the Geometric Analogy Experiment was quite successful in view of the small amount of error data available. Model III, the best model, accounted for 50.4% of the variance in the data. Model IV, as usual, was an extremely close runner up (50.5%). Model II was less close (47.0%), and Model I did much worse, accounting for only 36.8% of the variance in the data.

The final error model is shown in Table 9.3. The x_e parameter is rejected from the model, since it contributes only trivially to the stepwise multiple regression. These results are consistent with those of the People Piece Experiment. Encoding operations apparently lead to errors infrequently. In the People Piece Experiment, the contribution of encoding was so trivial as to lead to its elimination from the model, and in this experiment, encoding contributed only

TABLE 9.3
Final Geometric Analogy Component Model III for Errors

Parameter	Raw regression coefficient	Standard error	β	F_{Reg}	df
a_e	.05	.02	.12	4.3	1, 175
y'_e	.21	.06	.31	13.9	1, 175
z'_e	.15	.08	.17	.39	1, 175
t_e	.69	.14	.32	24.7	1, 175
c_e	.77				

	Stepwise multiple regression			
Parameter	Cumulative R^2	r	Cumulative F_{Reg}	Cumulative df
y'_e	.36	.60	102	1,178
t_e	.48	.58	80	2,177
a_e	.49	.27	56	3,176
z'_e	.50	.59	44	4,175
Rejected				
x_e	.50	.23	35	5,174

3% of the variance to error prediction. In both the People Piece Experiment and the present experiment, the self-terminating attribute-comparison operations, y' and z', were apparently responsible for large proportions of errors, whereas the exhaustive attribute-comparison operation, x, was responsible for hardly any errors at all. Self-terminating operations reduce solution time, but are more likely to lead to erroneous responses due to faulty or incomplete processing. As would be expected, justification (t) can often lead to erroneous responses; it is by no means always successful.

Multivariate component model. A multivariate component model was constructed using both solution time and error rate as dependent variables and the same independent variables as in the univariate component models for solution time and error rate. Parameter estimation and evaluation of model performance were done through canonical correlation analysis. (See Chapter 7 for a description of canonical correlation.)

Statistics for the multivariate component model are displayed in Table 9.4. Two significant canonical variates were obtained. The first accounted for 80% of the variance in the data, the second for 12% of the variance in the data. As noted in Chapter 7, successive canonical variates are mutually orthogonal.

The canonical coefficients for the dependent and independent variables show the same patterns as in the People Piece Experiment. In this experiment, solution time receives a weight of one on the first variate and error rate a weight of zero. Hence, the first canonical variate is essentially identical to solution time. Solution time receives a negative weight on the second canonical variate, and error rate a positive weight, also as in the People Piece Experiment. The

TABLE 9.4
Multivariate Component Model III: Geometric Analogies

Model Performance

Canonical variate	Canonical correlation	Variance (%)	Wilks' lambda	χ^2	Degrees of freedom
1	.897	80.4	0.17	310.1***	10
2	.352	12.4	0.88	23.3***	4

Canonical Coefficients

	Dependent Variables	
	Variate 1	Variate 2
Solution time	1.00	−1.13
Error rate	0.00	1.51

	Independent Variables	
	Variate 1	Variate 2
a	.26	−.12
x	.20	−.91
y'	.27	.48
z'	.24	.15
t	.43	.17

***$p < .001$.

canonical coefficients for the independent variables on Variate 1 are almost identical to the beta weights for solution time component Model III, as would be expected (since the first variate is essentially identical to solution time). All coefficients are positive. Not all coefficients for the second variate are positive, however. As in the People Piece Experiment, the coefficients for the two mandatory exhaustive parameters (encoding and inference) are negative, and those for the two mandatory self-terminating parameters (mapping and application) are positive. The coefficient for justification is positive. Thus, the coefficients for the three parameters associated with errors are positive, and those for the two parameters not associated with errors are negative (see component model for error rate above).

The relationships among the variables and between the variables and canonical variables can be better understood by examining the correlations between the variables and the canonical variates. These correlations are shown in Table 9.5. As would be expected, the correlation between solution time and dependent Variate 1 is 1.00. The two are identical. Error rate is also highly correlated with this variate. As in the People Piece Experiment, it receives a trivial weight not because it is uncorrelated with the variate, but because it is overwhelmed by solution time: With solution time held constant, the partial correlation between error rate and dependent Variate 1 is trivial (in this experiment, zero).

In this experiment, solution time is uncorrelated with Variate 2 (to two decimal places). Error rate, however, is highly correlated with the canonical variate. As in the People Piece Experiment, therefore, error rate turns out to be a complex variable. In one aspect, it is highly overlapping with solution time. In another aspect, it is nonoverlapping but still a source of significant variance in the independent variables. It thus taps a second source of variance that is nonoverlapping with solution time.

The correlations between the independent variables and the canonical variates are shown at the bottom of the table. All variables are highly correlated with the first canonical variate. However, the encoding and inference parameters show negative correlations with the second canonical variate, while mapping, application, and justification show positive correlations. This variate, therefore, identifies with positive loadings the sources of errors in analogy solution. This relation is independent of the magnitude of solution time (the first canonical variate).

To summarize, the multivariate component model enables one to assess simultaneously the relationships of solution time and error rate to the model parameters. Two significant canonical variates were extracted from the data. The first is essentially identical to solution time, but is also highly correlated with error rate. The second canonical variate is independent of solution time, but highly correlated with error rate. It distinguishes between those parameters that are sources of errors in analogies (independent of solution time) and those parameters that are negligible sources of errors.

Individual differences. Distinguishability of the models is poor for individual data. Where the models are distinguishable, it is almost always in the relatively poor fit of Model I relative to the other models. Model III accounts for the data of all subjects quite well relative to the other models, and there is no subject for whom the model is clearly inappropriate in comparison to other models.

TABLE 9.5
Correlations of Variables with Canonical Variate Scores

	Dependent variables		Independent variables	
	Variate 1	Variate 2	Variate 1	Variate 2
Dependent variables				
Solution time	1.00***	.00	.90***	.00
Error rate	.75***	.66***	.67***	.23**
Independent variables				
a	.49***	−.14	.55***	−.40***
x	.54***	−.26***	.60***	−.75***
y'	.67***	.15*	.75***	.43***
z'	.71***	.08	.79***	.24***
t	.72***	.06	.80***	.18*

$*p < .05.$ $**p < .01.$ $***p < .001.$

TABLE 9.6
Basic Statistics for Scores in Geometric Analogy Experiment:
Model III Component Scores (*N* = 24)

Component score	Mean	SD	Number of observations
a (encoding)	.65	.29	4,320
x (inference)	· .40	.24	4,320
y' (mapping)	1.08	.79	4,320
z' (application)	1.31	1.61	4,320
t (justification)	5.41	3.40	4,320
c (preparation and response)	.46	.99	4,320

Table 9.6 presents component score means and standard deviations across the 24 subjects. For two component scores, z' and c, standard deviations are actually larger than means. These distributions are both highly skewed.

Table 9.7 presents component score intercorrelations. Reliabilities of the component scores are presented in the diagonal of the correlation matrix. Reliabilities were determined by the split-halves method (odd-numbered versus even-numbered data points), and corrected by the Spearman–Brown formula. The reliabilities are disappointing. Only two component scores, z' and t, are reliable. Apparently, 180 observations per subject were too few to obtain six reliable parameter estimates for individual subjects.

There were two significant intercorrelations between parameters. The first was a large negative correlation between a and c ($-.81$), which replicates the findings of the previous experiments. The second significant correlation was that between z' and t (.61). Since the t parameter did not appear in previous experiments, this correlation could not have occurred in these experiments. The correlation

TABLE 9.7
Model III Component Score Intercorrelations

	a	*x*	*y'*	*z'*	*t*	*c*
a	−.10	.14	−.06	.21	.35	−.81***
x		.03	−.07	−.29	−.05	−.08
y'			.38	−.24	−.16	.20
z'				.54**	.61**	−.15
t					.78***	−.16
c						.28

**p < .01.   ****p < .001.

suggests that the process requirements of justification may be more similar to those of application than to those of other components. This is quite reasonable, since the need for justification arises during application: An application operation disconfirms (or confirms) both options, and an additional operation is needed to justify one or the other option.

EXTERNAL VALIDATION

Reference Ability Tests

Basic statistics. Means and standard deviations of the reference ability tests are displayed in Table 9.8. Two results are of special interest.

First, the results of the Culture-Fair Test of g, Level III, can be compared to those of the general population and of the subjects in the preceding two experiments. The mean raw score for the test represents a mean IQ of 122, and the standard deviation is about 12 IQ points. The comparable figures for the general population are 100 and 16, and the comparable figures for the subjects in the preceding two experiments are 126 and 12. Scores for the two sets of experimental subjects are comparable, $t(38) = 1.01, p > .05$. Both experimental group means, however, differ significantly from the population mean, $z = 6.50, p$

TABLE 9.8
Basic Statistics for Scores in Geometric Analogy Experiment:
Reference Ability Test Scores (N = 24)

	Mean	Standard deviation	Number of observations
Reasoning			
Word grouping	19.4	5.9	24
Letter series	21.5	5.5	24
Cattell culture-fair (form A)	29.3[a]	3.9[b]	24
French figure classification	130.8	36.3	24
Spatial visualization			
French figure rotation	84.0	18.1	24
Minnesota paper form board	44.2	9.4	24
French cube comparison	14.4	7.3	24
Vocabulary			
French vocabulary (level 3)	30.2	6.8	24
Lorge–Thorndike analogies	21.8	3.6	15

[a]This mean represents an IQ of 122 ($\overline{X}$ = 100 for normative population).
[b]This standard deviation represents a range of approximately 12 IQ points (SD = 16 for normative population).

$< .001$ for People Piece and Verbal Analogy Experiment subjects, $z = 6.74, p <$ .001 for Geometric Analogy Experiment subjects. This difference would be expected for a group of highly selected college undergraduates.

Second, the results for the Lorge–Thorndike analogies are only for the last 15 subjects tested in Session 2. Since order of testing was random, one would not expect this group to differ significantly in performance from the group formed by the remaining 9 subjects. The two groups do not differ significantly on any of the scores used in the experiment. The two groups will therefore be considered comparable.

Intercorrelations. Intercorrelations between tests are shown in Table 9.9. The tests were grouped a priori into three types: reasoning, spatial visualization, and vocabulary. The Lorge–Thorndike analogies were added later to compare performance on almost identical items administered in pencil-and-paper format versus tachistoscopic format. Inspection of the table of intercorrelations supports the separation of the vocabulary test from the other tests, but does not support the separation of tests into reasoning and spatial visualization groups. Correlations within these two groups are no higher than correlations between tests in the two groups, and in some cases they are lower. A factor analysis of the tests helps identify the dimensions along which individual differences tend to cluster.

Factor analysis. The factor analysis is presented in Table 9.10. Factors were extracted with communality estimates in the diagonal of the correlation matrix, and successive communalities were estimated until estimates reached a criterion of near-convergence. The three factors account for 65.5% of the variance in the ability test data. Consider first the last factor.

TABLE 9.9
Ability Test Intercorrelations

	WG	LS	CF	FC	FR	PF	CC	VO	LT
Reasoning									
Word grouping	1.00	.42	.19	.37	.40	.29	.48	−.05	.37
Letter series		1.00	.62	.64	.39	.80	.62	−.11	.71
Cattell culture-fair (form A)			1.00	.53	.15	.56	.46	.17	.73
French figure classification				1.00	.40	.56	.39	.34	.69
Spatial visualization									
French figure rotation					1.00	.24	.40	.23	.20
Minnesota paper form board						1.00	.58	−.21	.65
French cube comparison							1.00	.01	.40
Vocabulary									
French vocabulary (level 3)								1.00	−.12
Lorge–Thorndike analogies									1.00

TABLE 9.10
Ability Test Factor Analysis (Varimax Rotation)

	I	II	III	Communality
Reasoning				
Word grouping	.19	.67	−.07	.48
Letter series	.83	.42	−.11	.87
Cattell culture-fair (form A)	.72	.09	.17	.56
French figure classification	.62	.36	.33	.62
Spatial visualization				
French figure rotation	.16	.62	.20	.44
Minnesota paper form board	.83	.23	−.21	.79
French cube comparison	.51	.52	−.04	.53
Vocabulary				
French vocabulary (level 3)	.01	.05	.97	.94
Eigenvalue:	3.46	1.19	.59	

Total variance (%): 65.5%

The third factor is clearly a vocabulary factor. Only the vocabulary test has a substantial loading on this factor, a loading so high that the factor scores are interchangeable with the vocabulary test scores ($r = .998$).

The first factor loads highly on all the reasoning and spatial visualization tests except Word Grouping and French Figure Rotation. What unites these two seemingly dissimilar tests and differentiates them from the remaining tests? The two groups of tests, those loading on the first factor and those not loading on it, seem to be separated by one variable, setting of administration. Tests loading on Factor I were administered during geometric analogy testing sessions. Tests not loading on the factor were administered as initial screening devices in Psychology 1. Conversely, the highest loadings of tests on the second factor are for the two tests that were administered in Psychology 1. Two other tests, French Cube Comparison and Letter Series, also have substantial loadings on Factor II, and so this factor seems to tap more than purely situational variance.

Interval Scores and Component Scores

Correlations of reference ability test scores and factor scores with interval scores are not shown because they are all trivial. These trivial correlations are surprising, because one would expect geometric analogies to involve processes that are shared with the reference ability tests. Indeed, the geometric analogies (in pencil-and-paper form) were actually used as such a test: The items are taken from a standard test of mental ability. It thus seems almost incredible that more large correlations were not obtained.

Correlations of the ability tests and factors with the component scores are equally unimpressive. Since a, x, y', and c are not reliable, high correlations with these component scores could not be expected. However, z' and t are reliable enough to generate high correlations, but few are to be found.

Why don't the interval and component scores correlate with ability test scores? One possible explanation of the failure of the scores to correlate is failure to take into account error rates. A clear majority of error solution times were fast errors: Error times were lower than correct times. It is possible, therefore, that less able subjects are receiving faster component times than they deserve because of their commission of fast errors. If both error rate and response time are taken into account, perhaps then the geometric analogy scores will be correlated with the reference abilities.

Interval Scores Combined with Error Rates

Multiple correlations of interval scores and error rates with ability test scores are shown in Table 9.11. (Note that by definition, multiple correlations are always positive.) Taking into account error rate makes a huge difference in the magnitude of certain correlations. Four of eight multiple correlations between ability test scores and combined solution scores and error rates are statistically significant. The correlations between the Factor I score and the geometric analogy scores are also significant. In every case, both the multiple correlation *and* the contribution of solution time are significant. The former is indicated by asterisks, the latter by underscores (see note at bottom of table). Thus, the statistical significance of the multiple correlations is not due merely to error rate. The true extent of the correlation between solution times and ability test scores could not be shown without the incorporation of error rate into the equation.

The correlation in the two-cue condition reaches .80 with both the Cattell Culture-Fair Test of g and the Lorge–Thorndike analogies, the two tests that are most similar in content and process requirements to the geometric analogies. Correlations with Factor I, but not Factor II, are significant. Apparently, the better testing conditions under which the high-loading Factor I tests were administered made them better measures of reasoning ability as measured by the geometric analogies task.

Component Scores Combined with Error Rates

Multiple correlations of certain Model III component scores and error rates with ability test scores are shown in Table 9.12. It should be recalled that only the z' and t component scores are reliable enough to be considered.

This is the first experiment in which the application (z') score has been found to correlate significantly with measures of reasoning ability. It is the first experiment in which the justification parameter has been part of the analogical

TABLE 9.11
Multiple Correlations of Interval Scores and Error Rates
with Ability Test Scores[a]

	C0	C2	S0	S2
Reasoning				
Word grouping	.13	.27	.16	.27
Letter series	.38	.39	.58*	.56*
Cattell culture-fair (Form A)	.58*	.59*	.76***	.80***
French figure classification	.14	.43	.35	.35
Spatial visualization				
French figure rotation	.04	.25	.32	.28
Minnesota paper form board	.38	.32	.42	.41
French cube comparison	.14	.18	.54*	.52*
Vocabulary				
French vocabulary (level 3)	.20	.11	.12	.23
Factor I	.48	.45	.61**	.61*
Factor II	.45	.26	.27	.30
Factor III	.19	.12	.12	.22
Lorge–Thorndike analogies	.38	.45	.66*	.80**

[a]Single underscore indicates statistical significance of interval score at $p < .05$; double underscore indicates statistical significance of interval score at $p < .01$; triple underscore indicates statistical significance of interval score at $p < .001$.
*$p < .05$. **$p < .01$. ***$p < .001$.

reasoning model, and component scores for that parameter also were found to correlate with measures of reasoning. It thus appears that under the proper circumstances, all six component scores in the full model can be highly correlated with measures of reasoning ability. Five of these components are theorized to be *sources* of individual differences in reasoning. The positive correlation of encoding speed with reasoning was found to derive from differential strategies among high and low reasoning subjects: Subjects who score higher on reasoning tests appear to spend proportionately more time in stimulus encoding, thereby facilitating other information processes (see Chapter 8).

Percent-Variance-Accounted-For Statistic

The percent-variance-accounted-for statistic was unreliable; therefore, the statistic was not correlated with any other measure.

TABLE 9.12
Multiple Correlations of Model III Component Scores and Error Rates with Ability Test Scores[a]

	z'	t
Reasoning		
Word grouping	.14	.20
Letter series	.44	.57*
Cattell culture-fair (form A)	<u><u>.71</u></u>***	<u><u>.70</u></u>***
French figure classification	.24	.39
Spatial visualization		
French figure rotation	.27	.50
Minnesota paper form board	.29	.31
French cube comparison	.36	.35
Vocabulary		
French vocabulary (level 3)	.16	.30
Factor I	.49	.53*
Factor II	.19	.38
Factor III	.16	.30
Lorge–Thorndike analogies	<u><u>.70</u></u>*	.52

[a]Single underscore indicates statistical significance of component score at $p < .05$; double underscore indicates statistical significance of component score at $p < .01$.
*$p < .05$. **$p < .01$. **$p < .001$.

TABLE 9.13
Correlations of Component Scores with Interval Scores

	z'	t
Solution score		
$S0$	.62***	.71***
$S2$	.69***	.69***
Cue score		
$C0$	.01	.34
$C2$	.01	.28

***$p < .001$.

Relation between Component and Interval Scores

Correlations between the z' and t component scores and the interval scores are displayed in Table 9.13. Application and justification are sources of stable individual differences in the solution scores. Neither of the component scores correlates significantly with cue scores.

INTEGRATION

The results of the various models are integrated in the structural regression model shown in Figure 9.9. Figure 9.9 shows the structural regression for Factor I as the reference ability (Factor II appears to have been largely "situational,"

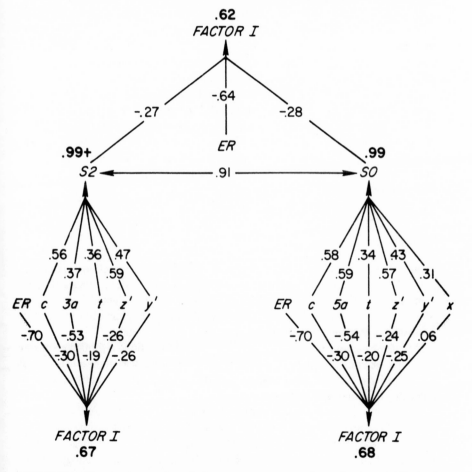

FIGURE 9.9 Structural regression relating component scores, interval scores, and Factor I reference ability.

and therefore of little interest). Error rate is included as an independent variable in correlations with reference ability scores, since it was found that error rate makes an important contribution to these correlations. Ideally, error rate would be broken down into error components a_e, x_e, y'_e, z'_e, t_e, and c_e (just as solution time is broken down into time components a, x, y', z', t, and c). While componential breakdown was possible for the group data, it was not possible for individual data due to the paucity of errors in individual protocols and the absence of repeated observations at single data points.

Figure 9.9 shows that the multiple correlation of solution scores and error rate with Factor I scores was .62. The path coefficients show that the largest variance contribution to this multiple correlation was made by error rate. Its path coefficient (standardized regression coefficient) is more than twice as high as that for either $S0$ or $S2$.

The multiple correlation of the component scores with the solution scores $S0$ and $S2$ was over .99 in each case. Thus, individual differences in solution scores are almost fully accounted for by individual differences in the component scores. Individual differences in overall analogical reasoning latencies are explicable in terms of individual differences in component latencies.

The multiple correlation of the component scores and error rate with Factor I scores was .68 in the zero-cue condition and .67 in the two-cue condition. The two multiple correlations differ only as a function of the inclusion of x as an independent variable in the multiple correlation for the zero-cue condition. The contribution of x is obviously trivial, since the multiple correlations differ by just .01. Once again, error rate makes the largest single contribution to the multiple correlation.

SUMMARY

Twenty-four subjects selected on the basis of scores on a reasoning test participated in an experiment investigating solution of geometric analogies. Experimental stimuli were 90 forced-choice geometric analogies selected from editions of the American Council on Education Psychological Examination for College Freshmen. Items were modified somewhat for use in the study.

The major dependent variable examined was solution time, although error rate was also examined. The major independent variable was item difficulty as measured by ratings of value changes and figure complexities and by amount of precueing information supplied to subjects.

Mean solution time for full analogies was 6.58 sec, a considerable increase over solution-time means in the People Piece and Verbal Analogy Experiments. Mean error rate was 4.6%, a large increase over that in the People Piece Analogy Experiment, but only a small increase over that in the Verbal Analogy Experiment.

Two general types of forced-choice models were examined, those with alternating option scanning and those with sequential option scanning. In the former type of model, a given attribute is tested on all options before proceeding to the next attribute. One alternates between options in scanning them.

With the justification parameter, Model III accounted for 80.4% of the variance in the data. Model III fit the data equally well when only full analogies (zero cues) were used, but there was some loss of predictive power when only nondegenerate items were used. The model fit the data slightly better in the second session than in the first.

Data collected by Cooper (1973) suggested that there may be no effect of stimulus complexity upon rate of mental rotation. This surprising result raised the possibility that rates of mental transformations might generally be independent of the complexity of the figures on which they are performed. However, figure complexity was found to have an effect upon solution times in this experiment, independent of numbers of value transformations and amount of precueing.

Several variants of models with sequential option scanning were tested. In these models, all scanning of one option is completed before scanning of another option begins. The performance of the best of these models was equivalent to (and indistinguishable from) the performance of the worst alternating option scanning model. Therefore, this whole class of models was rejected.

The final Model III accounted for 80% of the variance in the data, with six parameters (five regression parameters and a "constant") and 174 residual degrees of freedom. All parameters contributed significantly to the mathematical model, and thus all six components of the information-processing model appear to be psychologically necessary.

The distribution of component time in item solution shows that the largest amount of time is spent upon encoding processes. The amount of time spent on preparation—response was about the same as in the preceding two experiments, but since solution times were much longer, the proportionate amount of time spent on preparation—response was reduced. The proportion of time spent on attribute-comparison operations was greater in this experiment than in the preceding two experiments, as would be expected with items in which the value transformations are very complex.

Model III was quite successful in predicting numbers of errors at each of the 180 data points. The model accounted for 50% of the variance in the error data, which is quite satisfactory in view of the small number of errors made by subjects. The model did not contain the x_e parameter, since its variance contribution was found to be trivial.

A multivariate component model was constructed using both solution time and error rate as dependent variables. The parameters of the model were estimated and its performance assessed by canonical correlation. Two significant canonical variates were extracted from the data. The first is essentially identical to the variance tapped by solution time, but is also highly correlated with error rate. The second canonical variate is independent of solution time, but highly correlated with error rate. It distinguishes between those parameters that are sources of errors in analogies (independent of solution time) and those parameters that are negligible sources of errors.

Model III accounted for the solution-time data of all individual subjects reasonably well, and there was no subject for whom the model was clearly inappropriate (relative to other models).

Only two component scores, application and justification, were found to be reliable. These results suggested that many more than 180 observations per subject would have been needed for stable parameter estimates for individuals.

There were two significant intercorrelations between parameters, those between a and c and between z' and t. The former replicated results from the previous experiments. The latter could not have been previously found, since the optional t parameter did not appear in the People Piece and verbal analogy models. The correlation is interpretable, however, since the need for justification arises out of unsatisfactory results during application.

A factor analysis of the reference ability tests revealed three factors. The first identified those reasoning and spatial visualization tests given individually during geometric analogy testing. The second identified reasoning and spatial visualization tests given in Psychology 1, but some other tests had fairly high loadings as well. The third factor was a vocabulary factor. Thus, the factors confirmed the separation between vocabulary (verbal comprehension) and the other tests, but did not confirm a separation between the two hypothesized reference abilities of primary interest: inductive reasoning and spatial visualization.

It was suggested that since the majority of errors were "fast" errors caused by incomplete processing, it was possible that less able subjects received faster component estimates at the expense of accurate performance. Taking into account error rate made a huge difference in the magnitude of certain correlations. Four of eight multiple correlations between ability test scores and combined solution scores and error rates were statistically significant. The multiple correlations between the Factor I scores and the geometric analogy solution and error scores were also significant. In every case, both the multiple correlation and the individual contribution of solution time were significant. Thus, the geometric analogies did measure individual differences in abstract reasoning and visualization. The source of these correlations was traced through subsequent analyses to both reliable component scores — application and justification.

The structural regression model revealed that the component scores accounted for almost 100% of the individual differences variance in the solution scores. The multiple correlation of solution scores and error rates with Factor I was .62. Thus, Factor I appears to have been a factor tapping generalizable individual differences in reasoning and visualization. Factor II appears to have been largely a situational factor, and therefore of little interest.

10
The Animal Name
Analogy Experiment

Animal name analogies were introduced by Rumelhart and Abrahamson (1973) in a series of experiments designed to test their "parallelogram" theory of analogical reasoning. Details of the theory and experiments are presented in their article and summarized in Chapter 5 of this volume.

The animal name analogies used by Rumelhart and Abrahamson (1973) take the form $A:B::C:(D_1, D_2, D_3, D_4)$, where each analogy term is the name of an animal. A typical analogy is rabbit : cat :: mouse : (A. giraffe, B. horse, C. raccoon, D. wolf). Subjects were asked to rank order the answer options in terms of their closeness to the ideal answer. The "correct" ranking in the above example, determined by means to be described, is (1) C, (2) D, (3) B, (4) A.

A basic notion of the Rumelhart-Abrahamson theory is that analogies can be represented as parallelograms in a multidimensional semantic space. The distance from A to B should equal the distance from the C term to the ideal D term, which is labeled as I by Rumelhart and Abrahamson, and which has been called D' in this volume. Similarly, the distance from A to C should equal the distance from B to D' (or I). Rumelhart and Abrahamson used Henley's (1969) scaling results as the basis for the construction of analogies and the rank ordering of options. Each of 30 animal names is represented as a point in a three-dimensional space. Inspection of the three dimensions suggested that they could be labeled size, ferocity, and humanness. Rumelhart and Abrahamson used a Euclidean distance metric to compute distances between pairs of points in the three-dimensional space. (Thus, the distance between two points would be equal to the square root of the sum of the squared differences between the two points in their size, ferocity, and humanness coordinates.)

The present Animal Name Analogy Experiment differs from the previous experiments in that it is not a fully componential analysis. The experiment was designed with two considerations in mind.

First, the experiment permits a limited test of the componential theory of analogical reasoning with stimuli in which the latent attributes are identifiable but not at all obvious. In the People Piece Analogy Experiment, the latent attributes are identifiable (height, color, sex, girth) and obvious. In the Verbal and Geometric Analogy Experiments, the latent attributes are much less obvious, and identification of the attributes was bypassed by collecting ratings that estimated "value transformations." In the Animal Name Analogy Experiment, the identities of the attributes can be ascertained by multidimensional scaling or other algorithms to be discussed. The identities of the dimensions are not obvious, however, as they were in the People Piece Experiment. Hence, discovery of relevant attributes by subjects is important, as well as the testing of these attributes. Results of previous experiments suggest that discovery may be the primary source of individual differences in reasoning, while testing may be a much less important source. Hence, the animal name analogies are of special interest.

Second, the present experiment permits a number of tests to determine whether performance on a test of animal name analogies actually is related to performance on standard inductive reasoning tests. It has not been previously shown that there is a relation, and because of the unusual nature of the items, it is important to demonstrate that they tap variance nonspecific to the particular item type.

METHOD

Subjects

Three groups of subjects participated in the experiment. The first group was the same as that which participated in the People Piece and Verbal Analogy Experiments. These 16 subjects answered animal name analogies in the seventh and final session of their participation. The second group of subjects was that which participated in the Geometric Analogy Experiment. These 24 subjects answered animal name analogies in the first session of their participation. The third group of 20 subjects was otherwise uninvolved in analogy experiments. These subjects were included in order to stabilize the item data used in internal validation. Since these subjects took no tests other than the Animal Name Analogies test, no external validation was performed on their scores.

Materials

The stimulus material consisted of the 30 animal name analogies used in Experiment I of Rumelhart and Abrahamson (1973).[1] The procedure by which

[1] I am grateful to Adele A. Abrahamson for providing the 30 animal name analogies used in Experiment I of Rumelhart and Abrahamson (1973), and also for providing supplementary data from the Rumelhart and Abrahamson experiments.

animal name analogies were generated is described in detail by Rumelhart and Abrahamson. This procedure will only be summarized here.

The general procedure·was to select randomly and without replacement animal names from Henley's (1969) set of 30. The first name selected was used as the first term of the problem, the second name as the second term of the problem, and the third name as the third term of the problem. After ten analogies were created in this way, the pool of thirty names was exhausted. The entire set of animal names was replaced into the pool of possible analogy terms, and the selection procedure was repeated until 30 unique analogies were formed.

For each of the 30 problems, four alternative options were chosen that were at carefully graded distances from the ideal point of each particular analogy.

Design

All subjects received the identical animal name analogies and instructions for completing them. Two of the groups of subjects described earlier also received other types of analogies and reference ability tests.

Procedure

Instructions were the same as Rumelhart and Abrahamson's, except that subjects were asked only to select the best answer, not to rank order the answers. They were also asked to answer all items, even if they had to guess. Subjects were given as long as they needed to complete the analogies.

INTERNAL VALIDATION

Dependent Variables

In the previous experiments, solution time and error rate served as dependent variables. In the present experiment, four indices of item easiness were computed.

The first index of item easiness is the p value of the item: the proportion of times the best answer (defined as the answer closest in overall Euclidean distance to the ideal point) was selected as the preferred option. The mean value of p across the 30 analogies was .63, and the standard deviation was .18.

The second index is the z value (area under the normal curve) corresponding to the p value. The advantages of the z measure are that: (1) it is unbounded; and (2) it is normally distributed. The mean value of z was .43, and the standard deviation was .62.

The third index is the standard deviation (SD) of the number of subjects (out of 60) selecting each of the four options. The minimum possible standard deviation is zero, which is obtained when equal numbers of subjects select each of the four options. In this case, the number selecting each of the four options is 15, and the standard deviation of 15, 15, 15, 15 is zero. The maximum possible standard deviation is 25.98, corresponding to a response distribution of 60, 0, 0, 0. This measure, then, is like an uncertainty measure from information theory. The mean value of the SD index was 14.93, and the standard deviation across items was 5.14.

The fourth index is the variance (VAR) of the number of subjects selecting each of the four options, which is simply the standard deviation squared. The minimum value is 0, and the maximum value is 675. The mean value of VAR was 249.93, and the standard deviation across items was 154.86.

The advantages of these latter two measures over the former two are that: (1) they do not require any assumptions regarding which single option is the best answer; and (2) they take into account the distribution of responses across all four options, rather than just the number of subjects selecting one particular option, the preferred one (as measured by minimum Euclidean distance from the ideal point).

The four item-easiness measures are all very highly intercorrelated ($r > .95$ between all pairs of measures), and so it makes little difference which one or ones are used. Results will be shown for both z and VAR to point out that the same general patterns of results hold for both the proportion of subjects selecting the best answer and for the distribution of subjects selecting all the various responses.

Rated Distances

Henley obtained ratings of dissimilarity for all possible pairs of animals (Henley, 1969). Ratings were placed on a zero-to-ten scale, with zero indicating identity and ten indicating maximum dissimilarity. Correlations of rated distance (dissimilarity) and the two item-easiness measures were $-.41$ ($p < .05$) and $-.46$ ($p < .05$) between $D(A, B)$ and each of z and VAR respectively, but $-.06$ between $D(A, C)$ and each of z and VAR. The correlation of $D(A, C)$ with item difficulty was never significant in this experiment, and therefore will not be discussed further.

Rated distances may be analyzed by a number of data reduction algorithms that attempt to represent the psychological structure underlying the rated distances. If one of the representations does capture this psychological structure, and this psychological structure is relevant to the analogies task, then understanding of the analogical reasoning process will be enhanced by viewing the animal terms and the relations between them in terms of such a structure.

Spatial Representation

Overall distance. Correlations between the item easiness measures and overall scaled Euclidean distances from A to B were $-.33$ and $-.41$ ($p < .05$) with z and VAR. (City-block and supremum metrics yielded indistinguishable results.)

Intradimensional distance. In the distance computations described so far, all three dimensions are unweighted (except for weighting due to the fact that the variance of the projections of animal terms is greater on some dimensions than on others). The underlying assumption would seem to be that each dimension contributes equally to item solution. There is no a priori reason why this should be the case. It would seem as plausible, for example, that the more prominent dimensions are weighted more heavily than the less prominent dimensions in analogy solution. Thus, one might expect the size dimension to be weighted most heavily, and the humanness dimension to be weighted least heavily. Indeed, whereas subjects often mention size as a basis for discerning relations between animals, they rarely mention humanness. It would seem advisable, therefore, to compute distances separately for each dimension, and to correlate these separate intradimensional distances with the item-easiness measures.

The correlations with size and ferocity were all lower in magnitude than $-.3$ and nonsignificant. The $D(A, B)$ correlations for humanness were $-.45$ ($p < .05$) with both z and VAR. Only one dimension is of any consequence: humanness! The correlation of $D(A, B)$ with overall distance is apparently attributable to the correlation of the humanness distance with item easiness. Scatterplots between all distances and item-easiness indices were checked for presence of curvilinear trends, but none existed. The linear correlations well describe the relationships in the data.

The above results suggest that there is little justification for combining dimensions here in unweighted fashion, or even for including the first two dimensions in distance computations. The other two dimensions, of course, might be predictive of other types of dependent variables (other than item easiness), and they are apparently useful in predicting response distributions across answer options (Rips, Shoben, & Smith, 1973; Rumelhart & Abrahamson, 1973). But they appear to be of little or no use in predicting item difficulties across different items.

Coordinate values. So far we have been considering only distances, which are relevant for discovering the effects of inference, mapping, and application, but not of encoding. Because the Animal Name Analogy Experiment was not fully componential and did not use precueing, it was not possible to determine effects of amount of encoding on the basis of responses in different cueing conditions. This did not mean, however, that effects of encoding could not be determined in some other way.

It was shown in the Geometric Analogy Experiment that the effects of encoding may be estimated if different analogy terms are differentially difficult to encode. If, as in that experiment, some terms are more complex than others, then the effects of encoding may be estimated on the basis of stimulus complexity.

It would seem plausible that some animal terms are more difficult to encode than others. What type of index might serve as a useful measure of encoding difficulty? One set of indices that is readily available is the set of coordinate values on each of the three dimensions uncovered through multidimensional scaling. The relationship between coordinate values and item easiness, if there is any, might be curvilinear. It is possible, for example, that animal terms that are more extreme on a given dimension are easier to encode than animal terms that are not extreme. *Elephant* and *mouse,* for example, might be easily encoded as very big or very small, but *chimpanzee* is at neither extreme, and therefore might be more difficult to encode meaningfully on the size dimension.

Scatterplots were examined that related coordinate values to item easiness. No curvilinear trends were observed. There were certain linear trends, however.

Significant and strong correlations were obtained between coordinate values on the humanness dimension and item easiness, but correlations were much weaker for the other dimensions, and only one correlation for any other dimension was statistically significant. The correlations of the humanness coordinates for the $A, B,$ and C analogy terms were $-.38$ ($p < .05$), $-.35$, and $-.43$ ($p < .05$) with z, and $-.42$ ($p < .05$), $-.38$ ($p < .05$), and $-.48$ ($p < .05$) with VAR.

The correlations for the humanness dimension are, if anything, in the direction opposite to what might be expected. Greater amounts of humanness are associated with more difficult items. Since this correlation holds up for all three terms in the analogy stem, it seems unlikely to be due to a chance significant correlation.

Coordinate values are not independent of distances between pairs of coordinates. The correlation between $(A + B)$, the sum of the A and B humanness coordinates, and $D(A, B)_{\text{Hum}}$ is .41 ($p < .05$). This correlation is not high enough, however, to suggest that the coordinate sum and difference "measure the same thing."

Further analyses. The above patterns of results were so surprising that further data were collected in an attempt to elucidate some of these patterns of results.

It seemed possible that the failure to obtain significant correlations between the size and ferocity dimensions and item easiness might be due to differential weightings of the dimensions for different analogy terms. For example, ferocity might be a relevant dimension in evaluating relations between *tiger* and other terms, but might be irrelevant in considering relations between *chipmunk* and other terms. Twenty-three subjects otherwise uninvolved in any of the analogy experiments supplied ratings of the relevance of each of the dimensions — size, ferocity, humanness — for each of the 30 animal terms. These relevance ratings were then used to weight dimensions for each animal term. The ratings were also themselves used as independent variables in predicting item easiness. The ratings failed to have any predictive value.

Humanness does not seem like a compelling interpretation of Henley's third dimension, although there is no obvious better interpretation. It seemed possible that it was not humanness per se that was leading to high correlations between item easiness and coordinates and distances along the humanness dimension, but some variable that was highly correlated with but not identical to humanness. Four further variables were considered.

The first variable was production frequency for four-legged animals as measured by the Battig and Montague (1969) norms.[2] Only ratings for the A analogy term were significantly correlated with item easiness. While this single correlation was comparable to that for the humanness coordinate of the A term, the fact that all three stem terms correlated for humanness, but only one for the Battig–Montague norms, suggested that the humanness coordinates were the better measures for predicting item easiness.

Twenty-nine subjects otherwise uninvolved in the analogy experiments were asked to supply three ratings for each of the 30 animal name terms. The first rating was *representativeness* of each animal as a member of the category, *animal*. (See Footnote 2.) The second rating was *familiarity* with each animal. The third rating was *visualizability* of each animal. It seemed possible that the more "human" animals would be those that were more representative, familiar, or visualizable. No significant correlations were obtained for any of the rated values or distances between animal terms on any of these three scales.

The humanness dimension appears to be the source of the correlations, rather than some confounded variable. Since the dimension is the third and weakest one, a possible interpretation of these correlations is that there are relatively large individual differences in subjects' placements of animal terms along this dimension, and that these differences increase with the distance from A to B and the amount of humanness.

Cluster Representation

Do subjects actually compute distances along the size, ferocity, and humanness dimensions, either explicitly or implicitly? While introspective reports of subjects suggest that these attributes are used, they also suggest that: (1) they are not the only attributes used, (2) they are not necessarily used as spatial dimensions, and (3) they are not used in all comparisons between pairs of animals. Consider five subjects' descriptions of how they solved the animal name analogies:

> I tried to find any possible relation between the animals such as which was larger, which had hair, which had hoofs, and even which were domestic and which wild (usually).

> I picked any remote comparisons, such as: (1) Domestic vs. "wild"; (2) Same type of family (monkey–gorilla); (3) Size a) shape of body, b) ear lengths, c) neck lengths, d) skin texture; (4) Predation.

[2] I thank Edward E. Smith for suggesting the use of this scale as a predictor of animal name analogy easinesss.

I utilized such devices as: size, shape, function to man, domesticity, wildness, whether the animal operates on two or four legs, animal's temperament, etc.

Method — relationship in size, structure — two leg, four leg, tree, land, cattle, wild–domestic, native–foreign, predator–prey.

I tried solving the more difficult analogies by comparing the relative aggressiveness, domestication, and geographical area the animals possess. Sometimes, when no clearcut analogy could be made, I compared relative size and color. On the other extreme, the simpler ones seemed to automatically fall together by intuition or gut feeling. I can't account for this feeling, just as if someone said "peanut butter" and one would say "jelly."

Verbal descriptions are perhaps more consistent with the kind of representation achieved by a method of nonhierarchical additive clustering (ADCLUS) recently developed by Shepard and Arabie (Shepard, 1974; Shepard & Arabie, 1975). This method extracts overlapping clusters or subsets of elements that are highly intercorrelated. The ADCLUS method was applied to similarity ratings in an unpublished replication of the Henley (1969) study conducted by Arabie and Rips and cited in Arabie and Shepard (1973). The first ten subsets extracted by the algorithm, and the interpretations they were assigned, are given in Table 10.1. It can be seen that these subsets overlap in their contents, and also that they are quite interpretable.

The strategy subjects may have used is to attempt to find some common property for the A and B analogy terms, and then to attempt to apply this common property (or a closely related one) to arrive at a best solution. The more properties the animals share, the easier it should be to solve the analogy.

According to this notion, ease of inference might be measured by the number of common (overlapping) subsets in which the A and B analogy terms appear.

TABLE 10.1
Animal Subsets Extracted by ADCLUS

Rank	Elements of Subset	Interpretation
1	Monkey, chimpanzee, gorilla	Apes and monkeys
2	Rat, mouse	Rodent pests (lab animals)
3	Cat, lion, tiger, leopard	Cat family
4	Deer, antelope	Deer-like
5	Dog, wolf, fox	Dog-like
6	Bear, gorilla	Large–dangerous–humanoid
7	Horse, donkey	Domesticated horse-like
8	Sheep, goat	Bovidae family
9	Rat, mouse, squirrel, chipmunk	Small rodents
10	Cat, lion, tiger, leopard, wolf, fox	Wild predators

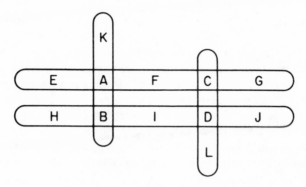

FIGURE 10.1   The concept of an ideal point in a nonhierarchical additive clustering representation.

The greater the number of common subsets, (1) the higher the probability of a subject's finding any relation between the animals; and (2) the higher the probability of a subject's finding a relation that can be carried over to the second half of the analogy. Thus, it would be relatively easy to solve analogies with the terms *rat* and *mouse* in the A and B analogy positions, because they appear together in four of the first twenty subsets. It would be difficult to solve analogies with *fox* and *zebra* in the first two terms, because they do not appear together in any of the first twenty subsets. The same notion might be extended to the A and C analogy terms.

Unfortunately, the clustering representation does not supply an automatic ideal point such as that supplied by the spatial representation; so it is not possible to obtain an overlap measure for each analogy between C and D' (since it is unlikely that any actual animal will fit an analogy perfectly). The overlap may be estimated by using the C and D_t analogy terms, but this is only a partially satisfactory substitute.

In theory, an ideal point could be constructed from a clustering representation. Figure 10.1 shows how this might be done.[3] In the analogy, *A:B::C:*(1. *F;* 2. *H;* 3. *D;* 4. *J*), D is the optimum answer, because it is the one term that is overlapping with both B and C in terms of cluster membership. It would seem, however, that only a small number of analogies would permit completion in this straightforward way.

A possible measure of encoding difficulty is the number of subsets in which each analogy term appears. Presumably, animal terms that appear in a large number of subsets are those existing in a rich associative network and that might be easily encoded in terms of a variety of properties. Animals that appear in few subsets are presumably those for which there is a more impoverished associative

[3] I thank Roger N. Shepard for suggesting how an ideal point might be constructed using a clustering representation and for devising this figure.

structure and that might be more difficult to encode in terms of salient properties.

The $A \rightarrow B$ cluster overlap measure is by far the best predictor of animal name analogy easiness of any of the variables that have so far been considered, correlating .68 ($p < .001$) and .69 ($p < .001$) with z and VAR respectively. The ($A + B$) cluster inclusion measure (number of clusters in which A is included plus number of clusters in which B is included) correlated .53 ($p < .01$) with z and .54 ($p < .01$) with VAR. These correlations are higher than those for the spatial representation, and suggest the usefulness of the nonhierarchical, additive cluster representation as an alternative to the spatial representation for animal name analogies.

Models of Analogical Reasoning for Animal Name Analogies

Overview. We have examined a number of variables that might be used in a model to predict easiness (or difficulty) of animal name analogies. It should be noted that these analogies are not in a form that is well suited to the type of modeling that has been done in the past three chapters. The reason for this is that the distances of the answer options from the ideal point were carefully controlled so that there is almost no variance across analogies. Rumelhart and Abrahamson (1973) were interested in predicting response patterns across options, and the construction of the analogies was well suited to this type of prediction. We are interested in predicting response patterns across items, and the analogies are less well suited for this purpose, because variance is large across options but not across items. In other words, there is a great deal of variance within each item in distances of answer options from the ideal point, but there is almost no variance across items in these relative distances. Since these distances are used to distinguish between self-terminating and exhaustive models of analogical reasoning, this distinction cannot be made in the present experiment. Nevertheless, we have seen that some prediction of relative item difficulties may be obtained using other sources of variance.

Spatial representation model. The two best overall predictors of animal name analogy easiness in the spatial representation are $D(A, B)_{\text{Hum}}$ and $(A + B)_{\text{Hum}}$. These two predictors are related, since $D(A, B)_{\text{Hum}} = |A - B|_{\text{Hum}}$. As was shown previously, however, they are not highly intercorrelated.

The distance between the A and B points along the humanness dimension may be viewed as the basis for estimating a confounded inference and application parameter, since the distance from A to B (used to estimate inference) is equal to the distance from C to D' (used to estimate application). Inference may be separated from application either through precueing or one parameter being estimated as exhaustive and the other as self-terminating. But precueing was not used in this experiment, and the distinction between exhaustive and self-terminating operations cannot be made due to lack of interitem variance in distances between D' and the various answer options.

The sum of the A and B humanness coordinates may be viewed as a basis for computing an encoding parameter. The evidence presented previously suggests that animals higher on this dimension are more difficult to encode, while animals lower on this dimension are easier to encode. As was also shown previously, humanness as measured by the third dimension in the Henley (1969) multidimensional scaling does appear to be the source of encoding difficulty.

There is no basis for including a mapping parameter in the model, because the A to C distance was found not to predict item easiness. This does not mean that the mapping component was absent from the solution process. As discussed in Chapter 6, the determination of whether a component is used in the analogy-solution process is possible only when solution time is the dependent variable. An operation may occur in real time, but not be a significant source of errors, in which case it will appear in the solution-time model, but not in the error model. This pattern of events was found in all three previous experiments.

Our first model using item easiness as the dependent variable is based upon two independent variables derived from the spatial representation of animal names, $D(A, B)_{Hum}$ and $(A + B)_{Hum}$. Taken together, these two variables account for 28% of the variance in the z measure of item easiness, and 31% of the variance in the VAR measure.

Cluster representation model. Our second model using item easiness as the dependent variable will be based upon two independent variables derived from the cluster representation of animal names, $A \to B$ and $(A + B)$. The first independent variable is the number of common (overlapping) clusters in which the A and B analogy terms appear, and will again serve as a confounded basis for estimating the inference and application parameters. The second independent variable is the total number of clusters in which A and B appear and will serve as a basis for estimating the encoding parameter. Once again, there is no basis for estimating a mapping parameter, since $A \to C$ failed to correlate with item easiness. The model accounts for 56% of the variance in z and 57% of the variance in VAR. These models, therefore, predict item easiness about twice as well as do the models based upon the spatial representation.

The cluster representation model performs better than the distance model, in spite of the relative crudeness of the cluster overlap and inclusion measures used. More sophisticated measures were also tried, using larger numbers of clusters (41) and cluster weights generated by the ADCLUS algorithm. These more sophisticated measures failed to result in substantial improvement of the cluster model's predictive power.

The cluster representation does have one distinct disadvantage relative to the spatial representation: It does not automatically furnish an ideal point. The conception of an ideal point remains, as discussed earlier. The mathematical specification, however, is elusive, and without such a specification, mathematical modeling of the solution process becomes more difficult.

These results do not permit and are not intended to yield a conclusive comparison between spatial and cluster representations. The assumptions underlying the two representations differ, and it is impossible to equate the two representations for number of structural parameters used in model fitting. The results do suggest, however, the utility of the alternative clustering scheme as one way in which subjects may represent information.

EXTERNAL VALIDATION

Overview

We now turn to external validation of the animal name analogies. The question of major interest here is whether these analogies provide a good measure of reasoning ability. It will be recalled that three groups of subjects solved the animal name analogies: (1) subjects in the People Piece and Verbal Analogy Experiments; (2) subjects in the Geometric Analogy Experiment; and (3) subjects otherwise uninvolved in the analogy experiments. External validation will be done separately for the first two groups of subjects, and the results will be considered together as well. Since no test results are available for the third group of subjects, other than their scores on the animal name analogies, the results for this third group will be ignored in subsequent analyses.

Basic Statistics

Basic statistics for the two groups of subjects are presented in Table 10.2 It can be seen that subjects in both groups answered about two-thirds of the 30 items correctly. The difference between group means is not significant, $t(38) < 1$. The reliability of the test was only moderate for each group, and was low relative to reliabilities usually obtained for good reasoning tests. At least twice the number

TABLE 10.2
Basic Statistics for Animal Name Analogy Subjects

	No. items	Mean	Standard deviation	Number of observations	Reliability
People Piece and verbal analogy group	30	19.44	3.74	16	.60
Geometric analogy group	30	19.54	3.26	24	.50

of items used in the test would have been required to attain reliabilities even in the .70s (as estimated by the Spearman—Brown formula).

Correlations with External Criteria

Table 10.3 presents correlations of animal name analogy scores with interval and component scores from the People Piece, Verbal Analogy, and Geometric Analogy Experiments. The correlations are not impressive. A few significant correlations were obtained with interval scores, and the correlation between the animal name analogy score and the standardized encoding component score is also significant. (All significance tests are two tailed.) Generally, there appears to be only a low to moderate level of overlap between these response time analogies and the animal name analogy scores.

Table 10.4 presents correlations between animal name analogy scores and scores on the reference ability tests. Consider first the correlations obtained with scores from tests in the People Piece and Verbal Analogy Experiments. The correlations with two out of the three reasoning tests are significant, and that with Word Grouping is particularly high. This, of course, is the one verbal reasoning test, and since the animal name analogies are also verbal, a higher correlation might be expected. The correlation with the reasoning factor score is also significant. None of the correlations with perceptual speed tests are significant. The correlation with the vocabulary score also does not reach significance.

Although the correlation with the reasoning factor score is statistically significant, the correlation drops down to a nonsignificant value with vocabulary (or vocabulary and perceptual speed) held constant. It is therefore of interest to see how the animal name analogies fared in the second group of subjects. None of the correlations with reasoning tests are significant. It would seem particularly surprising at first glance that the correlation with Word Grouping was trivial (and actually negative), since this correlation was extremely high for the first group of subjects. However, it should be recalled that Word Grouping for the second group of subjects did not end up loading on the primary reasoning factor (Factor I), but instead loaded on a specific factor (Factor II) that seemed to measure primarily situation-specific variance. Thus, the results of the Word Grouping test were not of much interest and probably not of much validity in the Geometric Analogy Experiment.

The correlation with the Minnesota Paper Form Board was significant, for no obvious reason. The correlation with vocabulary was not significant. The correlation with Factor I was significant, and the partial correlation between Factor I and animal name analogy scores with vocabulary held constant was actually higher than the simple correlation, although the difference was trivial.

Taken as a whole, these results are mixed and suggest that the animal name analogies probably do tap reasoning ability to some extent. It would have been

TABLE 10.3

Correlations between Animal Name Analogy Scores and People Piece, Verbal, and Geometric Analogy Scores

Cue Scores

	Overall				Session 1				Session 4			
	C0	C1	C2	C3	C0	C1	C2	C3	C0	C1	C2	C3
People Piece cue scores	-.44	-.50*	-.37	-.30	-.31	-.58*	-.52*	-.34	-.37	-.15	-.05	-.12
Verbal analogy cue scores	-.54*	-.33	-.39	-.35								
Geometric analogy cue scores	.09	.14										

Solution scores

	Overall				Session 1				Session 4			
	S0	S1	S2	S3	S0	S1	S2	S3	S0	S1	S2	S3
People Piece solution scores	-.28	-.35	-.43	-.34	-.27	-.38	-.41	-.15	-.41	-.31	-.47	-.43
Verbal analogy solution scores	-.28	-.32	-.31	-.59*								
Geometric analogy solution scores	-.08	.04										

Component scores

	a	x	y'	z'	c	t	a_β
People Piece component scores	.09	.09	-.32	-.32	-.32		.35
Verbal analogy component scores	.45	-.30	-.09	-.37	-.34		.51*
Geometric analogy component scores	-.33	-.26	-.20	.13	.23	.18	-.29

*$p < .05$.

TABLE 10.4
Correlations between Animal Name Analogy Scores and Reference Ability Test Scores

People Piece and Verbal Analogy Experiments		Geometric Analogy Experiment	
Reasoning		Reasoning	
Word grouping	.73***	Word grouping	−.14
Letter series	.25	Letter series	.32
Cattell reasoning	.60*	Cattell reasoning (form A)	.23
		French figure classification	.37
Perceptual Speed			
Same–different	.36	Spatial visualization	
Letter identification	.33	French figure rotation	−.22
French number comparison	.34	Minnesota paper form board	.46*
French identical pictures	.22	French cube comparison	.21
Vocabulary		Vocabulary	
French vocabulary (levels, 3, 4, 5)	.43	French vocabulary (level 3)	−.32
Factor I (perceptual speed)	.24	Factor I	.44*
Factor II (reasoning)	.53*	Factor II	−.14
Factor II (reasoning) Factor I constant	.50*		
		Factor III (vocabulary)	−.31
Factor II (reasoning) Vocabulary constant	.39	Factor I	
		Vocabulary Constant	.46*
Factor II (reasoning) Factor I Constant Vocabulary Constant	.37	Lorge–Thorndike analogies	.20

*p < .05.   ***p < .001.

helpful in assessing the validity of the animal names test if it were more reliable, and a test of at least 60 items would seem essential for any future research concerned with external validation of these items as measures of reasoning or any other ability.

SUMMARY

The Animal Name Analogy Experiment had two basic purposes. First, the experiment permitted a limited test of the componential theory of analogical reasoning with stimuli in which the latent attributes were identifiable but not obvious. Second, the experiment permitted a number of tests to determine whether performance on a test of animal name analogies actually is related to performance on inductive reasoning and other tests.

The stimulus material consisted of the 30 animal name analogies. All 60 subjects in the experiment received the identical analogies and instructions for completing them. Subjects were instructed to select the best answer to each analogy and were given as much time as they needed to complete the task.

Three types of representations were considered in analyzing the animal name data: rated distance, spatial representation (scaled distance), and cluster representation. In all three representations, the distance between the A and B analogy terms was significantly correlated with analogy easiness. The distance from A to C was not correlated with easiness.

In the spatial representation, three distance metrics were evaluated in an attempt to determine the metric for psychological distance in solving the animal name analogies. The data did not distinguish among the metrics. Overall distances were also broken down into their component intradimensional distances, and it was discovered that only the humanness dimension (the third dimension uncovered by Henley, 1969) contributed to the prediction of item easiness. Coordinate values along each dimension were also used as predictors and, again, only coordinates for the humanness dimension showed consistently high correlations with item easiness. The hypothesis was investigated that the correlations for the humanness dimension with item easiness might be due to a confounding of the humanness dimension with the true relevant dimension. However, no other dimension was found that yielded comparable prediction. Other dimensions investigated were Battig–Montague production frequency, representativeness, familiarity, and visualizability.

The cluster representation made use of nonhierarchical, overlapping subsets of animals. It was found that the number of common subsets in which the A and B analogy terms occurred and the number of subsets in which they occurred at all were better predictors of analogy easiness than comparable measures obtained from the distance representation. A model based upon the cluster representation was able to account for 56% of the variance in item easiness (as measured by the z transformation of proportion correct), but a comparable model based upon a distance representation was able to account for only 28% of the variance in the item easiness data. The cluster representation also accounts better for subjects' intuitions regarding how they solve the analogies.

External validation suggested that animal name analogies provide a measure of reasoning, but probably not a particularly good one. A more reliable test with more animal name items would have been desirable to provide a more exacting test of the validity of the animal name analogies as measures of inductive reasoning.

11
Miller Analogies

The Miller Analogies Test is a difficult 50-minute test consisting of 100 verbal analogies. The test is used for admission to graduate schools, for scholarship consideration, and for selection and placement in industry. A full description of the test is given in Sternberg (1974).

According to the Miller Analogies Test Manual (1970), the "Miller Analogies Test (MAT) was developed to measure scholastic aptitude at the graduate school level. . . . The test items require the recognition of relationships rather than the display of enormous erudition" (p. 3). This statement makes two strong claims about the test: (1) that it measures scholastic aptitude at the graduate school level, and (2) that it requires recognition of relationships rather than the display of enormous erudition. Many students who have taken the test would challenge both claims. Are the claims justified?

The first claim would be supported by research showing positive correlations between MAT scores and graduate school performance. The MAT manual presents the results of a large number of validity studies. In the large majority of studies reported, the test accounts for more than 1% of the variance in graduate school performance, but less than 15% of the variance in performance. On the average, it accounts for slightly more than 5% of the variance in various types of graduate school performance. The correlations, then, are almost uniformly positive, but also are almost all of low magnitude. It should be kept in mind that the correlations are reduced by the restriction of range that results when graduate school performance records are available only for students admitted in part on the basis of their test performance.

The second claim would be supported by research showing that the MAT is positively correlated with tests of reasoning ability, even after vocabulary or general information is held constant. I am unaware of any such study. There are experimental data, however, that cast doubt on the validity of the second claim.

Meer, Stein, and Geertsma (1955) investigated the relationship of MAT scores to scores on each subtest of the Wechsler—Bellevue Intelligence Scale (Wechsler, 1944). These authors found that by far the strongest correlation was with scores on the vocabulary subtest of the Wechsler—Bellevue ($r = .77$, $p < .01$). The second strongest correlation was with scores on the Information subtest ($r = .45$, $p < .01$). However, the correlation between MAT scores and scores on the verbal reasoning (similarities) subtest of the Wechsler—Bellevue was nonsignificant ($r = .27$, $p > .05$). The sample in this study was "50 subjects who are actively engaged in research in an industrial organization." Because of the atypicality of the sample, the results must be interpreted with caution. Nevertheless, the results are not compatible with the claim that the MAT measures recognition of relationships rather than erudition.

Guilford (1967) has also questioned the nature of the abilities measured by the MAT:

> To illustrate what may happen where vocabulary level is not controlled and one wants a reasoning test, we have the well-known Miller Analogies Test. This test was designed to be useful at the graduate-student level. The analogies form of item ordinarily involves relations as the kind of product. But in attempting to make the test difficult for testing purposes, the vocabulary level was apparently stepped up, which shifted the factorial nature of the test toward CMU [cognition of semantic units], which is already well represented in academic-aptitude tests. No factor analysis of the Miller Analogies Test is known to this writer, but its correlation with a good vocabulary test at the college level was reported to be about .85. (pp. 76–77)

The source of the correlation reported by Guilford is a personal communication from R. G. Watt, former director of the Testing Bureau of the University of Southern California.

The present series of investigations provided an unusual opportunity to discover what the Miller Analogies Test is measuring. First, a wide variety of reference ability test scores, including scores on tests of vocabulary and reasoning, were available for each subject. Second, component scores were available for each subject that would enable one to determine which component or components of analogical reasoning were correlated with scores on the MAT. There were also two disadvantages to the present context. The first was the small samples of subjects used in the investigations. The second was the age of the subjects, which averaged about three years younger than that reached by most students taking the MAT.

METHOD

Subjects were the 16 individuals who participated in the People Piece and Verbal Analogy Experiments. Each subject received 60 items taken from the *Bulletin of Information and List of Testing Centers with 60 Practice Items for the MAT*

(1972).[1] The booklet is distributed by The Psychological Corporation, publishers of the Miller Analogies Test. The test items were administered at the end of the seventh and final session for the 16 subjects who participated.

EXTERNAL VALIDATION

The mean score for the 16 subjects was 39.94 (67%), and the standard deviation was 7.19. The reliability of the test (split halves corrected by the Spearman—Brown formula) was .83, and the standard error of measurement was 2.96.

Correlations between the Miller Analogy Test scores and scores from the People Piece and Verbal Analogy Experiments are shown in Table 11.1. All significance tests are two tailed. The Miller scores did not correlate significantly with any of the cue scores in the People Piece Analogy Experiment, although they did correlate significantly with $C1$ and $C2$ from the Verbal Analogy Experiment. (Descriptions of the different types of scores from the People Piece and Verbal Analogy Experiments are contained in Chapters 7 and 8.) The higher correlations with the verbal analogy cue scores are presumably due to the verbal content common to the two tests. Several correlations with People Piece analogy solution scores are significant, and correlations with the verbal analogies solution scores are all significant. The higher correlations between the Miller and verbal analogies are probably again attributable in large part to the common verbal content.

None of the correlations with People Piece analogy component scores are significant, although the correlation with the inference score comes close ($p <$ .10) and might well have been significant with a more reliable component or Miller Analogy score. The correlation with the inference component from the Verbal Analogy Experiment is significant, as is the correlation with the preparation—response component and the standardized encoding component (beta weight) described in Chapter 8. The correlation with the standardized encoding component is positive, as were the correlations of this score with the reasoning tests examined in Chapter 8. These results, therefore, are quite favorable for the Miller Analogies Test. The test shows a strong correlation with inference in verbal analogies that are only slightly dependent upon vocabulary; and the correlations with two components that were found to be excellent measures of reasoning in the Verbal Analogy Experiment — preparation—response and standardized encoding — are also strong.

Let us turn, finally, to correlations between the Miller analogies and the reference ability tests and animal name analogies. These correlations are pre-

[1] I am grateful to Dr. David O. Herman, Assistant Director of the Test Division of The Psychological Corporation, for making arrangements permitting use of the Miller Analogy Test practice items in this study.

TABLE 11.1
Correlations between Miller Analogies and People Piece and Verbal Analogy Interval and Component Scores

Cue Scores

	Overall				Session 1				Session 4			
	C0	C1	C2	C3	C0	C1	C2	C3	C0	C1	C2	C3
People Piece cue scores	-.36	-.43	-.49	-.48	-.28	-.37	-.36	-.41	-.42	-.31	-.40	-.45
Verbal Analogy cue scores	-.46	-.63**	-.50*	-.48								

Solution Scores

	Overall				Session 1				Session 4			
	S0	S1	S2	S3	S0	S1	S2	S3	S0	S1	S2	S3
People Piece solution scores	-.51*	-.43	-.35	-.33	-.57*	-.40	-.06	-.15	-.42	-.43	-.56*	-.51*
Verbal Analogy solution scores	-.55*	-.59*	-.60*	-.63**								

Component Scores

	a	x	y'	z'	c	a_β
People Piece	-.05	-.44	-.35	.12	-.35	.28
Verbal Analogy	.41	-.64**	-.47	-.04	-.60*	.68**

$*p < .05.$ $**p < .01.$

sented in Table 11.2. The Miller analogies are highly correlated with all three reasoning tests. Scores on the Miller analogies are not, however, correlated significantly with scores on the perceptual speed tests, nor should they be. Miller analogy scores are very highly correlated with scores on the vocabulary battery. Indeed, this correlation of .76 is comparable to the correlation with the reasoning factor score of .77. Thus, these results replicate the strong correlation with vocabulary found in previous studies, but they also show strong correlations with reasoning tests. Does the correlation with the reasoning factor score hold up even after vocabulary is held constant? The partial correlation is .64, indicating that while the correlation decreases by .13, it still remains quite high. The correlation with the animal name analogy scores is a nonsignificant .34. While the animal name analogies are less confounded with vocabulary than the Miller analogies, they are also less highly correlated with reasoning scores. The low correlation between animal name and Miller analogies is probably due to lack of overlapping variance in both reasoning and vocabulary.

If the Miller Analogies Test is a fairly good measure of reasoning, even with vocabulary held constant, why are its correlations with performance in graduate programs so modest? A plausible interpretation of the pattern of data, similar to that of MacKinnon (1962), is that high performance on tests like the MAT is a necessary but not sufficient condition for successful performance in graduate

TABLE 11.2
Correlations between Miller Analogies and
Reference Ability Test and Animal Name Analogy Scores

People Piece and Verbal Analogy Experiments	
Reasoning	
Word grouping	.66**
Letter series	.72**
Cattell reasoning	.64**
Perceptual speed	
Same–different	−.09
Letter identification	.21
French number comparison	.12
French identical pictures	.30
Vocabulary	
French vocabulary (levels 3, 4, 5)	.76***
Factor I (perceptual speed)	.25
Factor II (reasoning)	.77***
Factor II (reasoning) Vocabulary constant	.64**
Animal name analogies	.34

**$p < .01$.   ***$p < .001$.

school and in subsequent careers. Once students are preselected on the basis of scholastic aptitude tests, the remaining variance in scores is of little use in predicting rank order among those selected. Other variables, such as motivation and creativity, may then become the critical sources of individual differences in performance.

SUMMARY

Sixty Miller analogies were administered to the 16 subjects who participated in the People Piece and Verbal Analogy Experiments. Scores on the Miller analogies were found to be highly correlated with some solution scores from the People Piece Analogy Experiment and all solution scores from the Verbal Analogy Experiment. None of the correlations with People Piece component scores reached significance, but correlations with the inference, preparation—response, and standardized encoding component scores of the Verbal Analogy Experiment were all significant. The Miller analogies thus tapped individual differences in components that were previously shown to be very good measures of reasoning ability.

Correlations with all reasoning tests but no perceptual speed tests were significant. In addition, the correlation with scores on a vocabulary battery was comparable to the correlation with the reasoning factor score. However, the correlation with the reasoning factor score remained quite high and statistically significant even after vocabulary was held constant. The results therefore suggest that Miller analogies may provide a good measure of reasoning as well as vocabulary. Because of the high correlation with vocabulary, the test would probably not be appropriate as a measure of reasoning for students who for one reason or another have unusually poor vocabularies relative to their reasoning abilities.

The high correlations of MAT scores with reasoning tests considered together with the relatively low correlations of MAT scores with graduate school and subsequent performance suggest the possibility that fairly high MAT scores may be a necessary but not sufficient condition for later success. Once students are preselected on the basis of MAT or similar scores, the remaining variance in the scores is of little use in predicting individual differences. Other variables such as motivation and creativity may then become the variables of importance.

12
Conclusions about Analogical Reasoning

This chapter presents 36 conclusions based upon the results described in the preceding five chapters. Only general conclusions are presented: More specific conclusions can be found in the individual chapters. Both solution time and error rate are used as dependent variables in all but one experiment (animal name analogies), and the range in difficulty of the analogies is quite large, as is shown in Figure 12.1. This figure shows the range and medians for solution times and error rates across subjects. Solution times are not available for animal name analogies.

In the following conclusions, the chapters from which the conclusions are drawn are noted after each conclusion.

BASIC UNIT OF INFORMATION PROCESSING

1. *Unit.* The basic unit of information processing is the component. (Chapters 7, 8, 9)

2. *Combinations of units.* Differences in performance across items and across subjects can be accounted for in terms of differences in contributions of components. (Chapters 7, 8, 9)

COMPONENTIAL THEORY

3. *Components.* Subjects solve all analogies using encoding, inference, mapping, application, and preparation–response components. Subjects solve some analogies using an additional justification component, and some using holistic processing. (Chapters 7, 8)

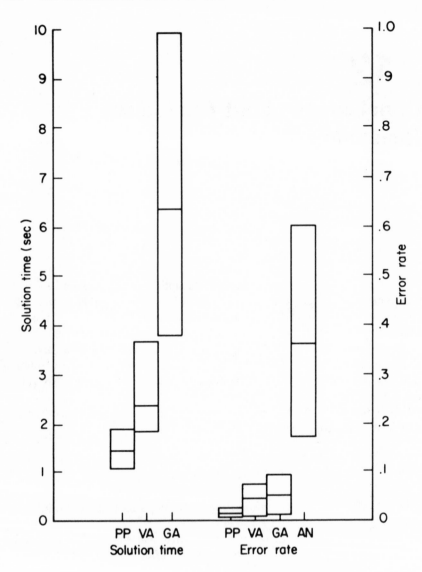

FIGURE 12.1   Relative difficulties of four types of analogies.

4. *Combination rule for components.* The combination rule for components is additive. (Chapters 7, 8, 9)

4. *Theory.* Conclusions 3 and 4 support the componential theory of analogical reasoning. (Chapters 7, 8, 9)

6. *Validity of alternative theories.* Both the mapping and application components, absent in some alternative theories, appear to be necessary components of an analogical-reasoning process model. (Chapters 7, 8, 9)

COMPONENTIAL MODELS: SOLUTION TIME

Mode of Component Execution

7. *Encoding.* Subjects encode analogy terms exhaustively. (Chapters 7, 8)

8. *Inference.* Subjects probably infer value transformations exhaustively, although the data do not permit an informed choice between exhaustive and self-terminating hypotheses. Subjects may use some combination strategy. (Chapters 7, 8, 9)

9. *Mapping.* Subjects map value transformations in self-terminating fashion. (Chapters 7, 8, 9)

10. *Application.* Subjects apply value transformations in self-terminating fashion. (Chapters 7, 8, 9)

11. *Model.* Conclusions 7, 8, 9, 10 support Componential Model III. Because it is uncertain in what mode the inference component is executed, the data do not convincingly reject Model IV. The data do seem to reject Model II, and overwhelmingly reject Model I. (Chapters 7, 8, 9)

Durations of Components

12. *Absolute time.* The absolute amount of time spent on the encoding, inference, mapping, application, and probably justification components is quite variable across different types of analogies. The amount of time spent on the preparation—response component is approximately constant across different types of analogies (400—500 msec). (Chapters 7, 8, 9)

13. *Relative time.* The relative amount of time spent on each component is quite variable across different types of analogies. In the analogies studied, (a) encoding always absorbed the greatest amount of time and (b) application always absorbed the least amount of time among the three mandatory attribute-comparison components. (Chapters 7, 8, 9)

Individual Differences

14. *Model.* There is no evidence of consistent individual differences in the models of analogical reasoning used by different subjects. (Chapters 7, 8, 9)

15. *Component intercorrelation.* The encoding and preparation—response components are negatively correlated across subjects. (Chapters 7, 8, 9)

COMPONENTIAL MODELS: ERROR RATE

Sources of Error

16. *Components.* Commission of errors is due largely to faulty or incomplete execution of self-terminating components and the justification component. (Chapters 7, 9)

Mode of Component Execution

17. *Inference.* The data do not permit an informed choice between the alternative hypotheses of an exhaustive versus a self-terminating inference difficulty component, nor is it clear that the inference difficulty parameter contributes significantly to the overall error model. (Chapters 7, 8, 9)

18. *Mapping.* The mapping difficulty component is self-terminating. (Chapters 7, 9)

19. *Application.* The application difficulty component is self-terminating. (Chapters 7, 9)

20. *Model.* Conclusions 15, 16, and 17 equally support Models III and IV, although III was chosen because of its consistency with the chosen solution-time model. The data probably reject Model II, and overwhelmingly reject Model I. (Chapters 7, 9)

Multivariate Componential Model:
Solution Time and Error Rate

21. *Aspects of solution time and error rate.* Predicted jointly, solution time has one "aspect" and error rate has two. Error rate, therefore, is the more complex dependent variable. The aspects are measured by canonical variates. (Chapters 7, 9)

22. *Aspect 1.* The first canonical variate is virtually identical to solution time. Error rate is also a measure of this canonical variate, but is a less valid measure than is solution time. (Chapters 7, 9)

23. *Aspect 2.* The second canonical variate, orthogonal to the first, distinguishes between components that contribute to error rate and those that do not. Error rate measures this canonical variate, but solution time does not. (Chapters 7, 9)

RELATIONS BETWEEN SOLUTION TIME AND ERROR RATE

24. *Across items.* Solution time and error rate are positively correlated across items (through the first canonical variate described above). (Chapters 7, 8, 9)

25. *Across subjects.* Solution time and error rate are negatively correlated across subjects. (Chapters 7, 9)

RELATIONS BETWEEN SOLUTION TIME AND REFERENCE ABILITIES

26. *Strength of relationship.* Lower solution times for full analogies are associated with higher reasoning scores, at least for verbal analogies. (Chapter 8)

27. *Amount of practice.* Correlations between solution time and reasoning scores increase with greater amounts of prior practice. (Chapter 7)

RELATIONS BETWEEN ERROR RATE
AND REFERENCE ABILITIES

28. *Strength of relationship.* Lower error rates are associated with higher reasoning scores if analogies are difficult enough. (Chapters 9, 10, 11)

RELATIONS BETWEEN SOLUTION TIME–ERROR RATE
AND REFERENCE ABILITIES

29. *Strength of relationship.* Lower solution times and error rates considered in conjunction may be associated with higher reasoning scores, even when neither variable considered alone is associated with reasoning. This situation arises when there is a speed–accuracy tradeoff. (Chapter 9)

RELATIONS BETWEEN COMPONENT TIMES
AND REFERENCE ABILITIES

30. *Encoding.* Higher encoding times are sometimes associated with higher reasoning scores, probably due to strategy differences between higher and lower reasoning subjects. Greater amounts of time spent on encoding may permit other operations to proceed more quickly. (Chapters 7, 8)

31. *Inference.* Lower inference times are sometimes associated with higher reasoning scores, probably only when the discovery of relevant attributes is a source of individual differences in inference time. Individual differences in time for testing relevant attributes do not appear sufficient to generate strong associations with individual differences in reasoning scores. (Chapters 7, 8)

32. *Mapping.* Lower mapping times are sometimes associated with higher reasoning scores, probably only when the discovery of relevant attributes is a source of individual differences in mapping time. (Chapters 7, 8)

33. *Application.* Lower application times are sometimes associated with higher reasoning scores, probably only in forced-choice items and possibly only in items in which no presented answer option is identical to the ideal one. (Chapters 7, 8, 9)

34. *Justification.* Lower justification times are associated with higher reasoning scores. (Chapter 9)

35. *Preparation–response.* Lower preparation–response times are associated with higher reasoning scores. (Chapters 7, 8)

RELATION BETWEEN
PERCENTAGE OF VARIANCE ACCOUNTED FOR
AND REFERENCE ABILITIES

36. *Strength of relationship.* The percent-variance-accounted-for by the overall best fitting model for each individual subject's solution-time data is positively associated with higher reasoning scores, but probably only when the discovery of relevant attributes is a source of individual differences in component times. (Chapters 7, 8)

Part IV
POSTSCRIPT

13
Toward a Theory of Intelligence

Although it is not possible at this time to present a full componential theory of intelligence, it is possible to present the beginning of a theory of intelligence, a description of the form that a full theory will take, and a synopsis of the major substantive and methodological issues arising out of the research described in this volume. The first two of these items are dealt with in the next section. The last item is dealt with in the final section.

PRELIMINARY SKETCH OF A THEORY OF INTELLIGENCE

A preliminary sketch of a theory of intelligence is presented in Figure 13.1. We begin our interpretation of Figure 13.1 starting at the bottom of the figure and moving toward the top.

Components

Components are the fundamental "units" of intelligence. They are the elementary information processes responsible for what we call "intelligent behavior." Because the components are processes rather than hypothetical "entities" of some kind, they are nonarbitrary. Component performance can be measured in terms of direct contribution to latency or error rate, not merely in terms of some arbitrary scale. Individual differences arise when some individuals perform components more quickly (lower values of latency parameters) or more easily (lower values of difficulty parameters) than other individuals.

Components may be either general or group. The category in which a particular component belongs depends upon the diversity of tasks under consideration. Hence, the categories are a convenience rather than a psychological property. Other categories could be used instead.

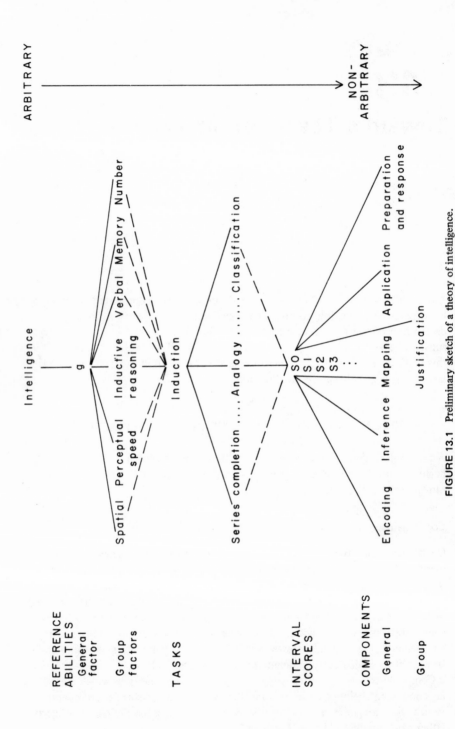

FIGURE 13.1 Preliminary sketch of a theory of intelligence.

A general component is mandatory in all tasks of a specified kind. In this volume, we have been concerned with analogical-reasoning tasks, and the five components theorized and shown to be general (at least to three quite different types of analogies) are encoding, inference, mapping, application, and preparation—response.

A group component is optional in all tasks of a specified kind. It is used in only a subset (or group) of the tasks being considered. One such component was demonstrated in this volume, the justification component. This component is used in the solution of forced-choice analogies in which the keyed option (D_T) is not identical to the ideal option (D').

A component that is general across tasks of one kind may be a group component across a wider range of tasks, and a group component may be general across a narrower range of tasks. Consider an example of each case. Mapping is theorized to be general to all analogical reasoning tasks, but is not theorized to be applicable to other inductive reasoning tasks such as series completion and classification, except under special circumstances. Over the full range of inductive reasoning tasks, it is a group component. Conversely, justification is a group component across analogical reasoning tasks, but is a general component if only a narrower range of tasks is considered — forced-choice analogy tasks in which no ideal answer is presented as an option.

Interval Scores

At the next higher level of Figure 13.1 are interval scores, which are scores on subtasks. Components are identified and their values estimated through mathematical modeling of subtask data. Performance on the full task is measured by the interval score $S0$, which contains all components. Performance on subtasks is measured by performance on successive interval scores, $S1$, $S2$, and so forth. These interval scores generally contain successively fewer components.

The number of subtasks used in an experiment will vary with the type of task studied and the information desired from the task. The breakdown of the task into subtasks is arbitrary, and usually could be accomplished in a variety of ways, some more revealing about psychological process than others.

Tasks

The next higher level of Figure 13.1 depicts tasks. The three most commonly used induction tasks are series completion, analogy, and classification. Because it has not yet been shown experimentally that series completion and classification tasks can be broken down into subtasks and then analyzed componentially, only dashed lines are drawn between these tasks and the lower level of interval scores.

All these tasks, like the subtasks, are arbitrarily constructed. A large variety of induction tasks could be constructed by varying task constraints such as type of response required, visual layout of the item, etc. These task variants would presumably require slightly different combinations of a relatively small number of components.

Reference Abilities

The next level of Figure 13.1 depicts reference abilities. Reference abilities are constellations of components showing common patterns of individual differences. The reference abilities are identified through factor analysis of task scores. The reference abilities used in this volume are the primary mental abilities of Thurstone, but the choice of reference abilities is one of convenience. A different set could be obtained by rotating factors in a different way, or by using different tests.

Analogy tasks and other tasks tapping individual differences in reference abilities can be constructed so as to measure different combinations of reference abilities. Presumably, analogy tasks (unless trivial) should always measure individual differences in inductive reasoning ability, and all the analogy tasks studied in this volume did measure them. Hence, a solid line is drawn from inductive reasoning through induction to analogy. It would be expected that by manipulation of the proper task variables, other reference abilities could also be measured by analogy tasks.

Consider some examples. Spatial analogies could be constructed by requiring the same degree of mental rotation from the C to D terms as from the A to B terms (Roger Shepard and Lynn Cooper, personal communications). Perceptual speed might be measured by constructing true–false analogies such as 138426: 138436::759162::759182, where the analogies are true if the third and fourth terms differ in the same digit position as the first and second terms, and are false otherwise. Verbal comprehension can be measured by analogies requiring a high level of vocabulary (such as the Miller Analogies Test). Memory might be measured by analogies with complex figural terms, in which the subject is not permitted to look back at an analogy term once it has been (successfully) encoded. Number might be measured by analogies such as 9:81::½:(a. ¼, b. 1), where the subject must select the better answer.

General Factor

The next level of Figure 13.1 depicts g, the general factor. A general factor may be obtained in at least two ways. One requires the use of an unrotated component or factor solution. With most factoring methods and tests, the resultant first factor will be a general one. A second way of obtaining a general factor requires factoring of an obliquely rotated component or factor solution. A "second-order" general factor will often be obtained if the original tests are all highly intercorrelated.

Intelligence

The highest level of Figure 13.1 is "intelligence." The notion of intelligence is largely arbitrary: History has shown that it can be defined in myriad different ways. Some definitions may prove more useful than others, just as some factor solutions, tasks, and subtasks prove more useful than others. But arguments about the "correct" definition will not lead to any resolution, because "intelligence" has no meanings other than those we assign it.

While we cannot supply a nonarbitrary definition of intelligence, we can define intelligence in terms of some nonarbitrary unit or units. In the componential theory of intelligence, this unit is the component.

Intelligence is defined in terms of: (1) the availability of components needed for information processing; (2) the utilities of the rules used for combining components; (3) the utilities of the modes used for component execution; (4) the utilities of the orders in which components are executed; and (5) the component values. Component values may be expressed either as latencies or difficulties, and the two are not necessarily correlated.

The term *utility* is used in a specific way. Higher utility is defined in terms of lower overall solution time and lower overall error rate. Greater intelligence is recognized through lower solution time and error rate, but is caused by the five sources described above. These sources of intelligence are all measurable through componential modeling of solution-time and error-rate data.

Much of the disagreement among theorists of intelligence has been over three issues. The first issue is the determination of the "correct" definition of intelligence. This issue is irresoluble, since there is no one correct definition. The second issue is the determination of the correct unit upon which to base a theory of intelligence. The component has been shown in this monograph to be a useful unit. The third issue is the determination of the correct way to partition the chosen unit. This has been a fundamental problem in factor analysis, and will continue to be a problem, because there is no one solution when the unit is arbitrary, as is the factor. Components are nonarbitrary (at a given level of analysis); therefore, this source of disagreement ceases to be irresoluble. While there may be disagreement over what the true components are, the disagreement can be resolved through experimental tests.

CURRENT ISSUES IN INTELLIGENCE RESEARCH

Substantive Issues

1. *Why does c correlate with reasoning?* One of the most surprising findings in the series of experiments was the strong correlation between the preparation–response component (c) and reasoning scores. Possible explanations of this

finding were discussed, but the data are only of minimal help in choosing among the explanations (motivation, attention, bookkeeping, decision, planning). What makes selection among explanations particularly difficult is that c is the unanalyzed component: It is confounded. In retrospect, this component might have been further subdivided, at least into separate preparation and response components, and possibly into a separate "bookkeeping" component as well.

2. *Under what circumstances do a, x, y', z', t correlate with reasoning?* All six components in the theory of analogical reasoning have been found to correlate with reasoning, at least under some circumstances. Hypotheses are ventured in the experiments and in the previous chapter as to what these circumstances might be. But these are only hypotheses, and the data just begin to distinguish among them. In particular, the distinction between attribute discovery and attribute testing seems to merit further attention. The preferred hypothesis at the present time is that attribute discovery taps individual differences in reasoning, but attribute testing does so only to a minimal degree.

3. *To what extent do individual differences at the theory and model levels contribute to differential task performance?* The data analyses presented in this volume did not seek out individual differences at the theory level (component identities and combination rule), and although individual differences at the model level were investigated, no substantial ones were found. These individual differences may be more pronounced in tasks other than analogy, and the componential method would seem to provide a useful way of discovering and then investigating them.

4. *What is the role of memory in complex task performance?* The analogy data have been interpreted in terms of a theory and model of reasoning, and relatively little has been said about the role of memory in analogy solution. Yet, memory must play an important role, since subjects must store and then retrieve attributes and must also relate the stimulus information to information already stored in long-term memory. The role of memory merits further investigation.

5. *How general are the components of analogical reasoning?* It has been claimed that four of the six components of analogical reasoning are general to all induction tasks and that two are group components of at least some generalizability. Since this volume has reported research only on analogical reasoning, the claim of generality is at this point only conjecture. The generalizability of the components remains to be demonstrated. This is a primary goal of the author's present research.

6. *How does intelligence develop?* Chapter 4 presented conjectures about how intellectual development might be understood in a componential framework. Development is understood in terms of the acquisition of components, combination rules, component modes, component orderings, and in terms of decreasing component values. Componential metatheory provides a potentially useful framework for understanding development, but at this point, the contribution is

only potential. It remains to be shown that the framework is useful in actual applications.

7. *Can intelligence be increased by training?* This question has been a major source of controversy, both in education and in psychology (e.g., Jensen, 1969). Chapter 4 presented conjectures about how training might proceed in a componential framework, taking into account deficiencies at the theory, model, and component levels. It was noted that most attempts have been at the component level; but this is probably the most difficult level at which to obtain improvements. A componential framework might be useful for improving training methods.

8. *What circumstances lead to the use of some modes of components as opposed to others?* Why do subjects use Model III in solving analogies, or any particular model in solving any particular task? The data unequivocally reject Model I, but they do not tell us why subjects do not use this model. Understanding of problem solving would be greatly enhanced if we knew what circumstances lead to the use of exhaustive versus self-terminating search, serial versus parallel search, or holistic versus particularistic processing.

9. *What are the components of intelligence?* The research described in this volume provides a start toward answering this question. Many more components must be involved in the performance of various intellectual tasks. A major goal for intelligence research is the identification of further components.

10. *Are components always additive, and if not, what other combination rules are used?* In the componential theory of analogical reasoning, component times and difficulties are theorized to be additive. The additive rule fits the data well. Additive models have the advantage of simplicity, but are they an oversimplification? Are there other combination rules that better represent psychological process? If so, the nature of these other rules remains to be demonstrated.

11. *In what form is information stored?* A format for the internal representation of knowledge has been suggested, but it is not the only one that might be consistent with the data. The issue of internal representation is an important one, and a complete theory of intelligence ought to describe in detail structure as well as process.

12. *Can intelligence be understood at a componential level?* It has been the assumption of this monograph that intelligence can be understood at the level of the component, componential model, and componential theory. But it is a long way from the experimental laboratory to everyday intellectual behavior, and it remains to be shown that intelligence can be fully understood in a componential or any other single framework.

Methodological Issues

13. *What should be the role of factor analysis in intelligence research?* Componential analysis uses factor analysis as an important analytical tool (in the

identification of reference abilities and the calculation of reference ability scores), but the role of factor analysis is much more modest than its role in differential research, or even in the contemporary research of Hunt (Hunt et al., 1973; Hunt et al., 1975). For example, Hunt factor analyzes model parameters (such as those from the Atkinson–Shiffrin memory model), whereas in componential analysis component scores are the root sources of individual differences, and, therefore, are not factor analyzed. The role of factor analysis in intelligence research is still a matter susceptible to further debate.

14. *What should be the role of mathematical modeling in theory development?* The componential analysis presented in this volume makes heavy use of mathematical modeling. It is understandable but less than reassuring, however, that as the modeled task became more complex, the ability of the mathematical models to account for the data declines. Is mathematical modeling a feasible way of studying complex processes, or does it begin to break down and become less useful after processes reach even a moderate level of complexity?

15. *Should individual differences be studied in terms of mean differences or correlations?* Hunt and his colleagues (e.g., Hunt et al., 1973) make extensive use of mean differences and some use of correlations in their research, whereas the present author uses correlations here almost exclusively. The correlational method has been preferred in these studies for four reasons. First, the correlational method permits a statement about the magnitude of a relationship as well as about its statistical significance. Second, the correlational method retains information about individual differences within groups (such as high and low reasoning) as well as between groups. Third, due to unreliability of measurement and consequent score fluctuations, the groups are not well defined entities. There are usually crossovers in scores on at least some tests. Fourth, multiple regression can be used to analyze relationships between a dependent variable and multiple independent variables. Two disadvantages of the correlational method are: (1) that it assumes linearity of the relationship between variables (nonlinear correlation can be used, but rarely is); and (2) it quickly loses statistical power with small samples.

16. *Can intelligence be studied meaningfully with small samples?* The research reported in this monograph makes use of small preselected samples, although large numbers of observations are collected from each subject. Questions of generalizability inevitably arise and are not easily answered. The power of statistical tests performed on the samples is implicitly increased by preselecting subjects with extreme test scores, but the preselection of subjects with extreme scores raises at least as many questions about generalizability as it answers. These problems become particularly troublesome in multiple regressions and factor analyses performed across subjects. More efficient testing methods are probably needed that will permit larger sample sizes.

17. *What should be the role of subjective analysis in identifying sources of individual differences?* Componential analysis leaves relatively little room for

subjective analysis. While the componential theory and models are to some extent subjective, they are always verified by experimental tests. The result is very slow progress: Much of this volume is devoted to the demonstration of the psychological reality and generalizability of just six components. Carroll (1974) has made extensive use of subjective analysis in identifying sources of individual differences in intellectual behavior. His method has the disadvantage of being backed by intuition rather than hard data, but it has the advantage of generating large numbers of hypotheses about sources of individual differences that can later be subjected to empirical test.

18. *Is componential analysis a general method?* It has been claimed in this volume that componential analysis is a general method for studying intelligence. The method has been shown applicable to a rather wide range of analogical reasoning problems and, in separate publications, will be shown applicable to other types of reasoning problems as well. But these are relatively limited classes of problems, and the applicability of componential analysis to a wide variety of complex tasks has not yet been demonstrated. This demonstration has a high priority for further research.

SUMMARY

A preliminary sketch of a theory of intelligence is presented. The sketch illustrates two basic types of constructs, arbitrary and nonarbitrary ones. All constructs are arbitrary except components. These components are theorized to be the fundamental "units" of intelligence. The components are elementary information processes, and correspond to latent traits.

Components may be either general or group. A general component is mandatory in all tasks of a specified kind, while a group component is optional in all tasks of a specified kind. The category in which a particular component belongs depends upon the diversity of the tasks under consideration.

Intelligence is defined in terms of: (1) the existence of components; (2) the utilities of rules for combining components; (3) the utilities of modes for executing components; (4) the utilities of orders for executing components, and (5) the component values. Higher utility refers to lower overall solution time and lower overall error rate.

Much of the disagreement among theorists of intelligence has been over three issues. The first is the determination of the "correct" definition of intelligence. This issue is irresoluble. The second issue is the determination of the correct unit of intelligence. The component is offered as this unit. The third issue is the determination of the correct way to partition the chosen unit. This issue is experimentally resoluble in the framework of componential analysis.

Eighteen current issues in intelligence research are enumerated and discussed, twelve of them substantive and six methodological. These issues suggest directions for further research on intelligence.

References

Ace, M. C., & Dawis, R. V. Item structure as a determinant of item difficulty in verbal analogies. *Educational and Psychological Measurement,* 1973, *33,* 143—149.

Achenbach, T. M. The children's associative responding test: A possible alternative to group IQ tests. *Journal of Educational Psychology,* 1970, *61,* 333—339.

Anderson, J. R. *Language, Memory, and Thought.* Hillsdale, N. J.: Lawrence Erlbaum Assoc., 1976.

Anderson, J. R. Verbatim and propositional representation of sentences in immediate and long-term memory. *Journal of Verbal Learning and Verbal Behavior,* 1974, *13,* 149—162.

Anderson, J. R., & Bower, G. H. *Human associative memory.* Washington, D.C.: Winston, 1973.

Arabie, P., & Shepard, R. N. Representation of similarities as additive combinations of discrete overlapping properties. Paper presented at the Mathematical Psychology Meetings, Montreal, 1973.

Bamber, D. Reaction times and error rates for "same—different" judgments of multidimensional stimuli. *Perception and Psychophysics,* 1969, *6,* 169—174.

Banks, C., & Sinha, U. An item-analysis of the Progressive Matrices Test and Binet. *British Journal of Psychology, Statistical Section,* 1951, *4,* 91—94.

Battig, W. F., & Montague, W. E. Category norms for verbal items in 56 categories: A replication and extension of the Connecticut category norms. *Journal of Experimental Psychology Monograph,* 1969, *80.*

Becker, J. D. The modeling of simple analogic and inductive processes in a semantic memory system. *Proceedings of the International Joint Conference on Artificial Intelligence.* Washington, D.C.: 1969. Pp. 655—668.

Bower, G. H. A multicomponent theory of the memory trace. In K. W. Spence & J. T. Spence (Eds.), *The psychology of learning and motivation. Volume 1.* New York: Academic Press, 1967. Pp. 299—325.

Bower, G., and Trabasso, T. Concept identification. In R. C. Atkinson (Ed.), *Studies in mathematical psychology.* Stanford, Calif.: Stanford University Press, 1964. Pp. 32—94.

Brown, W., & Thomson, G. H. *The essentials of mental measurement.* Cambridge, England: Cambridge University Press, 1921.

Bruner, J. S., Goodnow, J. J., & Austin, G. A. *A study of thinking.* New York: Wiley, 1956.

Bulletin of information and list of testing centers with 60 practice items for the MAT. New York: The Psychological Corporation, 1972.

326

Burke, H. R. Raven's Progressive Matrices: A review and critical evaluation. *Journal of Genetic Psychology*, 1958, *93*, 199–228.

Burt, C. *The factors of the mind*. London: University of London Press, 1940.

Burt, C. Alternative methods of factor analysis and their relations to Pearson's method of 'principal axes.' *British Journal of Psychology, Statistical Section*, 1949, *2*, 98–121.

Burt, C. The genetics of intelligence. In W. B. Dockrell (Ed.), *On intelligence*. Toronto: The Ontario Institute for Studies in Education, 1970. Pp. 15–28.

Butcher, H. J. *Human intelligence: Its nature and assessment*. London: Methuen, 1968.

Calfee, R. C. Sources of dependency in cognitive processes. In D. Klahr (Ed.), *Cognition and instruction*. Hillsdale, New Jersey: Lawrence Erlbaum Assoc., 1976. Pp. 23–50.

Campbell, D. T. Recommendations for APA test standards regarding construct, trait, or discriminant validity. *American Psychologist*, 1960, *15*, 546–553.

Carpenter, P. A., & Just, M. A. Sentence comprehension: A psycholinguistic processing model of verification. *Psychological Review*, 1975, *82*, 45–73.

Carroll, J. B. An analytic solution for approximating simple structure in factor analysis. *Psychometrika*, 1953, *18*, 23–38.

Carroll, J. B. Psychometric tests as cognitive tasks: A new "structure of intellect." RB-74-16. Technical Report No. 4. Princeton, N.J.: Educational Testing Service, 1974.

Cattell, R. B. *Abilities: Their structure, growth, and action*. Boston: Houghton-Mifflin, 1971.

Cattell, R. B., & Cattell, A. K. S. *Test of g: Culture Fair, Scale 3*. Champaign, Illinois: Institute for Personality and Ability Testing, 1963.

Chase, W. G., & Simon, H. A. The mind's eye in chess. In W. G. Chase (Ed.), *Visual information processing*. New York: Academic Press, 1973. Pp. 215–281.

Clark, H. H. Linguistic processes in deductive reasoning. *Psychological Review*, 1969, *76*, 387–404.

Clark, H. H. How we understand negation. Paper presented at the COBRE workshop on cognitive organization and psychological processes, Huntington Beach, California, 1970.

Clark, H. H. The chronometric study of meaning components. Paper presented at the CRNS Colloque International sur les problèmes actuels de psycholinguistiques. Paris, 1971.

Clark, H., & Chase, W. On the process of comparing sentences against pictures. *Cognitive Psychology*, 1972, *3*, 472–517.

Cliff, N. Orthogonal rotation to congruence. *Psychometrika*, 1966, *31*, 33–42.

Collins, A. M., & Quillian, M. R. Retrieval time from semantic memory. *Journal of Verbal Learning and Verbal Behavior*, 1969, *8*, 240–247.

Cooley, W. W., & Lohnes, P. R. *Multivariate data analysis*. New York: Wiley, 1971.

Cooper, L. A. Internal representation and transformation of random shapes: A chronometric analysis. Unpublished doctoral dissertation, Stanford University, 1973.

Cooper, L. A., & Shepard, R. N. Chronometric studies of the rotation of mental images. In W. Chase, *Visual information processing*. New York: Academic Press, 1973. Pp. 75–176.

Cronbach, L. J. The two disciplines of scientific psychology. *American Psychologist*, 1957, *12*, 671–684.

Dawis, R. V., & Siojo, L. T. Analogical reasoning: A review of the literature. Effects of social class differences on analogical reasoning. Technical Report No. 1. Minneapolis: University of Minnesota, Department of Psychology, 1972.

Day, R. Individual differences in cognition. Paper presented at a meeting of the Psychonomic Society, St. Louis, 1973.

DeGroot, A. D. *Thought and choice in chess*. The Hague: Mouton, 1965.

Donders, F. C. Over de snelheid van psychische processen. Onderzoekingen gedaan in het Physiologisch Laboratorium der Utrechtsche Hoogeschool, 1868–1869, Tweede reeks, *II*, 92–120.

Emmett, W. G. Evidence of a space factor at 11+ and earlier. *British Journal of Psychology, Statistical Section,* 1949, *2,* 3–16.

Esher, F. J. S., Raven, J. C., & Earl, C. J. C. Discussion on testing intellectual capacity in adults. *Proceedings of the Royal Society of Medicine,* 1942, *35,* 779–785.

Evans, T. G. A program for the solution of geometric-analogy intelligence test questions. In M. Minsky (Ed.), *Semantic information processing.* Cambridge, Mass.: M.I.T. Press, 1968. Pp. 271–353.

Eysenck, H. J. The logical basis of factor analysis. *American Psychologist,* 1953, *8,* 105–114.

Eysenck, H. J. Intelligence assessment: A theoretical and experimental approach. *British Journal of Educational Psychology,* 1967, *37,* 81–89.

Ferguson, G. A. On learning and human ability. *Canadian Journal of Psychology,* 1954, *8,* 95–112.

Feuerstein, R., Schlesinger, I. M., Shalom, H., & Narrol, H. The dynamic assessment of retarded performers: The learning potential assessment device, theory, instruments and techniques. Vol. II: LPAD analogies group test experiment. *Studies in cognitive modifiability,* Report No. 1. Jerusalem: Hadassah Wizo Canada Research Institute, 1972.

Fleishman, E. A. The prediction of total task performance from prior practice on task components. *Human Factors,* 1965, *7,* 18–27.

Fleishman, E. A., & Hempel, W. E., Jr. The relation between abilities and improvement with practice in a visual discrimination reaction task. *Journal of Experimental Psychology,* 1955, *49,* 301–312.

French, J. W., Ekstrom, R. B., & Price, I. A. *Kit of reference tests for cognitive factors.* Princeton, N.J.: Educational Testing Service, 1963.

Gabriel, K. R. The simplex structure of the Progressive Matrices Test. *British Journal of Statistical Psychology,* 1954, *7,* 9–14.

Garner, W. R., Hake, H. W., & Eriksen, C. W. Operationism and the concept of perception. *Psychological Review,* 1956, *63,* 149–159.

Garrett, H. E. A developmental theory of intelligence. *American Psychologist,* 1946, *1,* 372–378.

Gentile, J. R., Kessler, D. K., & Gentile, P. K. Process of solving analogy items. *Journal of Educational Psychology,* 1969, *60,* 494–502.

Glaser, R. Some implications of previous work on learning and individual differences. In R. M. Gagné (Ed.), *Learning and individual differences.* Columbus, Ohio: Merrill, 1967. Pp. 1–18.

Glucksberg, S., Trabasso, T., & Wald, J. Linguistic structures and mental operations. *Cognitive Psychology,* 1973, *5,* 338–370.

Greeno, J. G. Hobbits and orcs: Acquisition of a sequential concept. *Cognitive Psychology,* 1974, *6,* 270–292.

Guilford, J. P. When not to factor analyze. *Psychological Bulletin,* 1952, *49,* 26–37.

Guilford, J. P. *Psychometric methods* (2nd ed.). New York: McGraw-Hill, 1954.

Guilford, J. P. *The nature of human intelligence.* New York: McGraw-Hill, 1967.

Guilford, J. P. Rotation problems in factor analysis. *Psychological Bulletin,* 1974, *81,* 498–501.

Guilford, J. P., & Hoepfner, R. *The analysis of intelligence.* New York: McGraw-Hill, 1971.

Guttman, L. A new approach to factor analysis: The radex. In P. E. Lazarsfeld (Ed.), *Mathematical thinking in the social sciences.* Glencoe, Illinois: Free Press, 1954. Pp. 258–348.

Harman, H. H. *Modern factor analysis.* Chicago: University of Chicago Press, 1967.

Hebb, D. O. *The organization of behavior.* New York: Wiley, 1949.

Henle, M. On the relation between logic and thinking. *Psychological Review,* 1962, *69,* 366–378.

Henley, N. M. A psychological study of the semantics of animal terms. *Journal of Verbal Learning and Verbal Behavior,* 1969, *8,* 176–184.

Holzinger, K. J. Relationships between three multiple orthogonal factors and four bifactors. *Journal of Educational Psychology,* 1938, *29,* 513–519.

Horn, J. L. On subjectivity in factor analysis. *Educational and Psychological Measurement,* 1967, *27,* 811–820.

Horn, J. L., & Knapp, J. R. On the subjective character of the empirical base of Guilford's structure-of-intellect model. *Psychological Bulletin,* 1973, *80,* 33–43.

Hotelling, H. The most predictable criterion. *Journal of Educational Psychology,* 1935, *26,* 139–142.

Hoving, K. L., Morin, R. E., & Konick, D. S. Recognition reaction time and size of memory set: A developmental study. *Psychonomic Science,* 1970, *21,* 247–248.

Humphreys, L. G. The organization of human abilities. *American Psychologist,* 1962, *17,* 475–483.

Hunt, E. B. *Concept learning.* New York: Wiley, 1962.

Hunt, E. B. Quote the raven? Nevermore! In L. W. Gregg (Ed.), *Knowledge and cognition.* Hillsdale, N.J.: Lawrence Erlbaum Assoc., 1974. Pp. 129–157.

Hunt, E. B., Frost, N., & Lunneborg, C. E. Individual differences in cognition: A new approach to intelligence. In G. Bower (Ed.), *Advances in learning and motivation,* Vol. 7. New York: Academic Press, 1973. Pp. 87–122.

Hunt, E., Lunneborg, C. E., & Lewis, J. What does it mean to be high verbal? *Cognitive Psychology,* 1975, *7,* 194–227.

Hunt, E. B., Marin, J. K., & Stone, P. *Experiments in induction.* New York: Academic Press, 1966.

Hunt, E. B., & Poltrock, S. E. The mechanics of thought. In B. Kantowitz (Ed.), *Human information processing: Tutorials in performance and cognition.* Hillsdale, N.J.: Lawrence Erlbaum Assoc., 1974. Pp. 277–350.

Hurley, J. L., & Cattell, R. B. The Procrustes Program: Producing direct rotation to test a hypothesized factor structure. *Behavioral Science,* 1962. *7,* 258–262.

Jacobs, P. I., & Vandeventer, M. The learning and transfer of double-classification skills by first graders. *Child Development,* 1971, *42,* 149–159. (a)

Jacobs, P. I., & Vandeventer, M. The learning and transfer of double-classification skills: A replication and extension. *Journal of Experimental Child Psychology,* 1971, *12,* 140–157. (b)

Jacobs, P. I., & Vandeventer, M. Evaluating the teaching of intelligence. *Educational and Psychological Measurement,* 1972, *32,* 235–248.

Jensen, A. R. How much can we boost IQ and scholastic achievement? *Harvard Educational Review,* 1969, *39,* 1–123.

Johnson, D. M. Serial analysis of thinking. In *Annals of the New York Academy of Sciences.* Volume 91. New York: New York Academy of Sciences, 1960. Pp. 66–75.

Johnson, D. M. Serial analysis of verbal analogy problems. *Journal of Educational Psychology,* 1962, *53,* 86–88.

Johnson, S. C. Hierarchical clustering schemes. *Psychometrika,* 1967, *32,* 241–254.

Kaiser, H. F. The varimax criterion for analytic rotation in factor analysis. *Psychometrika,* 1958, *23,* 187–200.

Katz, J. J. *The underlying reality of language and its philosophical import.* New York: Harper & Row, 1971.

Katz, J. J. *Semantic theory.* New York: Harper & Row, 1972.

Katz, J. J., & Postal, P. M. *An integrated theory of linguistic descriptions.* Cambridge, Mass.: M.I.T. Press, 1964.

Kling, R. E. A paradigm for reasoning by analogy. *Artificial Intelligence,* 1971, *2,* 147–178.

Köhler, W. *The mentality of apes.* (Translated by E. Winter.) New York: Harcourt, Brace, & World, 1925.

Kotovsky, K., & Simon, H. A. Empirical tests of a theory of human acquisition of concepts for sequential events. *Cognitive Psychology,* 1973, *4,* 399–424.

Külpe, O. *Outlines of psychology.* Sections 69, 70. New York: Macmillan, 1895.

Levi, E. H. *An introduction to legal reasoning.* Chicago: University of Chicago Press, 1949.

Linn, M. C. The role of intelligence in children's responses to instruction. *Psychology in the Schools,* 1973, *10,* 67–75.

Lorge, I., & Thorndike, R. L. *The Lorge–Thorndike Intelligence Tests. Level 5.* Boston: Houghton-Mifflin, 1954.

Luce, R. D. *Individual choice behavior.* New York: Wiley, 1959.

Lunneborg, C. E. Individual differences in memory and information processing. EAC Reports. Seattle, Wash.: Educational Assessment Center, University of Washington, 1974.

MacKinnon, D. W. The nature and nurture of creative talent. *American Psychologist,* 1962, *17,* 484–495.

McNemar, Q. The factors in factoring behavior. *Psychometrika,* 1951, *16,* 353–359.

McNemar, Q. Lost: Our intelligence? Why? *American Psychologist,* 1964, *19,* 871–882.

Meer, B., Stein, M., & Geertsma, R. An analysis of the Miller Analogies Test for a scientific population. *American Psychologist,* 1955, *10,* 33–34.

Messick, S. Multivariate models of cognition and personality: The need for both process and structure in psychological theory and measurement. In J. Royce (Ed.), *Multivariate analysis and psychological theory.* New York: Academic Press, 1973. Pp. 265–303.

Miller, G. A. A psychological method to investigate verbal concepts. *Journal of Mathematical Psychology,* 1969, *6,* 169–191.

Miller, G. A., Galanter, E., & Pribram, K. H. *Plans and the structure of behavior.* New York: Holt, Rinehart, & Winston, 1960.

Miller Analogies Test manual. New York: The Psychological Corporation, 1970.

Neuhaus, J. O., & Wrigley, C. The quartimax method: An analytical approach to orthogonal simple structure. *British Journal of Statistical Psychology,* 1954, *7,* 81–91.

Newell, A. Production systems: Models of control structures. In W. G. Chase (Ed.), *Visual information processing.* New York: Academic Press, 1973. Pp. 463–526.

Newell, A., Shaw, J., & Simon, H. Report on a general problem-solving program. *Proceedings of the international conference on information processing.* Paris: UNESCO, 1960, 256–264.

Newell, A., & Simon, H. *Human problem solving.* Englewood Cliffs, N. J.: Prentice-Hall, 1972.

Noble, C. E., Noble, J. L., & Alcock, W. T. Prediction of individual differences in human trial-and-error learning. *Perceptual and Motor Skills,* 1958, *8,* 151–172.

Oppenheimer, J. R. Analogy in science. *American Psychologist,* 1956, *11,* 127–135.

Osherson, D. N. *Logical abilities in children.* Vol. 2: *Logical inference: Underlying operations.* Hillsdale, N.J.: Lawrence Erlbaum Assoc., 1974.

Pachella, R. G. The interpretation of reaction time in information processing research. In B. Kantowitz (Ed.), *Human information processing: Tutorials in performance and cognition.* Hillsdale, N. J.: Lawrence Erlbaum Assoc., 1974. Pp. 41–82.

Palmer, S. E. Visual perception and world knowledge: Notes on a model of sensory-cognitive interaction. In D. A. Norman & D. E. Rumelhart (Eds.), *Explorations in cognition.* San Francisco: Freeman, 1975. Pp. 279–307.

Poulton, E. D. Unwanted range effects from using within-subject experimental designs. *Psychological Bulletin,* 1973, *80,* 113–121.

Quillian, M. R. The teachable language comprehender: A simulation program and theory of language. *Communications of the ACM,* 1969, *12,* 459–476.

Raven, J. C. *Progressive Matrices: A perceptual test of intelligence, 1938, individual form.* London: Lewis, 1938.

Raven, J. C. *Guide to the standard progressive matrices.* London: H. K. Lewis, 1960.

Reitman, W. *Cognition and thought.* New York: Wiley, 1965.

Resnick, L. (Ed.). *The nature of intelligence.* Hillsdale, N. J.: Lawrence Erlbaum Assoc., 1976.

Restle, F. The selection of strategies in cue learning. *Psychological Review,* 1962, *69,* 329–343.

Rips, L., Shoben, E., & Smith, E. Semantic distance and the verification of semantic relations. *Journal of Verbal Learning and Verbal Behavior,* 1973, *12,* 1–20.

Royce, J. R. Factors as theoretical constructs. *American Psychologist,* 1963, *18,* 522–527.

Rumelhart, D. E., & Abrahamson, A. A. A model for analogical reasoning. *Cognitive Psychology,* 1973, *5,* 1–28.

Santesson, A. The perception of logical principles in a test of reasoning ability. *Reports from the Institute of Applied Psychology,* No. 45. Solna, Sweden: University of Stockholm, 1974.

Scheerer, M., Rothman, E., & Goldstein, K. A case of idiot savant: An experimental study of personality organization. *Psychological Monographs,* 1945, *58,* No. 4(Whole No. 269).

Schönemann, P. H. A generalized solution of the orthogonal procrustes problem. *Psychometrika,* 1966, *31,* 1–10.

Shalom, H., & Schlesinger, I. M. Analogical thinking: A conceptual analysis of analogy tests. In R. Feuerstein, I. M. Schlesinger, H. Shalom, & H. Narrol, *Studies in cognitive modifiability,* Report 1, Vol. II. Jerusalem: Hadassah Wizo Canada Research Institute, 1972. Pp. 260–313.

Shepard, R. N. Representation of structure in similarity data: Problems and prospects. *Psychometrika,* 1974, *39,* 373–421.

Shepard, R. N., & Arabie, P. Additive cluster analysis of similarity data. Paper presented at United States–Japan Seminar. Theory, methods, and applications of multidimensional scaling and related techniques, San Diego, 1975.

Shepard, R. N., & Feng, C. A chronometric study of mental paper folding. *Cognitive Psychology,* 1972, *3,* 228–243.

Shepard, R. N., & Metzler, J. Mental rotation of three-dimensional objects. *Science,* 1971, *171,* 701–703.

Shoben, E. J. Semantic features in semantic memory. Unpublished doctoral dissertation. Stanford University, 1974.

Simon, H. A., & Kotovsky, K. Human acquisition of concepts for sequential patterns. *Psychological Review,* 1963, *70,* 534–546.

Spearman, C. 'General intelligence,' objectively determined and measured. *American Journal of Psychology,* 1904, *15,* 201–293.

Spearman, C. *The nature of 'intelligence' and the principles of cognition.* London: Macmillan, 1923.

Spearman, C. *The abilities of man.* New York: Macmillan, 1927.

Spearman, C. Theory of a general factor. *British Journal of Psychology,* 1946, *36,* 117–131.

Sternberg, R. J. *How to prepare for the Miller Analogies Test.* Woodbury, New York: Barron's Educational Series, 1974.

Sternberg, S. The discovery of processing stages: Extensions of Donders' method. *Acta Psychologica,* 1969, *30,* 276–315. (a)

Sternberg, S. Memory-scanning: Mental processes revealed by reaction-time experiments. *American Scientist,* 1969, *4,* 421–457. (b)

Tatsuoka, M. M. *Multivariate analysis: Techniques for educational and psychological research.* New York: Wiley, 1971.

Thomas, J. C. An analysis of behavior in the Hobbits–Orcs problem. *Cognitive Psychology,* 1974, *6,* 257–269.

Thomson, G. H. *The factorial analysis of human ability.* London: University of London Press, 1939.

Thurstone, L. L. *Primary mental abilities,* Chicago: University of Chicago Press, 1938.

Thurstone, L. L. *Multiple factor analysis.* Chicago: University of Chicago Press, 1947.

Thurstone, L. L., & Thurstone, T. G. *SRA Primary Mental Abilities.* 1962 Revision. Chicago: Science Research Associates, 1962.

Tinsley, H. E. A., & Dawis, R. V. The equivalence of semantic and figural test presentation of the same items. The Center for the Study of Organizational Performance and Human Effectiveness. Technical Report No. 3004. Minneapolis: University of Minnesota, 1972.

Trabasso, T. Reasoning and the processing of negative information. Invited Address, Division 3, 78th Annual Convention, American Psychological Association, Miami Beach, 1970.

Trabasso, T. Mental operations in language comprehension. In J. B. Carroll & R. O. Freedle (Eds.), *Language comprehension and the acquisition of knowledge.* Washington, D.C.: Winston, 1972. Pp. 113–137.

Trabasso, T., Rollins, H., & Shaughnessy, E. Storage and verification stages in processing concepts. *Cognitive Psychology,* 1971, *2,* 239–289.

Underwood, B. J. Recognition memory. In H. H. Kendler & J. T. Spence (Eds.), *Essays in neobehaviorism.* New York: Appleton-Century-Crofts, 1971.

Verbrugge, R. R. The comprehension of analogy. Unpublished doctoral dissertation, University of Minnesota, 1974.

Vernon, P. E. The variations of intelligence with occupation, age, and locality. *British Journal of Psychology, Statistical Section,* 1947, *1,* 52–63.

Vernon, P. E. Intelligence. In W. B. Dockrell (Ed.), *On intelligence.* Toronto: The Ontario Institute for Studies in Education, 1970. Pp. 99–117.

Vernon, P. E. *The structure of human abilities.* London: Methuen, 1971.

Vygotsky, L. S. *Thought and language.* (Edited and translated by E. Hanfmann & G. Vakar.) Cambridge, Mass.: M.I.T. Press, 1962.

Wason, P. C., & Johnson-Laird, P. N. *Psychology of reasoning: Structure and content.* London: B. T. Batsford, 1972.

Wechsler, D. *Measurement of adult intelligence.* Baltimore: Williams & Wilkins, 1944.

Whitely, S. E. Types of relationships in reasoning by analogy. Unpublished doctoral dissertation, University of Minnesota, 1973.

Whitely, S. E., & Dawis, R. V. A cognitive intervention for improving the estimate of latent ability measured from analogy items. The Center for the Study of Organizational Performance and Human Effectiveness. Technical Report No. 3010. Minneapolis: University of Minnesota, 1973. (a)

Whitely, S. E., & Dawis, R. V. The effects of cognitive intervention on estimates of latent ability measured from analogy items. The Center for the Study of Organizational Performance and Human Effectiveness. Technical Report No. 3011. Minneapolis: University of Minnesota, 1973. (b)

Wiley, D. E. Latent partition analysis. *Psychometrika,* 1967, *32,* 183–193.

Williams, D. S. Computer program organization induced from problem examples. In H. A. Simon & L. Siklossy, *Representation and meaning: Experiments with information processing systems.* Englewood Cliffs, N. J.: Prentice-Hall, 1972. Pp. 143–205.

Willner, A. An experimental analysis of analogical reasoning. *Psychological Reports,* 1964, *15,* 479–494.

Winston, P. H. Learning structural descriptions from examples. Artificial Intelligence Laboratory. AI TR-231. Cambridge, Mass.: Massachusetts Institute of Technology, 1970.

Woodworth, R. S., & Sells, S. B. An atmosphere effect in formal syllogistic reasoning. *Journal of Experimental Psychology*, 1935, *18*, 451–460.

Zirkle, G. An evaluation of the postulates underlying the Babcock deterioration test. *Psychological Review*, 1941, *48*, 261–267.

INDEXES

Author Index

Numbers in *italics* refer to the pages on which the complete references are listed.

A

Abrahamson, A. A., 7, 92, 114, 115, 116, 117, 130, 145, 171, 172, 287, 288, 289, 291, 296, *331*
Ace, M. C., 127, *326*
Achenbach, T. M., 129, *326*
Alcock, W. T., 211, *330*
Anderson, J. R., 48, 57, 83, *326*
Arabie, P., 294, *326, 331*
Austin, G. A., 6, *326*

B

Bamber, D., 190, *326*
Banks, C., 103, *326*
Battig, W. F., 293, *326*
Becker, J. D., 121, 122, *326*
Bower, G. H., 84, 100, 130, *326*
Brown, W., 21, *326*
Bruner, J. S., 6, *326*
Burke, H. R., 102, 103, *327*
Burt, C., 11, 12, 13, 23, *327*
Butcher, H. J., 12, *327*

C

Calfee, R. C., 58, *327*
Campbell, D. T., 65, *327*

Carpenter, P. A., 40, 48, 56, 86, *327*
Carroll, J. B., 20, 65, 325, *327*
Cattell, A. K. S., 178, *327*
Cattell, R. B., 13, 31, 103, 178, *327, 329*
Chase, W., 41, 45, 47, 55, 64, 86, 187, *327*
Chase, W. G., 250, *327*
Clark, H. H., 41, 45, 46, 47, 55, 56, 64, 86, 187, *327*
Cliff, N., 31, *327*
Collins, A. M., 41, *327*
Cooley, W. W., 199, 203, *327*
Cooper, L. A., 48, 49, 264, 285, *327*
Cronbach, L. J., 65, *327*

D

Dawis, R. V., 100, 127, 128, *326, 327, 332*
Day, R., 65, *327*
DeGroot, A. D., 250, *327*
Donders, F. C., 41, *327*

E

Earl, C. J. C., 102, *328*
Ekstrom, R. B., 50, 178, 256, *328*
Emmett, W. G., 103, *328*
Eriksen, C. W., 83, *328*
Esher, F. J. S., 102, *328*
Evans, T. G., 113, 119, 121, 147, 256, *328*
Eysenck, H. J., 11, *328*

F

Feng, C., 48, 49, *331*
Ferguson, G. A., 211, *328*
Feuerstein, R., 112, 113, *328*
Fleishman, E. A., 211, *328*
French, J. W., 50, 178, 256, *328*
Frost, N., 65, 324, *329*

G

Gabriel, K. R., 103, *328*
Galanter, E., 37, 38, 39, *330*
Garner, W. R., 83, *328*
Garrett, H. E., 24, *328*
Geertsma, R., 7, 304, *330*
Gentile, J. R., 129, *328*
Gentile, P. K., 129, *328*
Glaser, R., 211, *328*
Glucksberg, S., 56, *328*
Goldstein, K., 128, *331*
Goodnow, J. J., 6, *326*
Greeno, J. G., 41, *328*
Guilford, J. P., 7, 13, 19, 22, 28, 29, 104, 105, 106, 109, 304, *328*
Guttman, L., 74, *328*

H

Hake, H. W., 83, *328*
Harman, H. H., 12, 14, *328*
Hebb, D. O., 118, *328*
Hempel, W. E., Jr., 211, *328*
Henle, M., 100, *328*
Henley, N. M., 114, 115, 287, 289, 290, 294, 297, 302, *329*
Hoepfner, R., 22, 106, 109, *328*
Holzinger, K. J., 21, *329*
Horn, J. L., 19, 32, *329*
Hotelling, H., 199, *329*
Hoving, K. L., 216, *329*
Humphreys, L. G., 12, 28, *329*
Hunt, E. B., 40, 65, 100, 123, 124, 324, *329*
Hurley, J. L., 31, *329*

J

Jacobs, P. I., 124, 125, *329*
Jensen, A. R., 323, *329*
Johnson, D. M., 72, 113, 114, 146, *329*
Johnson, S. C., 125, *329*

Johnson-Laird, P. N., 100, *332*
Just, M. A., 40, 48, 56, 86, *327*

K

Kaiser, H. F., 20, *329*
Katz, J. J., 109, 111, 130, 229, *329*
Kessler, D. K., 129, *328*
Kling, R. E., 121, *329*
Knapp, J. R., 32, *329*
Köhler, W., 26, *330*
Konick, D. S., 216, *329*
Kotovsky, K., 50, 51, 52, 53, 55, *330, 331*
Külpe, O., 59, *330*

L

Levi, E. H., 99, 100, *330*
Lewis, J., 48, 216, 324, *329*
Linn, M. C., 125, 126, *330*
Lohnes, P. R., 199, 203, *327*
Lorge, I., *330*
Luce, R. D., 115, *330*
Lunneborg, C. E., 48, 65, 216, 324, *329, 330*
Lunneborg, C. L., 65, 324, *329*

M

MacKinnon, D. W., 307, *330*
Marin, J. K., 100, *329*
McNemar, Q., 4, 28, 32, *330*
Meer, B., 7, 304, *330*
Messick, S., 65, *330*
Metzler, J., 48, *331*
Miller, G. A., 37, 38, 39, 125, *330*
Montague, W. E., 293, *326*
Morin, R. E., 216, *329*

N

Narrol, H., 112, 113, *328*
Neuhaus, J. O., 20, *330*
Newell, A., 37, 38, 40, 41, 65, 118, *330*
Noble, C. E., 211, *330*
Noble, J. L., 211, *330*

O

Oppenheimer, J. R., 99, *330*
Osherson, D. N., 137, *330*

P

Pachella, R. G., 42, 43, 57, 58, 59, 60, *330*
Palmer, S. E., 49, *330*
Poltrock, S. E., 40, *329*
Postal, P. M., 111, *329*
Poulton, E. D., 194, *330*
Pribram, K. H., 37, 38, 39, *330*
Price, I. A., 50, 178, 256, *328*

Q

Quillian, M. R., 41, 111, 113, *327, 330*

R

Raven, J. C., 102, 125, *328, 331*
Reitman, W., 41, 45, 118, 119, *331*
Resnick, L., *331*
Restle, F., 100, *331*
Rips, L., 117, 131, 171, 224, 291, *331*
Rollins, H., 41, 45, 47, 64, *332*
Rothman, E., 128, *331*
Royce, J. R., 13, *331*
Rumelhart, D. E., 7, 92, 114, 115, 116, 117, 130, 145, 171, 172, 287, 288, 291, 296, *331*

S

Santesson, A., 125, 269, *331*
Scheerer, M., 128, *331*
Schlesinger, I. M., 110, 111, 112, 113, 131, 146, *328, 331*
Schönemann, P. H., 31, *331*
Sells, S. B., 100, *333*
Shalom, H., 110, 111, 112, 113, 131, 146, *328, 331*
Shaughnessy, E., 41, 45, 47, 64, *332*
Shaw, J., 118, *330*
Shepard, R. N., 48, 49, 294, *326, 327, 331*
Shoben, E. J., 117, 131, 171, 224, 229, 291, *331*
Simon, H. A., 37, 38, 40, 41, 50, 51, 52, 53, 55, 65, 118, 250, *327, 330, 331*
Sinha, U., 103, *326*
Siojo, L. T., 100, *327*
Smith, E., 117, 131, 171, 224, 291, *331*

Spearman, C., 20, 21, 102, 106, 107, 108, 109, 146, *331*
Stein, M., 7, 304, *330*
Sternberg, R. J., 7, 303, *331*
Sternberg, S., 41, 42, 43, 44, 57, 58, 59, 74, 244, *331*
Stone, P., 100, *329*

T

Tatsuoka, M. M., 199, *332*
Thomas, J. C., 41, *332*
Thomson, G. H., 21, *326, 332*
Thorndike, R. L., *330*
Thurstone, L. L., 12, 13, 20, 22, 32, 103, 105, 175, *332*
Thurstone, T. G., 22, *332*
Tinsley, H. E. A., 128, *332*
Trabasso, T., 41, 45, 47, 56, 64, 100, *326, 328, 332*

U

Underwood, B. J., 130, *332*

V

Vandeventer, M., 124, 125, *329*
Verbrugge, R. R., 129, 130, *332*
Vernon, P. E., 13, 23, 24, 32, 33, 102, 103, *332*
Vygotsky, L. S., 211, *332*

W

Wald, J., 56, *328*
Wason, P. C., 100, *332*
Wechsler, D., 304, *332*
Whitely, S. E., 126, 127, *332*
Wiley, D. E., 126, *332*
Williams, D. S., 122, *332*
Willner, A., 128, 129, *332*
Winston, P. H., 121, *333*
Woodworth, R. S., 100, *333*
Wrigley, C., 20, *330*

Z

Zirkle, G., 128, *333*

Subject Index

A

Abilities, 21–26, 32–33, 36, 41, 54, 80, 102, 105, 109–110, 122, 206–209, 245, 304, *see also* Reference abilities
  crystallized, 103, 131
  fluid, 103, 131
  general (*g*), 102–103, 106, 318, 320
Additive clustering, 294–295
Additive-factor method, 41–44, 54, 58–60, 62–63, 76
Additivity, assumption of, 73–76, 94, 182–184, 220, 260, 323
Alternating option scanning, *see* Analogical reasoning, option scanning, alternating
American Council on Education (ACE) Psychological Examination for College Freshmen, 255, 259, 284
Analogical reasoning
  combination rule for, 135, 137, 148, 310
  component modes
    exhaustive, 139–140, 143, 148, 158, 161, 186, 192, 196, 199, 202–203, 220, 232–233, 262, 264–265, 273–274, 296, 311–312, 323
    holistic, *see* Analogical reasoning, dual processing
    self-terminating, 140, 143, 148, 159, 161, 171, 186–187, 192, 196, 199, 202–203, 220, 232, 262, 264–267, 273–274, 296, 311–313

Analogical reasoning (*contd.*)
  component processes in, 148–149, 173, 203, 319
  application, 109, 111, 113, 132, 135–136, 138–144, 146–148, 151, 153, 155, 157–161, 163, 165–167, 169–171, 185–186, 191–193, 196, 199, 206, 212, 233, 238, 244, 246, 274–277, 280, 283, 286, 291, 296–297, 309–313, 318–319
  encoding, 109, 112, 135–136, 138–143, 146–160, 162–170, 185–187, 192, 196–197, 199, 206, 212, 231–232, 235, 238, 244, 246–247, 252, 261–264, 269, 272, 274–276, 281, 285, 291, 297, 299, 305, 308–309, 311, 313, 318–319
  inference, 109, 111, 113, 132, 135–136, 138–143, 146–150, 152, 154, 156, 158–162, 164, 167–168, 170–171, 185–186, 191–192, 194, 196, 199, 206, 212, 233, 238, 243, 246–247, 250, 253, 274–276, 291, 294, 296–297, 305, 308–309, 311–313, 318–319
  justification, 135–136, 147, 163, 165–167, 169–170, 262–263, 268, 272–277, 280, 283, 286, 309, 311, 313, 318–319
  mapping, 109, 112, 135–136, 138–143, 146–148, 150, 152,

Analogical reasoning
  mapping (*contd.*)
    155–156, 158–162, 164, 166–168,
      170–171, 185–187, 191–192, 196,
      199, 206, 212, 232–234, 238, 243,
      246–248, 250, 253, 272, 274–276,
      291, 297, 309–313, 318–319
  preparation-response, 109, 112, 135,
      137, 139, 140–142, 146, 148, 151,
      153, 155, 157, 159, 160–161, 163,
      165–167, 169, 185–186, 196–197,
      205–206, 212, 221, 231, 235, 238,
      243, 246–248, 252–253, 269, 272,
      276, 285, 305, 308–309, 311, 313,
      318–319, 321
  dual processing, 190–191, 194, 220,
      231–232, 252, 262, 309
  models of
    Model I, 138–139, 148–151, 161–163,
      166, 168–172, 185–186, 191–192,
      194, 197, 199, 204, 220, 231–232,
      236, 238, 262–265, 267, 272,
      311–312, 323
    Model II, 139–143, 148, 152–153,
      161, 167, 170–171, 185–187,
      191–192, 194, 197, 199, 204, 220,
      231–232, 236, 238, 262, 264, 272,
      311–312
    Model III, 141–143, 148, 154–155,
      161, 164–165, 167, 170–171,
      185–187, 191–192, 194–201,
      204–205, 219–220, 231–234,
      236–239, 242, 248–249, 252–253,
      262–264, 267, 270, 272, 274–276,
      280, 282, 285–286, 311–312, 323
    Model IV, 142–143, 148, 156–157,
      161, 167, 170–171, 185–187,
      191–192, 194, 197, 199, 204, 220,
      231–232, 236, 238, 262–264, 272,
      311–312
  option scanning
    alternating, 143–144, 148, 170–171,
      262, 265, 267, 285
    sequential, 143–144, 148, 170–171,
      264–265, 267, 285
  parameters, 185, 187, 190, 194–195,
      198–199, 202, 204, 220, 231,
      233–234, 248, 252, 260, 267–268,
      270, 273–275, 281, 285–286, 296
  difficulty. 137
  duration, 137, 149

Analogical reasoning (*contd.*)
  session effects, 194, 211, 258, 261–263,
      300, 313
  theories of
    componential, 118, 134–135, 145, 148,
      192, 199, 230–231, 233, 248,
      252–253, 267, 288, 301, 309–310,
      322–323
    differential, 101–106, 131
    information-processing, 101, 106–131,
      287
  types of component models
    multivariate, 199–201, 220, 273–275,
      285, 312
    response-error models, 137, 148, 186,
      198, 220, 236, 272–273, 312
    response-time models, 137, 148,
      194–195, 220, 270, 311
  types of component processes
    attribute comparison, 135–136, 145,
      147, 158, 187, 190, 192, 194, 211,
      220–221, 232, 234–235, 244, 249,
      253, 262, 272–273, 285, 311
    attribute identification, 135, 147, 252
    control, 135–136, 147–148
Analogies, 72–75, 84, 86–87, 89–90, 92,
      99, 101–103, 105, 110, 118–120,
      122–123, 126–128, 130–132,
      136–137, 144, 147, 173, 177, 181,
      196–198, 204, 216, 222–224, 235,
      248, 251, 255–256, 259, 266, 286,
      289–290, 302, 309, 320
  content
    animal name, 115–118, 145–146, 172,
      287–289, 293, 296, 298–300, 302,
      305, 307, 309
    behavioral, 105
    cartoon, 105
    color name, 117
    figural, 104–106, 110–113, 128,
      130–132, 320
    geometric, 119, 123, 132, 145–146,
      214–215, 236, 255, 258, 270–274,
      279, 284, 300
    letter, 104–105, 122, 132
    nonverbal, 110
    pattern, 103–104
    People Piece, 145–146, 173–174, 176,
      195, 200–201, 210, 213–215, 219,
      225, 231–232, 235–236, 254, 300,
      306

Analogies
    content (*contd.*)
        perceptual speed, 320
        spatial, 320
        verbal, 103–106, 110–113, 118–119,
            122, 126–133, 145–146, 214–215,
            222–224, 228–231, 234–235, 237,
            239, 249, 251–252, 254, 300, 303,
            305–306, 312
    format
        forced-choice, 134, 144, 147–149, 255,
            258, 268, 313, 319
        true-false, 134, 144, 147, 149, 173, 177,
            222, 251, 258, 320
    Miller analogies, *see* Miller Analogies Test
    parts
        domain, 134, 230
        range, 134, 230
    task
        option ranking, 171–172
        option selection, 171–172, 262
    types
        degenerate, 179, 181, 185, 189, 191,
            197–198, 200, 222–223, 226, 232,
            251, 256, 259–260
        nondegenerate, 179, 181, 187–191,
            197, 200–201, 222, 226, 229, 232,
            251, 256, 260, 263, 285
        semidegenerate, 179, 181, 185, 187,
            189, 191, 197–198, 200, 222–223,
            226, 232, 251, 256, 259–260
ANALOGY (computer program), 119–123,
    132
Analytic processing, *see* Analogical
    reasoning, dual processing; Component
    processes, mode of execution,
    particularistic processing
Animal name analogies, *see* Analogies,
    content, animal name
Animal Name Analogy Experiment, 287–302
Application, *see* Analogical reasoning,
    component processes in, application
Apprehension of experience, *see* Principles
    of cognition, apprehension of experience
Aptitude Test Taker, 122, 132
Arbitrary constructs, 318–319, 321, 325
ARGUS, 118–119, 122–123, 132
Artificial intelligence, 40–41, 45, 54, 62
Association, *see* Word association
Assumption of pure insertion, *see* Pure
    insertion, assumption of

Attention, 212, 215–217, 322
Attribute comparison, *see* Analogical
    reasoning, types of component
    processes, attribute comparison
Attribute discovery, 215, 250, 254
Attribute fixedness, 214–215, 243, 253
Attribute identification, *see* Analogical
    reasoning, component processes in,
    encoding; Analogical reasoning, types of
    component processes, attribute
    identification
Attribute testing, 215, 250, 254
Attribute-value representation, *see*
    Representation, attribute-value

B

Behaviorism, 4–5, 26, 37
Bookkeeping operations, 149, 215, 217,
    253, 322

C

Canonical correlation, 199–200, 203, 220,
    273
Canonical variate scores, *see* Score types,
    canonical variate
Capacity, processing, *see* Processing capacity
Cattell Culture-Fair Test of *g*, 178,
    206–207, 246, 258, 277, 280
Children's Associative Responding Test
    (CART), 129
Cluster representation, *see* Representation
    of information, attribute-value, cluster
Clustering, *see* Additive clustering;
    Hierarchical clustering
Cognition
    of relations, 104–105, 109–110, 131, *see
        also* Analogical reasoning, component
        processes in, inference
    of units, 110, 132, 304, *see also*
        Analogical reasoning, component
        processes in, encoding
    principles of, *see* principles of cognition
Combination rule, *see* Analogical reasoning,
    combination rule for; Component
    processes, combination rule
Communalities, *see* Factor analysis, diagonal
    entries in correlation matrix, commu-
    nalities; Variance, partitions, commu-
    nality

Component model, *see* Componential model; Factor analysis, models of, component model

Component processes, 6, 16, 29, 32–34, 36, 48, 54, 61–63, 65–71, 76, 78–81, 83, 85, 89–91, 93–95, 217, 309, 317–318, 320–323, 325, *see also* Analogical reasoning, component processes in

accuracy of execution, *see* component processes, difficulty of execution

combination rule, 6, 48, 66–70, 90–91, 93, 321–322, 335, *see also* Analogical reasoning, combination rule for

difficulty of execution, 68–70, 91, 93–94, 321–322

duration of execution, 68–70, 91, 93–94, 321–322

mode of execution, 66–70, 91, 93, 321–323, 325

exhaustive processing, 6, 67, 93, 323, *see also* Analogical reasoning, component modes, exhaustive

holistic processing, 6, 67, 93, 323

parallel processing, 6. 66–67, 93, 323

particularistic processing, 6, 67, 93, 323

self-terminating processing, 67, 93, 323, *see also* Analogical reasoning, component modes, self-terminating

serial processing, 6, 67, 93, 323

order of execution, 6, 66–70, 91, 93, 321–322, 325

speed of execution, *see* component processes, duration of execution

types of

general, 317, 319, 325

group, 317, 319, 325

Component scores, *see* Score types, component

Componential analysis, 3, 7, 36, 64–66, 70–71, 75–78, 80, 84, 87–91, 93–95, 217, 228, 287, 322, 324–325

Componential model, 6, 66–70, 76–77, 81–83, 85, 90, 93–95, 148, 220, 311, 321, 323, 325

error model, 77, 220, *see also* Analogical reasoning, types of component models, response-error models

solution-time model, 77, 220, *see also* Analogical reasoning, types of component models, response-time models

Componential theory, 3, 6–7, 66–70, 85, 87, 90, 93, 323, 325

Componential theory of analogical reasoning, *see* Analogical reasoning, theories of, componential

Componential theory of intelligence, *see* Intelligence, theories of, componential

Components (principal), 17–18, 35, 199–200

Composite score, *see* Score types, composite

Composite task, *see* Task level, composite task

Computer simulation, *see* Simulation

Computer theory, *see* Theory, type of, computer

Concept formation, 100

Connection formula, 110, 132, 146

application of, 110, 112–113, 132, 146

formation of, 110, 112–113, 132, 146

Construct validation, *see* Validation, construct

Control structures, 40

Convergent production of relations, *see* Production, convergent, of relations

Convergent validation, *see* Validation, convergent

Converging operations, 83–84

Criteria for evaluating theories, 5, 100, 105, 109–110, 112–113, 117–118, 122–123, 130–131, 145, 148–149

Crystallized ability, *see* Abilities, crystallized

Cue score, *see* Score types, interval, cue

Cue time, *see* Score types, interval, cue

Cueing, *see* Precueing

D

Decision, 215, 322

Deductive operation, 113–114, 146, *see also* Analogical reasoning, component processes in, application

Degenerate analogies, *see* Analogies, types, degenerate

Degrees of freedom, 56–57, 63, 85, 87, 265, 285

Development of intelligence, *see* Intelligence, development of

Diagnosis, 89–90

Differential approach to intelligence, *see* Intelligence, approaches to, differential

Differential theories of analogical reasoning, *see* Analogical reasoning, theories of, differential

Difficulty of component processes, *see* Component processes, difficulty of execution

Discriminant validation, *see* Validation, discriminant

Distance, psychological, *see* Psychological distance; Representation of information

Divergent production of relations, *see* Production, divergent, of relations

Domain, *see* Analogies, parts, domain

Dual processing, *see* Analogical reasoning, dual processing

Duration of component processes, *see* Component processes, duration of execution

E

Eduction of correlates, *see* Principles of cognition, eduction of correlates

Eduction of relations, *see* Principles of cognition, eduction of relations

Elementary information processes, 38, 47, 50, 53–54, 61, 65, 75, 87, 93, 148, 317, 325, *see also* Component processes

Encoding, *see* Analogical reasoning, component processes in, encoding

Error models, *see* Analogical reasoning, types of component models, response-error models; Componential model, error model

Executive, 118–119, 123, 216, *see also* Control structures; Planning

Exhaustive processes, *see* Analogical reasoning, component modes, exhaustive; Component processes, mode of execution, exhaustive

Extensive task analysis, *see* Task analysis, extensive

External validation, *see* Validation, external

F

Factor analysis, 4, 11–14, 16–19, 23–36, 72, 76, 79–80, 88, 94, 106, 110, 200, 208, 278–279, 286, 320–321, 323–324
diagonal entries in correlation matrix
communalities, 14, 17, 35, 208, 278

Factor analysis
diagonal entries (*contd.*)
reliabilities, 14, 17, 35
unities, 14, 17, 34–35
fundamental factor theorem, 18
input matrix, 14, 17
limitations of, 29–34, 36
methods, 18, 23
centroid, 18
confirmatory maximum likelihood, 29
principal-component, 18, *see also* Components (principal)
principal-factor, 18
misuses of, 28–29, 36
models of
common factor model, *see* Factor analysis, models of, factor model
component model, 16–18, 24, 35, 199–200
factor model, 16–18, 24, 35
output matrices
factor pattern, 17–18, 35
factor structure, 17–19, 35
purpose of
hypothesis formation, 12, 34
hypothesis testing, 12, 34
Factor axes
criteria for placement
Procrustes, 31–32
quartimax, 20
simple structure, 20, 22, 25, 31
varimax, 20
indeterminacy of placement, 18, 31–32, 36
relation among axes
oblique, 20
orthogonal, 20, 32
rotation of, 19–20, 24, 28–29, 31–32, 34–35, 54, 63, 77, 85, 88, 208, 279, 320
objective, 19–20, 31
subjective, 19–20, 31–32
Factor scores, *see* Score types, factor
Factor space, 18, 25, 31, 77
Factorial approach, *see* Intelligence, approaches to, differential
Factors, 13–14, 16–37, 61, 77–81, 88, 94, 101, 200, 286, 321
invariance of, 19, 26, 31
nature of
causal, 13, 34
descriptive, 13, 34

Factors (*contd.*)
    number of, 19, 24, 30–31
    types of
        bipolar, 19, 25, 31
        common, 16, 24
        error, 23–24
        general, 19, 21–25, 31, 33–34, 318,
            320, *see also* Abilities, general
        group, 21–23, 25, 31, 33–34
        multiple, 22, 31
        second-order, 22, 25, 320
        specific, 21, 23–24, 31, 33–34
        unique, 16, 24
Fast processes, 41, 53–54, 62
Fluid ability, *see* Abilities, fluid
Forced-choice analogies, *see* Analogies,
    format, forced-choice
French Kit of Reference Tests for Cognitive
    Factors, 177–178, 256, 258–259
Fundamental factor theorem, *see* Factor
    analysis, fundamental factor theorem

G

General ability, *see* Abilities, general
General component processes, *see*
    Component processes, types of, general
General factor, *see* Abilities, general (*g*);
    Factors, types of, general
General Problem Solver, *see* GPS
Geometric analogies, *see* Analogies, content,
    geometric
Geometric Analogy Experiment, 203,
    255–285, 288, 291, 298–299, 301
Gestalt psychology, 26
GPS, 118
Group component processes, *see* Compo-
    nent processes, types of, group

H

Hierarchical clustering, 125, 133
Holistic processing, *see* Analogical
    reasoning, dual processing; Component
    processes, mode of execution, holistic
    processing

I

Ideal point, 115–116, 132, 266, 287,
    289–290, 295–297
Image, 37–39

Indeterminacy of factors, *see* Factor axes,
    indeterminacy of placement
Individual differences, 4, 14, 24, 26–27,
    32–33, 35, 48, 54, 57, 60, 63–65,
    68–72, 76, 78–80, 85, 88–94, 101,
    104, 106, 110, 133, 204, 211,
    213–215, 219, 221, 227, 238, 240,
    243, 245, 247–248, 250–253, 275,
    281, 283–284, 286, 288, 308, 311,
    313–314, 317, 320, 322, 324–325
    in analogical reasoning, 131, 204, 206,
        209–210, 213–214, 272
Inductive operation, 113–114, 146, *see also*
    Analogical reasoning, component
    processes in, inference
Inductive reasoning, *see* Reasoning,
    inductive
Inference, *see* Analogical reasoning,
    component processes in, inference
Information processes, *see* Component
    processes; Elementary information
    processes
Information-processing approach to
    intelligence, *see* Intelligence, approaches
    to, information processing
Information-processing theories of
    analogical reasoning, *see* Analogical
    reasoning, theories of, information-
    processing
Intelligence, 3–4, 7, 12, 20–21, 24, 26–27,
    29, 32–37, 41, 44–45, 47, 62, 99, 101,
    103–104, 118–119, 125, 211,
    317–325
    approaches to
        componential, *see* Componential
            analysis
        differential, 3–4, 11–12, 27–29, 35,
            37, 44, 61, 63–65, 71, 77, 79–80,
            84, 93, 95, 105, 324
        information-processing, 3–5, 37, 40,
            44–45, 48, 53, 60–61, 63–65, 72,
            79, 84, 92–93, 95
    artificial, *see* Artificial intelligence
    development of, 85, 91, 322
    tests of, 7, 101–106, 119
    theories of
        anarchic, 21
        bi-factor, 21, 24, 35
        bonds, 21, 35
        componential, 317, 321, 325
        hierarchical, 23–24, 35
        monarchic, 21, 25

Intelligence
  theories of (*contd.*)
    multiple-factor theory, *see* Intelligence,
      theories of, primary mental abilities
    oligarchic, 21
    primary mental abilities, 22, 35, 64,
      103, 175, 211, 320
    structure-of-intellect model, 22, 32, 35,
      104
    two-factor theory, 20–21, 25, 35, 102
Intensive task analysis, *see* Task analysis,
  type, intensive
Internal representation, *see* Representation
  of information
Internal validation, *see* Validation, internal
Interval score, *see* Score types, interval

J

Justification, *see* Analogical reasoning,
  component processes in, justification

L

Latent partition analysis, 126, 133
Latent trait, *see* Trait, latent
Lorge-Thorndike Intelligence Tests, 259,
  277–278, 280–282, 301

M

Manifest trait, *see* Trait, manifest
Mapping, *see* Analogical reasoning,
  component processes in, mapping
Markers, *see* Representation of information
  markers
Mathematical theory, *see* Theory, type of,
  mathematical
Memory, 52, 114, 130, 135, 138, 318, 320,
  322, 324
Miller analogies, *see* Miller Analogies Test
Miller Analogies Test, 7, 128, 303–308, 320
Minnesota Paper Form Board, 258, 299
Mode of component processes, *see*
  Analogical reasoning, component
  modes; Component processes, mode of
  execution
Models, *see* Componential model; Reference
  ability model; Simplex model;
  Structural regression model
Models of analogical reasoning, *see*
  Analogical reasoning, models of
Motivation, 212, 215–217, 308, 322

Motor speed, 212, 229
Multidimensional scaling, 7, 115, 288, 292,
  297
Multidimensional space, *see* Representation
  of information, multidimensional space
Multiple regression, 185, 194–195,
  199–201, 219, 231, 268, 270,
  272–273, 324
Multivariate component model, *see*
  Analogical reasoning, types of
  component models, multivariate
Multivariate regression, *see* Canonical
  correlation

N

Nonarbitrary constructs, 318, 325
Nondegenerate analogies, *see* Analogies,
  types, nondegenerate
Nonhierarchical clustering, *see* Additive
  clustering

O

Objective rotation, *see* Factor axes, rotation
  of, objective
Option ranking, *see* Analogies, task, option
  ranking
Option scanning, *see* Analogical reasoning,
  option scanning, alternating; Analogical
  reasoning, option scanning, sequential
Option selection, *see* Analogies, task, option
  selection
Order of component processes, *see*
  Component processes, order of
  execution
Overlapping clustering, *see* Additive
  clustering

P

Parallel processing, *see* Component
  processes, mode of execution, parallel
  processing
Parameter space, 54, 88
Parameters of analogical reasoning, *see*
  Analogical reasoning, parameters of
Particularistic processing, *see* Analogical
  reasoning, dual processing; Component
  processes, mode of execution,
  particularistic processing
Path coefficients, 218–219, 221, 250, 284

People Piece analogies, *see* Analogies, content, People Piece
People Piece Analogy Experiment, 173–221, 225–236, 238–240, 242–244, 246–251, 253–254, 265, 269, 272–275, 278, 284, 288, 298–299, 301, 304–305, 307–308
Perceptual speed, 105, 173, 175–176, 178, 207–210, 213, 219, 221, 240–242, 246–249, 253, 299, 301, 307–308, 318
Plan, 39–40, 47, 62
Planning, 215–216, 322, *see also* Control structures; Executive
Practice effects, *see* Analogical reasoning, session effects
Precueing, 73–74, 94, 183, 185, 187–188, 193, 219, 220, 222, 225–226, 255, 258, 260, 285, 291, 296
Predictability of behavior, 70
Preparation-response, *see* Analogical reasoning, component processes in, preparation-response
Primary mental abilities, *see* Intelligence, theories of, primary mental abilities
Principal components, *see* Components (principal)
Principles of cognition
    apprehension of experience, 107–110, 132, *see also* Analogical reasoning, component processes in, encoding
    eduction of correlates, 107–110, 113, 132, 146, *see also* Analogical reasoning, component processes in, application
    eduction of relations, 107–110, 113, 132, 146, *see also* Analogical reasoning, component processes in, inference
Processes, *see* Component processes; Elementary information processes; Fast processes; Slow processes
Processing capacity, 137
Procrustean rotation, *see* Factor axes, criteria for placement, Procrustes
Production, 38–40, 62
Production, convergent, of relations, 105, 109–110, 132, *see also* Analogical reasoning, component processes in, application
Production, divergent, of relations, 105
Production system, 39–40, 62, *see also* Production

Progressive Matrices, 102–103, 106, 123–126, 133
    algorithms for solving
        analytic, 123–124, 132
        Gestalt, 123–124, 132
    colored, 125
    error types
        conglomerate, 126
        matching, 126
    matrix types
        elimination (E), 125–126, 133
        prediction (P), 125–126, 133
Psychological distance, 114, 132, *see also* Representation of information
    rated, 117, 178, 193, 224, 229, 252, 259, 290, 302
    scaled, 117, 193, 230, 290–291, 302
        city-block metric, 290
        Euclidean metric, 290
        supremum metric, 290
Psychological theory, *see* Theory, type of, psychological
Psychometric approach, *see* Intelligence, approaches to, differential
Pure insertion, assumption of, 58–60, 63

R

Range, *see* Analogies, parts, range
Ratings, *see* Psychological distance, rated
Raw score, *see* Score types, composite
Reasoning, 114, 173, 175–176, 178, 207–211, 213–219, 221, 240–243, 245–247, 249–250, 253, 277–282, 284, 286, 288, 299, 301, 304–305, 307–308, 312–314, 321–322, 325
    analogical, *see* Analogical reasoning
    deductive, 100
    inductive, 22, 50, 75, 100, 102, 104–105, 122, 131–132, 286, 288, 301, 318–319, 322
Reference abilities, 78–83, 87, 92, 94–95, 208–209, 212, 217, 283, 312–314, 320, 324, *see also* Abilities
Reference ability model, 80, 82–83, 94–95, 217–218, 221, 250, 318
Reference ability scores, *see* Score types, reference ability
Reference ability tests, 75, 89, 206–210, 219, 240, 247, 286, 289, 299, 305, 307
Reflex, 37–38
Regression, multiple, *see* Multiple regression

Regression, multivariate, *see* Canonical correlation
Relational network, *see* Representation of information, relational network
Relations
  ideal, 108–109
  real, 108
Representation of information, 48–50, 65, 110–111, 113, 117, 122, 132, 135, 323
  attribute-value, 119, 130, 135–136, 138, 143, 145
  cluster, 293, 295–298, 302
  markers, 111, 229
  multidimensional space, 114–118, 132, 145, 287, 290, 293, 295–298, 302
  relational network, 111, 113
Response-time models, *see* Analogical reasoning, models of; Analogical reasoning, types of component models, response-time models; Componential model, solution-time model
Rotation, *see* Factor axes, criteria for placement; Factor axes, rotation of

S

Score types
  canonical variate, 202–203, 275
  component, 75–77, 80–83, 87–89, 91, 94–95, 185, 205, 211–212, 214, 217–219, 221, 229, 239, 242–244, 246–248, 250–251, 253, 260–261, 276, 279–284, 286, 299–300, 304–306, 308, 313, 318–319
  composite, 75–76, 82–83, 86, 88, 91, 94, 280, 282
  factor, 16, 34, 77–81, 88–89, 94, 202, 208, 240, 243, 246, 248, 250, 253, 279, 299, 301, 307–308
  interval, 72–77, 80, 82–83, 86–88, 94–95, 181–182, 184, 205–206, 211, 214, 217–218, 221, 226–227, 231, 240, 242, 247–251, 253, 260–261, 263, 279–283, 299, 306, 318–319
  cue, 73, 94, 181–183, 206, 209, 212, 221, 226–227, 240–241, 247, 252, 260–261, 282, 300, 305–306
  solution, 73–74, 81, 94, 181–184, 206, 210–211, 217, 219–221, 226–229, 240–242, 247, 250, 252, 260–261, 282, 284, 300, 306

Score types (*contd.*)
  reference ability, 77, 80–83, 91–92, 94–95, 207–210, 212–213, 218, 221, 241–242, 249, 251, 253, 279, 281–284, 301, 304, 318, 324
Second-order factor, *see* Factors, types of, second-order
Selection rule, 110
Self-terminating processes, *see* Analogical reasoning, component modes, self-terminating; component processes, mode of execution, self-terminating
Semantic space, *see* Representation of information, multidimensional space
Semidegenerate analogies, *see* Analogies, types, semidegenerate
Sequential option scanning, *see* Analogical reasoning, option scanning, sequential
Serial analysis, method of, 72, 113
Serial exposure, method of, *see* Serial analysis, method of
Serial processing, *see* Component processes, mode of execution, serial processing
Sessions, *see* Analogical reasoning, session effects
Similes, 129, 133
Simple structure, *see* Factor axes, criteria for placement, simple structure
Simplex model, 74, 76, 82–83, 94–95, 182–184, 217, 220, 227–228, 252, 260, 263
Simulation, 40–41, 53–55, 62
Slow processes, 41, 53–54, 62
Solution score, *see* Score types, interval, solution
Solution time, *see* Score types, interval, solution
Solution-time models, *see* Analogical reasoning, models of; Analogical reasoning, types of component models, response-time models; Componential model, solution-time model
Spatial representation, *see* Representation of information, multidimensional space
Spatial visualization, 48–50, 256, 258, 277–279, 281–282, 286, 318
Speed-accuracy tradeoff, 185, 213–214, 229, 243, 252–253, 313
Speed of component processes, *see* Component processes, duration of execution

Stages of processing, 42–45, 58–60,
    62–64, 74, 76
Strategy, 245–246, 249
Structural regression model, 80–83, 95,
    217–218, 221, 250–251, 283, 286
Subjective rotation, see Factor axes,
    rotation of, subjective
Subtasks, see Task level, subtasks
Subtraction method, 41–42, 53–55,
    57–59, 62–63

T

Task analysis
    type
        extensive, 70–71, 83–84, 93, 95
        intensive, 70–71, 82–83, 93, 95
Task level
    composite task, 72–74, 78, 94, 318–319
    subtasks, 72–74, 81, 86, 93, 95, 319
Task score, see score types, composite
Theories of analogical reasoning, see
    Analogical reasoning, theories of
Theories of intelligence, see Intelligence,
    theories of
Theory
    componential, see Componential theory
    criteria for evaluation, see Criteria for
        evaluating theories
    type of
        computer, 53–55, 62–63
        mathematical, 29–31, 36, 53–54, 57,
            62–63
        psychological, 29–31, 36
TOTE, 38–40, 62
Trait
    latent, 54, 63, 72, 75, 77–79, 82–83, 93,
        325
    manifest, 72, 75, 78–79, 82–83
Transformation vector, 149, 158, 160, 170
True-false analogies, see Analogies, format,
    true-false
Truth index, 149, 159, 161, 166–167,
    170–171

U

Utility, 321, 325

V

Validation
    construct, 65, 82–84, 103
    convergent, 75, 77, 82–83, 94
    discriminant, 75, 77, 82–83, 94, 209
    external, 57, 63, 71, 75, 77–78, 82–83,
        85, 87, 93–94, 173, 206, 240, 253,
        256, 288, 298, 302
    internal, 71, 74, 76, 78, 82–83, 93–94,
        173, 181, 226, 260, 289
Variance, 14, 16–20, 30–35, 70, 72, 80,
    86–87, 95, 205–206, 227, 245,
    247–250, 252, 275, 285–286, 288,
    296–297, 307–308
    partitions
        communality, 14–15, 17
        error, 14–15, 17, 19, 24, 34
        reliability, 14–15
        specificity, 15, 17, 19, 24, 34
        total, 14–15
        uniqueness, 14–15
Verbal analogies, see Analogies, content,
    verbal
Verbal Analogy Experiment, 222–254, 272,
    278, 284, 288, 298–299, 301,
    304–305, 307–308
Verbal comprehension, 45–48, 62, 75, 286,
    320, see also Vocabulary
Vocabulary, 7, 22, 75, 105–106, 110, 123,
    131, 173, 207, 209, 213, 222–223,
    241–242, 249, 252, 258, 277–279,
    281–282, 286, 299, 301, 303–305,
    307–308, 320, see also Verbal
    comprehension

W

Wechsler-Bellevue Intelligence Scale, 304
Weighted models, 193
Word association, 128–131, 133, 224, 252

Z

ZORBA, 121

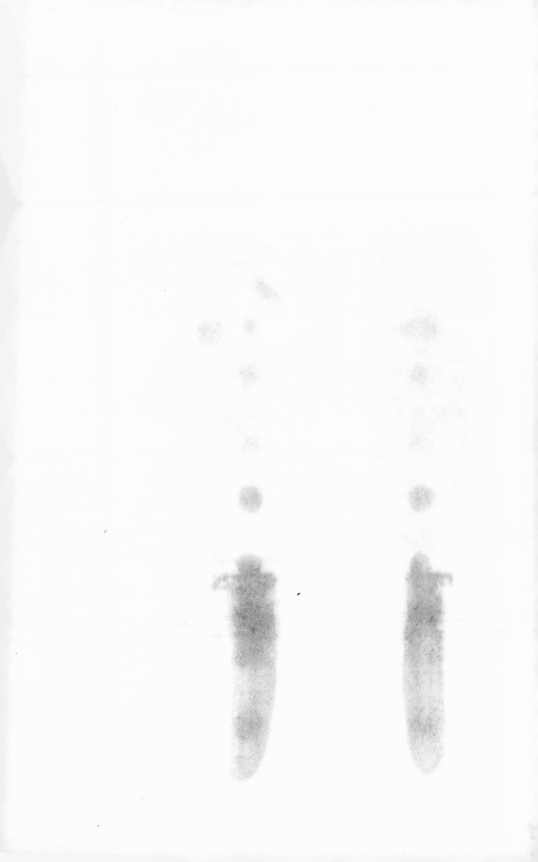

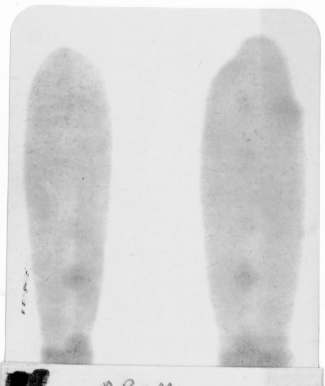